ROME RESURGENT

Ancient Warfare and Civilization

SERIES EDITORS:
RICHARD ALSTON ROBIN WATERFIELD

In this series, leading historians offer compelling new narratives of the armed conflicts that shaped and reshaped the classical world, from the wars of Archaic Greece to the fall of the Roman Empire and the Arab conquests.

Dividing the Spoils:
The War for Alexander the Great's Empire
Robin Waterfield

By the Spear:
Philip II, Alexander the Great, and the Rise and Fall of the Macedonian Empire
Ian Worthington

Taken at the Flood:
The Roman Conquest of Greece
Robin Waterfield

In God's Path:
The Arab Conquests and the Creation of an Islamic Empire
Robert G. Hoyland

Mastering the West:
Rome and Carthage at War
Dexter Hoyos

Rome's Revolution:
Death of the Republic and Birth of the Empire
Richard Alston

The Plague of War:
Athens, Sparta, and the Struggle for Ancient Greece
Jennifer T. Roberts

Rome Resurgent:
War and Empire in the Age of Justinian
Peter Heather

ROME RESURGENT

War and Empire in the Age of Justinian

Peter Heather

OXFORD
UNIVERSITY PRESS

OXFORD
UNIVERSITY PRESS

Oxford University Press is a department of the University of Oxford. It furthers the University's objective of excellence in research, scholarship, and education by publishing worldwide. Oxford is a registered trade mark of Oxford University Press in the UK and certain other countries.

Published in the United States of America by Oxford University Press
198 Madison Avenue, New York, NY 10016, United States of America.

First issued as an Oxford University Press paperback, 2020

CIP data is on file at the Library of Congress
ISBN 978–0–19–936274–5 (hardcover) | ISBN 978–0–19–750053–8 (paperback)

CONTENTS

MAPS

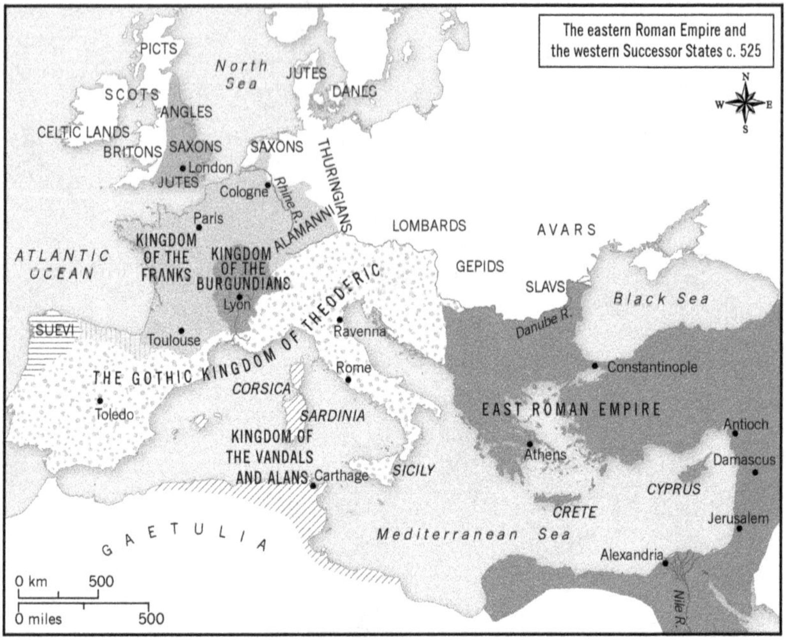

MAP 1

East Rome and the Western Successor States AD 525

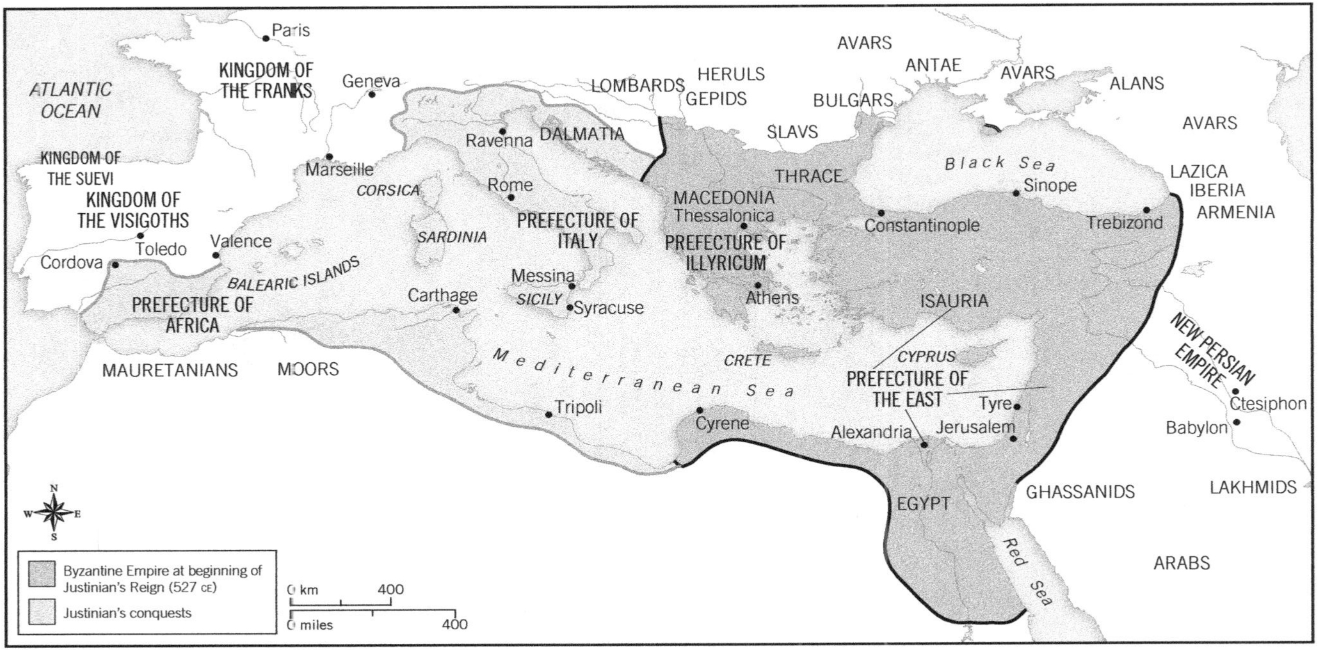

MAP 2
The Conquests of Justinian

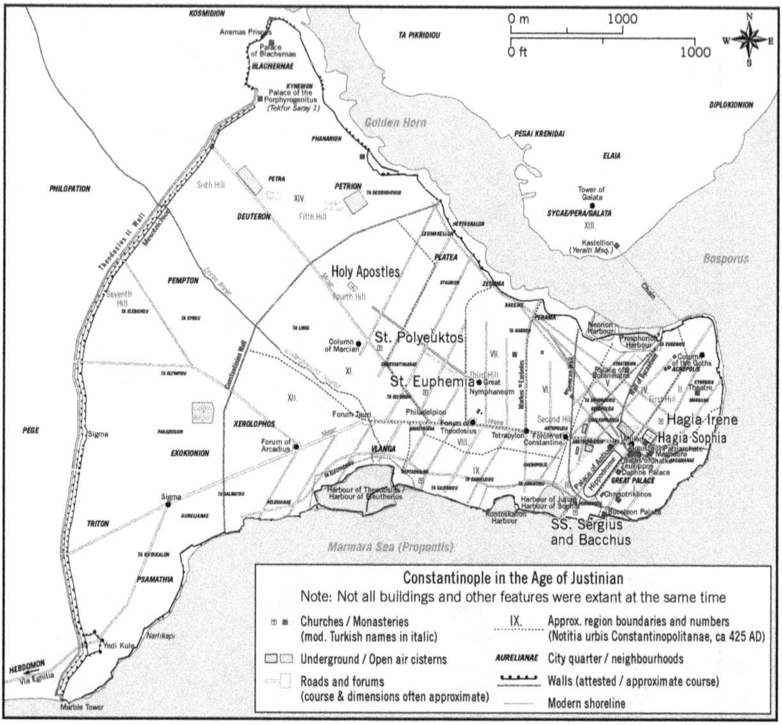

MAP 3
Constantinople in the Age of Justinian

MAP 4
The Conquests of Italy

MAP 5
The Conquests and Subjugation of Africa

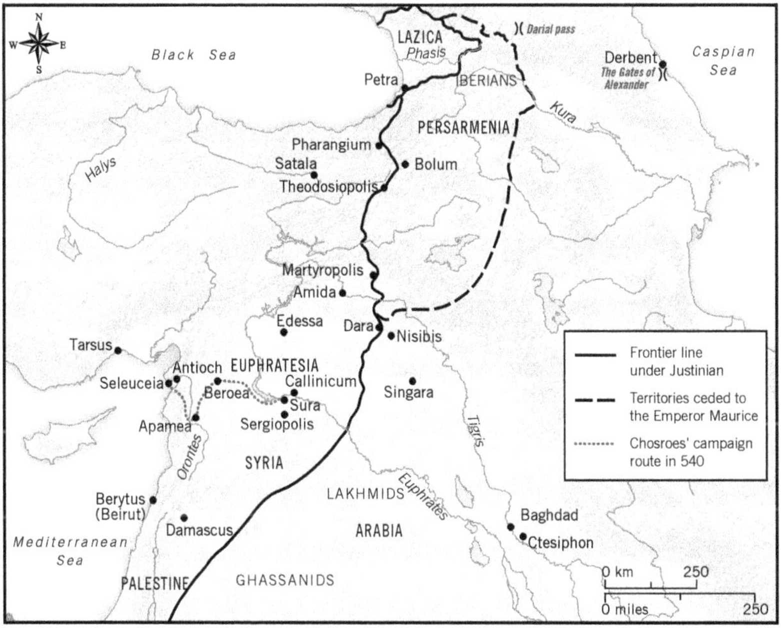

MAP 6
The Eastern Front: Justinian and Afterwards

INTRODUCTION

JUSTINIAN AND THE FALL OF THE ROMAN EAST

IN THE MID-SIXTH CENTURY, the imperial authorities in Constantinople began construction of a brand-new city atop a small plateau between two small rivers in the central Balkans: the Svinjarica to the west and the Caricina to the east. The north-western extremity of the plateau was occupied by an acropolis, surrounded by massive ramparts made irregular by the terrain and studded with five huge towers and just the one gate (Figure I.1). Within, a huge episcopal complex (basilica, baptistery, and audience hall) faced an equally ornate seat of secular authority across a colonnaded square. Lower down, another set of walls marked off the five hectares of the upper town. Here were more churches, arcaded streets, and a substantial granary, together with several rich residences and some of the paraphernalia of water management usual to the more arid parts of the ancient Mediterranean, including a cistern and water tower. Outside, a lower town occupied three more hectares, where excavations have thrown up still more churches, another huge water tank, and two massive bath blocks. No economic, administrative, religious, or strategic necessity generated this extraordinary exercise in civil engineering. This is Justiniana Prima (modern Caricin Grad in Serbia), built solely to commemorate the sixth-century Emperor Justinian I, born Peter Sabbatius in precisely this corner of the Balkans in the early 480s.[1]

As emperors go, Justinian is pretty well known, not least because he has left us a range of striking monuments. You don't have to enjoy

FIGURE I.1
Justiniana Prima, the emperor's birthplace went from village to regional imperial capital as Justinian sought to memorialize his birthplace.

poking around Balkan ruins (as I confess I do) to have your breath taken away by the great cathedral church of Hagia Sophia in modern Istanbul. And the beautiful mosaic panels depicting Justinian and his supporting courtiers on one side, with, opposite, his wife, the Empress Theodora, and hers annually draw thousands of visitors to Saint Vitale in Ravenna. There are also two excellent pen portraits in contemporary sources which agree on all the key points. As the Chronicler Malalas puts it,

> He was short with a good chest, a good nose, fair-skinned, curly-haired, round-faced, handsome, with receding hair, a florid complexion, with his hair and beard greying.[2]

But he is not as well known as he would be, I suspect, had he lived in the first century AD, and the extraordinary nature of his reign makes him well worth his place alongside the stars of *I Claudius*.

Justinian came to throne in 527, divinely appointed ruler of a self-styled Roman Empire which was still coming to terms with a previous century which had seen its western half evaporate into non-existence. After five hundred years of existence (a time span which puts nineteenth- and twentieth-century European empires firmly into perspective), the largest and longest-lived empire western Eurasia has ever known saw its western provinces fall under the control of a series of foreign military powers in the third quarter of the fifth century: Angles and Saxons in Britain, Franks and Burgundians in Gaul, Visigoths and Sueves in the Iberian peninsula, Vandals and Alans in the western half of North Africa (modern Libya, Tunisia, and Algeria). Italy, the ancient seat of empire, and home, of course, to the city of Rome itself, was ruled by a refugee prince of the Sciri called Odovacar, who had fled to Italy when his father's kingdom had been destroyed in the 460s and then led a coup d'état which ousted the last Western emperor, Romulus Augustulus, in the summer of 476, after which he pointedly sent the Western imperial regalia off to Constantinople. The intervening half-century before Justinian came to the throne had seen some further changes, of which the most important were the extension of Merovingian Frankish power south and west from an original power base in modern Belgium and Theoderic the Ostrogoth's conquest of Odovacar's Italian kingdom between 489 and 493 (Map 1).

The causes of this astonishing imperial unravelling have been intensely debated since the time of Gibbon and before, but recent years have seen the emergence of a revisionist literature which has sought to minimize both the role of outsiders in the events of the fifth century and the amount of violence involved. In this view, various Roman interest groups decided to stop participating in the structures of empire and used semi-outsiders (such as the Franks and Ostrogoths), who were already part of a broader Roman world, to help them negotiate the path to local autonomy. A book about the Emperor Justinian is no place for a full discussion of this hotly debated issue. But in the chapters which follow, we will need to think a bit more about the Vandal-Alans and Ostrogoths in particular, who were targeted by Justinian's armies, and although the revisionist discourse has gained considerable traction in some scholarly circles, in some important respects it does not add up to a fully satisfactory account of the overall process of Western imperial dismemberment.

You do find western provincial Roman elites engaged in intense negotiations with rising outside powers (such as Visigoths and Vandal-Alans) already established on Roman soil in the third quarter of the fifth century. But this was the final stage of a several-generation process whose earlier stages—when these groups had first established themselves on Roman soil—had been decidedly violent. Visigoths and Vandal-Alans were new coalitions put together on Roman soil out of manpower deriving from two bouts of unprecedented migration across the imperial frontier (between 376 and 380 and 405 and 408) so that they were in origin outsiders to the empire per se (see Figure I.2). Both forced the Roman state to accept their long-term existence on Roman soil by winning a series of major military victories (such as the nascent Visigothic coalition's victory at Hadrianople

FIGURE I.2
Justinian's uncle and predecessor, the Emperor Justin.

in August 378 which saw the death of the Emperor Valens and the destruction of two-thirds of his army on one dreadful day). Not only did the creation of these coalitions destroy Roman armies, but acceptance of their existence involved ceding them territories (south-western Gaul to the Visigoths, North Africa—eventually—to the Vandal-Alans) which reduced Western imperial revenues and made it increasingly difficult to sustain large enough military forces to prevent further, militarily driven territorial expansion on the part of the new, emergent power blocs of the Roman West: not just Visigoths and Vandal-Alans but Burgundians and Franks, too, and some smaller migrant groups who also ended up on Roman soil in the different political crises associated with the rise and fall of the Hunnic Empire in the mid-fifth century.

This process undermined central imperial control of the western provinces, drastically reducing the Western Empire's tax revenues; it also created a new political context in which provincial Roman landed elites had no choice but to do deals with the new kings around them. The wealth of these elites all came in the form of real estate, which made it highly vulnerable, since it could not be moved. If you suddenly found that a Frankish or a Gothic king was the most important ruler in your vicinity, you simply had to do a deal with him, if you could, or risk losing everything. Such deals always involved some financial losses, in fact, but the threat was there—as clearly happened in Roman Britain and north-western Gaul, where pre-existing Roman elites utterly failed to survive the fifth-century collapse—that they might lose the entirety of their wealth, and losing something was infinitely preferable to losing everything. But to describe this, overall, as a largely peaceful and voluntary process of imperial collapse is, to my mind, to privilege the final element of the story over the total picture which emerges from the whole body of relevant evidence.[3]

Through all this fifth-century mayhem, however, which included its own large-scale outside attacks, particularly in the heyday of Attila's Hunnic Empire in the 440s, the eastern half of the Roman Empire stood firm. For reasons explored in chapter 1, by the late third and fourth centuries it had become common for the vast stretches of the later Roman world to be governed by more than one emperor from two political centres: Constantinople in the East and Trier on the Rhine or Milan/Ravenna in northern Italy in the West. Eastern and Western emperors often quarrelled and sometimes fought, but it remained firmly one empire as demonstrated by its overarching legal and cultural unities, which the rise and fall of different imperial regimes never threatened.[4] And whereas central imperial authority in the West was eventually destroyed by the loss of too much of its provincial tax base (the loss of the rich North African provinces to the Vandal-Alans in the 440s being a moment of particular disaster), Constantinople retained its key tax-producing territories more or less intact. Egypt, Syria, Palestine, and western Asia Minor (modern Turkey) were the economic powerhouse of the Eastern Empire, and Attila's armies, though brutally successful on the battlefield, were never able to get past Constantinople and out of the Balkans.

As a result, the state inherited by Justinian in 527—even if it was centred on the eastern Mediterranean and run by largely Greek-speaking elites—retained its characteristically late Roman cultural and institutional structures. This surviving eastern half of the Roman world was governed by recognizably the same basic means and operated with the same broad mechanisms of economic organization as the old whole had done before the disasters of the fifth century. It was also recognizably still an imperial power with greater resources than those available to any of the new western successor kingdoms. This changed, in fact, only in the seventh century, when the Eastern Roman Empire suffered a similar fate to that of the West. Somewhere between two-thirds and three-quarters of its territories fell into the hands of the rampant armies of newborn Islam, exploding out of the sands of the Arabian desert, and what survived was forced to transform itself—culturally, economically, and institutionally—in such profound ways that it is best regarded from this point as another successor state, like the early medieval western kingdoms, rather than as a further direct continuation of the old Roman Empire. This is why many historians, myself included, prefer to use the term Byzantine Empire to differentiate this post-Islamic eastern successor state from the eastern half of the Roman Empire which preceded it.[5]

But if the prevailing zeitgeist of the mid-first millennium AD was one of Roman imperial disintegration, the collapse of the Western Roman Empire in the fifth century being followed by the evisceration of its eastern counterpart in the seventh, someone clearly forgot to tell the young Peter Sabbatius. By the time of his death in 565, well past the age of eighty, Constantinople's armies had not only prevented any eastern replay of fifth-century Roman territorial losses in the West but, ably commanded by Justinian's famous general Belisarius, had even put the process decisively into reverse. Unlike his emperor, no picture of Belisarius survives from antiquity, but he is said to have been tall and handsome, with a fine figure, cutting rather a dashing contrast, one imagines, to the diminutive, balding Justinian (see Figure I.3).[6] But however much an odd couple in physical terms, emperor and general together brought the old North African provinces conquered by the Vandal-Alans, Sicily, and Italy, the north-west Balkans, and even parts of southern Spain back under central Roman control, even if this was now the Eastern Roman Empire of Constantinople. Also, two of the early 'barbarian' successor kingdoms of the West—the Vandals and the Ostrogoths—were utterly extinguished.

These extraordinary events prompt two fundamental questions about the reign of Justinian. By the mid-530s, in the tenth year of his reign, Justinian's propaganda was claiming that his burning desire all along had been to restore the western territories lost in the fifth century to Roman control, a claim which, up to the 1980s, was generally taken very much at face value, although more recent literature has become much more sceptical.[7] There is also not the slightest doubt that his conquests put huge strains on the human and financial resources of the core eastern provinces of his empire, as well as causing death and dislocation on a massive scale in the territories at which they were directed. Justinian even persisted with his western ambitions when the whole Mediterranean world was gripped by an outbreak of plague in the 540s. For many commentators, therefore, even those taking a positive view of Justinian as romantic Roman imperial visionary, the overall balance sheet of his reign raises serious questions. Given all the strain, death, and destruction, were Justinian's conquests in any sense worth it? The conquest of Italy eventually took the best part of twenty-five years, but within a decade of Justinian's death, most of its northern plains fell swiftly into the hands of invading Lombards. Still worse, the early seventh century saw an utterly unprecedented series of disasters much closer to home. The

FIGURE 1.3
A triumphant Justinian conquering submitting 'barbarians' in the famous Barberini ivory diptych.
Credit: © RMN-Grand Palais / Art Resource, NY

core revenue-generating heartlands of Constantinople's Eastern Roman Empire—Syria, Palestine, and Egypt—fell first temporarily into the hands of the Persians and then permanently to the armies of Islam, reducing Constantinople from capital of a world empire to a regional power at the north-eastern corner of the Mediterranean. This raises the very real possibility that Justinian's obstinate campaigning had so overstretched his empire's resources as to make it an easy target for outside predators. Alongside visions of Justinian as a romantic visionary, therefore, you often find the supposition that his campaigns of western conquest fatally damaged the internal structures of his empire. It is the central purpose of this book to explore how much truth there might be in either of these received images of the age of Justinian.

EMPEROR AND HISTORIAN

To allow us to explore these two fundamental questions which lie at the heart of any overall judgment on the extraordinary historical phenomenon which is Justinian, a wide range of sources is available. Apart from the physical evidence of Justinian's still-standing buildings, like Hagia Sophia in modern Istanbul (there are other churches, too), a vast body of recent archaeological evidence now makes it possible to explore not only particular sites, like Justiniana Prima, but the general functioning of the society and economy over which the emperor presided. There are also smaller physical survivals besides, from exquisite silver plate to coins to manuscript illuminations and mosaics. And while certainly in the midst of important processes of cultural transformation, most of the traditional genres of classical culture continued to flourish. As a result, important poetic, philosophical, and even grammatical works have come down to us from the mid-sixth century, some of which, like the epic Latin poetry of Corippus, play an invaluable role in narrative reconstruction and help to establish the general cultural context of the reign.[8] If nothing else, too, Justinian was an emperor who liked to legislate, and a vast, hugely valuable corpus of legal rulings survive from his reign, illustrating not only Justinian's responses to practical issues but—equally important—the rhetorical justifications in which he couched them (which perhaps bore little relationship to the real reasons behind them). The mid-sixth century also witnessed an important phase in the continuing development of the still nascent Christian religion. Justinian, again, played a major role in church affairs, not least in convening the fifth ecumenical council of the entire Christian Church in Constantinople in 553. So Christian authors—not just in Latin and Greek but also in oriental Christian linguistic traditions such as Syriac and Coptic—have much to tell us about his reign.[9] And often, particularly in the then still developing genre of ecclesiastical history, supplemented by the increasingly influential fashion of writing chronicles of world history starting from creation and working their way down to the present day, church writers were concerned with far more than what we now might think of as religious history, offering valuable insights into political and military events as well.[10] As will become clear, religious policy could never be divorced from the other dimensions of imperial activity in Justinian's Christian empire, so that even apparently more straightforward religious matters turn out to be deeply entwined with the wars of conquest.

That said, this is fundamentally a book about the wars of Justinian: an attempt to provide narrative and analysis of their causes, course, and consequences. As such, it has to depend on one type of source material above all: the ancient genre of classicizing historiography with its ruthless focus on war, politics, and diplomacy. A whole run of authors from the later third to the early sixth century, writing mainly in Greek but also including Ammianus Marcellinus in Latin, provide detailed contemporary narratives of the structures of Roman imperialism in action.[11] As a whole, they provide a bedrock understanding of what the empire actually was and how it functioned in practice, on which any thoroughgoing analysis of Justinian's regime and its actions will need to be based. And for Justinian's reign itself, several different exponents of this specialized art provide much of the specific information we have about his conquests. The annoyingly wordy and numerically hyperbolic, if otherwise well-informed Agathias, known to us also as a poet, completes the story of Justinian's wars, recounting the final campaigns of the mid-550s in Italy and the East. A military officer by the name of Menander, whose fabulously detailed and precise work sadly survives only in excerpts, likewise covers the emperor's final years, providing diplomatic information of the highest quality.[12] But there is one classicizing historian in particular who must stand centre stage in any account of Justinian and his regime, whose work both Agathias and Menander set themselves to continue: Procopius of Caesarea.

Procopius doesn't tell much about his own background, but he clearly belonged to the Eastern Empire's landowning gentry. His works make it clear that he had enjoyed the extensive private education in classical Greek language and literature which was the preserve of his class (and above). Since he appears in his own writings as an *assessor*—legal advisor—to Justinian's most famous general, Belisarius, he must then have moved on to legal studies, the costs of which again confirm the kind of privileged background from which he came. It was Belisarius, with Procopius in tow, who led first Justinian's conquest of Vandal Africa (in 533) and then the initial phases of the war in Italy. Our historian was thus an eyewitness to and occasional active participant in some of the events at the heart of this book.[13]

Procopius's account of Justinian's reign takes the form of three separate works. The longest is a dense narrative history of Justinian's wars focusing on the years 527–52/3. Books 1 through 7, taking the story down to around 550, were published together in 551; book 8, covering subsequent fighting in Italy and the East, followed in 553. They were all written according to the literary conventions governing this type of classicizing history in the late Roman period, which gives them some peculiar features. You were not allowed to use any vocabulary which had not been sanctioned by the ancient, founding Greek grammarians of the classical period. Amongst other things, this meant finding alternative words for Christian bishops, priests, and monks, none of whom had existed in Athens in the mid-first millennium BC. Introductory digressions to amuse and show off learning, rather than actually explain anything, were de rigueur, and subject matter was strictly prescribed. Characteristic of the genre was an unrelenting focus on military and diplomatic history, and it had become customary, though not essential, for an author to have participated personally in some of the events he describes, both to provide extra interest and to guarantee its essential accuracy.[14]

Procopius was well aware of the limiting effects of some of these conventions, complaining at one point that he wasn't allowed to discuss Justinian's religious initiatives in the same breath as the wars of conquest. But the genre poses other problems, too, of which our author was much less aware. Not least important, in his first seven books Procopius chose to present Justinian's wars on a theatre-by-theatre basis; he broke with this approach only partly in book 8, which covers both Italy and Lazica, but, again, in discreet chunks. Since the regime was always having to balance priorities in the face of multiple, simultaneous demands on its available resources all the way from Persia to North Africa, treating the different theatres separately places serious obstacles in the way of any proper understanding of the development of imperial policy. Equally important, Procopius shared the ancient predilection for the 'great man' view of history: that human affairs are largely driven by the virtues and vices of those in charge. Individual competence is obviously not unimportant when it comes to understanding any sequence of historical events, but ancient historiography has little to say about logistic, fiscal, and administrative constraints which always provide a vital context for understanding what choices were made and often fundamentally dictate them.

Despite these limitations, Procopius's war narrative contains a huge amount of detailed information that there is no serious reason to doubt, even if its overall quality is patchy. Part of this patchiness reflects Procopius's presence and absence. His accounts of Belisarius's African and Italian campaigns down to 540 have a vivacity and overall density of information which stem directly from the fact that he was a first-hand witness and sometime participant. But other factors also sometimes intrude. Procopius was certainly present for Belisarius's defeat at the hands of the Persians at Callinicum in 531, yet that battle narrative is vague and evasive. A comparison with the excellent account he produced of Belisarius's victory over the same foe at Dara the year before makes it clear that a desire to protect the general's reputation has got in the way. Even when he was not an eyewitness, Procopius's writing can still be excellent, presumably because he used his time with Belisarius to build a chain of informants in East Roman military circles who helped him sustain narrative intensity. There is no sign that Procopius ever went anywhere near Lazica, for instance, but his account of Bessas's siege of Petra is vivid and detailed.[15]

As to his reporting of troop numbers and casualties, that classic bugbear of any encounter between ancient and modern historiography, Procopius's record is patchy. Sometimes he gives them, and sometimes he doesn't. And where he does give them, they can be more or less convincing.

It has long been noticed, for instance, that there is a substantial disconnect between an overall figure he gives at one point for the total size of the army of Ostrogothic Italy and the scale of Gothic contingents actually reported as taking part in engagements. Likely this discrepancy reflects a tendency to add lustre to Roman victories by exaggerating the scale of the opposition. But in general terms, the numbers he includes carry much more conviction than anything found in the hyperbolic continuations of Agathias. Often, at least on the Roman side, they are highly plausible and sometimes very specific—as in his record of the original expeditionary forces Belisarius led to Africa and Italy and the subsequent flow of Roman reinforcements into the Italian theatre of war down to 540.[16] Overall, all its generic peculiarities and limitations aside, the body of data transmitted in the eight books of *Wars* is so vast that it actually poses a further challenge. The biggest problem for any historian of Justinian's reign is not to fall into the deeply seductive trap of writing out Procopius in one's own words with the addition of just a little extra comment.

If all this did not pose problems enough, our author's oeuvre as a whole serves up another, still greater challenge. The second of Procopius's works—the *Buildings*—devotes four lengthy books to Justinian's construction works. They contain much useful information but also raise some substantial difficulties. In this text, the emperor is everything that he ought to be. Divinely ordained, holy, and pious, his many construction works ornament and safeguard the empire, according to the general and sometimes even the specific will of the almighty Christian God. There is such an overtly propagandistic tone to the treatment that historians have long been worried that there might be a sizeable gap between the reality of Justinianic building programmes and Procopius's obviously idealized portrait of them, a specific issue to be addressed in due course.[17] A still more fundamental problem emerges when it is set alongside the third and shortest of Procopius's surviving works: the *Anekdota*, or *Secret History*.

Anekdota's preface tells us exactly why Procopius wrote it, after having just recently published the first seven books of the *Wars*.

> In the case of many of the events described in that previous narrative, I was compelled to conceal the causes which led up to them. It will therefore be

> necessary for me to disclose in this book, not only those things which have thus far remained undivulged, but also the causes of those occurrences which have already been described.[18]

Afraid of 'a most cruel death' and of being discovered by the emperor's 'multitudes of spies', Procopius had been forced up to this point to produce a sanitized account of Justinian's wars of conquest. Now he promises to tell the whole unvarnished truth, both in terms of facts previously omitted and, above all, concerning the real causes behind events already reported.

This 'truth', famously, turns out to be a tissue of scandal. The supposedly divinely appointed and suitably pious Justinian turns out to be the son of a demon, whose night-time visit to her bed at the point of his conception was explicitly confessed to by his mother. The emperor's face would also sometimes disappear when you were talking to him late at night, and a visiting holy man could not enter the imperial audience chamber because he saw the 'Prince of the Demons' sitting on the throne. Justinian's wife, the Empress Theodora, is not just an actress but an extremely enthusiastic prostitute, utterly enslaved to physical pleasure, who slept her way to the top. Put in power not by God but by supernatural powers of evil, husband and wife were united in a love of avarice, caring not a jot about the colossal scale of the destruction which Justinian's wars unleashed on the entirety of mankind.[19] Nor does his erstwhile employer and Justinian's right-hand man, the general Belisarius, escape the wrath of Procopius's pen. The general's chief fault is a pathetic subservience to his wife Antonina, an old friend of Theodora from her days in the theatre. Antonina utterly dominates their relationship—the ancient ideal was, of course, male superiority—and she was just as lacking in virtue as her empress. Despite the fact that she has countless other lovers, she twists Belisarius around her fingers and prompts him not only into nasty murders to cover up affairs but also into serious derelictions of his public duty. Above all, we are told, it was his desire to rejoin her and put a stop to any further love affairs that allowed the Persians to beat Belisarius's army at the battle of Callinicum.[20]

The problem all this poses for using any of Procopius's works to write about the reign of Justinian is straightforward. When the same author tells you in *Buildings* that the emperor is the God-appointed salve of mankind but in *Anekdota* that exactly the opposite is true, serious issues of credibility are raised, issues that cannot but spill over into the detailed narratives of the *Wars* on which so much of our knowledge of the reign depends. What did Procopius think about Justinian? And how much credibility, anyway, should one afford an author capable of such volatility of response? There have been many different reactions to this problem over the years, but careful reading and much thought has brought prevailing scholarship some way towards consensus. Although published together, the tone of Procopius's writing strikingly darkens over the first seven books of the *Wars*, the author not hiding his increasing disenchantment with the progress and effects of Justinian's wars of conquest. This becomes still more marked in the eighth and final book, whose hero is in many ways the Gothic king Totila. *Anekdota* was composed somewhere between the two instalments of *Wars*, and the negativity of its overall tone does at least find a general fit with the disillusioned Procopius of the later *Wars*.[21]

From this perspective, *Buildings*, with its enthusiastically positive vision of the pious Justinian, is really the outlier. It was certainly written later than *Anekdota* and the final book of *Wars* (though how much later exactly is uncertain). So did Procopius, who starts so positively in the *Wars* before his mood darkens, alter his judgment about the emperor yet again, swinging back from the demonic to the divine? Maybe, but both the preface to *Buildings* and its contents strongly suggest that the only plausible audience for this extraordinary work—a four-book, hundred-plus-page eulogy of the emperor's building works—was Justinian himself. That being so, there is no real need to worry about its sincerity. The later Roman Empire was a form of one-party state in its basic political culture (see chapter 1), and in a work aimed at the court, no sane author was ever going to do much more than reflect straight back at his ruler a clever, elaborated, self-promoting version of the basic message that he already knew, from regime propaganda, the emperor wanted to hear. It seems most unlikely, therefore, that *Buildings* represents a genuine swing back towards the positive in Procopius's overall assessment of his emperor.[22] But if extreme volatility of opinion can be removed from the list of potential charges against Procopius's overall credibility, how are we to reconcile the extraordinary juxtaposition of *Anekdota*'s claims to reveal the full and final truth about the regime with its pornographic portrayal of Theodora and its utterly diabolical Justinian? The stakes here are high. Who would place serious trust in a witness who could unleash such an overblown barrage of vituperative invective?

There have been many different answers to this question, but *Anekdota* contains a host of clues within the text that Procopius is playing with his readers—not that he isn't utterly serious in his condemnation of the regime but in the sense that neither does he expect us to accept its contents as 'truth' in a straightforward, literal sense. The response of nearly every student I have ever taught (female or male) to the pornographic portrayal of Theodora has been laughter. It can be dangerous to judge the cultural values of another time and place, but I am confident that this is precisely the response Procopius was after. And when one looks for sources, it becomes obvious that he cobbled together a portrait of the empress which was not only the exact opposite of what she ought to have been but which drew recognizably on stories about famous prostitutes of the classical past.[23] The account of Justinian is equally funny (although historians have been less inclined to laugh at it), especially the cock and bull story Procopius puts together about the striking facial resemblance between Justinian and the worst Roman imperial tyrant of all, Domitian. All of the tyrant's portraits were destroyed after his death, Procopius tells us, but in Rome he happened to have seen the one exception, which Vespasian's wife made after her husband's death, by sewing his face back together after the crowd that killed him had ripped it apart. The disappearing face and 'emperor's mother shagged a demon' stories are not only worthy of the *National Enquirer* but are also carefully framed with phrases like 'it is reported' and 'they say' that strongly steer readers as to how they should take them. I am very confident, in other words, that the Procopius of *Anekdota* is a clever, funny satirist who did not think that Justinian was literally a demon or his wife the world's greatest harlot. Demonization and sexual humiliation were long-standing strategies for ridiculing enemies in the ancient literary canon (as they remain today), and in *Anekdota* Procopius deploys them to brilliant effect to make the overarching point that the reality of Justinian's regime was the precise opposite of the claims made by its own propaganda.[24]

This is in one sense comforting. Procopius was neither breathtakingly volatile in his opinions—as you might initially think, given the apparent volte-face of *Buildings*—nor so credulous as a literal reading of *Anekdota* might lead you to suppose, all of which makes it more reasonable to continue to take seriously the vast amount of detailed narrative evidence that he offers in *Wars*. But this still leaves a fascinating and, in some ways, more difficult problem. Somehow, we now have to take account of the fact that Procopius was not only an extremely well-informed author but also an artful, playful one. This might seem a paradoxical concern, but it is not. The more clever the writer, especially in the case of an extremely well-informed one like Procopius, the more difficult it is to escape the interpretative web that he or she has artfully constructed.

That, in essence, is the task facing this book. Readers might in the end decide that they wish to echo the overall judgement of the disillusioned Procopius of *Anekdota* and the later *Wars*: that Justinian's conquests were a futile waste of human life. But given the overall persuasiveness of Procopius's rhetoric, it would not be sensible to do so without exploring other possibilities first, despite the fact that he is often the main or only source. Not being prescient, readers also need to ask a question that Procopius could not himself ask. Is it the case, beyond short-term losses, that Justinian's conquests fatally undermined the integrity of the Eastern Roman Empire, paving the way for the disastrous territorial losses of the seventh century? Other sources do, of course, provide some kind of control on Procopius's world view, but it is even more important, in my view, to frame the account of Justinian's reign within the kind of introductory, explanatory digression that the conventions of classicizing history made it impossible for Procopius himself to write.

Before even beginning to explore Justinian's regime and the role played within it by policies of western expansion, let alone the effects of these policies, it is crucial first to explore the political and institutional backdrop against which all this unfolded. What was this East Roman imperial entity that Justinian inherited from his uncle in August 527? How did it function in practice, and what was the nature of the political culture that bound it together? These questions have fallen somewhat out of favour in the last scholarly generation, not least under the influence of the Cultural Turn which has tended to push academic history away at least from detailed analysis of the political process and its broader consequences. This book will argue, however, that testing Procopius's account of Justinian's reign against both the demands and practical limitations imposed by the structures—ideological and practical—of the later Roman Empire provides its own kind of control on the interpretative presentations of our central source and helps unravel properly both the causes and effects of his extraordinary career of western conquest.

1

'IN THIS SIGN CONQUER'

THE CHRISTIAN ROMAN EMPIRE inherited by Justinian on 1 August 527 began as a dream. In the autumn of 312, Constantine advanced over the Alps and was moving south towards Rome and his immediate enemy: Maxentius. On the eve of battle,

> Constantine was advised in a dream to mark the heavenly sign of God on the shields of his soldiers and then give battle. He did as he was commanded and by means of a slanted letter X with the top of its head bent round, he marked Christ on their shields. Armed with this sign, the army took up its weapons.[1]

On 28 October, Constantine scored a thumping victory, and the rest, as they say, is history. The victorious emperor thanked his divine protector by unleashing a process of Christianization which transformed the political and religious culture of the later Roman Empire out of all recognition. Constantine's legacy remained the foundation stone of Justinian's empire. In the *Buildings*, Procopius describes the monumental equestrian statue Justinian raised to himself in the heart of Constantinople:

> In his left hand he holds a globe, by which the sculptor signifies that all the land and sea have been subjected to him, yet he has neither sword nor spear nor any other weapon, but a cross stands upon the globe which he carries, through which alone he has obtained his empire and victory in war.[2]

Thanks to Constantine's dream, *Nika*—'win' or 'conquer'—became the watchword of Rome's armies, protected by the symbols of the Christian God.

The familiarity of this juxtaposition must not hide its fundamental paradox. When asked in the Gospels about what to do if someone hit you in the face, Christ replied 'turn the other cheek'.[3] Understanding exactly how it was that late Roman armies came to seek military victory under the sign of the Cross helps unlock the key role that warfare played in the ideological and practical functioning of Justinian's empire.

IDEOLOGY AND EMPIRE

The Roman imperial state claimed to be a superior form of political organization not only to any other that then existed on the planet (where the limitations of late antique geographical knowledge helped curtail the range of potential comparisons) but to any political society that *might* exist: any time, any place. This claim was based on a cocktail of ideas, mostly inherited from classical Greek philosophy and political thought, brought together under a Roman imperial umbrella. The starting point was a specific understanding of human beings and their place in the created universe. In this view of the cosmos, humans occupied a uniquely liminal position between the spiritual realms above, inhabited by superior, entirely rational beings, and the irrational purely physical world of everything else below. Human beings—unlike any other entity in creation—were composed of both rational soul and irrational physical body, which meant that they had an inherent capacity to become either fully rational, with rational souls controlling their irrational bodies, which is what the divinity destined them to become, or utterly irrational, like animals, where the desires and drives of the body were allowed to predominate. All superior, utterly spiritual beings could not help but be rational, and all inferior, entirely physical beings could only be irrational. Only human beings might go either way.

This gave the classical Graeco-Roman concept of civilization an equally specific meaning. Civilization—*civilitas* in the Latin—consequently signified an order of social organization which allowed human beings to become the fully rational beings their divine Creator wished them to be. In concrete terms, classical theory identified a number of specific cultural elements (different theorists giving them different weightings) which gave Graeco-Roman society this unique civilizing force. Its characteristic elite classical education centred on grammar, rhetoric, and literature (in Greek or Latin) was understood as essential first preparation. Grammar taught logic and ordered thought, rhetoric the capacity to express both, and literature was a moral database from which key lessons could be learned about types of behaviour and their likely outcomes. From Alexander the Great, you could learn not to get so drunk at dinner that you threw spears at your best friend, but there were more complex lessons besides. Barbarians, in the Roman view, were ridiculously emotional; the slightest success and they thought they had conquered the world, the smallest setback and they collapsed in a heap. Studying life and character through literature allowed you to avoid both pitfalls.

The importance of rational written law was also singled out, although in different contexts it could be cause or effect. Some theorists portrayed written law as curbing unruly self-interest. In other formulations, education made individuals rational enough to subordinate their self-interest to the greater good by accepting the rule of written law. Living in towns run by self-governing councils—*civitates*, singular *civitas*—was a further critical prop. Meeting with your peers to decide matters of importance by reasoned debate again developed rationality in a way that living at home on your estates with your slaves and your womenfolk never could. The latter, as far as Graeco-Romans was concerned, was the true path to idiocy (from the Greek *idiotes*, someone living privately instead of engaging in the kind of public life which led to reason and *civilitas*).[4]

As a model, it was unashamedly elitist. Only members of the landowning elite could afford a private classical education, and Graeco-Roman town councils defined their memberships on the basis of landed property qualifications. It was also patriarchal. The model could envisage the concept of fully rational women, but they were seen as exceptional. No limitations at all, however, were attached to the overall significance Graeco-Romans ascribed to the superiority of their social institutions. In a view descending from the philosophers Pythagoras and Ptolemy, they detected one organizing principle at work throughout the cosmos, providing everything with an underlying order, so that distances from earth to the planets mirrored harmonic ratios in music and exact proportionality.[5] Which is why human rationality was so important. It really did represent human beings realizing the Creator's fundamental design. This also explains why—in a final but for our purposes crucial ideological twist—the divinity could be understood to take a unique interest in the fate of the Roman state. Again, there were a couple of converging lines of thought. First, cosmological order extended into the realm of human politics. No earthly ruler could hold power unless the divinity ordained it. Second, because the cultural and social order perfected under Roman rule was so uniquely in tune with the divinity's overall purposes for humankind—the empire being God's tool for perfecting fully rational humans—then its health and good purposes had unique access to divine support.[6]

All of these lines of thought were well-established when Constantine had his dream. They were part and parcel of the elite education, which by this date was shared by the Roman elite—gentry landowners and above—across the vast expanse of imperial territory. All the way from Scotland to Iraq, these ideas were transmitted, along with a linguistic and literary education in Latin and/or Greek, by the grammarians who were to be found in every larger market town of the empire and whose educational product was the sine qua non for acceptance into the imperial elite—and for any real chance of a profitable career in the political and administrative structures of the empire. There were better and worse grammarians, better and worse educations, but the same basic values and ideas were a staple of the grammarians' teaching and gave a surprising degree of cultural unity to the empire's geographically dispersed landowning classes.[7]

On most levels, Constantine's new religion made spectacularly little difference to any of these claims. In the emperor's own lifetime, the first entirely positive Christian theorist of empire, Bishop Eusebius of Caesarea, stated that it was no accident that Christ had been born during the reign of Augustus, the first Roman emperor. Christianity and the empire were bound together in the mind of the divinity, and with the advent of Christian emperors, it was Rome's destiny to bring all of humankind to Christianity. In this Christianized version of existing imperial ideologies, the emperor was no less than Christ's vicegerent, ruling on earth in His place until the Second Coming, and the imperial state on earth was understood as a direct extension of the majesty of heaven. Every state event was marked by direct verbal and ceremonial expressions of this central claim, and an aura of Christian sacrality surrounded the imperial person and his officers. Everything was 'sacred', from his bedchamber to his tax office.[8]

There were, to be fair, some more significant changes other than the slight reidentification of the divinity who was so concerned with the empire's welfare as the God of the Old and New Testaments. It was unclear, for instance, whether the divine plan of the pre-Christian empire had the slightest interest in peasants (85–90 per cent of its population) who had no access at all to the rationality-generating structures (education, town councils, etc.) of the Roman world. Christianity, on the other hand, was uncompromising in its teaching that everyone had a soul and that the salvation of each and every soul was of equal importance in the eyes of God. For this reason, the rule of written law, rather than education or participating in urban self-government, increasingly starred as the decisive cultural characteristic distinguishing rational, divinely ordained Roman society from its inferior—'barbarian'—neighbours in the post-Constantine versions of comparative discussions which have come down to us. One Roman author famously has the Visigothic king Athaulf say that he gave up on the idea of replacing the Roman Empire with a Gothic one precisely because his followers couldn't obey written laws. The best option he could come up with was to use Gothic military might to support Rome. Another author equally famously reduces a Roman merchant turned prosperous Hun to tears at the memory of the overall quality of life that written law could sustain. And within the post-Roman West as a whole, issuing a written law code, however virtual and impractical, would become tantamount to a declaration that your polity belonged to the club of civilized Christian nations.[9] Law was well suited for this role since everyone, superior or inferior, had a designated place within the legally prescribed social structure. Written law was God's gift to order mankind, and it allotted all their due place.

Christianity also affected the religious dimension of the imperial job description. Emperors had always had religious functions. From Augustus onwards, the title *Pontifex Maximus* had been theirs alone, combining ultimate general responsibility for maintaining divine favour towards the empire with the specific function of performing certain expiatory rituals when omens or events suggested that divine support was lacking. Under Christianity, a religion that came equipped with professionals responsible for all divine ritual, everyone quickly realized that the emperor could no longer be thought of as straightforwardly a priest. On the other hand, as God's vicegerent, he stood in a unique relationship to the divinity and certainly retained religious authority of an overarching kind. This made his relationship to the Christian priesthood complicated—so complicated that it took some time for emperors and bishops to negotiate how the former could attend public mass without their overarching religious authority being compromised by priests who were apparently able to do something that emperors could not.[10] You also find individual Christian leaders of different kinds questioning particular emperors' religious authority in specific circumstances. Holy men and bishops, for instance, are sometimes portrayed giving occupants of the imperial throne a stiff talking to. At the end of the fifth century, Pope Gelasius wrote to the Emperor Anastasius in Constantinople using a metaphor of two swords to suggest that imperial authority didn't extend to the sacred.[11]

But at this date Gelasius no longer had to deal with resident emperors, the western half of the empire having ceased to exist a generation before, and this was not the kind of sentiment late Roman churchmen, however exalted, tended to utter in the imperial presence. They would sometimes say rude things in private communications to their own supporters about individual emperors with whom they disagreed, but the overall picture from Constantine to Justinian shows that emperors exercised massive authority over the Church both de facto and de jure. In reality, Constantine's conversion set in motion a massive revolution in the nature and operation of the Christian religion that was at least as important as any transformation the religion effected upon the structures and ideologies of empire. Key doctrines such as the Trinity were defined, new authority structures erected—establishing the rights and duties of bishops, archbishops, and priests—and new rulings on appropriate religious and moral behaviour brought into being. In all of this, emperors played a central role. Above all, they called, presided over, and even set agendas for the sequence of major councils notionally of the entire Christian Church—hence ecumenical councils—from Nicaea in 325 onwards in which much of this was decided.

The most senior churchmen of the late Roman era were the five patriarchs—bishops of Rome, Alexandria, Antioch, Jerusalem, and Constantinople—who held sees which had been founded by one of the Apostles (or in the case of Constantinople, because it was the city of New Rome and should therefore have all the honours possessed by Old Rome). Rome considered itself the most prestigious of the five, but that view was not shared by the other four, and papal authority as it came to be in the High Middle Ages did not yet exist. Only emperors could call ecumenical councils, patriarchs being limited to regional councils, and this symbolizes the overarching level of religious authority that the imperial office possessed. In practice, too, emperors enforced conciliar decisions, appointed senior churchmen, and even generated a series of important formal rulings for the church through their own legislation. The most ambitious formal legal claim to papal authority over the Western church from the late Roman period only emphasizes the point. Composed in 445, it declared that 'nothing should be done against or without the authority of the Roman Church'. That its strictures were utterly ignored in practice is one key point about this ruling (it would take another seven hundred years for it to have much effect). The other is that it is to be found in the legislation of the Western emperor Valentinian III. In reality, as the imperial view of the divine source of an emperor's authority might suggest, late Roman emperors functioned as the head of the rapidly developing Christian Church, and that church itself was essentially a department of the imperial state. It was still accepted, in other words, by the vast majority of the inhabitants of the empire, ecclesiastical and otherwise, that emperors had a perfect right to exercise overarching religious authority.[12]

This redefinition of its religious authority left most other dimensions of the imperial office fundamentally unchanged. In civilian matters, it was an emperor's duty to maintain the key institutions of *civilitas* by setting the appropriate overall tone for his officials and the regime that together they constituted. According to the fourth-century imperial spin doctor Themistius, the key imperial virtue here was *philanthropia*: love of mankind (that is, *all* mankind, not particular favourites or groups). In Graeco-Roman ideological constructs, this was the divine virtue par excellence; it enabled emperors to care properly for the entirety of their subjects by maintaining the key social and cultural institutions which supported *civilitas*. In practice, this meant that an emperor had to act (at least be seen to act) appropriately in a number of key areas. Judicially, he had to maintain the legal structures that late Romans viewed increasingly as the central feature which distinguished their civilized society from all its barbarian neighbours'. From the late third century onwards, emperors dominated lawmaking in the Roman world and were themselves customarily viewed as law incarnate: *nomos empsychos* in the Greek.[13] They could therefore make (and sometimes break) laws as they wished, but because of law's central ideological importance, in doing so they had to be able to present what they were doing as supportive of the ideals of rational *civilitas*, even if the reality was often blatantly different.

A second core function of the civilian emperor was to appoint all the high officials who between them constituted a functioning imperial regime. Emperors were supreme autocrats, but like any supreme autocrat ruling vast territories with limited bureaucratic machinery, they ruled in practice through officials who exercised much autonomous power. The early stages of any reign were consequently consumed with appointing new officials at the centre and making relationships with a whole series of local power brokers in order to create a working regime. Again, much of what happened was dictated by realpolitik, but as Themistius put it, an emperor shaped the character of his regime by the personal qualities of the 'friends' whom he appointed to positions of power. At the very least, therefore, the process of regime building had to be presentable as one—through appointees who possessed the correct personal qualities—that could be seen as strengthening *civilitas*.[14] For similar reasons, even if it was often largely window dressing, emperors liked to create the right kind of cultural photo opportunities where they could show themselves off as supporting the educational and local governmental structures which were seen as central to *civilitas* in all its glory. Endowing professorships was always a good move, as was anything which looked supportive of local self-government by city-based elites. In reality, central interference had slowly undermined local civic autonomy, but these cultural ideological imperatives still exercised force in the Christian empire of the sixth century. In the *Buildings* again, Procopius gives most weight to Christianity and defence, but the importance of the city as the only possible context for a proper, fully civilized life, is certainly there. Writing about Caput Vada (in modern Tunisia) in the 550s, where Belisarius's invasion force landed twenty years before, he describes what had happened since in a very particular manner:

> The rustics have thrown aside the plough and lead the existence of a community, no longer going the round of country tasks but living a city life. They pass their days in the market place and hold assemblies to deliberate on questions which concern them; and they trade with one another, and conduct all the other affairs which pertain to the dignity of the city.

The ancient civilizing mission of local self-government, at least in theory, was still alive and kicking.[15]

Emperors chosen personally by the Christian divinity also had key military responsibilities. This was obviously the case when emperors themselves functioned as active military commanders. Through most of the fourth century, emperors still often either commanded in the field or were appointed in dynastic interregna—as with Valentinian I and Theodosius I—in part because they were generals with established reputations. More important, the imperial office retained an overall military function or, perhaps better, *responsibility*, even when, from the late fourth century, emperors ceased to campaign in person. In 402, the poet Claudian reckoned the victory of Western Roman armies over the Gothic forces of Alaric to have been the personal achievement of the Emperor Honorius. But Honorius was a twelve-year-old boy who had gone nowhere near the battlefield. It wasn't even so much a victory as a draw. What matters here is not historical truth, however, but Claudian's reasons for highlighting Honorius's contribution to this well-imagined outcome.[16]

Throughout imperial history, the prime virtue required of all Roman emperors was victory: the capacity to win on the field of battle. This changed not a jot with the advent of Christianity, for an extremely straightforward reason. Military victory had an ideological and political impact which neither the religious nor civilian dimensions of the imperial job description could possibly match. Both of the latter *could* be trawled (and regularly were) for possible signs of divine favour (excellent doctrinal settlements; laws which secured the operation of *civilitas*, etc.), but an emperor's actions on these fronts were always open to question. Doctrinal settlements always involved losers, who continued to deny, often for decades, the legitimacy of what had been decided. The dispute over the person of Christ in the Trinity, originally 'settled' at Nicaea in 325, actually rumbled on for another three political generations. In the same way, as the chapters which follow show, Justinian in the mid-sixth century was still having to deal with a further dispute which had notionally been settled at the Council of Chalcedon in 451. No law, likewise, was equally beneficial to absolutely everyone (whatever imperial propaganda might claim).[17] Military victory, by contrast, had a legitimizing power which no other form of imperial activity could even begin to match. There could be no clearer sign of favour from an omnipotent divinity than a thumping military victory over barbarian opponents who, by definition, stood in a lower place in the divine order of creation. Throughout imperial history, therefore, while huge effort was put into presenting every imperial act as fully in tune with the divine plan for humankind, winning military victories possessed an overwhelming ideological cache. Even if an emperor, like the young Honorius, did not campaign in person, his divinely chosen legitimacy could still be made incontestably manifest through the military victories of his generals. The ideological circle was thus closed. A legitimate emperor brought divine support, which meant nothing if not victory on the battlefield. Correspondingly, military success generated a level of political legitimacy which no other imperial action could ever hope to reach.[18]

As a result, claiming military victory—because it was the ultimate sign of divine support—loomed large in the propaganda of all Roman rulers, early or late. From the time of Constantine's immediate predecessors—the tetrarchic emperors Diocletian and his colleagues—emperors claimed and carefully recorded victory titles: adding adjectival forms of the names of defeated enemies to the lists of their own titles. Thus *Parthicus, Alamannicus, Gothicus*, and many others were added to *Caesar, Augustus*, and *Pontifex Maximus*. The tetrarchs even added numbers after each title to indicate just how many times they or one of their colleagues had defeated a particular opponent. Titles like *VII Carpicus*—'victor seven times over the Carpi'—became commonplace. The fixation with number declined after Constantine but not that with victory. Whenever an emperor's name was mentioned, whether they liked it or not, his subjects were confronted with a litany of victory which underscored the legitimate, divinely supported nature of the regime.[19]

These occasions were many and varied. Imperial titulature appeared in all official imperial pronouncements: everything from brief letters to formal laws. It also featured on many inscriptions, most of which were dated by the names of consuls, an office which emperors regularly held in the late Roman period. Most of the public life of the empire, whether central and imperial or more local, involved formally shouted acclamations where an emperor's titles would also figure. Every meeting of the many hundreds of town councils of the late Roman world began with such acclamations (although the minutes of only one have come down to us), as did every formal imperial ceremony, not least those carefully orchestrated moments of arrival—*adventus*—which greeted an emperor's entry into any of his cities. On all these occasions, an emperor's military record was not only held up to general public view in titulature outline but usually discussed in more detail. Most imperial ceremonies also involved a formal speech of praise—panegyric—in the emperor's honour, given by some lucky orator who could use it to advance his own career. These speeches could take many forms, but a commonly utilized model devoted a specific section to an emperor's deeds in war. Even where another form was adopted, some reference to the current emperor's success in warfare was still de rigueur.[20]

Beyond such specific references, the point was reinforced by a great deal of more general allusion to the fact that divine support had shown itself in the current emperor's capacity to generate victory. The figure of a submitting barbarian played a huge role in late Roman iconography. A staple of coinage types—often accompanied by an appropriate inscription such as *debellator gentes* ('conqueror of peoples')—was the supine barbarian lying at the bottom of the reverse just to remind everyone that the emperor defeated such enemies as a matter of course. Similarly defeated barbarians of various kinds also appeared regularly in the engraved reliefs, not least on the triumphal victory arches, with which emperors liked to decorate the larger cities of their empire.[21] Submitting barbarians were the natural accompaniment of divinely supported, victorious Roman emperors, spreading the general message that the current regime was ticking all correct ideological boxes.

The ideologies of Roman imperium, only slightly modified by Christianity, thus defined an overarching imperial job description, not directly in terms of dictating a series of day-to-day functions but, at least as important, by setting a series of targets which had somehow to be hit. A legitimate Roman emperor was not a secular ruler in modern understandings of the term but one chosen directly by the supreme creator divinity of the entire cosmos to maintain the key pillars of rational Roman civilization—education, city life, the rule of written law, the welfare of the Christian Church—by which humankind was destined to be brought into line with the divine plan and in return for which the divinity would guarantee that ruler's success against all comers. All of these targets were centuries old by the time that Justinian came to the throne in 527, but their potency was not one jot reduced. Whatever else it did, his regime was going to be judged by its capacity to demonstrate that its functioning ticked all the boxes of legitimate Roman government, of which by far the most important, because it was ostensibly so easy to measure, was military success. Nor, it must be emphasized, was ticking these boxes some abstract exercise in a regime's strategies for self-presentation. The overwhelming ideological imperative attached to divinely appointed legitimacy, hence above all to military victory, had huge knock-on effects for the political process in the late Roman world.

THE POLITICS OF VICTORY

That all individual emperors claimed to be personally appointed by the divinity did not mean in the slightest that all politically engaged parties immediately rolled over and accepted it. The empire's Panglossian ideology, that it was the best possible state shored up by a divinity who hand-picked its rulers, certainly made it difficult to air dissent in public. Imperial ceremonial was actually dedicated to providing a series of public photo opportunities where the great and even the only moderately good—all lining up in their correct order of social precedence—could demonstrate their unqualified assent to the fundamental idea that they formed part of a perfected, divinely ordained political structure, whose perfection consequently commanded their consent. The bizarre, orchestrated chanting in the Roman Senate which greeted the presentation to them of a new imperial legal text—the Theodosian Code on Christmas Day 438—is only one example of the formal unanimity that this political culture demanded.[22] Who but a barbarian could *not* give support to such a perfected social order, and any public expression of dissent was fraught with danger. As John Matthews showed, the late fourth-century Senator Symmachus could only signal in most oblique terms when he didn't like someone, especially someone—one of the emperor's 'friends'—who had been rewarded with an important position.[23] But the fact that the public life of the empire demanded formal public consent on an industrial scale did not prevent intrigue, not to mention out and out plotting, from constituting a basic constant of political life.

Succession still does not get the amount of discussion that it should do in analyses of the late Roman world, even though the operations of modern politics confirm its overriding importance. All grandees in a court-based political structure had an immediate stake in it. For everyone doing well under the current regime, succession was hugely threatening. Would the next regime show them the same degree of favour? By the same token, those currently out of favour could hope for substantial change for the better, and those doing moderately well would always be looking for possible advancement. In other words, as soon as succession became an issue, every existing political alliance and relationship was immediately up for potential renegotiation, because the creation of a new regime was the moment when long-suppressed hopes could come decisively to the fore. And as was seen in recent succession shenanigans in the United Kingdom, when Michael Gove suddenly turned from cheerleader in chief for Boris Johnson to leading assassin, even what seem to be solid political alliances can be burnt away in a moment by the fires of untrammelled ambition.

In the late Roman world, the range of parties with a vested interest in all matters to do with succession was extensive. First in line, of course, was the current imperial family, home to the most obvious contenders for the purple, but the net here could extend widely, even to collateral connections of past dynasties. After the death of Leo I, the 470s and 480s in Constantinople saw a whole series of collateral cousins, brothers-in-law, and even ex-imperial wives involved in a decade and more of unrest at court.[24] But it was not just greater and lesser royals who figured in calculations about succession. Contenders could also come from outside the dynasty, especially if there was no obvious male heir. It is traditional in these kinds of paragraphs to talk about the army as a political force, but this is shorthand for the officer cadres of one specific component of the Roman military: its elite field armies. Senior commanders of these forces always had purple potential in the right circumstances. Valentinian I was a prominent soldier before his elevation, as was Theodosius I and so too the later emperors Marcian and Justinian's uncle Justin.[25] Senior bureaucrats and court officials could also figure, if more occasionally. After Julian's death, the purple was offered to his chief financial and legal officer, the Praetorian Prefect Salutius Secundus, and the Western usurpers Eugenius (392–4) and John (423–5) were both senior bureaucrats, while Justinian's predecessor but one, Anastasius, was a senior court dignitary prior to his accession.[26] Even when conditions dictated a dynastic succession, the same range of military and civilian dignitaries were still intimately involved, carefully calculating which specific member of the dynasty to back for the future, if there was any choice, while still manoeuvring for position under the current ruler.

Others further down the pecking order also had a major stake in the process. Medium-level bureaucrats were often tied to grander patrons, whose success or failure had serious implications for their own prospects. In the mid-350s, medium-level financial officials fed the Caesar Julian crucial information which allowed him to bypass the control of the chief financial officer, the Praetorian Prefect Florentius, foisted on him by Constantius II, and establish de facto political independence. Other functionaries in the eastern half of the empire had earlier encouraged Julian's half-brother, the Caesar Gallus, towards a similar but in this case ill-fated bid for autonomy, which ended in Gallus's death. In both cases, the officials were motivated by perceptions that their respective Caesar's star was on the rise and hopes for the potential benefits of early service. This dynamic was alive and well in the sixth century. John Lydus's prosperity was closely tied to the success of his much grander patron Zoticus, the Praetorian Prefect of the East. In the late 540s, likewise, one group of only moderately well connected military plotters tried to interest Germanus, Justin's nephew and highly plausible if by no means official heir, in a plan which would have led to the emperor's murder and his nephew to an early collection on his (as yet only potential) inheritance.[27] Still further away from the centre, imperial regimes functioned at the local level by recruiting loyal agents who made sure that the crucial tax revenues flowed. In return, such men—a classic case in point being Synesius from Cyrene in the early fifth century—used their connections at the centre to dominate the politics of their home territories, so that they too had a substantial, if less direct, stake in the minutiae of imperial politics.[28] Though certainly court-centred, the political process of the late Roman world involved a substantial cross-section of its landowning elite. For all these parties, succession always raised the normal political temperature close to boiling point and with the added excitement, in the late Roman world, that it was usually not possible to sort it all out smoothly in advance.

For one thing, you never knew when the current emperor was going to die. Average lifespans are hard to calculate, and history always throws up somebody who comfortably beat the odds. Constantine made it to sixty-five, and Anastasius to an astonishing eighty-seven, but both were unusual. Most active males pegged out somewhere between their mid-forties and mid-fifties, like Constantius II, the only one of Constantine's sons to die in his bed, or Theodosius II, who was forty-nine on his demise in 450.

And death could come suddenly. Valentinian I, admittedly in his mid-fifties so people would already have been watching him closely—went from apparent health to death via a stroke in a matter of hours. But forty-five to fifty-five is an average, which means that quite a few holders of the office went earlier still: Arcadius and Honorius, sons of Theodosius I, both died in their thirties.[29] And because, before ca. AD 400, the imperial system did not in practice tolerate child emperors, the relatively youthful age at death of emperors could generate more succession complications in the form of offspring who were not real contenders for power. The infant son of the Emperor Jovian, for instance, disappeared from public life (maybe private life, too) immediately after his father's sudden demise in the spring of 364.

That death tended to come unexpectedly, however, was only part of the problem. Even if an emperor had an adult male heir already holding the reins of power, he could, of course, change his mind. Mid-reign, Constantine deposed and executed his adult son Crispus, from an earlier liaison, in favour of younger sons by his current wife.[30] This must have derailed a great deal of existing political calculation.

Much more fundamentally, the basic nature of late Roman political life meant that even if there were plausible dynastic heirs, regime change was rarely smooth. All late Roman regimes were balancing acts, combining—immediately below the reigning emperor—a series of lieutenants who were all-powerful in their own right and who were usually vying among themselves for maximum influence within the regime. For all the emphasis on public, ceremonial consensus, we need to think in terms of the kind of rivalries and tensions that are so well documented in court societies of the early modern era, such as that of Henry VIII of England. Against such a backdrop, even dynastic succession was usually a dogfight. Valentinian I left two sons: Gratian, aged sixteen, and Valentinian II, aged four. On his sudden death from a stroke, one set of grandees immediately proclaimed Gratian emperor at Trier, where Valentinian's court was customarily established. In what was essentially a coup d'état, however, another group grabbed the young Valentinian II, who was on campaign with his father at Aquincum in the Middle Danube, and did the same. There then followed a lengthy process of negotiation and elimination, which saw a whole host of Valentinian I's senior lieutenants fall bloodily from power, including the father of the future Emperor Theodosius I, before a new coalition emerged from the wreckage.[31]

Valentinian II himself survived the carnage and was quietly put out to grass, but this doesn't hide two basic truths. First, regime change in the late Roman world, even within a ruling dynasty, was usually nasty, as those close to the throne sought to settle old scores and grab power by isolating and eliminating potential rivals. Second, because you never knew when death might strike, those with any substantial stake in the political system always had to have a functioning plan B already half in place, reinsuring their position against the potential for future loss by keeping an eye on how to construct an equally sympathetic future regime or actively calculating how to secure for themselves a much better position than they currently enjoyed.

This dynamic interplay between mortality, succession, and political ambition meant that plotting—at least in terms of planning carefully for a range of potential future scenarios—was a constant fact of late Roman political life. It could also easily lead you to cross the thin line separating legitimate concern for the future from outright treason. Some important officials got themselves into serious trouble in Antioch in the early 370s by using a tripod device in a seance to divine the name of the next emperor. The current Emperor Valens was less than impressed, especially when the tripod appeared to spell out the name of one of the participants, prompting him into some active political campaigning. The tripod got as far as THEOD, and the participant was a senior bureaucrat called Theodorus. Unfortunately for him, the next emperor would in fact be named Theodosius[32]—which underlines one final key point about the practical implications of prevailing imperial ideologies.

For all that the ideologies underpinning public life demanded unrelenting political consensus for the current, divinely ordained ruler in the best of all possible worlds, they still accepted that it was possible for emperors to come to power without divine support or, at least, for divine support to be switched subsequently from the current incumbent to a rival contender. A beautiful case in point is provided by two speeches given by the orator Themistius in 364 for two different imperial regimes: first that of

Jovian, on 1 January, then that of Valentinian and Valens later the same autumn. In the first speech, to celebrate Jovian's consulship, Themistius duly identified the elements in the emperor's rise to power which demonstrated that he had been chosen by God. Unfortunately, Jovian died in mysterious circumstances just a couple of months later. This made it crushingly obvious that Jovian could not in fact have been the divinity's real choice. Otherwise, God would have protected him from such an early demise. In the second speech Themistius implicitly acknowledged the point, pointedly contrasting the elements in the new regime's establishment which guaranteed that, this time, fallible human beings had properly understood the divine will when selecting their new emperors.[33]

In this instance, Themistius's recognition of the illegitimacy of Jovian's accession was *post* de facto, hardly amounting to a license to plot, but it reinforces the point that signing up to a public life committed to consensus never prevented any interested party from testing the water. Was the current ruler really God's preferred choice? Political calculation of some kind was constantly demanded of you anyway by the uncertainties of succession, and the number of successful usurpations or semi-usurpations—even the raising of Constantine by his father's close supporters in York against the will of most of the tetrarchy or later of Valentinian II was a kind of usurpation—demonstrates that plotting, even aside from succession matters, was pretty much a constant feature of late Roman political life and one that no emperor, least of all Justinian, who, as we shall explore in more detail, did not hail from some long-established dynasty, could ever afford to ignore. There were, however, particular moments when regimes were more vulnerable than others and when the intensity of plotting, hence the likelihood of successful usurpation, increased accordingly.

The early years of any regime provided one set of such moments. A recent work on the Carolingian empire of Charlemagne and his successors convincingly argues that it took a Carolingian ruler between five and ten years firmly to grasp the reins of power, because it took that long to establish solid relationships with a series of reliable local agents who actually ran the constituent parts of their kingdoms on the ruler's behalf. The Roman Empire operated with more of a functioning administrative bureaucracy than Charlemagne's empire but not that much more, and it was also much larger than any Carolingian realm. In practice, therefore, successful Roman regimes likewise depended on a series of power brokers who ran local communities in ways, particularly in terms of revenue collection and the preservation of social order, that worked to their advantage. The early stages of any emperor's rule were consequently spent cultivating such relationships by identifying potentially loyal power brokers and distributing a raft of favours. But such relationships took time to bed down.[34]

In my view, the Carolingian parallel is not a bad rule of thumb to have in mind for Roman imperial regimes, too, and the time frame of early vulnerability could be longer still when the break with a previous regime was substantial, where, for instance, there had been an enforced change of dynasty or outright usurpation. Valentinian's brother Valens—following the short and unsuccessful reigns of Julian and Jovian—seems never to have established a secure hold on the loyalties of large sections of the politically important players of the Eastern Empire throughout his fourteen-year reign. That one usurpation would often beget another was a further basic rule of late Roman political life: from the unravelling of the tetrarchy in the early 300s, to the overthrow of Constantine's son Constans in the West in the late 340s, to Constantinople in the 470s under the reign of the Isaurian imperial outsider Zeno.[35]

Outside events could also destabilize regimes. In the early 380s, the Emperor Gratian shifted his court from Trier, on the Rhine frontier, to northern Italy and incorporated large numbers of Alans into his elite field army. These Alans had been displaced from their old haunts above the Black Sea in the chaos currently being generated in eastern and central Europe by the Huns, which is also what moved Gratian to shift his centre of operations to Milan, closer to the new epicentre of threat. But while perfectly sensible in themselves, these moves so disturbed existing patronage distributions within Western field armies, particularly those stationed in Gaul, that the General Maximus was able to exploit the resentment to generate a (temporarily) successful usurpation. The disappearance of figures other than a senior Augustus, likewise, could throw court politics into chaos. In the late 410s, Constantius III, following a highly successful military career, married Galla Placidia, sister of the childless Emperor

Honorius, fathered the young Valentinian III—heir presumptive for the next generation—and was duly raised to the purple alongside Honorius. But all balance quickly disappeared from Western politics with his sudden death in 421, even though Honorius still sat on the throne. We don't have all the details, but in his absence, contending voices quickly pulled brother and sister—previously reported as extremely affectionate towards one another—apart. Eventually, the two fell out so badly that Galla was forced to flee to Constantinople with her son; her flight, on Honorius's subsequent and sudden death, laid open a path to the throne for the usurper John.[36]

But of all the various possibilities, it was always military defeat which posed the most dramatic challenge to political stability, sometimes for obvious reasons. Valens's whole regime disappeared into thin air when he perished on the field of battle at Hadrianople along with many of his leading officials on 9 August 378. Even less mortal setbacks could have dire effects. The failure of Majorian's Vandal expedition in 461 undercut his political support to such an extent that the patrician General Ricimer felt free to have him deposed and executed. Stilicho's inability, likewise, to deal with the Rhine invasion of 406 and the usurpation of Constantine III (the latter itself, arguably, a product of Stilicho's perceived inability to secure the Roman northwest from attack) eventually undermined his strong hold over the Emperor Honorius, built up over a decade and more in power from 395. Other voices inserted themselves into the imperial ear, and the result was Stilicho's fall and execution in August 408. When the policies adopted by Stilicho's immediate successors failed to restore stability, their support evaporated in turn. There followed a whole sequence of short-lived regimes, punctuated by nasty deaths for their chief protagonists.[37]

Outright defeat, even *perceived* military incapacity, was politically toxic not just for simple practical reasons—like the death of an emperor—but because of the ideological license it afforded to more intensive plotting. Since there was no greater sign of divine favour—and hence legitimacy—than military success, because it was ostensibly so easy to measure, the opposite was also true. Nothing screamed louder that the current regime lacked divine favour, hence fundamental legitimacy, than a record of military failure, with dire consequences for its political stability. Not surprisingly, therefore, regimes were ready to be economical with the truth in every possible way imaginable to portray themselves as victorious in battle.

Turning draws into victories or minor victories into major ones were obvious strategies, repeated almost ad nauseam in the speeches of Themistius for various regimes across the middle decades of the fourth century. Oration 1 claimed that Constantius II's advance on Singara in 344 had frightened the Persian Shapur to death, glossing over the fact that there had been no battle at all. Inventive rhetorical colour was used to portray Valens's summit meeting with Athanaric in 369 as a massive triumph (with gibbering, grovelling Goths lined up on the riverbank) when (actually *because*) the new agreement acknowledged much greater diplomatic equality than its predecessor, despite three highly frustrating years of Roman campaigning. Theodosius's inability to win an outright victory over the Goths in the aftermath of Hadrianople, likewise, was shrouded in a series of arguments proclaiming that the new treaty was actually a different and greater kind of victory.[38] So common were these kinds of presentational strategies that it was equally common to accuse rivals of gross exaggeration. Constantius II's regime aimed to limit the potential political fallout from Julian's stunning victory over the Alamanni at Strasbourg in 357 by proclaiming that any fool could beat a bunch of 'naked savages'. The real test was facing up to the Persians in the East.[39]

This overriding political imperative to win—or to be seen to win—military victories easily spilled over from the presentation of policy into its actual formation. If nothing else, emperors liked to be seen building fortresses in unlikely parts of the frontier. Whether any more of these were really required by the time of Valentinian and Valens must be questionable, but such constructions made for excellent photo opportunities, sometimes with unexpected results. Valentinian at one point pushed fortifications into an area where it had previously been agreed that the empire would not build, prompting an outbreak of violence from outraged Alamannic inhabitants. Early in his reign, Valentinian had also wanted to present himself to his taxpayers as tough on barbarians. Hence he unilaterally lowered the value of the annual gifts presented to the kings of the Alamanni. But the kings recycled these gifts to express prestige and reinforce their own patronage networks at home, so the result was another howl of Alamannic protest in the form of still more trouble on the Rhine frontier. It has even been argued that the empire was primarily responsible for initiating *every* recorded bout of dispute with the Alamanni in the late imperial period, as the product of emperors hard pressed by the need to record some kind of victory. In my view, this pushes the argument too far and unwisely removes any sense of agency from those living beyond the frontier. But it is certainly the case that an internal political imperative to score a recognizable victory sometimes drove imperial foreign policy.[40]

Still more dramatically, the same imperative could even lead emperors to cover up defeat. In the late summer of 363, the Emperor Julian was killed in a skirmish trying to extract his army from Persian territory. As Ammianus's account makes clear, Julian's force, if tactically undefeated, was strategically trapped, and his successor Jovian was forced to make a humiliating peace deal which handed over to Persia the Roman regional capital, Nisibis, and a host of territories east of the river Tigris. In propaganda terms, the option was clearly there to blame all of this on Julian's folly. This is how most modern governments, for whom blaming their predecessors for every current problem is almost second nature, would surely have handled it. One the reasons I left H.M. Treasury for academia was the puerile nature of its official briefing document for handling press enquiries where the answer to every question was 'Yes, but under the last (opposition) government, the situation was much worse . . . '. But as both Jovian's coinage and a speech on his behalf by Themistius make clear, the new regime took the much more difficult option of claiming that the humiliating peace terms actually represented a victory. No one believed it, especially when the surrender of Nisibis and so much other eastern territory duly followed, but that wasn't the point. Such was the ideological and political imperative of claiming victory that, even at the start of a reign when it could plausibly be blamed on a predecessor, no Roman emperor could afford to acknowledge defeat, especially not one on such a scale against the auld enemy.[41]

An interconnecting web of ideological and practical political necessities thus made successful warfare an overarching priority for all Roman imperial regimes. To fail, even to be perceived as failing, the test of battle automatically raised difficult questions of legitimacy and risked destabilizing what was always the shaky and improvised political balance which underpinned every functioning imperial regime. Despite an imposing ceremonial frontispiece of unanimous, unrelenting consent for a unique, divinely supported imperial order, all imperial regimes rested in practice on a delicate web of alliances, both at the centre, in and around the court, and between the centre and its constituent localities, with military victory playing a critical role in convincing key political players that they should not be looking for an immediate alternative. As was true for all Justinian's late Roman predecessors, it was this extremely demanding balancing act, with perceived military success at its heart, that would dictate the overall fate of Justinian's own regime. Given the overarching ideological and political importance of victory within this system, it is not surprising to find, either, that much of late Roman governmental administration was actually geared towards the practical mechanics of effective war making, and this, too, had profound implications for the working of political process in the empire of Justinian.

2

THE MILITARY-FISCAL COMPLEX

THE PERCEIVED TASK OF government in much of the modern world is to provide services for its citizens in return for taxes. Health, pensions, education, income supplements, infrastructure projects: all have long been funded out of taxation in the developed world, where the nation state model evolved, providing a blueprint that developing countries have generally sought to follow. It is also funding social spending, particularly the ever expanding costs of health care and of pensions for rapidly ageing populations, which lies behind the budgetary problems which have led so many Western governments to adopt policies of financial austerity since the crash of 2008. But in historical terms, all of this is extremely new, the product of the extraordinary amounts of surplus wealth generated by industrialization and post-industrial economic development. Throughout most of human history, pretty much up to any point before the mid-nineteenth century, no government—with a fiscal base consisting of relatively unproductive, overwhelmingly agricultural economies—could raise anything like enough surplus wealth to undertake such a range of activities. In the premodern world, the Roman Empire was no different; the central, often the *only* real function of premodern government was making war. In consequence, it was the prevailing nature of warfare which usually dictated the basic shape of governmental administration in different eras of human history, as well as the political relationships between rulers and ruled which underlay it.

There were two basic patterns by which premodern states, operating with much lower incomes and only limited bureaucratic capacity, could set about organizing effective war making. The first, in some ways simpler, alternative was to draw on all or usually an elite portion of their constituent populations for personal military service, characteristically defined as a certain time period per year, owed in return for the lands that provided those elites with their annual incomes. These elite militias would usually be supplemented by relatively small numbers of more professional forces serving on a permanent basis, provided for out of whatever tax revenues (or in the simplest cases, basic food renders) might be available. The second option which prevailed in the Roman world was much more complicated in administrative terms: raise enough revenue in direct taxation to fund fully professional armies.

SOLDIERS OF THE EMPIRE

The sixth-century army of Justinian's era, like its earlier counterparts, was an entirely professional force, but it no longer conformed to the patterns of the Roman army of Caesar or Augustus: overwhelmingly a force of heavy infantry, divided into legions composed of Roman citizens supported by non-Roman auxiliaries. The classic Roman legion of the early empire numbered about five thousand soldiers organized into ten cohorts, each commanded by a centurion, with more or less the same number of noncitizen auxiliary troopers organized in supporting infantry cohorts and cavalry *alae* (wings). The number of legions slowly increased from the time of Augustus until, in the Severan period in the early third century, it reached a grand total of thirty three, implying a total paper strength, with an equal quantity of supporting auxiliaries, of around 350,000 men. More or less the entirety of this military establishment was distributed along the empire's vast frontiers: in northern Britain, along broadly the rivers Rhine and Danube on the European continent, and in Mesopotamia and Armenia facing up to the Persians, while smaller forces patrolled the desert fringes of Egypt and the rest of North Africa as far west as modern Morocco. When larger forces were required for major campaigns, contingents were pulled together from all the legions within reach, but whole legions—each a small expeditionary force in its own right—were moved around the empire only occasionally.[1] By the time of Justinian, the Roman army had changed out of all recognition under the pressure of two sequential periods of military crisis.

The nearest fully comprehensive listing of the Roman army's order of battle to the time of Justinian is preserved in the eastern portions of the famous *Notitia Dignitatum*, dating to the 390s. Fifth-century legal materials dealing with military matters and some more episodic pictures of the East Roman army in action provided by fifth- and early sixth-century narrative sources make it clear, however, that the basic pattern of military organization did not alter in the intervening 130 years. Periods of heavy fighting could destroy individual units, and new threats demanded particular recruiting efforts. Sixteen regiments of heavy East Roman infantry were never reconstituted after their destruction at the battle of Hadrianople in August 378, and the Hunnic wars of the 440s both caused more heavy casualties and occasioned major recruitment drives in Isauria (south-central Anatolia).[2] But if individual units came and went, the overall shape of East Roman military organization remained broadly stable. By the late fourth century and on into the mid-sixth, the old pattern of large legionary units stationed at intervals along the major frontier lines had given way to a more complex set of unit structures and dispositions. There were now three broad types of East Roman army grouping: in descending order by status, central ('praesental') field armies, organized in two separate corps each with its own commanding general (*Magister Militum Praesentalis*); three regional field armies (one in Thrace, one in Illyricum, the third on the Persian front, each again with its own *Magister Militum*); and a whole series of frontier guard troops (*limitanei*) stationed in fortified posts on or close to the frontier line. The last were organized in more local, regional clusters each commanded by a *dux* ('duke').

The number and type of military unit found within each grouping had also evolved. The word 'legion' survived in the title of many units, particularly of the *limitanei*, some of which were direct descendants of very old formations. *Legio V Macedonica* had originally been raised by Julius Caesar in 43 BC; it still existed in Egypt in the seventh century AD. Like all its late Roman peers, however, it had become a completely different type of unit, for which the standard term was now *numerus* in Latin, *arithmos* in Greek. No individual late Roman unit was anything like as large as the old legion of 5,000 men (about the size of a modern brigade). We don't have exact information, but even the notional manpower of larger infantry formations was no more than 1,000 to 1,500 (much more like a regiment). There were also many more cavalry units in both the frontier *limitanei* and in the regional and praesental field armies than there used to be; these were smaller still, consisting of no more than 500 men.

The old binary divide between citizen legionaries and noncitizen auxiliaries, likewise, had been replaced by three main categories of soldiers, who received differing rates of pay and enjoyed varying grades of equipment. The highest-ranking *palatini* and second-ranked *comitatenses* were distributed across the central and regional field armies, while frontier forces were composed of *limitanei* and/or *ripenses*.[3] Differences in status materially affected military capacity. When a cavalry unit operating against desert raiders in Cyrenaica was downgraded from field army status (as *comitatenses*) to *limitanei*, it lost the right to the extra remounts and supplies, making it potentially much less effective against troublesome desert raiders, much to the chagrin of Synesius of Cyrene. The men themselves presumably also didn't much enjoy the resulting pay cut. But it is a mistake to write off the effectiveness of *limitanei* altogether. It used to be fashionable to envisage them as part-time soldier farmers who would have struggled to cope with anything more demanding than a little patrolling and the odd customs inspection. But while it is conceivable that their state of readiness and overall training may have varied substantially on different frontiers, the *limitanei* of the eastern and Danubean fronts were battle hardened. Warfare in the East largely took the form of extended sieges, and in this theatre the garrison forces of many of the major Roman fortresses were composed of *limitanei*. As such, they bore the brunt of much of the initial fighting in many campaigns. The same was also true of the Danubean front, where heavy fighting had been endemic throughout the fifth century. For really major campaigns, units of *limitanei* were sometimes also mobilized alongside designated field army formations.[4]

Much of this reorganization can be traced back to the period of extended military and political instability known as the third-century crisis. The fundamental destabilizing factor here was the rise of Persia to superpower status under the Sassanian dynasty, which displaced its Arsacid rivals in the 220s and found new ways to unite the massive resources of what are now Iraq and Iran and turn them against Roman possessions in the East, with extremely negative effects upon the overall strategic position of the Roman Empire. The third-century Persian King of Kings Shapur I (AD 240/2–270/2) set out the record of his achievements in a great rock inscription, the *Res Gestae Divi Saporis.*

> I am the Mazda-worshipping divine Shapur, King of Kings ... , of the race of the Gods, son of the Mazda-worshipping divine Ardashir, King of Kings. ... When I was first established over the dominion of the nations, the Caesar Gordian from the whole of the Roman Empire ... raised an army and marched ... against us. A great battle took place between the two sides on the frontiers of Assyria at Meshike. Caesar Gordian was destroyed and the Roman army was annihilated. The Romans proclaimed Philip Caesar. And Caesar Philip came to sue for peace, and for their lives he paid a ransom of 500,000 denarii and became tributary to us. ... And the Caesar lied again and did injustice to Armenia. We marched against the Roman Empire and annihilated a Roman army of 60,000 men at Barbalissos. The nation of Syria and whatever nations and plains that were above it, we set on first and devastated and laid waste. And in the campaign [we took] ... thirty-seven cities with their surrounding territories. In the third contest ... Caesar Valerian came upon us. There was with him a force of 70,000 men. ... A great battle took place beyond Carrhae and Edessa between us and Caesar Valerian and we took him prisoner with our own hands, as well as all the other commanders of the army. ... On this campaign, we also conquered ... thirty-six cities with their surrounding territories.[5]

It actually took the Roman Empire three political generations to recover from this cataclysm of humiliating defeats and restore balance to the eastern front and thereby to its own internal workings.

The most immediate level of response, as you might expect, was a revolution in the empire's overall military capacity. Some of this came in the form of new unit types. Persian elite forces of the third century AD characteristically took the form of heavily armed lancers—cataphracts—who were responsible for much of the carnage inflicted on the armies of Gordian, Philip, and Valerian. In response, Rome substantially increased the number of cavalry units at the disposal of its commanders and, in particular, created from scratch a number of heavily armoured cavalry units, the plate-mailed *clibanarii*. These units still formed part of the Eastern praesental field armies at the end of the fourth century.[6]

For the most part, however, the response took the form of a huge expansion in the size of the traditional heavy infantry arm of the Roman military. Because the notional paper strength of the new unit types is far from certain, the exact scale of this expansion is impossible to calculate. But a whole range of evidence, from the size of extant barrack blocks to pieces of specific information, provides the basis for worthwhile calculation. From these materials, no serious student of the late Roman army thinks that its notional manpower strength increased by less than 50 per cent in the century after 230, and a pretty good argument can be made that it actually doubled in size. There could be no more eloquent testimony to the scale of the strategic problem posed by the emergence—better, perhaps, re-emergence (Shapur's great inscription was placed near the tombs of the great Achaemenid kings of antiquity, Darius and Xerxes)—of Persia as a rival superpower to Rome. As a result of this expansion, the Persian threat had been broadly contained by the turn of the fourth century. The first serious Roman victories came in the final decade of the third century, and while one side or the other often held a short-term advantage in subsequent years, the fourth century saw no repetition of the stunning victories recorded by Shapur I.[7]

But the effects of increasing Persian power and of consequent Roman military expansion were felt not just on the battlefield. The rise of Persia to superpower status gave a new importance to the eastern front, which in the longer term destabilized existing political balances of command and control within the empire as a whole. Once Persian power became such a basic fact of life, it demanded imperial-level oversight be available more or less constantly for the eastern front, since only an emperor could safely command the kind of resources that war making in this theatre now required. In the *Notitia Dignitatum*, about 40 per cent of the entire Roman imperial army was positioned to deal with a potential Persian threat, and this was far too large a force to leave under the control of an unsupervised general, since few could resist the opportunity that such an army provided to bid for the imperial throne. Moreover, given the enormous size of the empire, stretching from Scotland to Iraq, and the catatonically slow speed of movement—Roman armies could move on average twenty kilometres a day for three to four days at a time before needing a rest day[8]—this in turn meant, in practice, that an additional source of command and control had to be available for the empire's other major European fronts, where a smaller but nonetheless significant increase in the level of threat posed by the new, largely Germanic-dominated confederations of the Rhine and Danube was another characteristic feature of the late imperial period.[9]

After a long period of experiment in the third century, punctuated by repeated usurpations as undersupervised generals made successive bids for the purple, the result was a general tendency in the late imperial period—for as long as the Western Empire remained in existence—for political power to be divided between two or more emperors. The knock-on political effects of military reorganization also help explain the relatively complex structure of central and regional field armies. Logistics meant that regional commanders required sufficient forces to respond to most 'normal' levels of threat. It generally took at least a year to concentrate the necessary food supplies and animal fodder and then move the actual troops required for major campaigns, and this was obviously far too long a delay for most frontier problems.[10] But since army commanders also had a long track record of usurpation, emperors wanted to make sure that individual generals did not have so many troops at their disposal that they could easily make a bid for the throne. The field army organization of the fourth to the sixth centuries can be seen as compromise. It redistributed elite portions of the army to allow for quicker, more effective responses to the new strategic demands of the late Roman period but tempered the potential political consequences by carefully dividing units, even of the central, praesental field army, between two separate commanders whose political influence could be counted on more or less to cancel each other out.

The same kind of balance is also visible in another military innovation which had become a characteristic feature of East Roman armies by the time of Justinian. It is not clear when exactly it emerged, but by the sixth century field army generals, the *Magistri Militum*, all seem to have had substantial forces of officers and soldiers—'guardsmen and spearmen', as Procopius calls them—who were recruited by them personally and tended to follow their generals on campaign even to far-flung corners of the Mediterranean. Belisarius's guards served with him in the East, in Africa, and in Italy, and when the commanding general in Armenia was assigned to the Balkans in preparation for an Italian campaign, his guards came with him. The normal term for these soldiers is *bucellarii*, and the institution clearly grew out of the tendency of the great and good, military and civilian, in the late Roman world to maintain personal armed retinues. The *bucellarii* of the sixth-century Roman military, however, were different. They were supported at least in part out of state funds (although rich generals, such as Belisarius became, might also employ some of their own money in recruiting and equipping their men, just like richer ships' captains in Nelson's navy), and they swore an oath of loyalty to the emperor as well as to their own general. The state funding increased their numbers—at one point Belisarius's guards amounted to 7,000 men, but 500 to 1,500 seems much the more usual range—and rather than think of them as an expanded personal retinue, they are better understood as elite striking formations whose permanent attachment to successful generals (successful at least in the sense of having been promoted to *Magister Militum*) meant that they enjoyed higher levels of training and equipment. It is also clear that by the sixth century, *bucellarii* were being recruited from both outside 'barbarians' and the empire's own citizens. Here, too, we see the desirability of heightened military effectiveness being balanced by the necessity of preventing individual generals from becoming politically dangerous.[11]

If the size, geographic distribution, and command structure of Justinian's army can be traced back to the military convulsions of the third century, its unit forms and tactical doctrines had their origins in a quite separate crisis. From the late fourth century, the rise of Hunnic power in eastern and central Europe generated an unprecedented level of threat to the empire's Rhine and Danube frontiers. One casualty of this second strategic revolution, as we have seen, was arguably the whole Western Empire.[12] The East, by contrast, survived relatively intact, since the Huns were never able—directly or indirectly—to undermine central imperial control of its key revenue-producing heartlands in Egypt, the Near East, and Asia Minor. Nonetheless, the level of strategic shock engendered by the Huns even for the Eastern Empire was again enormous. Particularly in Attila's pomp in the 440s, the empire found itself on the European front facing an opponent capable of effectively besieging major fortified bases (such as Singidunum and Sirmium) and of defeating imperial field armies in open battle. In 447, two imperial armies—those of Thrace and then the Praesental forces—were defeated, and a whole series of fortresses across the Balkans destroyed.[13]

The overall Roman military response to the Hunnic menace was no quicker nor more straightforward than it had been to the rise of Persian power in the third century. Most immediately, it proceeded by employing groups of Hunnic mercenaries, a common feature of the later fourth- and early fifth-century Roman campaigns.[14] New sources of military manpower were also developed, some of them from inside the empire. In the 440s, the East Roman army was transformed by a sustained recruiting drive among the population of what had previously been largely the bandit country of Isauria: rough Cilicia in south-west Asia Minor. As the recruited Isaurians became increasingly prominent in Constantinople, this was to have important political consequences for a generation of imperial politics from the later 460s to the mid-490s (see chapter 3).[15]

Recruitment also went on vigorously among displaced groups from the empire's European periphery who were keen to escape Hunnic domination. A large force of Goths, for instance, rescued from Hunnic control in the 420s and allocated land to settle on in Thrace, remained a recognizable part of the Eastern Empire's military establishment down to the 480s. These were *foederatii*—'federates'—and held their land on innovative legal terms that had evolved in the later fourth and early fifth centuries. These involved a commitment that the group concerned would provide military units for the imperial armies over the long term on a hereditary basis—a bit like Roman veterans, whose sons had a particular liability for service—but with the added proviso that the *foederatii* could preserve their own existing communal and political structures and would always serve under their own leaders.[16] The use of mercenary contingents from beyond the imperial frontier, hired in for particular campaigns, also remained a regular feature of the sixth-century East Roman army. Procopius records a whole range of such contingents, from groups as diverse as the Germanic-speaking Lombards of the Middle Danube to the Turkic-speaking Bulgars (whom he calls Massagetae) from north of the Black Sea.[17] But the empire continued to maintain largely autonomous groups of *foederatii* on Roman soil, too, even after the departure of the Thracian Goths for Italy in 488, with Heruli in particular playing an important role in Justinian's campaigns.

In the long term, however, the most important military response to the era of Hunnic domination was tactical. The Romans first met the Huns as small-scale cavalry raiders equipped with a more powerful version of the reflex bow, which had long been a characteristic weapon of Eurasian steppe nomads. This gave different Hunnic groups sufficient military edge rapidly to establish hegemony over large numbers of the semi-subdued, largely Germanic-speaking clients of Rome—Goths and others—who controlled the territories beyond the defended imperial frontier. As a result, the military problem posed by the Huns in the era of Attila evolved into a much more complex one, since the great Hunnic warlord disposed of the combined forces of both the Hunnic core of his empire and of a host of conquered subject peoples: other steppe nomads, such as the Alans, and the largely infantry forces of Germanic Goths, Gepids, Suevi, Sciri, and others. The range of weaponry that Attila could deploy was accordingly varied; it encompassed mounted archers to heavy, mailed shock cavalry equipped with lances to dense groupings of infantry.

The full story of all the experimentation which underlay the Roman adaptation to new patterns of warfare in the Hunnic era cannot be recovered, but its overall effect upon the sixth-century army emerges clearly from the battle narratives of Procopius's histories and contemporary military manuals, above all the *Strategicon of Maurice*. As seen in action in these texts, the East Roman army of the sixth century was characterized by a much greater reliance upon its cavalry arm. Now often deployed in the front of the battle line instead of just as flank protection (as had still generally been the case in the fourth century), it comprised two distinct elements. Occupying the van were the lighter cavalry (*koursoures* in the terminology of the *Strategicon*) characteristically armed with Hunnic-type reflex bows, whose archaeological remains, in the form of bone stiffeners (see Figure 2.1), start to appear in Roman military contexts in the early fifth century. The *koursoures* were the first to engage an enemy, using their projectile weaponry at least to inflict some initial losses on an enemy or, at best, to spread disorder in his tactical formations. If this initial assault was successful, the heavier shock cavalry—*defensores*—could then be deployed almost literally to ram home the advantage. They were armed not only with bows but with cavalry lances to break up an opposition line. Alternatively, if the *koursoures* ran into trouble, the heavy cavalry would cover their retreat.[18] Procopius's battle narratives indicate that the new elite cavalrymen of the sixth-century army tended to be concentrated in the *bucellarii* of the *Magistri Militum*, but regular field army

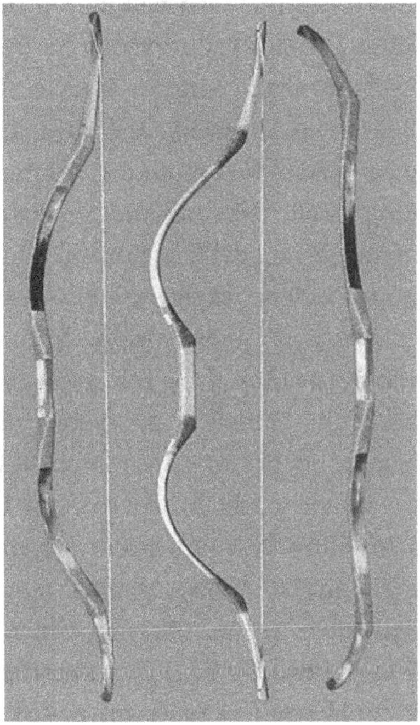

FIGURE 2.1
The reflex bow of the Huns. Fighting the Huns kick-started the revolution in East Roman tactics and equipment which paved the way for Justinian's conquests.

cavalry units, and some of the *foederatii* too, were intensively trained in the new battlefield practices.

I suspect, too, that the *bucellarii* of field army generals also provided the key military structure of institutional continuity which allowed new weaponry and the tactics to exploit them fully first to be developed and then passed on across the generations. This is partly an argument from silence. There were no officer training schools or military academies in the later Roman Empire where they might have been able to develop new doctrines by discussion in the classroom, which is how modern armies operate. But it is a bit more than that, too. The *bucellarii*, the new elite arm of the Roman army of the sixth century, enjoyed the highest rates of pay and best equipment on offer from the state factories (not to mention any extras that their often rich commanders chose to provide), so that they could generally attract the best recruits. The officer cadres of the *bucellarii* were also a source of new field army generals. At least two of Justinian's initial tranche of his own appointees to the rank of *Magister Militum* in command of key field army formations in the late 520s—not only Belisarius who will play such an important role in this book but Sittas as well—had served in his *bucellarii* when the future emperor first held the rank of *Magister Militum Praesentalis* in the early 520s; several of Belisarius's household and underofficers from the original African campaign would find promotion to the rank of magister in turn as the reign progressed.[19] Not only were the *bucellarii* a key element in their own right of the new model East Roman army of the sixth century; they also transmitted military expertise across the generations.

Even if the most striking feature of this military revolution was its transformation of the role and equipment of Roman cavalry, it did also affect the battlefield operations of the infantry. Both the lighter and heavier cavalry units were trained to operate in integrated fashion with the infantry, which remained the largest element in every Roman field army and whose tactics and equipment had also been revamped accordingly. The latest interpretation suggests that defensive armour was indeed lightened—as the military commentator Vegetius complained in the later fourth century—but to increase the infantry's battlefield mobility so that it could work in more integrated fashion with the rapidly developing cavalry arm. The range of infantry equipment was also increased to include more bows and other projectile weaponry so that foot regiments could perform a wider variety of roles: everything from reinforcing and driving home a tactical advantage created by successful cavalry assault to providing a strong covering force should the horsemen be forced to retreat. Experience of combat in the Hunnic era eventually taught Roman commanders that it was no use operating the infantry in dense, relatively static formations, since Hunnic-style horse archery was likely to cause mayhem within the massed ranks before the heavy infantry's brute force could be brought tellingly to bear at close quarters. The infantry had to become more mobile and less vulnerable to sustained missile and cavalry attack and, by the time of Justinian, had been reordered accordingly. By this stage, it even operated with portable anti-cavalry barricades—*munitiones*, as an early sixth-century commentator labels them—to help protect it from the unwelcome attention of horse archers.[20]

Two strategic crises, therefore, shaped the armed forces available to the Emperor Justinian on his accession to the throne in 527. The old heavy infantry legions which had conquered an empire had been forced to adapt: numerically, to the threat posed by a newly united Persian superpower in the third century, and tactically, to the intrusion of large numbers of steppe nomads into eastern and central Europe in the later fourth and fifth. Such was the importance of war making in both practical and ideological terms to the overall functioning of the empire that a military revolution on this scale was bound to have equally profound effects on the workings of its internal structures.

COSTING THE EARTH

The reason is straightforward. The army was far and away the largest item on the expenditure side of the imperial budget. We can only use informed guesswork and analogy, but most estimates suggest that military expenditure consumed somewhere between half and three-quarters of annual imperial revenues, and my preference lies towards the upper end of this range. This immediately brings into focus the enormous scale of the financial problem involved in increasing the size of the army in response to the rise of Persian power. Modern governments find it extremely difficult to find an extra percent or two increase for items of expenditure, such as health care, which make up only a little more than 10 per cent of their total outgoings. If we take the most conservative estimates and suppose that army numbers increased by 'only' 50 per cent in the third century and that the military was 'only' 50 per cent of imperial expenditures, that still means that imperial revenues had to increase by 25 per cent overall to fund the military expansion needed to fend off renewed Persian aggression. In fact, the necessary increase was probably substantially larger, but finding even an overall increase of one-quarter represents a fiscal and administrative problem of colossal proportions.[21]

The signs of the resulting stress are unmistakable. In fiscal terms, the third century was marked by a series of stopgap measures which reflected an all too desperate search for cash. The last remaining independently controlled funds of the empire's constituent city territories were confiscated in the 250s. From that point on, the revenues accruing from local endowments and taxes still had to be collected by local administrators, but the proceeds were handed over to the centre.[22] There are also plenty of references to hastily imposed emergency supertaxes to generate extra revenue, and the sheer number of even legitimate emperors thrown up in the third century—twenty in fifty years without even counting usurpers and co-emperors—is itself testimony to problems with military pay, since this was always the issue which pretenders to the throne would exploit to win military support. Above all, however, the increasing desperation of Roman imperial administrators and their political bosses shows up in the progressive debasement of the silver coins—*denarii*—in which soldiers were customarily paid. Unlike modern governments, the Roman centre did not maintain a coin stock for the general use of its overall population; cash was a tool of government, fundamentally for raising and disbursing military pay. The problem with the money supply was straightforward. As the army increased in size, there was simply not enough silver bullion available to pay the extra soldiers in full-value silver coins, so the precious metal was cut with increasing quantities of base metal to generate the requisite quantity of cash. Comparative examples suggest that it took about a month for everyone to realize that the new coins were worth less, by which time many of the soldiers would have spent their pay, and the immediate crunch moment—keeping the army happy on pay day—had passed. The end result, however, as the debasements continued on into the early fourth century, was inflation on a huge scale, so that in terms of silver *denarii*, a measure of wheat cost two hundred times more in AD 300 than it had in the second century. This prompted still further stop-gap measures, not least the famous Maximum Prices Edict of 301, which made it an offence to charge soldiers more than stipulated amounts for an enormous range of goods and services—a desperate attempt to make traders accept the devalued coinage in which the imperial soldiery was now being paid.[33]

The longer-term answer to this problem lay in a complete overhaul of the fiscal systems of the empire and the mechanisms by which soldiers were actually paid. On the one hand, the empire was taxed more directly and intrusively than ever before. In proper biblical fashion, Diocletian and his fellow tetrarchs instituted a vast survey of the empire's economic and demographic assets, which were overwhelmingly agricultural, with farming generally reckoned to have generated at least 80 per cent of imperial GDP. On the basis of the vast amount of information gathered (in some places it survives in the form of stone inscriptions, as though, bizarrely, the rural world was now forever fixed), each city territory was allocated a certain number of tax units—*iugera*—which were designed to generate the same amount of revenue per year. Depending on the shape of local economies, there might be several (or many) less wealthy taxpayers to a single *iugum*, or the estates of a particularly rich landowner might amount to several *iugera*, and since it was a unit of value, not geographical size, a *iugum* of good land was much smaller than a *iugum* of poorer-quality soil. As the new system developed out of what already existed, it was not exactly the same in each region of the empire. Some provincial populations had to pay a poll tax as well as hand over a percentage of their annual agricultural production, whereas others did not. Overall, it represented a Domesday Book–level of administrative effort in terms of collecting and analysing basic information but carried out all the way from Hadrian's Wall to the Euphrates. The end result was to divide the empire into a known number of equal-value tax units, making it possible for the first time for something close to actual budgeting to take place, in the sense that the overall sum required in any given year could be divided between the total number of tax units to generate a figure for the amount of taxation to be demanded from each *iugum*. The allocation of tax bills at the micro level was up to local city administrators, who also had to collect what was due.[24]

The nature of what was in fact due was dictated by the second major plank of reform. Since there was not enough silver bullion available empire-wide to pay the expanded army in good quality silver coin, military remuneration was switched to a combination of in-kind supplies supplemented by occasional payments in gold (on recruitment, on retirement, and in the form so-called donatives, to celebrate major imperial anniversaries in between). The new tax system was geared up to produce the necessary mixture of in-kind revenues and gold, and imperial administrators operated it to maximum convenience, the obvious problem with in-kind taxation, of course, being the problems and costs involved in transporting bulky, heavy agricultural produce from where it was produced to the fringes of the empire, where much of the army was still stationed. The arrangements for the collection of a tax designed to produce woollen military cloaks in 377 provides an excellent illustration of how the system worked. Actual cloaks were demanded of taxpayers in regions where the army was stationed in large numbers, such as the Balkans and Mesopotamia, or regions of intensive pastoral farming, such as Isauria. Elsewhere, the payment was commuted to gold.[25] There were also additional taxes in gold on senators and a supposedly voluntary crown gold paid by the empire's cities notionally every five years to honour the anniversary of imperial accessions, both of which played a crucial role in providing the necessary bullion for periodic military donatives. This is not to say that everything functioned smoothly. In the fourth and fifth centuries, supertaxes were still demanded, and especially if they were stationed far from the centre, soldiers could face substantial pay arrears.[26] But there was no repetition of the systemic usurpation and inflation-via-debasement patterns of the third century: the telltale signs of a chronically underfunded military. At the cost of a huge administrative effort, the confiscation of local revenues, and a major hike in its overall tax take, the Roman imperial state eventually found the necessary resources to pay for a huge expansion of the military. It is clear testimony to the scale of the necessary effort, however, that it took the best part of three political generations from the first appearance of the Persian problem in the 230s for a workable long-term solution finally to emerge from a series of ad hoc experiments.

Understandings of just how significant the overall cost of military expansion actually was for the empire as a whole have evolved over time. For much of the twentieth century, it was assumed to have been overwhelming. This conclusion was drawn from papyrus evidence that hyperinflation had set in by the 280s and from an astonishing fall-off from about AD 250 in the number of commissioned stone inscriptions (the annual rate fell by about 80 per cent), combined with fourth-century references to peasants being tied to their lands and to deserted fields (*agri deserti*). The fourth-century empire may have regained a kind of stability after the crisis of the third century, it was supposed, but only by employing draconian legal measures to keep the peasantry farming and by raising taxes to such high levels that land fell out of production. At the same time, the incomes of wealthier citizens had been destroyed by hyperinflation (along the lines of post–World War I Germany); its effects were only too visible in the disappearance of the old patterns of participation in local city government, which the now almost extinct inscriptions had often used to celebrate before the mid-third century fall-off.[27]

All of this added up to a satisfactory model of economic collapse,[28] which has made the new archaeological evidence that has become available since the 1970s all the more exciting. Using surface finds of highly datable Roman pottery, archaeologists developed new field survey techniques whose analysis has allowed the overall temperature of the agricultural powerhouse of the imperial economy to be measured more or less directly for the first time, at least in terms of the number of functioning farming settlements that existed at different moments of the Roman imperial era. The results are revolutionary. A few areas aside (such as northern Britain and the region immediately behind the lower Rhine frontier), the fourth century has turned out, against all expectation, to be the period of maximum, not minimum, rural occupation across the overwhelming majority of the empire's provinces. This directly contradicts the expectations of the old model (although a few wise heads had already begun to doubt its most pessimistic iterations) and necessarily forces us to rethink the economic and social consequences of the fiscal restructuring which paid for late Roman military expansion. Tax rates were evidently not high enough to drive land out of production. On the contrary, the late imperial period saw much relatively marginal land come under cultivation in many parts of the empire, so that tax rates could not have been as punitive as used to be imagined. The new archaeology has also forced a rethink of the term *agri deserti*. It is now understood to mean 'land not paying taxation', with no necessary implication that it had ever done so. The new evidence does not mean that individual peasants were everywhere well off, since a highly populous countryside implies downward pressure on agricultural wages and overall conditions. But it is certainly no longer possible to think that the third-century arms race bankrupted the empire. The necessary economic costs and administrative effort were both protracted and enormous, but enough assets were eventually mobilized to sustain the new military establishment without fundamentally damaging the productive fabric of the empire. It is impossible to escape the overall conclusion, in fact, that imperial GDP was at an overall maximum in the fourth century, despite its more demanding fiscal regime.[29]

This is not to say that the process of structural fiscal adjustment had been easy, however, or that the overall tax burden was light. It was manageable in normal conditions, as all the new archaeological evidence demonstrates, but there was probably not much to spare. Fourth-century sources consistently report, for instance, that turning a large portion of the army out to fight a sustained campaign over several seasons imposed heavy extra burdens, which taxpayers found difficult to meet. For really major campaigns troop rosters were suddenly filled to the maximum, a great deal of extra equipment was needed, massive baggage trains (and the extra animals to pull them) had to be put together, and perhaps above all, huge quantities of provisions and animal fodder had to be concentrated in the relevant sector of the frontier.

All this stretched fiscal administration and logistic capacity (the latter often taking the form of mobilized labour corvées, another form of taxation) close to breaking point. Our sources specifically comment, for instance, on one occasion when the necessary resources for a big campaign were found *without* imposing unpleasant strains on taxpayers—a highly revealing form of negative evidence.[30] More explicitly, the narratives of Julian's sustained sequence of campaigns on the Rhine frontier in the mid-350s indicate that it was a considerable struggle to find sufficient food stockpiles to keep his army in the field year on year. The campaign of 357 used up the last major reserves available in Gaul itself—and even in that year the arrival of a wagon train of grain from Aquitaine was a hugely welcome surprise—while for 358, the Caesar had to turn to British stockpiles. The preparations for major campaigns normally generated costly extra taxation, hence a great deal of local political stress. Julian's preparations for his Persian campaign in 362/3 caused severe economic problems in and around his campaign headquarters at Antioch; the same city responded in 387 with a famous riot, when imperial statues were toppled over, to the extra taxation in cash and kind currently being raised by the Emperor Theodosius I to underwrite the costs of his campaign preparations against the Western usurper Maximus.[31] Although a kind of equilibrium had been reached by the early fourth century, it didn't take much to knock it off balance. Hence, too, tax rates quickly went through the roof in the embattled western half of the empire in the mid-fifth century, after it lost control of large parts of its tax base but still had to face major Hunnic and other military threats.

Another reflection of the overall scale of this fiscal recalibration is visible in the extent to which it remade patterns of elite life within the empire. Roman elites were characteristically landowners. Even if they made a fortune by other means, as was true for many other pre-industrial elites the money was quickly invested in land, which was the one sure source of an annual income. There were, of course, infinite individual variations, but three broad levels of wealth can be identified within the landowning elite as a whole. Some, like many senators of the city of Rome, were staggeringly wealthy, with large, dispersed portfolios of estates, which sometimes stretched right across the empire. Old Roman senatorial families tended to possess inherited lands in central and southern Italy, Spain, North Africa, and Italy, which their ancestors had acquired in the early centuries of empire, then supplemented this older stratum of holdings with newer acquisitions picked up in the course of their careers and marriage alliances. This level of wealth was characteristic, however, only of a numerically highly restricted imperial-level aristocracy. Much more usual was either gentry-level wealth, where a family held substantial but local landed holdings, usually concentrated in just one city territory, or the greater wealth of regional aristocrats, who had estates in several city territories but usually all within one region of the empire and who could not match the massive, widespread holdings of the imperial aristocracy.

Up to the third century, the local political lives of all but the imperial aristocracy revolved around the local town councils (formed after the model of the ancient Greek polis), which ran the empire's city communities. You qualified for membership on these councils by owning land (the precise amount varying according to the size and wealth of the particular city territory), and an essential part of the self-justificatory myth of these local elites was that they gave of their time and wealth selflessly for the good of their fellow citizens. In reality, of course, investing time and money to win prominence in your local city generated a whole series of personal benefits. In the earliest period, when Roman citizenship was rare outside Italy, holding the leading administrative posts within your city, under the standard form of municipal constitution granted uniformly across the empire in the first two centuries AD, granted you the legal right to claim it. That was a time when Roman citizenship was a sine qua non for serious prosperity in what quickly became a thoroughly Roman world. The same constitution also allowed cities to raise local funds through taxes and tolls, and being in charge of your city allowed you to decide how to spend both of these revenue flows, not to mention the annual proceeds of the endowments and gifts which gradually built up within the cities over time (not least as competitive landowners made gifts to their cities to make themselves popular enough to be voted into office).[32]

This pattern of local political life slowly evolved over the first two centuries AD as Roman citizenship spread, as the empire increased its control over the sums being raised and spent in local communities, and as the imperial elite began (very) slowly to encompass some richer landowners of provincial origin as well as the senators and equestrians of the city of Rome itself. But the military expansion of the third century, combined with the fiscal restructuring which paid for it, changed the old situation out of all recognition by fundamentally recasting the incentives operating in local elite politics. Negatively, the empire confiscated the annual flows of funds—from taxes, tolls, and endowments—which had made it worthwhile for local landowners to win power at city level. The monies still existed and still had to be raised, but the proceeds were now handed over to the central state; all the work and none of the play were left for local elites.

More positively, the central bureaucracy of the imperial state began, simultaneously if slowly, to increase its numbers to run the more intense administrative mechanisms which the new fiscal regime required. In AD 249, there were only 250 senior imperial administrators for the entire imperial land mass, so that as fiscal adjustment required both greater revenue extraction and closer supervision of the process, numbers were bound to increase. Not surprisingly, as its numbers and functions increased in importance, so did the rewards and privileges of imperial service. The old orthodoxy—as found in the relevant chapters of the first editions of the Cambridge Ancient and Medieval Histories—was that the emergent imperial bureaucracy was an alien force in the late Roman world that destroyed existing patterns of elite membership and life. The fact that many of these chapters were being written in the 1920s and 1930s, a time when totalitarian administrations were ripping up the old order in much of central and eastern Europe, is no accident. On close inspection, however, extensive fourth-century sources demonstrate that the vast majority of the new imperial bureaucrats were actually recruited from the old city-level gentry and above, the same class that had previously run the city councils. The fourth-century letters of Libanius, which are so numerous that their recipients amount to roughly an astonishing one-third of everyone we know about from the fourth century, include many letters of recommendation for posts in the emerging bureaucracy and new Senate of Constantinople. The overwhelming majority of these are in favour of individuals from old curial stock. The same point emerges, more specifically but more intensely, from the Egyptian papyri. By the early sixth century, the Apion family, who owned estates in the Oxyrhyncite nome (maybe others, too), had emerged from Egyptian curial roots to hold high imperial office at court.[33]

Equally significant, bureaucratic expansion was increasingly by consumer demand. From the 330s onwards, emperors periodically attempted to control the process but generally failed, and they came under pressure—to which they usually responded positively—to increase both bureaucratic numbers and privileges, and, indeed, to create whole new dispensations which further increased the number of individuals with a direct stake in the imperial system. Waiting lists beyond the actual establishment (for which children could be put down at an early age), honorary grants of office, eventually honorary grants of ex-office-holder status, which counted as being as important as real office holding (as surprising as that may be): all appeared, while length of service decreased markedly, and periods of lengthy absence were increasingly tolerated.[34]

The overall effect of all this was massively to increase the extent to which local landowning elites had a direct stake in the imperial administrative system. By AD 400, the 250 senior administrators of the mid-third century had been replaced by 3,000 in each half of the empire. These 3,000 served only for ten years, so that more than one individual held each job in a single political generation. This figure also doesn't take account of all the honorary grants. An attachment to the burgeoning imperial bureaucracy in some way, shape, or form had actually become the new way to exercise influence in local society, if that was one's interest, as well as of amassing wealth and influence at the centre for the more ambitious. Among the interesting jobs accorded ex- and even honorary imperial bureaucrats by the end of the fourth century were sitting with the local provincial governor, while he tried legal cases, to help him find the right verdict and running the periodic reassessment/reallocation exercises of the imperial tax burden at city level, which supposedly took place every fifteen years. Add to that the chance to make friends and influence people that came with a period in imperial service and all the favours that could follow from that, plus the fact that most cities now had no independent revenues to control, and it is easy to see why imperial service became so popular in the fourth century. The empire's fiscal refit may not have completely destroyed the old gentry and regional aristocracies, as used to be thought, but it revolutionized the incentives which dictated prevailing patterns of elite life. The empire's new fiscal structures, generated originally to fund military expansion, quickly became the new organizing principle behind the public career choices of the local and regional political elites of the empire.[35]

These same structures also generated an enormous new flow of wealth running through the spine of late Roman political life, which quickly revolutionized the private concerns, too, of the empire's local, regional, and even imperial elites. Even out of office, a first priority for members of the landowning elite became maximizing their position in relation to what was in fact the largest flow of wealth ever to have been generated by any society of the ancient Mediterranean. For those in official positions, the most obvious response was to try to siphon off a portion via scams of different kinds. Some were small scale, such as unit commanders who reported the existence of phantom soldiers on their formal rosters and pocketed the extra pay (one reason why large campaigns occasioned desperate recruiting campaigns). The scale of potential misappropriation increased in direct relationship to the seniority of the officials concerned. In one fourth-century case, a trusted imperial henchman split the cash he had been given to cover the pay arrears of the Roman army in Africa with their regional commander; cash could 'go missing' at every level, however.[36] There is less information at the micro level, but again, a bit of thought suggests an equally wide range of possible scams. Hiding the full extent of production has a long history as a rural response to the prying eyes of taxmen, and the fact that tax bills were reallocated only every fifteen years must have made it irresistible, for those with the necessary flexibility, to bring unrecorded assets into production in the intervening period and enjoy the proceeds untaxed.

The sources also demonstrate, more systematically, that Roman gentry and aristocratic landowners customarily positioned themselves politically to achieve the most tax-efficient outcomes possible from the internal operations of the system. All the vital information was kept at the local level. City council offices contained registers which recorded every estate within that city's territory, with a note of the owner, a statement of the notional annual value of the surplus it could produce, and its associated tax liability. This meant that moments of local revaluation, coming every fifteen years, were of huge importance. Being well-connected to the officials charged with this process—usually, as we have seen, retired ex-bureaucrats and often enough, too, from somewhere nearby—offered the opportunity of having the lowest possible tax valuation attached to your estate. By the same token, these officials had huge powers of patronage within their local communities, and it is reasonable to suppose that they were used to the full. The significance of holding such posts also emerges with striking clarity from particular case studies where the evidence happens to be dense. The rise of the Apion family from local Egyptian gentry to imperial aristocracy in the fifth century, for instance, was clearly based on the new roles played by its founding fathers, Strategius I and Apion I, in imperial tax collection. Its continued prominence in the sixth century, likewise, was based, at least with Oxyrhychus itself, on acquiring the no doubt lucrative responsibility to account to the central authorities for the tax of a large proportion of the total owed by the entire nome.[37]

The actual payment system also offered interesting possibilities. Tax was paid in three separate instalments across the year, and the well-connected deployed whatever influence they could muster to delay payments on the grounds of adverse weather conditions or other problems. Indeed, there was excellent reason to employ every possible device one to pay as little as possible up front and then delay the remainder, because emperors, who liked to appear beneficent to cultivate general popularity among the politically important landowners of the empire, would periodically grant tax amnesties, forgiving all arrears currently on the books. Making sure that you were well connected enough both at city level, where the money was actually paid, and higher up the system, where track was kept of outstanding arrears, to ensure that year-on-year payments were minimized was obviously a strategic priority.[38]

Not only, in other words, did the recalibration of the empire's fiscal structure to pay for military expansion generate a complete reorganization of local political priorities among its constituent landowning elites, disincentivizing their continued participation in city councils and pushing them towards imperial service, but it articulated a whole new patronage structure within the empire, organized around the colossal flow of fiscally generated wealth now running through the heart of the system. Detailed records do not survive, but it seems likely that emperors at the top end and local powerbrokers further down manipulated the possibilities for maximum political leverage, in the same way King John and later his son Henry III used the fine rolls of his English kingdom in the thirteenth century. These recorded all the sums that greater and lesser landowners owed the Crown for a whole variety of reasons, but year-on-year analysis shows that how much any individual actually had to pay was largely dictated by political calculation. If even very large debtors were in good odour with the king or his high officials, they had to pay only small amounts. Falling out with either, however, might suddenly result in having to pay everything up front.[39] The Roman Empire—even just the eastern half of it after 476—was much larger than the medieval kingdom of England, whose gentry and aristocratic elite after 1066 constituted only about two thousand landowning families of significance. Its emperors could have taken a direct interest, therefore, only in a much smaller proportion of the state's constituent landowners than good King John, and intermediary imperial officials must have dictated the fate of many. But the basic principles of the situation were analogous. Taxation of the wealthy and well-connected is always a political matter, and the new taxation system of the later empire relocated the focus of local elite political jockeying towards building up the connections which would allow navigation of the new system in the most efficient manner possible.

Such, in outline, was the imperial system inherited by the Emperor Justinian in 527. The job description had other important components besides, especially maintaining religious orthodoxy and the structures thought necessary to *civilitas*, but imperial regimes tended to succeed or fail according to their fate on the battlefield. Ideologically, victory was the acid test of legitimacy. An emperor's armies could not lose if the divine creator of the cosmos was behind them, but He would support only an emperor who was really fit for purpose, so military defeat immediately raised difficult questions of legitimacy and intensified the perennial political calculations of the great and good, which could easily run over into actual plotting. More directly, military success also allowed a regime to protect itself from external and internal enemies, but paying for the expanded and remodelled military of the late Roman period had also revolutionized the fiscal and administrative structures of the imperial state and, hence, modes of local elite engagement with these new systems.

The success or failure of individual emperors depended on their ability to exploit these systems and their prevailing constraints to respond effectively to the threats and opportunities that arose in the course of their regime's existence. The demands put on the empire's structures by the conquest policies of the Emperor Justinian would test them to the limit and, many have thought, beyond. Before we can begin to consider that issue, however, we need to explore the political processes which brought Justinian to the throne in the first place and their impact upon the developing policies of his reign.

3

REGIME CHANGE IN CONSTANTINOPLE

On 1 August 527, Justinian succeeded his uncle and adoptive father Justin I as emperor of the Roman world. At this point, his succession came as no surprise, because Justin had formally associated Justinian in the rule of the empire the previous spring, proclaiming him fellow Augustus on 1 April. Justinian's wife, the famous Theodora, had also been crowned Augusta three days later. This was the first time that a son of any description had inherited the throne of Constantinople from his father since the boy emperor Theodosius II in 408, the best part of 120 years before. To understand the intense political backstory which underlay Justinian's direct but highly unusual inheritance of the purple and how fundamentally it dictated the initial policy choices of his regime, it is necessary to step back briefly in time to the reign of his uncle/father's immediate predecessor, Anastasius I.

THE FAILURES OF ANASTASIUS

A detailed account of Anastasius's election has been preserved in a tenth-century text, the *Book of Ceremonies*. The year is 491, the month April, and the Isaurian Emperor Zeno has just died. His widow, the Empress Ariadne, daughter of Zeno's predecessor but one, Leo I, came to the Hippodrome, which could hold 100,000 spectators. For such a moment, it was probably full. She displayed herself to the assembled populace of the imperial capital to hear what qualities they wanted of their new emperor. As was the norm, communication between ruler and ruled took the form of shouted acclamations. They began conventionally:

> Ariadne Augusta, may you be victorious!
> Holy Lord, give her long life!
> Lord have mercy!
> Many years for the Augusta!

So far, it was highly reminiscent of the opening acclamations with which the assembled senators of Rome greeted the arrival of a new imperial law book, the Theodosian Code, on Christmas Day 438. Then, just as happened with the code ceremony, the acclamations moved from the general to the specific. The capital's populace had two qualities in mind for its new emperor. He should be orthodox and he should be Roman.[1] Ariadne took these thoughts back with her to the nearby imperial palace; an enclosed passage led from the Hippodrome's royal box into the palace complex. After discussion with the assembled senators, it was agreed that the empress herself should make the final choice. Her vote went to the sixty-year-old Anastasius, a long-serving palace insider—officially a *silentarius*, but the standard translation of this term as 'usher' gets nowhere near its importance. She then married him to provide the new imperial regime with the stamp of legitimizing continuity.

As with most public ceremonials of the later empire, there is every reason to suppose that the substantive contents of Ariadne's meeting with her Constantinopolitan focus group had been carefully choreographed. In the Hippodrome, the factions (Blue, Green, Red, and White) reigned supreme, and the way to get the answer you wanted was straightforward. They were part supporters' clubs for the great chariot-racing teams, part mafia-type organizations who ran or took a cut from a whole range of businesses in their specific corners of the city. But they also had responsibilities for keeping basic social order in return. If you wanted something shouted in the Hippodrome, you needed to make the faction bosses an offer they couldn't refuse. Often this would be cash, but in this case, the acclamations themselves suggest something more specific. The chief interface between the factions and imperial government was the office of the city's prefect, Constantinople's (unelected) mayor. How the prefect chose to run the city directly affected the key interests of the factions. Before enquiring what qualities it wanted in an emperor, Ariadne had asked the crowd what it wanted of her. The people shouted back that they wanted a new prefect, to which Ariadne—again likely by prior arrangement—duly agreed.[2]

The demand that the new incumbent should be 'Roman' had, in context, an extremely specific meaning. What he should not be, in other words, was an Isaurian outsider, like Ariadne's ex-husband, Zeno. In particular, the demand seems to have been framed to exclude one prominent candidate for the throne: Zeno's brother Longinus. Longinus had supported his brother through thick and thin—virtually the whole of Zeno's reign had been spent in a desperate struggle to hold onto the throne—even to the extent of spending ten years as a hostage in the hands of Zeno's fellow Isaurian warlord, Illus. When Longinus finally regained his freedom in 485, Zeno lavishly rewarded him. He was appointed commanding general of the senior of the two central field armies—the empire's senior military command—and immediately made consul for 486. Between 485 and 491, he featured prominently in the public life of the empire as a leading member of the inner cabal of Isaurians with whom the emperor surrounded himself, including a second Isaurian Longinus, who served as chief administrative officer with control of much of the imperial bureaucracy—*Magister Officiorum*—for the latter half of Zeno's reign (484–91). The normal tenure for such posts was usually closer to a year than a decade, which only underlines the point. Against this backdrop, to get 100,000 people baying in the Hippodrome that they wanted the next emperor to be a 'proper' Roman was tantamount to demanding that, whoever else was chosen, it must not be Longinus, who had been actively campaigning to fill the imperial vacancy.[3] The meeting in the Hippodrome, in other words, was part of a carefully orchestrated coup d'état that Ariadne and her confederates pulled off at a crunch moment in the unfolding succession process.

Given such highly charged beginnings—it was always possible for someone else to make the factions a better offer, so you never quite knew what was going to happen (as Hypatius would find to his horror in 532: see

p. 111)—it is in some ways harsh to categorize Anastasius's reign as a failure. It was no small achievement, in fact, that he would die quietly in his own bed at the grand old age of eighty-seven. Isaurian involvement in Constantinopolitan politics was born out of military necessity. Faced with the fifth-century explosion of Hunnic power, Constantinople needed new troops and needed them fast. The Isaurians were part of the answer to the military problem, but recruiting them into imperial field armies in such large numbers and promoting their officers accordingly had major political consequences. As Isaurian officers became field army generals (*Magistri Militum*), they began to exercise considerable influence at court. By the 460s, under Ariadne's father, Leo I, they had become so numerous and so deeply entrenched within Constantinopolitan politics that the emperor had married off his daughter to one of them, viewing them as a counterweight to the power of an overmighty general, the great Aspar, who had particular ties to the large body of Thracian Gothic *foederatii* (see p. 158). Eventually Leo had Aspar murdered (hence Leo's nickname, 'the butcher'), while the Thracian Goths dropped out of the picture. In the 480s, most of them signed up to the new coalition that Theoderic the Ostrogoth built up in the Roman Balkans in the 470s and 480s and led into Italy just before Zeno's death (488/9). By 491, not only were the leading Isaurians a well-entrenched element within Constantinopolitan politics, but they also had a strong record of fighting extremely hard and exploiting long-standing ties of loyalty to particular groups of Isaurian soldiery to hold on to power.[4]

Zeno's rise had begun in the 460s when he fought off the influence of rival generals from among the Thracian Goths eventually to make good on a potential claim to the imperial throne by marriage. He became sole emperor in 474, following the twin deaths of both his father-in-law and his own infant son by Ariadne, Leo II; but that was only the beginning. He had subsequently had to fight tooth and nail to hold on to his throne against other forces within the Constantinopolitan establishment, particularly his mother-in-law, Leo's widow, Verina, along with more Goths and even rival Isaurian warlords (above all Illus, who held Longinus hostage for a decade). This included an eighteen-month exile back home in Isauria during the usurpation of Basiliscus, Verina's brother, in the mid-470s, from which he eventually returned to Constantinople in triumph, and a four-year war against another usurper, the general Leontius, who had the backing both of Verina and Illus. Zeno's reign is a story of warfare, exile, manoeuvring, and assassination, both attempted and successful, and it all adds up to the basic point that the Isaurians were never going to go quietly just because Ariadne and her associates managed the Hippodrome crowd with aplomb on the morning after Zeno's death.[5]

Within a year, the new regime had safely exiled Zeno's brother to an Egyptian monastery, separating him from his family, whose other members were sent to Bithynia, beside the Black Sea. But the other Longinus, Zeno's ex-*Magister Officiorum*, was still at large, and Zeno's henchmen were not easily excluded from the inner circles of empire. By 492, a large section of the Isaurian military had risen in revolt against the new emperor, under the leadership of Conon, who resigned as bishop of Apamea, and the current governor of the Isaurian region, Lilingis. It was a dangerous moment, but the regime found enough loyal troops in the eastern and praesental field armies to defeat the rebels in battle at Cotyaeum (modern Kutahya) and kill Lilingis. At that point, the attempt to unseat the regime by force was broken, and the surviving rebels fled back to their mountains, where they continued to cause serious disturbances throughout most of the rest of the decade. Slowly, however, their leaders were hunted down. Conon was killed in 493, and Longinus captured in 497; his head was sent on a pole to Constantinople amid great rejoicing. Two other leaders (one of them yet another Longinus) remained at large but were finally cornered in 498. Brought to Constantinople alive, this time, they were paraded through the streets to ridicule before the third Longinus was sent off to Nicaea to be tortured and executed. With that, the Isaurian rebellion was finally crushed.[6]

Surviving this initial crisis was no small achievement for Anastasius's regime; it had meant rooting out a political generation of unbalanced Isaurian influence at the heart of the empire. One might say that Anastasius's reign was subsequently characterized by careful and, in late Roman terms at least, relatively efficient administrative competence. Not least, the tax system was overhauled, with in-kind exactions being commuted substantially into cash payments, which greatly eased processes of collection and distribution (if not necessarily of payment). The sources also preserve generally positive judgements about how the empire was run.[7] In one key respect, however, Anastasius's rule was a conspicuous failure: succession.

Anastasius was sixty years old when he came to the throne. His empress, Zeno's widow, was about forty, so they might just about have had children but did not (whether by accident or design is not known, but I suspect the latter). The lack of an heir from his own body, however, did not prevent Anastasius from promoting close family members to positions of prominence. He had three nephews, the children of two different sisters: Pompeius, Probus, and clearly the favourite, Hypatius. Pompeius was honoured with the consulship for 501, before holding an important military command (probably general of the Thracian field army) towards the end of Anastasius's reign. Probus was consul in 502, but he was not in a senior post of any kind until the reign of Justin. Hypatius, on the other hand, already held a significant military command during the Isaurian insurrection and was the first of the nephews to receive the consulship (in 500); he then held a string of commanding generalships throughout the first two decades of the sixth century: *Magister Militum Praesentalis* ca. 503 and again a decade later, punctuated by spells as commander of both the Thracian and the eastern field armies. There is no doubting the strength of his uncle's favour, nor that Hypatius had aspirations towards the purple; these surfaced clearly in the early 530s. Nonetheless, Anastasius made no moves to secure the succession for his favourite nephew. The contrast with Justin's elevation of Justinian in the 520s (Caesar in 525, Augustus in 527) is striking and normally understood (in my view correctly) to mean Anastasius lacked the political capital to be able to make such a move without it generating overwhelming opposition among the other interested parties at his court.[8] In part, this reflected the nature of his original candidacy, but it was also reinforced by the overall history of his reign.

In origin, Anastasius was a compromise candidate. A sixty-year-old court fixer with no children and little likelihood of having any, he was a candidate that all those with an interest in blocking Longinus's succession could unite behind. As already noted, he lived to be eighty-seven, but this was well above average for the period (see p. 33); just like picking an elderly pope now, Anastasius's backers in 491 probably saw him as a short-term solution to their immediate Isaurian problem, which would not involve so many hostages to fortune as putting a family line on the throne that might seize the purple for the long term (as the Theodosian dynasty had done from the late fourth century through to the mid-fifth). The fact that Anastasius proceeded to occupy the throne for so much longer than might have been expected certainly offered him the chance, over time, to take a firm grip on the reins of power. As events turned out, however, most of his reign, even after the defeat of the Isaurian insurrection, turned into a dogged struggle for survival in the face of intense pressure from two different directions.

His first problem was the renewal of war with Persia, in the second decade of his reign, after only the briefest of respites following the suppression of revolt in Isauria. The rise of Persia to superpower status in the mid-third century had fundamentally changed the strategic context in which the Roman Empire was operating and forced its structures into a revolutionary process of internal transformation (see Chapter 2). Thanks to military expansion and the fiscal transformation which paid for it, there were few repetitions, from the 290s onwards, of the disasters of the third century, even though major bouts of conflict between the two empires recurred periodically down to the 370s. At that point, however, the pattern changed. Where previously both empires had taken every opportunity to cause trouble for their arch-rival, both now sought to minimize the effects of the kinds of disturbance they previously exploited to the hilt. In 456, for instance, a Roman client king of Lazica, at the eastern end of the Black Sea, became restive under Constantinopolitan tutelage and looked to the Persians for assistance in establishing greater independence. The Persians refused to make anything of the opportunity, however, so the client king was forced to hand over the crown to his son and go to Constantinople to explain himself. Such a cooperative approach to potential bones of contention was utterly typical of fifth-century relations between the two empires.[9]

It is important to understand that this extended period of cooperation was not completely voluntary, however, in the sense that it was forced on these previously bitter imperial rivals by outside circumstances. The extended period of peace was based on Rome's acceptance of two substantial reverses to its overall strategic position as it had stood in the first half of the fourth century. First, the defeat of Julian's Persian expedition in 363 led to the surrender of Nisibis and a series of Roman territories on the far side of the Tigris. Second, in the 380s, the Emperor Theodosius I accepted a partition of Armenia that turned about three-quarters of it (Persarmenia) into a Persian protectorate, with only a rump remaining within the Roman sphere of influence (see Map 1).[10] That both of these setbacks were simply accepted by a sequence of fifth-century Roman imperial regimes owed nothing to a sudden outbreak of generosity towards Persia. This was the era when the rise of Hunnic power in central and eastern Europe was posing an entirely unprecedented level of threat to East Rome's European frontiers, and there was simply no military capacity left over for unnecessary quarrels with Persia. For their part, not only had the Persians achieved about as much as they could reasonably hope for, but they, too, were facing new pressures from steppe powers to their north—in particular, the so-called Hephthalite, or 'White' Huns, who expanded outwards from an original power base, it seems, in northwestern Afghanistan to conquer Sogdia and Khurasan in the early fifth century and make themselves into highly predatory eastern neighbours of the Persian Empire. If and exactly how, they may have been related to the Huns who made themselves such a nuisance to both halves of the Roman world continues to be debated. Crucially, however, as their power base expanded, the Hephthalites won a series of victories over the Persians in the later fifth century, including a Persian equivalent to Hadrianople at the battle of Herat in 484, which saw the defeat and death of the Persian king of kings, Peroz (459–84).[11]

Both empires had excellent reasons to keep the peace in the fifth century, therefore, and this did not change overnight. To help fight the Hephthalites, the Persians had pressured Constantinople for financial support in the time of Zeno, and he does seem to have responded with occasional assistance. In the 490s, however, Persian demands increased, especially when the latest Persian ruler, Khavad, had to pay for Hephthalite support to win back his throne. Nonetheless, Anastasius's regime, in the face of considerable provocation, continued to maintain the fifth-century pattern of peaceful cooperation, refusing to exploit a revolt of Christian Persarmenians in the 490s as an opportunity for stirring up trouble for their increasingly demanding imperial neighbour. By the start of the sixth century, however, Khavad was desperate enough for cash actually to go to war instead of just threatening it.[12]

If none of this was the fault of Anastasius's regime, the lack of serious preparations for war on the Persian front was. In 502, Khavad's invasion army enjoyed almost complete freedom of manoeuvre right across the Roman east. His initial invasion route ran through Armenia, where he quickly swept up the main Roman base of Theodosiopolis. His forces then turned south, leaving Martyropolis in peace in return for the two years' worth of taxes that its governor had in his strong boxes, before ending up outside Amida. There were no Roman *limitanei* in the city, but its civilian inhabitants defended their homes with determination for three months until the city was finally stormed. One in ten of its surviving male inhabitants was executed, the rest sold into slavery, and all the wealth of the city dragged off to Persia. At the same time, Khavad's Arab allies raided right across the Roman east, all the way from Edessa to Constantia.

Stung by defeat, Anastasius despatched a huge army to Mesopotamia for the campaigning season of 503. It reportedly numbered forty thousand men (far larger than any single force put in the field under Justinian) and operated in three divisions, one of them, significantly, commanded by the emperor's nephew Hypatius. Two headed for Amida, now held by a Persian garrison of three thousand, the third for the Persian regional capital at Nisibis. All three divisions were decisively defeated later in the year, however, when Khavad counterattacked, although he found it impossible in turn to make any substantial additional gains, being held in check by the Roman fortifications at Constantia and Edessa. The war in Mesopotamia was rapidly approaching stalemate; the most dramatic action of the year came in the form of Persia's Lakhmid Arab allies, under Al-Mundhir, invading the Roman provinces of Arabia and Palestine. According to Cyril of Scythopolis, they laid 'everything waste, enslaving countless thousands of Romans, and committing many lawless acts'.

That was more or less that. The easy gains having been made, Khavad had no interest in continuing the war. The Romans tried again to recapture Amida but were unable to do so. Truce and then permanent peace negotiations began in 504, and there was no more fighting of substance. The resulting peace agreement was no humiliation for Anastasius, who avoided having to agree to the kind of annual payments which the Persians had been demanding before the war and won back control of Amida. He also set in motion major improvements to Roman defences in Mesopotamia, not just at Amida but at Edessa and Batnae as well, while constructing a brand-new Roman forward base for the region, right on the frontier line at Dara. On the other hand, the defeats of 502/3 were not avenged on the battlefield; Amida was regained only by negotiation, and Anastasius did make some kind of payment to his Persian rival. None of this was disastrous, but it provided neither the emperor nor his favourite nephew, whose campaign to retake Amida had not gone well, with the kind of political capital which might have allowed them to shake up the court's factional balance decisively in their own favour in Constantinople.[13]

The same was even more true of the second great issue of Anastasius's reign: division within the Christian Church of the East. The importance of this issue was signalled right at the start of Anastasius's reign, when the crowd in the Hippodrome demanded—again probably by prior arrangement—that the new emperor should be 'orthodox'. The current divide had emerged in response to the definition of faith enshrined in the declarations of Chalcedon, the fourth great ecumenical council of the late Roman era, held in 451. The underlying issue was continuing debate over how divine and human were combined in the person of Christ, an issue that had powerful implications for understandings of how exactly Christ had saved humanity. Did Christ as God die on the Cross? Is that the miracle which banished death for the saved? But can an immortal, eternal divinity actually die? In the generation before Chalcedon, Nestorius, patriarch of Constantinople (428–31), had been deposed by a body of hostile opinion orchestrated by his archenemy, Cyril, patriarch of Alexandria, for arguing that Immortal God could not have suffered on the Cross and it was only the human part of Christ that had died. In response, Cyril had asserted the indivisible 'one incarnate nature of God the Word': God and human utterly inseparable. Everyone agreed that Nestorius could not be correct, but for some, Cyril's one-nature language, especially as interpreted by some of his more radical supporters, left no room for Christ's humanity. Chalcedon attempted to calm this dispute by affirming that after the Incarnation, Christ continued to exist 'in two natures' while it at the same time reaffirmed the condemnation of Nestorius. This could just about be made compatible with Cyril, because in one document, the Formula of Union (433), when under imperial pressure to be conciliatory, the patriarch had stated to John, his fellow patriarch of Antioch, that it was not necessarily illegitimate to discuss the two natures of Christ so long as it was not supposed that only His human element had suffered and died on the Cross. The current pope also contributed a treatise to Chalcedon, the *Tome of Leo*, which restated the standard Western understanding of the matter: 'one person in Christ but two natures'.[14]

As usual, gathered together just over the Bosporus and under the watchful eye of the Emperor Marcian, who had called the council, and his officials, who ran it, the assembled bishops had all signed up to Chalcedon at the time. Once released from close imperial oversight, however, dispute began again. For many of the Eastern bishops, 'in two natures' just sounded too much like Nestorius and, the Formula of Union aside, contradicted what they understood as the touchstone of Cyrillian orthodoxy. As debate continued over the next generation, official imperial policy was simply to enforce Chalcedon. But questions were being asked about its viability behind the scenes, given the extent of visible division it had provoked and to which the usurper Basiliscus (474–6) had responded by condemning the council's teaching.

With the Eastern Church ever more bitterly divided, Zeno decided to act. In 482, perhaps drawing on a peacemaking initiative that had been tried out locally in Palestine, the emperor published his 'unifying statement': the *Henotikon*. This stated that the faith had been satisfactorily defined once and for all in the fourth century at the ecumenical Councils of Nicaea (325) and Constantinople (381). Chalcedon was not condemned outright, but there was no need for it to be a source of such dissension. Zeno's edict successfully restored formal peace to the Eastern Church, as all four Eastern patriarchs (Alexandria, Antioch, Constantinople, and Jerusalem) officially endorsed its contents. As a strategy, however, it had two substantial drawbacks. First, by 482 the Western Empire had ceased to exist, and Italy was controlled by Odovacar, whose relations with Zeno were fundamentally hostile. This meant that the emperor currently had no leverage at all over the fifth Patriarch of the late Roman Church: the bishop of Rome. Because the *Tome of Leo* had been formally incorporated into its proceedings, Rome had a strong stake in upholding Chalcedon's full legitimacy as an ecumenical council. Negotiations got nowhere, and two years later, Pope Felix III held a synod denouncing the *Henotikon* and formally deposing and excommunicating Acacius, the current patriarch of Constantinople. Rome and Constantinople were now formally in schism. Second, the fact that churchmen were no longer publicly attacking one another in the East did not mean that the underlying dispute had been resolved. The imperial capital was home to various monasteries, above all that of the *Akoimetoi* ('Sleepless') monks, who were fierce supporters of Chalcedon. In Syria and Palestine, it had equally fierce opponents.[15]

As a result, it is hard to know exactly what the Hippodrome crowd meant when it shouted at Ariadne that the new emperor should be 'orthodox'. If this was an orchestrated event, it presumably meant that the new regime should uphold the status quo as enshrined in the *Henotikon*. If not, then given the strong tendency of at least part of the capital's population towards Chalcedon, it was shouting for the *Henotikon* to be rescinded. Either way, the new regime had inherited an intractable problem which, again, was fundamentally not of its own making.

There is reason to think that Anastasius's own sympathies lay with the anti-Chalcedonians. Either that or, by the second half of his reign, he and his advisers had concluded that the best way to restore overall peace to the Eastern Church was to undermine the pro-Chalcedonian sympathies which still prevailed within the imperial capital and bring it into line with an anti-Chalcedonian position. In 508, the intellectual heavyweight of the anti-Chalcedonian leadership, Severus, was allowed to come to Constantinople with two hundred highly partisan monastic supporters from Palestine. In due course, he was even introduced to the emperor by one of Anastasius's nephews, Probus, who seems to have been part of Severus's network. This prepared the ground for more explicit moves. On

20 July 511, the congregation in the great Church of Hagia Sophia found that an anti-Chalcedonian addition had suddenly been introduced to one of the standard prayers of the liturgy, the Trisagion. This was chanted before the daily psalm and usually went 'Holy God, Holy Strong, Holy Immortal, have mercy upon us.' Late in the 460s, however, as part of the hostile reaction to Chalcedon, an additional 'who was crucified for us' was inserted into the prayer in some churches, as a phrase which no supporter of Chalcedon could possibly utter. The *Henotikon* was still officially in force in 511, but regime policy was moving in an anti-Chalcedonian direction, as was made clear by the depositions of the patriarchs of Constantinople and Antioch, Macedonius and Florian, the same summer. Both had signed up to the *Henotikon*, but both had enough Chalcedonian sympathies to resist any more radical moves towards the council's formal condemnation. Confirmation that this was indeed the regime's underlying direction of travel came with the appointment of Severus to replace the deposed Florian. An overt anti-Chalcedonian now held the see whose intellectual traditions had been most strongly represented in the original council.[16]

So far so good: Anastasius's regime had decided on its preferred solution and was attempting to make it happen. The underlying weakness of the regime shows up, however, in what happened next. Having pushed for one kind of resolution to the religious divide, it was quickly shunted back in the opposite direction. In 512, the imperial capital witnessed such large-scale Hippodrome riots in favour of Chalcedon that they nearly cost the emperor his throne. Anastasius was forced to appear in person in the Hippodrome, without his imperial diadem, and beg forgiveness from the crowd for his ham-fisted handling of religious policy.[17] The Sleepless monks had played a leading role in orchestrating the violence, but it is also quite likely that court grandees hostile to the regime's positively anti-Chalcedonian policies—or just hostile to anything that might give Anastasius a stronger hold on the reins of power—were also involved. Soon afterwards, the regime was further rocked by the outbreak of rebellion in a large section of the Balkans' military establishment under the leadership of Vitalian. His official position at this point was probably commander of the numerous *foederatii* who held land in different parts of the Balkans. The *foederatii* were a major contributory party to the revolt, which began life, as so many military revolts did, as a dispute over shortages of pay and supplies. But it quickly spread to many of the region's *limitanei* and field army units, however, as Vitalian won over or assassinated their officers, until, in early 513, a force of up to fifty thousand men advanced as far as the Hebdomon, seven miles from Constantinople, where new emperors were often raised to the purple. In discussions with regime officials, however, Vitalian said nothing about wanting to be emperor. His troops wanted their pay, but they also wanted a restoration of Chalcedonian orthodoxy and the reinstatement of the Patriarch Macedonius.

Through his representatives, Anastasius gave the required undertakings but then reneged; so Vitalian advanced a second time in 514. Five thousand pounds of gold richer, he withdrew once more on the specific promise that Anastasius would reinstate the two deposed patriarchs (Macedonius and Florian) and call a church council for 515 to restore religious union with Rome. The death of Pope Symmachus in July 514 opened a window of opportunity, as there was always hope that his successor might be more amenable, and Anastasius duly wrote to Pope Hormisdas about a possible reconciliation in the second half of the year. The emperor remained wedded to the *Henotikon*, however, and Hormisdas would not compromise. The Acacian schism, as it was known in the West (after Pope Felix's excommunication of the Patriarch Acacius; see p. 80), could not be healed, therefore, and Vitalian advanced on the capital a third time in 515, bringing with him a fleet that might make it possible this time actually to storm the city. To landward, Constantinople was protected by the triple-belt fortifications of its Theodosian Walls, which no enemy succeeded in breaching until the invention of cannon.[18]

A bit like the Persian war, the final outcome was not the disaster that originally threatened. Under one of Anastasius's most trusted officials, the Praetorian Prefect Marinus, the regime's forces used the famous Greek fire—a lethal compound of sulphur which continued to burn on water—to incinerate Vitalian's fleet in the Bosporus. As there was no other way for his forces to break into the city, further negotiations saw him agree to go into exile while his forces were paid off. Anastasius had held on to power but only just, and he made no further moves in an anti-Chalcedonian direction. In short, the regime's record on religious matters can be characterized as one of vacillation, increasing conflict, and a total lack of concrete achievement. With the emperor now in his mid–eighties, the regime had ground to a halt, and nothing substantial was going to happen until a new regime came to power. In this context, it is plain exactly why Anastasius was unable to exercise any decisive influence over succession, and in his final years, when he might have died at any moment, it is striking that his two most prominent nephews were kept actively away from the capital. Pompeius was commanding general in Thrace with a watching brief over the exiled Vitalian. Hypatius was in Antioch, commanding general of the eastern field armies. Neither would be close enough to the palace to play any role in the political horse-trading which was bound to follow the death of an officially heirless emperor.

'PURPLE DEATH'

On the night of 8/9 July 518, the eighty-seven-year-old Anastasius died in his sleep. An almost infinite number of succession possibilities will have been intensively discussed among the interested parties within the army, court, and Senate over the previous few years, precisely because Anastasius so conspicuously lacked the authority to settle matters before his death. According to one maxim of the ancient world, one that would be picked up in due course by the papacy, only someone who didn't actually want supreme authority was worthy to exercise it. Since emperors were divinely chosen, human ambition should not come into the equation. Taking on such a level of responsibility should also feel like an enormous burden, not something to be positively desired—which is why the Emperor Julian, on being appointed Caesar and riding in the imperial carriage with his cousin, the Augustus Constantius II, was heard to mutter the (slightly adapted) Homeric tag 'a purple death and a mighty destiny have seized me.'[19] According to one story, therefore, Justinian's uncle showed completely the wrong spirit on the morning of 9 July. He was given a large sum of money by the chief palace eunuch, the *Praepositus*

Sacri Cubiculi Amantius, to bribe the palace guards to support the eunuch's own candidate, but Justin used it instead to win them over to his own candidacy. This is probably no more than scurrilous gossip,[20] but even according to the better evidence, Justin still fails the test. By 518, his eyes were firmly fixed on the throne.

On hearing of Anastasius's death, the crowd duly assembled in the Hippodrome shouting, this time, that they wanted a general. Strangely enough, Justin just happened to be a general. From the northern Balkans, Bederiana, near Naissus (modern Niš), he had enlisted in the army to escape poverty, enrolling in the *excubitores*, one of the two palace guard units (the other was the *scholarii*). Little is known about his subsequent career, because our sources are fixated on his much more famous nephew. But Justin served in all the major campaigns of Anastasius's reign. By the 490s, he was a senior field army officer (*comes rei militaris*, one rank down from *Magister Militum*) during the Isaurian revolt. He fought in the Persian war of 503/4 and was on a ship in the Bosporus when Vitalian's fleet met its match. At that point he was appointed *comes excubitorum*, commander of the palace guard unit in which he had originally enrolled. This was not as important a command as general of a field army, but it was a highly prominent one and had the distinct advantage of being a palace posting—close to the centre of power.[21]

Justin was in the right place, therefore, during Anastasius's last few years to advance his claims among the great and the good at the court, which leads one to wonder about those shouts in the Hippodrome. There is no way to be certain, but some carefully distributed cash probably was behind the crowd's highly convenient demands for a general. It was also Justin who formally announced to the assembled senators and court dignitaries, after they had been called to the palace, that Anastasius was dead. Again, the fact that he was given such a prominent task might indicate his name was being firmly put up in front of court opinion. Not everything, however, could be stitched up beforehand. As Michael Gove's sudden backstabbing of Boris Johnson in the aftermath of Brexit so vividly reminded us, even the best-laid succession plans can take surprising turns.[22] Even now, Justin's name did not come unanimously to everyone's lips. The other palace guard unit, the *scholarii*, acclaimed the only other general of any standing available in the palace: the commander of the central field army, Patricius. Plans could easily have gone awry at this point, even though the 'loyal but rather slow-witted' Patricius didn't actually want the job, especially once the *excubitores*, presumably batting for their own commander, threatened to kill him. Justinian then made a decisive intervention; he jumped in to rescue Patricius and persuaded him to make a hasty exit stage left, at the cost, it seems, to the future emperor of a punch in the face. By now there had been enough of delay that the crowd was getting restive. Worried that it might acclaim its own candidate, the senators and dignitaries unanimously went for Justin, and the palace eunuchs released the imperial regalia. Within minutes, the properly attired emperor entered the royal box and addressed his people, who cheered lustily. He also promised all the palace guardsmen a substantial pay rise.[23]

There are too many small but telling coincidences here for us not to see Justin's elevation as the end result of some careful planning. No doubt other people had alternative plans (some evidence of what they might have been emerges in the aftermath of his election), but he had used his position as palace guard commander to put himself forward beforehand and won enough support to prevail over other possible challengers on that crucial morning in the palace—as well, perhaps, as having bribed enough of the crowd to make sure that it made the appropriate demand for a general. To many of these supporters, he may, like Anastasius before him, have seemed like a good compromise candidate, one who would not exercise the reins of power with undesirable firmness. He was not one of Anastasius's nephews, he had not previously held high administrative office, and he was, again, over sixty with no children of his own, even if he had already, apparently, adopted his favourite nephew, Justinian. If that was the calculation, his backers were in for a nasty shock. The new regime exploited the policy failures of Anastasius's rule to seize power with a vengeance.

Its first priority was to clean out potential opposition within the palace. Within a week, hostile shouting in the great Church of Hagia Sophia compared the current chief eunuch, Amantius, to the infamous Chrysaphius, chief eunuch to Theodosius II, who had given strong support to the religious opposition in the run-up to Chalcedon. These shouts were probably elicited by the new emperor, whose hostility towards Amantius is also suggested by the story of the money that he supposedly gave Justin to back a different candidate. Palace eunuchs could be extremely powerful, but were also highly vulnerable to regime change. Because they lacked any broader network of political supporters, they could be executed without alienating anyone of importance. Amantius was executed within ten days of Justin's accession, together with a fellow eunuch called Andreas—a sign, perhaps, that he had been the committed backer of an alternative candidacy. Some of Anastasius's grander supporters followed them through the palace door, though by dismissal, since they had supportive networks, rather than execution. Anastasius's chief of administration, the *Magister Officiorum* Celer, who had been in office since 503, lost his job more or less immediately, and others soon followed. Hypatius had been dismissed as commanding general on the eastern front by 519, as had Marinus, Anastasius's Praetorian Prefect for the eastern provinces. The sources record that Marinus at one point decorated a public bath in Constantinople with the story of Justin's impoverished arrival in the capital. This may have been in revenge for his dismissal, but that would probably not be a smart move if Justin were already emperor. I suspect that it rather belongs to the final years of Anastasius, a stratagem perhaps to discredit Justin as a potential candidate for imperial power.[24]

There was a further pattern to these dismissals, however, which shows that the new imperial regime had much more in mind than just securing its control of the palace. Dismissals are always matched by appointments, and Justin made one highly significant one. Vitalian, the rebellious *comes foederatorum* of Anastasius's later years, was not only rehabilitated but promoted commanding general of one of the central field armies (Patricius remained the other; his reward, perhaps, for stepping aside so gracefully in the heat of the moment). The main ideological justification for Vitalian's revolt had been the desire to heal the schism with Rome, and many of Justin's other moves pointed firmly in the same direction. Amantius was compared to Chrysaphius, remember, because of his opposition to Chalcedonian theology, and both he and his fellow eunuch Andreas would eventually be celebrated as anti-Chalcedonian martyrs.

Celer, too, had been strongly implicated in the dismissal of the patriarch of Constantinople, Macedonius, in the summer of 511. For good measure Severus was quickly dismissed from his position as patriarch of Antioch. Both Justin and his wife, Euphemia, were strong supporters of Chalcedon, and the ground was being prepared for a swift volte-face.

The emperor wrote to the pope for the first time on 1 August to announce his accession to the throne. A second letter went with an imperial legate on 7 September, asking the pope to send envoys back to Constantinople to end the schism. They were accompanied by a letter from Justinian asking if the pope might like to visit Constantinople in person. The legates and their messages did not reach Rome until 20 December, but by January, a papal delegation was on its way. Its arrival was carefully timed for Monday, 25 March, the start of Holy Week, the legates being met at the tenth milestone from Constantinople by a high-powered reception committee consisting, appropriately, of Justinian and Vitalian, and, interestingly, of Pompeius, one of Anastasius's three nephews. Three days later, Patriarch John of Constantinople signed the letters from Rome, and Acacius's name was erased forever from diptychs, the official listing of true-believing patriarchs. The schism was over.[25]

Justin's regime had enjoyed an extraordinary few months (Donald Trump eat your heart out). A reasonably smooth succession had been followed by a ruthless clear-out both of the palace and of many of the top jobs of empire, a process geared to a decisive shift in religious policy, and all pushed through inside a year. There is no reason to think that the new emperor was anything other than genuine in his adherence to Chalcedon, and the deposition of Severus was only the beginning. In 519, Bishop Paul of Edessa received his marching orders when he refused to accept Chalcedon, and others soon followed. By Justin's death, in 527, about thirty anti-Chalcedonian bishops had been exiled from their sees. The contrast with the hesitant vacillation of the previous regime could not be more marked. Stepping away from the detail, one sees an imperial regime which not only enforced policy for its own sake but used enforcement as a mechanism for taking complete control of the reins of power. Its key moves over the next two years extended the pattern, making clear that the consolidation of power was deliberate and self-conscious.

One of the most extraordinary moves of those first few months was the rehabilitation of Vitalian. Partisan of Chalcedon he may have been, but he had also threatened the imperial capital, and if his fleet had not gone up in smoke in 515, an actual assault on the city could have been catastrophic. Justin not only rescued him from exile, however, but rewarded him with a top military appointment and granted him the consulship, the highest dignity of the Roman world, for 520. Vitalian's star at this point could hardly have been more ascendant, and as one recent study has underlined, the correspondence of Pope Hormisdas, generated by the ending of the schism, treated him virtually as co-emperor. In June 520, however, having just attended a set of chariot races held to honour his consulship, Vitalian was walking back through the Delphax, one of the main courtyards of the imperial palace, when he was set upon and assassinated with two of his senior aides. Procopius claims that Justinian killed him personally, which may or may not be true, but Justinian was certainly the prime beneficiary from his death. Up to this point, despite his adroit footwork over Patricius and the *scholarii*, Justinian had received no official advancement from his uncle's accession, although his unofficial prominence, as shown by his role in the ending of the Acacian schism, was clear enough. This changed immediately after Vitalian's assassination. Justinian, now thirty-six years old, replaced him as *Magister Militum Praesentalis* and was also announced as consul designate for 521. For the first time, Justinian's public profile began to reflect the informal influence that he was obviously exercising within the regime.[26]

What is fascinating about all this is that Justin was able to eliminate Vitalian with no obvious consequences. The Balkans' military showed no signs of revolt, which strongly suggests that some carefully targeted distributions of pay and supplies had been used to win them over. At court, too, the ground had been carefully prepared. The other striking feature of the summer of 520 is that Anastasius's favourite nephew, Hypatius, suddenly returned to high office as commander on the eastern front. He was back in command by 7 August, when he received a letter from the emperor, and the chronology really can't be a coincidence.[27] Justin's self-advancement had, of course, been at the expense of Anastasius's nephews, but they were extremely well connected within Constantinople and well worth conciliating if at all possible. One of the other nephews, Pompeius, had clearly come to terms with Justin early, playing a major role, as we have seen, in the ending of the Acacian schism. Hypatius's sudden rehabilitation in the summer of 520, just after Vitalian's murder, suggests that Justin reinsured himself against potentially dangerous fallout at court by using Vitalian's assassination as an opportunity not only to advance Justinian but also to rebuild relations with the important court factions associated with Hypatius. As a result, an official announcement could be made that Vitalian had paid the price for all his previous rebellions against the state, going from celebratory consular games at one moment to the mortuary at the next, and no one batted an eyelid. Eliminating Vitalian, whose prominence had been a potential obstacle to his nephew's future, while simultaneously advancing Justinian's public profile to such a dramatic extent, even if this was balanced by some careful fence-mending with the Hypatians, strongly suggests that Justin was already looking to manoeuvre Justinian into an unchallengeable position as his successor.[28]

Another indication that this was so, from the same period, takes a particular form. The emperor's favourite nephew somehow, somewhere, got himself entangled with an extraordinary former actress, a blonde by the name of Theodora. You can't believe any of the lurid details Procopius provides for her earlier life in *Anekdota* (cf. p. 16), but she was an actress, and that was problem enough because actresses and other individuals of lesser social status had long been banned from making legitimate marriages to individuals of high rank, such as the *illustris* Justinian. In 521/2, out of the blue, Justin changed the law. Several extracts from his new ruling survive in the Code of Justinian, preserving not just the legal details but also, unusually, their rhetorical justifications. As has often been argued, this new law was clearly framed to license one marriage in particular. After an introduction which rehearses all the moral failings of the theatrical profession, the first substantive clause asserts that, nonetheless, it would not be right to leave those who repented of their previous loose way of life with no hope of making a legitimate marriage. They might therefore petition the emperor to achieve the same status as women 'who had never sinned'. A second, highly significant clause, then rules that children born of such marriages would be fully legitimate and could inherit from their fathers. Six more detailed clauses follow, but the basic point of the law could not be clearer. Justinian could marry his actress, and their children would be his legitimate heirs.[29]

It is worth pausing a moment to think exactly what it was that Justin had just done for his nephew. Justin's wife, Euphemia, we are told, hated Theodora, because of her disreputable past and her anti-Chalcedonian religious leanings. The old laws banning such marriages had been in place for over two hundred years, but the attitudes behind them were much older than that. The landowning elites of the ancient world took an extremely dim view of any kind of marriage that crossed the boundaries of established social standing. Going to such lengths to allow Justinian to form a fully legitimate union with Theodora, instead of just keeping her as his mistress (which would have worried no one), generated an enormous amount of scandalized opposition within the rigid, status-obsessed world of the Constantinopolitan court. And not only from Justin's wife: the degree of fun that Procopius has with the story emphasizes how scandalous it all was. Pushing the new law through in the face of this resistance so that Justinian could marry his Mrs Simpson represented a huge investment of the regime's political capital and, along with the generalship and consular appointment that came his way after the elimination of Vitalian, sent out a clear signal that Justinian was already Justin's intended heir, even if this was not yet a done deal.

That the marriage issue strained the emperor's patience or was perhaps thought to have done is suggested by a strange story which surfaces in a variety of versions. At its heart was a serious outbreak of faction violence on the part of the Blues in 523, particularly in Constantinople but in some the empire's other major cities, too. In several versions but not the earliest, this prompted an official enquiry, which concluded that it was all being orchestrated by Justinian. He was about to be named, when a furious Justin intervened to shut down the process. It is hard to know what to make of these stories both because of their internal contradictions and because they fail to provide Justinian with a credible motive. But there were many at court who would have been happy to discredit Justinian and make Justin think again about the succession, and this may be a reflection of one effort in that direction.[30] If so, it didn't work; 523 is also the year in which Justinian received the honorific title of Patrician, giving him entry to the most exclusive status group in the empire. Relations between uncle and nephew were clearly back on track at this point, and both were clearly of one mind, again, when relations with Persia, the second great issue of Anastasius's reign, pushed its way back into the imperial in tray in the mid-520s.

A foretaste of the regime's general attitude to Persia had been provided, a little earlier, by an incident dating to 521 or 522. King Tzath of Lazica, at this point a Persian client kingdom again, suddenly contacted Constantinople. Khavad was trying to reinforce his regional domination by pressing the Lazi to accept the Zoroastrian religion, and Tzath wanted both to be baptized a Christian and to secure East Roman assistance to fend off this increase in Persian hegemony. It was a mirror-image analogue, in other words, to the situation in 456, when, with Lazica then a Roman client, the Persians had refused to interfere in a Roman sphere of influence (cf. p. 75). Justin's regime was not willing to pass up an opportunity, however, to advance its prestige. King Tzath was received in Constantinople and baptized there with full honours, dressed in gorgeous silk robes complete with embroidered likenesses of the Emperor Justin. He was then sent home with a high-born Roman wife and a Roman military mission. When the Persian ambassador complained, he was dismissed with the (inaccurate) putdown that Lazica had always been Roman. This wasn't true—Lazica made a habit of swapping imperial protectors as a strategy for maximizing its independence—but with the cooperative traditions of the fifth century still partly alive, Khavad decided not to go to war.[31]

The reason why became clear when a new Persian embassy arrived in Constantinople, probably in 525. It may have been a myth, but by the early sixth century, both empires understood the long period of broadly cooperative relations between them as having begun, at the start of the fifth century, with an agreement between the Emperor Arcadius and the Persian King Yazdegerd that the latter would adopt Arcadius's young son Theodosius II. The arrangement was to smooth Theodosius's accession in case of Arcadius's early death, and the arrangement proved prophetic. Arcadius died in 408 when Theodosius was just six.[32] Citing this precedent, Khavad now asked Justin to adopt his son Chosroes. Chosroes was the king's third son, but he had broken off relations with his eldest, and the second was barred from the throne because he had lost an eye. Chosroes was now Khavad's preferred choice, and the king feared that his succession would be hotly contested after his own death.

As the story is told by Procopius, Justin and Justinian were overjoyed at the Persian proposal and immediately drew up the necessary documents. Then the Quaestor Proculus, the regime's chief legal officer, intervened:

> This embassy openly and straight from the very first words means to make this Chosroes, whoever he is, the adopted heir of the Roman Emperor. And I would have you reason thus in this matter: by nature the possessions of fathers are due to their sons, and while the laws among all men are always in conflict with each other by reason of their varying nature, in this matter both among the Romans and among all barbarians they are in agreement and harmony with each other, in that they declare sons to be masters of their fathers' inheritance. Take this first resolve if you choose: if you do you must agree to all its consequences.[33]

It's a wonderfully dramatic story but not one to be taken at face value. Proculus's argument is nonsense. To become emperor, any candidate had to win sufficient backing from a critical mass of the key constituencies: major senatorial landowners, leading bureaucratic administrators, court officials, and senior army officers. An adopted Chosroes would still have lacked support from any of these key groups and had not the slightest hope of succeeding to the throne of Constantinople, any more than Yazdegerd's adoption of Theodosius II (if it happened) gave him a claim to its Persian counterpart.

But on the basis of this flimsy legal pretext, instead of complying with the Persian request in full, Justin offered alternatively to adopt Chosroes as son-at-arms, following a practice East Roman emperors now often used with the rulers of western successor states and other so-called barbarians. This counter-offer was transmitted to the Persians at a formal summit meeting held beside the River Tigris, right on the frontier line between the two powers. Anastasius's nephew Hypatius, still eastern *Magister*

Militum, led the Roman delegation, and the Persian king's son Chosroes was present in person. Procopius records the impact of the message:

> Chosroes left and went off to his father with nothing accomplished, deeply injured at what had taken place and praying that he might exact vengeance for their insult to him.[34]

It is utterly unconvincing, in my view, to draw any conclusion from this episode other than that Justin's regime had acted with deliberate provocation. To reject Khavad's approach on the basis of such a legal absurdity and to announce a demeaning alternative at a formal summit with the king's son present in person was a deliberate red rag to the Persian bull. Rather than accept the proffered olive branch, Justin opted instead to try to help destabilize the Persian Empire by refusing his formal blessing to Chosroes's succession. It was the continuation on a much grander scale of the new, more aggressive approach towards Persia, which Justin's regime had already displayed over Lazica.[35]

That this is the correct way to read the events is confirmed by a third incident. At more or less the same time as Khavad sent in his adoption request, a message came to Constantinople from Gourgenes, the King of Iberia, in the south-eastern Transcaucasus. Where Lazica regularly swapped allegiances, Iberia had belonged to the Persian sphere of influence without interruption since the late fourth century. In the 520s, however, Khavad tried to make the Christian Iberians, too, adopt Zoroastrian religious practices. Again, his attempted cultural imperialism misfired. Encouraged by the enthusiastic Constantinopolitan response to his Lazican neighbour, Gourgenes asked Justin for similar assistance. In practice, Iberia was too far from the Black Sea for the emperor to provide any direct military assistance, but he encouraged the Iberians' revolt, nonetheless, and paid for some indirect support for them in the form of a nomad intervention against Persia from north of the Caucasus. This had little effect, and Gourgenes was quickly driven from his kingdom, but the refusal to adopt Chosroes was clearly only one element in a profound reversal of policy. Confrontation had replaced cooperation as the watchword of relations with Constantinople's great imperial neighbour.[36]

There may also have been an internal political dimension to this second great volte-face of Justin's reign. Procopius tends to treat the different issues separately, but the Tigris summit meeting was meant to broker a comprehensive peace agreement with Persia to cover the Transcaucasus—Lazica and Iberia—as well as the prospective adoption. As a whole, the available sources suggest (as does Procopius's story of Proculus's dramatic intervention) that imperial policy had initially been receptive to Khavad's request before it eventually hardened. The question is: when exactly did it harden? The fact that Chosroes turned up at the Tigris summit in person strongly suggests that he was expecting a positive answer. The same is also suggested by comments in our sources that the chief Roman representative on the Tigris, Hypatius no less, was later accused of having conspired with Chosroes against Justin's interests. The evidence doesn't allow for certainty, but it begins to look as though a comprehensive peace deal, including Chosroes's adoption, had been brokered by Hypatius, Justin's commander in the East, but that his preferred approach was then derailed at the last minute by the imposition of a much harder line from the centre. If so, this would provide us with another example of Justin's regime using policy initiatives as vehicles for isolating and outmanoeuvring its Constantinopolitan political rivals.[37]

It was in precisely these middle years of the 520s that Justin's domination of court politics reached its apogee. In 525, amid discussion of what response to make to Khavad's adoption request, Justin formally elevated Justinian to the rank of Caesar. This not only signalled that Justinian's succession was now unambiguously official regime policy—I strongly suspect that this had been true for some time—but also that Justin felt politically secure enough to formalize the arrangement, despite all the other parties at court who had alternative preferences. According to Procopius, Justinian was always really in charge throughout Justin's reign: his uncle was little more than a front man.[38] This may have been true in Justin's last years, but Justinian's pre-eminence at that point was the end result of a long and complicated process of political manoeuvring in which his uncle had taken the lead, first of all to put himself on the throne, of course, and then to secure his nephew's succession. There had been many challenges along the way, to Justin himself in the reign of Anastasius and to others in his own reign who did not want Justinian to get two hands on the imperial sceptre. Anastasius's supporters had to be rooted out, Vitalian eliminated, and Hypatius outmanoeuvred. We should not discount the possibility, either, that uncle and nephew may have come close to falling out over a combination of Justinian's marriage to Theodora and the outbreak of faction violence, just as, in an earlier era, Constantine had eventually decided to eliminate Crispus from the succession (see p. 34). But even if we can't recover all the details, one point shines out clearly. Neither Justin nor Justinian was seized unwillingly by Julian's purple death. Both had actively sought power and framed broader policy choices at least in part to secure it. As a result, Justinian inherited from his uncle in August 527 not just a throne but a set of existing decisions, which would decisively shape the opening years of his reign.

4

THE LAST DESPERATE GAMBLE

COMPARED TO THE EXPERIENCES of Anastasius and Justin, Justinian's final promotion to the position of sole ruler of the Roman world on 1 August 527 was remarkably smooth. All the hard work had already been done. But no emperor could count himself secure until he had conclusively shown himself to be God's choice for ruling His chosen people, and here Justinian faced real difficulty. Together with his uncle, he had been responsible for two bold policy choices: restoring the full authority of Chalcedon and steering the empire away from a century and more of broadly cooperative relations with its great Persian neighbour. In the short term, these choices had tremendous political impact and allowed Justin's regime to take full control of the court in Constantinople. But both were bound to have problematic longer-term consequences.

Most immediately, war with Persia was looming. Justin's insulting response to Khavad's adoption request, combined with a new willingness to stir up trouble among Persia's Transcaucasian clients, made it inevitable. The baptism of King Tzath (see Chapter 3) had made excellent propaganda, and sabotaging the peace negotiations may have cleverly undermined the standing of Hypatius, but the policy's real effectiveness was about to be tested on the field of battle. On the religious front, healing the split with Rome had played to magnificent effect in the imperial capital, where there were strongly pro-Chalcedonian religious interest groups. It had gone down less well across the Eastern Church as a whole, however, where many still found Chalcedon's 'two natures' an impossible formula. Now, thanks to Justin's hard line on enforcement, there were fifty-five exiled anti-Chalcedonian bishops adding further fuel to the fires of entrenched religious resentment.[1]

There is good reason to think that Justinian was significantly less committed to a blanket enforcement of Chalcedon, in fact, than he was to war with Persia. The second of these policy shifts had come so late in the reign that it is impossible to think that Justinian was not involved in the decision to provoke Khavad. He had also been involved by letter in the negotiations which ended the schism and had greeted the papal delegation at Constantinople's tenth milestone in 519. But in 520 he consulted Pope Hormisdas about a possible initiative which might have allowed the East's anti-Chalcedonians to accept a slightly watered down version of the council's proceedings. The pope gave this initiative short shrift and Justinian dropped it, but his empress, Theodora, was known to have ties to some of the anti-Chalcedonian leadership networks, and her husband clearly had every intention of using them.[2] We do not hear of any formal approaches to the anti-Chalcedonians in Justinian's early years, but in 532 formal conversations were held in Constantinople, and there must have been an informal backstory to these meetings. Even if there was no immediate shift in policy, backdoor conversations to begin to heal the hurt generated by seventy years of religious division—talks about talks—clearly got under way at some point between 527 and 532. In the meantime, Justinian opened his reign with a series of persecutions of highly marginal religious groups (pagans, Manichees, and Samaritans, amongst others), whom both parties to the dispute could agree to hate.[3]

A bold approach to both religious and Persian policy had brought immediate political gains in the time of Justin, but the gains of both were now pretty much exhausted and the potentially much less attractive longer-term consequences of previous choices about to be felt, whether in terms of war against Persia or long and difficult negotiations to find some path back to church unity. At the same time, like all new emperors, Justinian needed to establish the authority of his regime, to show that he was indeed God's personally chosen ruler for the Roman world. Once again, as if dealing with a Persian war and a bitterly divided Christian Church were not enough, the emperor made the bold choice. Within a few months of his accession, Justinian had identified an entirely new field of action, which would allow him to demonstrate that he was, unquestionably, God's chosen one.

BY THE AUTHORITY OF GOD

On 13 February 528, the emperor announced the commissioning of a new codification of Roman law. As a flagship home affairs project for his new regime, it was a brilliant choice. In the later Roman Empire, as we have seen (Chapter 1), state ideology identified its structures of written law as the crucial factor which distinguished the divinely protected Roman world as a higher order of human society from any other that might exist. As Justinian himself put it in *Deo Auctore*—'by the authority of God'—the order which set in motion a second element of legal reform on 15 December 530,

> Nothing in any sphere is found so worthy of study as the authority of law, which sets in good order affairs both divine and human and casts out all injustice.[4]

There was no more important way to demonstrate your divinely chosen legitimacy, in the internal running of the Roman state at least, than to bring a major legal reform project to a successful conclusion.

This initial legal project of Justinian's regime came in two parts. First, a commission of eight senior administrators-cum-politicians of high standing within the regime, acting with two practicing barristers, was charged with collecting all new imperial legislation issued since the last such collection, the Theodosian Code of 438 (which had done a similar job with imperial legislation issued ca. AD 300 onwards). Second, the commissioners then had to combine their new selection from the last ninety years of imperial legislation with the three earlier codes of imperial laws currently in use: that of Theodosius and two earlier codes compiled by Hermogenianus and Gregorianus in the 290s, which between them provided a selection of imperial law dating back to the

130s. The end result would be a single-volume selection of the most important imperial decisions; it would entirely supersede all earlier collections, not least the three volumes of Hermogenianus, Gregorianus, and Theodosius.

The task was far from straightforward, but the commission's working parameters at least were clear when it came to dealing with the new post-Theodosius imperial laws, since they could follow the model set out by both the Theodosian Code proper and subsequent smaller collections of new legislation (*Novellae*, 'novels'), such as that sent in 448 to his Western colleague Valentinian III by Theodosius II.

a) They began by rejecting laws which applied only to one individual case; anything included had to have more general significance (the operative Latin concept being *generalitas*).
b) The chosen laws were then carefully edited, often by discarding most of the self-justificatory rhetoric in which emperors customarily framed their legal pronouncements, although this sometimes survived, as in the case of Justin's marriage law (p. 89).
c) Third, they had to separate out the various subsections of a law which related to different topics, because emperors often issued composite laws covering several topics.
d) Finally, they arranged these edited extracts under thematic chapter headings within numbered books while maintaining chronological order within the individual chapters.

What was different this time was the fifth and final stage, which came when the new materials assembled by the commission had to be integrated into one volume with a selection from the three existing codes of imperial law. The first four stages were pretty straightforward, since the major departments of state now maintained archives of important legal materials, and all the basic procedures for editing the original laws, together with most of the book and chapter titles could be taken over from the three older codes, which had themselves preserved for the most part a traditional topic order inherited from older Roman legal texts. The much harder task was to decide what to keep from the three older works and how to integrate these materials with the selections the commissioners had just made from more recent imperial legislation.

The commission proved itself up to the task, however, and the completed Codex Justinianus was formally promulgated on 7 April 529. This was an extraordinary achievement. In comparison, it had taken the commissioners responsible for the Theodosian Code nine years to complete only the first four tasks, and they never even tried to produce any kind of combined volume. So slow was the progress in that case that a second commission was set up six years after the initial promulgation of the project, with many new members, to finish the job. The experience of the Theodosian era emphasizes, once again, Justinian's boldness. A new emperor at the start of his reign, with some difficult issues in the offing, couldn't afford to announce a high-profile, high-stakes project only for it to get bogged down like its predecessor. Better-established bureaucratic habits of collection and the fact that they had a model to follow certainly made some aspects of life easier for Justinian's commissioners, but to edit the new laws and integrate all imperial legislation from the three previous codes into one book—and to complete all this within thirteen months, start to finish—showed extraordinary administrative energy.[5]

Justinian's regime had its propaganda coup. It had successfully fulfilled part of the remit of a fully legitimate, divinely appointed Roman ruler by bringing rational order to part of the written law which, at least according to its own self-understandings, distinguished this unique, divinely supported imperial world from every other society on earth. Against all expectations, the job had been completed in just over a year, and it was the very speed of this success, I suspect, which then encouraged Justinian to set up a second commission in December 530 to pursue a second, much more ambitious legal reform project altogether.

By the sixth century (and for several centuries previously), two main types of legal authority were normally cited in court: imperial rulings of various kinds (as just pulled together in the Codex Justinianus) and the writings of lawyers licensed by a sequence of earlier emperors to give authoritative legal opinions (the jurisconsults). The jurisconsult material had built up between the first and third centuries AD and was both vast and intractable. Late Roman lawyers had long recognized in principle that the problem needed resolution. Theodosius II had originally announced that his legal commission would tackle the jurisconsult material after completing its collection of imperial legislation. But when just the first project took the best part of a decade, tackling the jurisconsult problem was quietly dropped.

Having seen his law commission deal with imperial legislation so promptly, however, Justinian was encouraged to aim much higher. On 15 December 530, the new imperial order *Deo Auctore* announced the creation of a second commission and set out its working principles.

> We command you to read and work upon the books dealing with Roman law, written by those learned men of old to whom the most revered emperors gave authority to compose and interpret the laws [i.e. the jurisconsults], so that the whole substance may be extracted from them, all repetition and discrepancy being as far as possible removed, and out of them one single work may be compiled, which will suffice in place of them all ... so that nothing may be capable of being left outside the finished work ... but that in these fifty books the entire ancient law—in a state of confusion for almost fourteen hundred years, and rectified by us—may be as if defended by a wall and leave nothing outside itself. All legal writers will have equal weight and no superior authority will be reserved for any author, since not all are regarded as either better or worse in all respects, but only some in particular respects.[6]

Chairing the new commission was Tribonian, one of the two barristers who had worked on the code. He had clearly distinguished himself in that project and had certainly been doing some preparatory work between its publication in April 529 and the announcement of the reform in December 530. In *Deo Auctore*, Justinian, already knowing that his new law book would contain fifty books, set out the commission's working principles: no prejudging by traditional repute; every individual jurisconsult opinion was to be weighed on its merits.[7] However, Justinian's second legal project was not destined to progress as smoothly as his first.

WAR IN THE EAST

In the meantime, war with Persia had begun equally promisingly. The Persian front can be divided, in practice, into three separate zones of conflict. Most of the huge battles of the past had taken place on the open, central Mesopotamian front up and down the lines of the Tigris and the Euphrates. It was here that Shapur I had destroyed three Roman armies in the third century and here, too, that the Emperor Julian's great thrust towards Ctesiphon in 363 had eventually come to grief. By the sixth century, both sides had studded this world of ancient cities with massive fortifications, and warfare tended to take the form of lengthy sieges. Further north, in Armenia and Transcaucasia, the landscape was broken up into relatively isolated valleys connected by a network of passes. Forts and garrisons had a role here, too, but campaigns here, as in the cases of Lazica and Iberia, were fought as much in the hearts and minds of the nobles who ran their localities as virtually independent fiefdoms, especially when cut off by the snows of winter. The southern flank, by contrast, was arid and dry: home to Bedouin Arabs. The Emperor Diocletian had constructed a fortified road to control the desert fringes here around the year 300, but that was an inefficient response to the security problems of a region, where conventional armies were unable to operate. By the sixth century, both Rome and Persia had long since concentrated on building up reliable allies among the Arab groupings of the desert fringe. Persia put its weight behind the dominant confederation of Lakhmids, while Constantinople operated through a series of smaller, separate allies.[8]

It was two limited but tangible successes in the north, which saw Transcaucasian dynasts (i.e. Tzath and Gourgenes; see Chapter 3) change sides, which had helped push the regime of Justin and Justinian towards confrontation with Persia. It was also in the north that Justinian made it plain that there was going to be no swift return to older patterns of cooperation with Persia under his sole rule, making the first substantial change to the overall disposition of East Roman field armies since the fourth century. An entirely new field army command was created for Armenia, with troops being transferred in from elsewhere. The new force was quickly in action. In 527 and 528, its new commander, Sittas, raided Persarmenia, returning with a host of prisoners. On the southern front, too, Justinian prepared for action, creating a new, lesser military command based in the city of Palmyra. Limited operations were also conducted in Mesopotamia, with the Romans raiding Persian territory and attempting in 528 and 529 to construct a number of small forts closer to the frontier. This prompted a Persian counterstrike which drove off the Roman covering force and led Justinian to appoint a brand-new field army commander for the East in the person of Belisarius, who was destined to play a major role in the unfolding history of this regime.[9] Like Sittas, as we have seen (p. 54), Belisarius had been an officer in Justinian's *bucellarii* in the early 520s, when the emperor was still *Magister Militum Praesentalis*. There is a real sense in which the early years of Justinian saw the blooding of a whole new generation of senior officers who would continue to play important roles throughout the reign.[10]

Thus far Justinian's forces had held the initiative, but by late 529, Khavad was fully mobilized for the coming campaigning season. In January 530, a huge Persian army, reportedly numbering forty thousand men, advanced on the city of Dara, Rome's forward base on the Mesopotamian front. Our knowledge of the subsequent battle relies heavily on Procopius; on this occasion, already appointed legal adviser to Belisarius, he gives a clear, eyewitness account of the fighting. It is also worth looking more closely at the action because it demonstrates that, even by 530, the sixth-century tactical transformation of the East Roman army (see Chapter 2) was well under way. Belisarius had only twenty-five thousand men, but he knew the Persians were coming and made elaborate preparations. A series of deep trenches were dug as basic protection for the infantry in the centre, punctuated by a series of crossing points. If he had had less time, the portable *munitiones* described in sixth-century tactical manuals would presumably have been used instead. On both flanks, the trench network was thrown forward and the Roman cavalry was massed, some of it on the left flank concealed by high ground. Procopius doesn't use the terms *koursoures* and *defensores*, but the flanking cavalry was divided into heavier and lighter units, Belisarius's plan being—contrary to the pattern laid out in the *Strategicon of Maurice*—that should the heavier cavalry be forced back by Persian attack, the lighter units (composed here of irregular non-Roman allies) could infiltrate the flanks and attack from the rear. The first day, as the Persians sized up the opposition, saw just a light skirmish and some individual challenges. Both went the way of the Romans, which was good for morale, but no one was in any doubt that the main event was still to come.

One reason for the Persian commander's inaction became apparent the next morning, when another ten thousand troops arrived from the main Persian base at Nisibis. But still there was no fighting as Belisarius and his opposite number exchanged messages and taunts; it was only on the third day that the armies deployed in earnest. The Persians deliberately began the fighting around noon, timing the action to prevent the Roman army from being fed (whereas the Persians were accustomed to eating later in the day), thinking that this would weaken their resolve. The battle started with a barrage of missiles, but the Romans enjoyed a substantial following wind; hence, despite weaker numbers, they had the better of the opening exchanges. Hand-to-hand combat followed when the Persian right wing advanced. It seemed to drive back the Roman cavalry, but Belisarius's plans went like clockwork. After the Persians were drawn forward, the Roman light cavalry reserves broke from behind the high ground and hit them from their outer flank to devastating effect. Battered and demoralized, the Persian attackers fled back to the main body, leaving, Procopius tells us, three thousand dead. While this was going on, the Persian commander unleashed his main assault, including the elite corps of Immortals, on the opposite flank. Again, the Persian advance drove back the initial Roman defensive line, but Belisarius unleashed a large cavalry force over the crossing points of the defensive trench and was able to hit the advancing Persians, this time from the inside flank. The effect was pretty much identical. The retreating Roman right wing rallied as Belisarius's counterattack was launched, and the Persians found themselves caught in crossfire. These attackers retreated, too, this time leaving five thousand dead. Faced with such a heavy loss of life, the Persian main body dropped its weapons and fled. Belisarius prevented his soldiers from chasing after them in case it led to disaster. As Procopius comments: 'on that day the Persians had been defeated in battle by the Romans, a thing which had not happened for a long time.'[11]

The dose was repeated almost immediately in Armenia, where Khavad unleashed a second invasion force in the summer of 530. Bypassing the Roman base of Theodosiopolis, the Persians advanced as far as Satala, where the Roman army of Armenia under its new commander, Dorotheus, reinforced by some central field army forces under his predecessor and newly promoted *Magister Militum Praesentalis* Sittas, were waiting. According to Procopius, the fifteen-thousand-strong Roman force was outnumbered two to one. In line with the new military zeitgeist, however, Sittas hid his best cavalry in some high ground while the Persians moved forward to invest the city, which Dorotheus and the rest of the Roman army were conspicuously defending. At the telling moment, Sittas unleashed his ambush. The sudden flank attack caused the Persians stiff casualties and, probably more important (although Procopius's account—he was not there—is much less good), threw them into general disorder. Dorotheus advanced from the city with the rest of the Roman army and, after stiff fighting against the rallying Persians, forced them into a complete retreat. In the aftermath, the Romans captured two important fortresses, Bolum and the particularly valuable Pharangium, where the Persians had significant gold mines.[12]

God had shown His hand. Not only had the new emperor brought order to three hundred years of imperial legislation, but smaller Roman forces had inflicted two heavy defeats on the armies of the empire's greatest enemy. This was more than enough divine validation for one war, and Justinian was keen to get out while the getting was good. His armies went no further, and his diplomats besieged Khavad with peace offers. The emperor was even willing to make a one-off cash payment to sweeten the deal.

But Khavad had his own political imperatives, and making peace after two humiliating defeats would do nothing to stabilize Chosroes's succession. The spring of 531 saw another Persian invasion of Roman territory, therefore, this time taking an unconventional route. Making use of Lakhmid expertise under their long-established leader, al-Mundhir, a mixed Persian-Arab force of fifteen thousand horsemen advanced through Euphratesia and Syria I, ravaging every soft target in their path. In response, Belisarius left most of his forces to guard the cities of the central

Mesopotamian front, in case this was just a diversion, and moved south to Barbalissos to cut off the Persian advance with three thousand of his cavalry, where he was met by five thousand of his own Arab allies under the Ghassanid Harith, who had just been appointed to a pre-eminent position as overking (*phylarch*) of Rome's Arab allies, and further reinforcements mobilized by the *Magister Officiorum* Hermogenes, making a grand total of twenty thousand men. Faced with the Roman advance, the Persians retreated back along the Euphrates, with Belisarius following about a day's march behind. Exactly what happened next is difficult to know. The Romans were beaten in a major confrontation close to the city of Callinicum, but quite how and why is unclear, because Procopius does everything in his power to deflect any blame from Belisarius. In the run-up to the battle, he carefully lays doubts in our minds about the reliability of the newly promoted Harith and stresses that Belisarius did not want to fight, because a) the Persians were retreating without accomplishing anything anyway and b) it was Holy Week, the day before Easter Sunday to be exact, and the Roman army was fasting and hence physically below par. The army, however, was passionate about fighting to the point of insubordination and forced Belisarius to give battle.[13]

Whether or to what extent any of this is true is impossible to know, but the battle was a certainly a disaster. Belisarius put the Arabs on the right, his own heavier cavalry in the centre, and the infantry on the left. After exchanges of missiles, the Persians routed Harith's men and fell on Belisarius's cavalry from behind. The cavalry fought hard but suffered heavy casualties—eight hundred of the three thousand he had brought with him and most of a further group of two thousand Isaurians—and were eventually rolled back on the main body of infantry, who had wheeled in retreat to put their backs to the river. There the Romans fought it out until nightfall and the arrival of boats from the other side of the river to rescue them from the Persians' further attentions. Procopius carefully avoids giving overall casualty figures for the Roman army, merely commenting that the 'Persians did not find their own dead less numerous than the enemy's' in yet another attempt to play down the scale of defeat.[14]

But defeat it was, a disastrous one for Justinian's regime. The emperor was forced to dismiss Belisarius in the early summer and set up a commission of enquiry into the defeat. This suggests that the emperor needed to placate disgruntled opinion at court, which might well have included Hypatius, who had been commander in the East for long periods under both Anastasius and Justin. Khavad, on the other hand, was emboldened into greater adventures. Raids into Armenia were repulsed, but a huge Persian army moved forward to lay siege to Martyropolis through most of the summer, and the back end of the year saw a devastating raid on parts of Mesopotamia by Sabir Huns whom the Persians had paid to move south through the Caucasus.[15]

Not only was the war going badly, but the second tranche of Justinian's flagship legal reforms began to run into difficulties. Part of the problem with the jurisconsult material was its sheer scale. By its own account, Justinian's commission had to read legal opinions totalling 2,000 books and 3 million lines. In the end, they would reduce this mass to 50 books and 150,000 lines, but a much more difficult problem was its intractability. The key thing to remember about lawyers, even academic Roman ones, is that they make their living from clients, and clients employ lawyers to win cases. Going to law, especially in non-criminal cases—and it was mostly non-criminal, civil law that jurisconsults wrote opinions on—is a costly activity whose purpose is normally to protect or achieve some kind of financial benefit. Hence, not surprisingly, the chief problem Tribonian's commissioners found in the jurisconsult material was the fact that its leading practitioners often disagreed with one another. Many of these disagreements had presumably originally been generated by the need to provide no doubt ingenious arguments for the interests of particular clients. Cutting the jurisconsults down to size was therefore not just an editing problem but one of constant and contentious decision making. Which among the competing opinions on any particular issue would the commission chose to support, and why? To complete their work, Tribonian and the rest of Justinian's lawyers had to cut through the Gordian knot of Roman legal authority; they proceeded to do so via the so-called Fifty Decisions, which tackled a sequence of legal cruxes one by one, setting out in each case the preferred resolution under the authority of a new piece of imperial legislation.

In practice, there were more than fifty of these, and they were battered through between 1 August 530 and 30 April 531 (another indication that preparations were well in hand before the project was officially announced in December 530). But some of these problems had been around for centuries, and resolving them quickly was less a question of logical argument than of making an argument, any argument, stick in the face of the vested interests which had preserved them, no doubt to their profit, over preceding generations.[16] At precisely the same moment, therefore, as the Persian war started to go spectacularly wrong, Justinian and Tribonian were twisting arms and banging heads together to generate momentum for legal reform, which was clearly both a difficult process and one that generated substantial opposition. By late 531, the storm clouds were gathering. Dara aside, the Persian gambit had failed. After Callinicum, Justinian could no longer claim that military success proved that God was sustaining his rule. The political vultures started to circle, awaiting the opportunity to pounce. It came from an unexpected direction.

NIKA

The Roman equivalent of football was chariot racing. Charioteers were sporting superstars, commanding massive salaries, and their movements between teams—Greens and Blues being the most popular, Reds and Whites the also-rans—generated fanatical responses. At least in the largest cities of the empire, as their role in regime change has made clear, the factions behind these teams were far more than supporters' clubs (Chapter 3). Normally, they worked hand in glove (perhaps 'pocket' would be more appropriate) with city officials, but in a world of intense poverty and little policing, lines of acceptable extortion could easily be crossed, and there was a limit to how much intimidation could be tolerated, especially within the imperial capital. Hence on Sunday, 11 January 532, seven members of the two largest factions—the Greens and the Blues—were due to be hung, but two ropes broke, and one survivor from each faction fled to a nearby church.

The following Tuesday was another day of chariot racing, and in line with the established tradition of using such occasions to ask for favours by organized, mass chanting—acclamation again—the assembled crowd in the Hippodrome asked the emperor, present in the royal box, to pardon the prisoners. Justinian refused, at which point the Greens and Blues started to riot en masse. Using the codeword *Nika*—'victory', the traditional battle cry of the Roman army—they stormed the capital's prison, releasing all the inmates. More chariot racing was due for Wednesday, which the emperor, fearing still worse trouble should he ban it, allowed to go ahead. There were more chanted demands, which this time took an overtly political turn. Now the crowd was demanding the dismissal of three of Justinian's leading ministers, including an obvious target, the emperor's hugely unpopular chief financial officer and tax collector, John the Cappadocian, as well as Tribonian, who had just rammed through the Fifty Decisions and was currently engaged in writing up the resulting final selection of jurisconsult material.

Unnerved, Justinian dismissed all three, but on Thursday matters escalated. A vast crowd went to the house of Probus, one of the nephews of Anastasius, to raise him to the purple. Probus was careful not to be in the city, but this kicked off three days of rioting and arson which devastated the ceremonial centre of Constantine's great capital. In the middle of the mayhem, on Saturday, Justinian decided to expel some of the leading senators who had taken refuge in his palace. These included Anastasius's two other nephews, Hypatius and Pompeius. On Sunday, another huge crowd gathered in the Hippodrome, whose royal box was connected to the palace by an enclosed passage. The crowd had come partly in response to an announcement—following the precedent established by Anastasius during the religious riots of 512 (p. 81)—that Justinian would humble himself before the crowd and offer an unconditional amnesty to all the rioters. But what happened was something totally different. The crowd—or part of it—acclaimed Hypatius emperor, and he ended up in the royal box surrounded by the baying crowd. Exactly, how many of the Hippodrome's one hundred thousand seats were occupied at this point is unclear.

Justinian had reached the ultimate crunch moment for all dictators faced with rebellion: do I run or order in the troops? Justinian's first instinct, Procopius reports, was to leave, but Theodora renewed his resolve, declaring, in a nearly accurate classical quotation: 'Purple makes a fine burial shroud.'[17]

She would rather die than give up the throne. The eunuch Narses, going into the crowd alone, sought out the leaders of the Blues and promised them gold; he even had some of it with him. He also reminded them that Hypatius had long supported the Greens. In the middle of Hypatius's coronation, the Blues simply got up and left, leaving the Greens stunned. Astonishment turned to panic as the departing Blues were replaced by the regime's most loyal troops: Belisarius's *bucellarii*, fresh from the Persian front, and Herulian *foederatii* from the Balkans, led by Mundus, troops with no ties to the population of Constantinople. Belisarius's original plan was to storm the stadium from the royal box, but the palace guards wouldn't unlock the gate at the end of the passage from the palace. Belisarius and his men had to work their way round to another entrance, at which point, hearing the tumult, Mundus burst in through the Black gate opposite (see Figure 4.1). The Greens' thugs were no match for crack imperial troops, and as the slaughter unfolded, no one even tried to defend Hypatius and Pompeius. Held overnight, Hypatius claimed that he had been forced to accept the purple against his will, but Justinian was implacable. Both were executed the next morning, their bodies thrown into the sea, and all their property confiscated to the treasury.

The regime had held onto power, but the cost was huge. Around thirty thousand people died in the street fighting and Hippodrome massacre. This is slaughter on the same scale as that required to keep the previous president Assad in power in Syria in the early 1980s, and that's without taking account of relative scale. The population of Constantinople had peaked ca. AD 500 at around half a million, so that Nika killed around 5 per cent of its inhabitants, the equivalent of, say, four hundred thousand dead among the current population of New York City. The fires also destroyed the great palace Church of Hagia Sophia, its smaller neighbour Hagia Irene, the Senate House, many of the palace's outer buildings, and several of the ceremonial arcades at the heart of the city. It would be hard to overestimate, therefore, the extent of the dissent and destruction.[18]

FIGURE 4.1

The eunuch general Narses. He commanded the final conquest and subsequent subjugation of Italy.
Credit: Art Resource, NY

Despite the many details preserved in the surprisingly full sources, a number of key questions remain. Who was behind Wednesday's politicization of the uprising, when demands for the pardon of a couple of thugs were replaced, over the following forty-eight hours, by calls, first, for Justinian to emasculate his regime by jettisoning its most prominent officials and then for an entirely new emperor? What was Justinian's thinking when he threw Anastasius's nephews out of the palace? Was he trying to engineer a showdown by bringing latent opposition into the open? And should we really believe Procopius's description of Theodora putting the fight back into Justinian? Her famous phrase is a misquotation. The original reads '*Tyranny* makes a fine burial shroud.' So it looks like the Procopius of the *Secret History* reckoned he could use the lack of a proper classical education in the higher reaches of the regime to crack a little recherché joke at the imperial couple's expense.[19] But the story of the empress's courage appears in the *Wars*, which was published openly, so it presumably encapsulates a reading of the riot that the regime was happy to endorse ca. 550.

Some of these questions are unanswerable, but the presence of Belisarius and Mundus suggests that the emperor may have anticipated a need for reliable military muscle.[20] This suggests in turn that there may have been an element of entrapment in his expulsion of Anastasius's nephews, although this can also be explained as a desire to forestall the possibility of an overnight palace coup at the hands of suborned palace guards; indeed, their refusal to unlock the gate to the royal box and let Belisarius and his guards into the Hippodrome through the royal box suggests that they had had some contact with the opposition. Publicly, Justinian had no doubts where responsibility for the politicization of the violence lay, and mass shouting in the Hippodrome was often produced to someone's order. Not only were Anastasius's unfortunate nephews executed, but another eighteen senators were banished from the city, their estates confiscated.[21] There was probably an element of score settling in this, with the emperor's officials not being overly sparing in the accuracy of their condemnations, but the emperor was surely correct that halfway through that dreadful week, conspiracy at the highest levels hijacked the hooliganism and directed it towards toppling an imperial regime which, like many before it, had become distinctly vulnerable in the aftermath of military defeat (see Chapter 1).

In the event, the regime survived and by 550 could use Nika to celebrate the courage of Justinian's imperial consort. But at the time, none of this would have lifted the air of doom and disaster that hung over Constantinople. The political opposition had used the failings of the new regime to attempt to replace it. The deliberate quarrel picked with Persia had led to defeat, the chief architect of the emperor's legal reform and two other leading loyalists had been dismissed, 5 per cent of the capital's population lay dead in its streets, and its ceremonial centre was a smoking ruin. None of this was remotely compatible with the claim that Justinian was ruling with the direct assistance of the divinity. The current outburst of opposition may have been cut off, but one usurpation often generated another in the world of late Roman politics, and by the end of that terrible week in January 532, the regime had forfeited all obvious consent to its rule. It had held on at sword's point but was teetering on the brink, and Justinian did not have sufficient political capital, after all the mayhem, even to bring back into office the favourites he had been forced to dismiss.[22]

GO WEST

It is against this stark backdrop that the western reconquest policy, generally considered a leitmotif of Justinian's reign in older scholarship, started to emerge. For many historians, launching it had always been Justinian's underlying aim. A Latin-speaking traditionalist from Illyricum, he was desperate to recover Rome's lost glory. As his propaganda put it:

> We are inspired with the hope that God will grant us rule over the rest of what, subject to the ancient Romans to the limits of both seas, they later lost by their neglect.

But this is Justinian's first statement of what is often supposed to have been his fundamental aim, and it dates from 536: the emperor's tenth year.

It also followed the almost bloodless acquisition of Sicily in 535 and the successful conquest of Africa in 533/4, which was originally justified on alternative, purely religious grounds:

> That which the omnipotent God has now ... deemed proper to demonstrate through us exceeds all wonderful acts which have happened in the course of all time—namely that freedom should, through us, in so short a time be received by Africa, which 105 years before was captured by the Vandals who were enemies of both mind and body. ... By what language, therefore, or by what works worthy of God that He deemed it proper that the injuries of the Church should be avenged through me, the least of His servants.[23]

It was only after these two initial successes, when Justinian was eyeing further gains in Italy, that we hear any whisper of an underlying aim to reconquer the lost Roman west, and as a result, more recent studies have either been sceptical of the existence of an underlying plan or have firmly contested its existence.[24] So was there a plan, and if there wasn't, how did western expansion become such a central feature of the policies of Justinian's reign?

The chronology of Justinian's propaganda statements has never been in doubt, but it has nonetheless been thought that he came to the throne with a plan to reconquer Rome's lost western territories, which, as soon as peace could be made with Persia, he was determined to put it into action. Everything indicates that this was not the case. The key point here is that the regime of Justin and Justinian deliberately provoked a war with Persia in the mid-520s, when the opportunity was clearly there to reaffirm, even strengthen, long-established patterns of peaceful cooperation. This was quite far on in Justin's reign, at a point when Justinian's influence was already large and certainly on the increase. Indeed, if the argument about Hypatius's championing of a more conciliatory policy towards Persia is correct, then an aggressive stance in the East was even being used as a further means to consolidate his power. If Justinian had really wanted to devote his energies to the lost Roman west, he could have dropped all the nonsense about Chosroes's adoption and stopped stirring up trouble in Transcaucasia (p. 91).[25] In reality, the policy of western expansion emerged only slowly and in highly contingent—that is to say *unpredictable*—circumstances.

The first of these conquests, that of the Vandal's North African kingdom of Proconsularis, Byzacena, and Numidia (see Figure 4.2), was triggered by an unpredictable sequence of events that were internal to the Vandal realm and outside of Constantinopolitan control. Justinian's initial celebration of his military success in North Africa concentrated on religion, because unlike most of the other western successor states, where non-Catholic but Christian monarchs generally maintained good relations with their Catholic subjects, the Vandal kings had periodically persecuted theirs.[26] The pattern had finally been broken by King Hilderic, who succeeded to the Vandal throne in May 523, ushering in a new era of religious peace. Suspending all persecution, he allowed the Catholic Church of North Africa to function without impediment, even to hold its first full regional council for two generations in Carthage (525). His new religious policy was part of major realignment of the Vandal kingdom, away from the hegemony of the Ostrogothic Italian kingdom (see Chapter 6) and towards an alliance with Constantinople, a new beginning that was marked by many exchanges of friendly letters and diplomatic

FIGURE 4.2
The Vandal King Gelimer. He eventually gave in to despair as his kingdom was destroyed in four months of campaigning.

presents.[27] But this happy new state of affairs within the Vandal kingdom quickly ran into problems from a different quarter. On its fringes, the indigenous, nomadic Berber groups had been growing in size, organization, and military effectiveness in the later fifth and early sixth centuries. In 529/30, one of these nomad coalitions inflicted the latest in a series of defeats on Hilderic's armies in the province of Byzacena. This was enough to trigger a coup d'état led by his royal cousin Gelimer. Gelimer seized the throne on 19 May 530 and took full control of the kingdom, not only purging Hilderic's Vandal supporters but also reversing some of his pro-Catholic policies.[28]

Hilderic had been a loyal ally of Justinian, but when news arrived in late 530 of his overthrow, the emperor was still hopeful of a good outcome to his Persian war. As yet, Callinicum lay in the future. The emperor therefore contented himself with a couple of stiff diplomatic messages, one to Gelimer's Vandal court making disapproving noises and the other to the Italian Ostrogothic King Athalaric advising him not to recognize the new Vandal king. It was only two years later, in the summer of 532 (it is important to keep the chronology clear), that Justinian began to show the slightest interest in doing anything more than write a few letters. By this time, two intervening events had revolutionized the political context. Nika had come and gone, leaving the prestige of Justinian's regime lying in smoking heaps of rubble at the heart of his imperial capital. The prevailing sense of disaster had also been reinforced by the terms of the so-called Eternal Peace which in the spring of 532 finally brought Justinian's first Persian war to an end, soon after the riot. Khavad had died late in 531; the new king, Chosroes, was keen for peace so that he could concentrate on establishing his rule in the face of considerable opposition. This halted Persian offensive operations, but it is a sign of the underlying weakness of Justinian's regime at this point that even in these ostensibly more favourable circumstances, he was ready to concede everything the Persians demanded. Captured forts were returned, and the emperor agreed to pay an annual indemnity, supposedly in return for Persian defence of the Caucasus, which arguably protected both empires from the incursions of dangerous steppe nomads to the north. Different emperors had been resisting such demands since the 480s, but Justinian was ready to concede even this. Not even a Persian succession crisis offered him a clear path back from the defeats of 531. Justinian simply accepted whatever terms he was given.[29]

By the spring of 532, reeling from the Nika riot and the evident failure of his Persian war, Justinian's regime was desperate for political success, and it was this which finally put a military intervention of some kind in North Africa firmly on the menu. The expedition sailed only in the early summer of 533, but given how long it took to accumulate food, fodder, and men in the ancient world, preliminary preparations for some kind of expedition, especially one involving such a large quantity of shipping, must have already been under way in 532. Both Belisarius's *bucellarii* and some of the Herulian *foederatii* (though not Mundus himself), the bodies of troops who stormed the Hippodrome in February 532, eventually sailed with the expedition, so their presence in the vicinity of the capital in late winter of 532 might just be an early sign of first preparations. The Ostrogothic regime in Italy would also provide the expedition with crucial logistic support once the fleet had reached Sicily; this, too, required careful negotiation beforehand. But there are good reasons to think, nonetheless, that even if preparations were under way in 532, a final decision had not yet been taken.

For one thing, our sources report that the emperor was extremely hesitant about authorizing the expedition; he had excellent reasons for being so. Landing a large military force on a hostile shore is one of the most dangerous military operations there is, and since the Vandals captured Carthage in 439, there had been three serious Roman attempts to recapture the lost North African provinces. All ended in disaster. Justinian would have had in mind, in particular, the fate of the great fleet despatched under the command of Basiliscus by Leo I in 468. It had been destroyed, with horrendous loss of life, by Vandal fireships, and the whole effort had left the Eastern Empire bankrupt for years.[30]

Equally important, an African expedition was not the only avenue the regime was exploring to win back some of its lost prestige in the early months of 532. Shortly after Nika had wreaked its trail of destruction through the capital, Justinian's representatives initiated a set of formal 'conversations' to explore possible means of healing the current divisions within the Eastern Church. This formal, quite public event can be seen only as the end result of private, backdoor contacts, which having an empress with links to important anti-Chaledonian circles had made possible since 527 (p. 98). Five representatives from each side discussed the issues, and important progress was made on how the theological differences might be resolved, with Justinian, significantly, showing himself both in a hurry to achieve some kind of settlement and surprisingly flexible in his approach to the status and authority of Chalcedon. The emperor, as might be expected in the circumstances, was desperate for success. In the end, however, the conversations failed to reach a positive conclusion. The main stumbling block turned out to be not theology but the fifty-five exiled anti-Chalcedonian bishops left over from his uncle's reign. As Justinian was not willing simply to reinstate them, the meeting broke down.[31] Religious affairs had failed to provide the desperately needed success, and the emperor was left contemplating, again, whether or not to take a high-risk African option.

According to Procopius, divine inspiration eventually resolved the dilemma. God told Justinian to launch the attack in a dream. The emperor may have had a dream, but another set of contingent events helped prompt him finally to launch the attack. Over the autumn and winter of 532/3, two important pieces of news reached Constantinople. First, at the eastern end of the Vandal kingdom, a revolt against Gelimer's rule erupted in Tripolitania (modern Libya) led by a local notable called Pudentius. No actual Vandals had settled this far east in the Vandal kingdom, so there was no actual fighting—at least not much—to be done to declare independence. Pudentius immediately asked for Tripolitania to be taken back under direct East Roman rule. A second revolt within the Vandal domains then pushed a possible African expedition right to the top of the imperial agenda. This time Godas, the governor of the island of Sardinia, Gelimer's northernmost holding, declared independence and, again, wrote to Constantinople asking for support. This message, which also arrived in the autumn/winter of 532/3, was enough to make Justinian finally commit his forces. With two revolts convulsing Gelimer's kingdom, there was a much greater chance of success.[32]

Accordingly, preparations for an expeditionary force were brought to completion in the spring and early summer of 533, its fleet of nearly six hundred ships assembling in the quiet waters of the Bosporus and the Golden Horn. Under the command of Belisarius, it left Constantinople in mid-June and made slow progress first to the eastern coast of Italy and then on to Sicily, where it anchored in the shadow of Mount Etna. Two Hunnic mercenaries had had to be executed for killing one of their comrades while drunk, and an astonishing five hundred men died from eating infected bread. These must have seemed ill omens at the time. Procopius was sent forward to the port of Syracusa and came back with vital intelligence. Gelimer was completely unprepared for invasion. The Vandal kingdom's fleet and seven thousand of its best soldiers had just been despatched to Sardinia to quell Godas's revolt.[33]

It was at this exact moment, just off Taormina with its wonderful Greek theatres, that Justinian's western conquest policy was finally born. As Procopius tells us, it was only on hearing that the Vandal fleet was elsewhere that Belisarius took the fateful decision to head straight for the heart of Gelimer's kingdom. This makes it clear that Belisarius had left Constantinople still with only contingent orders. Justinian and his key advisers knew that there was disruption in the Vandal kingdom, but news travelled so slowly in the ancient world, even around the Mediterranean, that what was known in the imperial capital in mid-June 533 was weeks if not months out of date. Slow communications also made it impossible for Belisarius, when he did find out more, to send back to Justinian for further orders. As Procopius puts it, the general was given absolute monarchical authority over the expedition, and this was entirely necessary.[34] Only when he got to Sicily would Belisarius be in a position to assess the current military and political situation, and he would need to decide at that point, entirely by himself, exactly how ambitious a campaign to mount.

In reality, Justinian's orders must have set out several options, from least to most ambitious, depending on what Belisarius actually found. The expedition was a large one, comprising altogether about sixteen thousand soldiers. So one of the options was clearly to land somewhere in North Africa and undertake some serious warfare, perhaps even the outright conquest of the kingdom. But the deposed Hilderic was still alive at this point, and on landing in North Africa, Belisarius immediately declared that his forces were there to put the rightful Vandal ruler back on his throne.[35] Even if he could manage to land his army in North Africa, therefore, outright conquest of the Vandal kingdom was not the only possible option. If the military situation looked less promising, if the Vandal fleet was armed and waiting, as it had been in 468, then Belisarius's ships could alternatively just sail on to Tripolitania, and by securing, at minimum, that province, confirm at least some kind of 'victory' for Justinian's propaganda to celebrate. Once ashore in Tripolitania, then, he had enough soldiers to do more, but given the current state of the regime, the commander would certainly have been told not to risk another maritime disaster like that suffered by Basiliscus's expedition in 468.

But now Procopius returned from Syracuse with the electrifying news that the Vandal fleet was off the west coast of Italy and the chance was there to pursue the most ambitious of the options that had been discussed exhaustively back in Constantinople before the fleet's departure. Set against the twists and turns of Justinian's early reign, the western conquest policy turns out to have been not the long-standing plan of a romantic visionary but another type of phenomenon altogether, one much better known to historians: overseas adventurism as the last desperate gamble of a bankrupt regime. Between them, Nika and defeat at the hands of the Persians had placed Justinian's still nascent regime in deepest jeopardy. As contingent factors unfolded around them, the emperor and his advisers eventually decided, three years after the event, that avenging their erstwhile Vandal ally Hilderic offered the best available means of re-establishing the standing of the regime. It was now Belisarius's task to put the policy into practice on the field of battle.

5

FIVE THOUSAND HORSE

To get the job done, Belisarius had substantial forces at his disposal. His army was carried in a huge armada of five hundred merchantmen escorted by ninety-two warships, manned by no fewer than 30,000 seamen. In their care was an army, a powerful one, of nearly 15,500 men, consisting of 10,000 infantry and 5,000 cavalrymen, with a smaller force of 400 destined for Sardinia, to provide direct military assistance for the revolt of Godas. Everyone else was to be committed to whatever war in North Africa Belisarius eventually decided to fight. Crucially, it had been agreed beforehand with the Ostrogoths that not only food but large numbers of horses would be available for the expedition to purchase during its stay off the coast of Sicily.[1] Otherwise, the horses would have been stuck on board ship, unexercised, for the best part of three months. The infantry were all regulars, the cavalry a mix of East Roman regulars stiffened with Belisarius's own elite *bucellarii*, and about 1,000 others: 400 Herulian *foederatii* under their own leader from inside the empire, and 600 Hunnic Massagetae (i.e. Bulgar), steppe nomads from beyond the frontier hired especially for the expedition.[2] What, exactly, was the task facing this assemblage of Constantinopolitan firepower?

KINGS OF THE VANDALS AND ALANS

Writing from the perspective of what turned out to be a victorious campaign, Procopius played up the notion that Belisarius's opponents had been corrupted into decadence by the wealth of their North African kingdom.

> Since the time … they gained possession of Libya, [the Vandals] used to indulge in baths, all of them, every day and enjoyed a table abounding in all things, the sweetest and best that the earth and sea produce. And they wore gold very generally, and clothed themselves in the Persian garments which they now call 'seric' [= silk] and passed their time, thus dressed, in theatres and hippodromes and in other pleasurable pursuits, and above all else in hunting … and they had a great number of banquets and all manner of sexual pleasures were in great vogue among them.[3]

Before the Vandals took possession of Carthage in AD 439, the grain of Proconsularis and Numidia, together with the olive oil and wine of Byzacena and Mauretania, had long fed the city of Rome and been exported far and wide across the Mediterranean, along with truly vast quantities of pottery by a guild of merchant traders who enjoyed a roster of financial privileges—so much, in fact, that an extra harbour had been brought into commission at Carthage in the late Roman period to carry all the traffic, and there were several other major North African port cities besides.[4]

Procopius was interested, according to the time-honoured norms of classical Graeco-Roman historiography, in supplying a moralizing explanation for the Vandals' defeat. In this classical view, historical outcomes were dictated by the virtues and vices of the principal actors involved. Virtuous individuals generated good outcomes, while disaster was the product of moral weakness (p. 12). Even treating Procopius's explanation for the Vandals' defeat with caution, his description of elite lifestyles finds plenty of confirmation in other sources within the kingdom itself. There have been archaeological finds of rich villas and town houses from the Vandals' hundred-year occupation of Rome's old North African provinces, and the exports did continue to flow, if in slightly reduced quantities and slightly different directions, generating plentiful overseas earnings. The imagery, ceremonial ritual, and even the dress styles of the Vandal court, likewise, directly imitated luxurious late Roman norms. Even more striking is a collection of classical Latin verse, which has come down to us via just one ninth-century manuscript: the Latin Anthology. Alongside many works from a much deeper past, the text preserves the work of no less than fifteen Latin poets who wrote in and around Carthage during the reigns of its different Vandal kings. Supplemented by the independently preserved work of the best poet of them all, Dracontius, this material makes it clear that the Vandals soon enjoyed a decidedly Roman style of life. Educated, classical Latin was still being taught in functioning schoolrooms across the kingdom, and rulers liked to be celebrated in classical verse, according to the received canon of classical virtues. The poetry also confirms Procopius's description of the Vandals' enjoyment of baths, theatre, and horse racing, not to mention the all-important but perhaps less surprising joys of the hunt. Vandal Africa kept much of its Roman administrative shape, too: provincial governors were overseen by a proconsul with headquarters in Carthage. As Belisarius's fleet left its anchorage in the shadow of Mount Etna, it was sailing towards what was recognizably a sub-Roman kingdom on the other side of the Libyan Sea.[5]

The rich and recognizably Roman character of the Vandal court by ca. AD 500 reflects several generations of internal evolution; it must not be allowed to hide either the degree of violence which had originally brought the kingdom into existence or the recent non-Roman origins of its defining elite. Most of the kingdom's peers, as successor states to the West Roman Empire, had grown slowly in physical size and political autonomy, to some extent by default as central imperial power melted away, its tax revenues declining in the third-quarter of the fifth century. The Vandal kingdom of North Africa had been created a generation earlier, carved by violence out of the still living body politic of the old Roman west.

Its origins lay in an unlicensed crossing of Rome's Rhine frontier—probably using the military bridge at the fortress of Mainz rather than, as has sometimes been imagined, the ice of the frozen river—by a loose coalition of outsiders on the final day of the year 406 during the second major bout of upheaval in short order on Rome's European borders (p. 4). Its main components were two separate bodies of Vandals, the Hasdings and the Silings; a numerically dominant force of Alans, under at least two separate kings; and Suevi and other, smaller population fragments. None of these had previously occupied territory close to their crossing point, and only the Suevi had lived right beside a part (a different one) of Rome's European frontiers in the fourth century. The bulk of the coalition had moved substantial distances, therefore, even before reaching the Roman frontier. In the fourth century, both Vandal groups probably occupied the Upper Theiss region of what is now Slovakia, close to a thousand kilometres (600 miles) from the bridge at Mainz. The Alans had come from still farther afield. As late as 376, their main stomping grounds had been territories north of the Black Sea and east of the river Don, more than two thousand kilometres from the Rhine.

Trouble had clearly been brewing between the upper and middle Rhine and the western arc of the Carpathian Mountains, in the central zone of Rome's European frontiers, for several years before this coalition crossed into Roman territory. In 402 and 403, Vandals were already disturbing the frontier province of Raetia, well away from their Slovakian homelands, a locale in which they never appear in fourth-century sources, and the crossing of 406 was preceded by another substantial explosion of population from the same central frontier zone in 405. Led by a king called Radagaisus, this expedition headed south over the Alps into Italy, rather than west across the Rhine, but it originated in the same general area. While smaller migration flows had always been part and parcel of general frontier life, such large-scale population explosions were highly unusual, so something momentous was clearly going on in central Europe in the middle of the first decade of the fifth century to generate two such major outpourings in quick succession. What that was, our fragmentary Roman sources do not report, concentrating instead upon both expeditions' dramatic impact on the Roman west. In my view, however, the fact that Hunnic power had become dominant in the same central European frontier zone by the year 410 at the latest, whereas its epicentre before 400 clearly lay on the eastern side of the Carpathian Mountains, is extremely unlikely to be a coincidence. The closest analogy to the surges of 405/6 is provided by the arrival of large numbers of Goths from Rome's east European frontier zone north of the Black Sea in 376, a generation earlier. That event was directly generated by the initial build-up of Hunnic power north of the Black Sea. By far the likeliest cause of both Radagaisus's expedition (405) and the Rhine crossing (406) was the western relocation of the European epicentre of Hunnic power, a move that was designed to put the Huns closer to the ultimate Roman source of all the new wealth that was coming in their direction and was complete by the end of the first decade of the fifth century.

The other big issue surrounding the Rhine invasion is its likely scale. Historians of previous eras, influenced by nationalist ideas of identity, sometimes in straightforwardly racist ways, tended to think of groups like Vandals as 'peoples', by which they meant large population aggregates, mixed in age and gender, who possessed their own distinct material and non-material cultures, which kept them utterly insulated from any other population groups around them. The Vandals who conquered North Africa were demonstrably not a 'people' in that sense, however, but a coalition that reconstituted itself on Roman soil. More recent social scientific understandings of group identity have demonstrated that individuals often can and do change identity. For some revisionist scholars, therefore, the trope of migrating 'peoples' has been replaced by one of intrusive warbands on the make. When you push against it, the warband hypothesis is not very precisely defined, but it seems to mean largely warrior, hence overwhelmingly male, groups of hundreds—not thousands—of fighters on the move with only limited numbers of dependents rather than a full complement of women and children. The overall effect of the hypothesis, of course, is dramatically to reduce the numbers of original migrants envisaged as crossing the frontier and to suggest that where, as with the Vandals, one of these warbands became the core of a kingdom, this followed a large-scale process of culturally random recruiting on Roman soil.[6]

There is no place for a full discussion of this thorny issue in a book on the wars of Justinian, but while the Vandals who conquered North Africa were certainly a product of their experiences on Roman soil, this doesn't license us to reduce the numbers of original migrants to the extent that a warband hypothesis requires. For one thing, this isn't what our chronicle and other sources, such as they are, imply. They describe, already in 406, a seriously large demographic phenomenon, and accordingly, even most of the self-styled revisionist writing about the Rhine crossing thinks it must have encompassed at least tens of thousands of individuals. This supposition is reinforced by both analogy and the best surviving evidence. The

Goths of 376 were, two years later, numerous enough, with only limited reinforcements, to kill over ten thousand elite Roman soldiers on a single day at the battle of Hadrianople. This outcome was clearly a fluke, but not a fluke that could have been performed by an assembled maximum of four warbands of even a thousand men each. Radagaisus's expedition, likewise, required a Roman army of thirty regiments (again, well over ten thousand men) reinforced by numerous Hunnic and Alanic auxiliaries to bring it to heel, and its dismantling saw twelve thousand elite fighters drafted into the Roman army: their dependents placed as hostages in various Italian cities.[7] To get across the Rhine, for their part, the Hasding Vandals had to fight their way past intense Frankish resistance which cost them, reportedly, twenty thousand casualties, a potential disaster from which they were rescued only by Alanic intervention. Over the next two years the invaders affected pretty much the entirety of Rome's Gallic provinces, creating, as the poets put it, one vast 'funeral pyre'. Even without envisaging racially distinct 'peoples', we are still faced with a loose migratory coalition which originally numbered many tens of thousands of people, potentially over a hundred thousand in total. What happened after Gaul, however, once the coalition moved over the Pyrenees into Spain, played a still more important role in creating the Vandal phenomenon which faced Belisarius and his invasion force when they arrived in North Africa.[8]

In the early autumn of 409—'certainly on a Tuesday', as the chronicler Hydatius tells us—the Rhine invaders moved definitively south of the Pyrenees. Within two years, they divided up most of Roman Spain: the Hasding Vandals and Suevi took Gallaecia in the north-west, the Siling Vandals, Baetica in the south, and the Alans, the broad stretches of Lusitania and Carthaginensis in between. All modern commentators, surely correctly, have concluded that this distribution must reflect the relative power in 411 of the different groups, emphasizing that the Alans (as their earlier rescue of the Hasding Vandals from the Franks also suggests) were the dominant force within the partnership at this point.[9] Nothing suggests that this seizure of provinces was an authorized settlement rather than an annexation, and as soon as it had its house in order, the West Roman state organized a series of joint campaigns, with Visigothic assistance, against the coalition, starting in 416. The results, as Hydatius reports, were catastrophic:

> All of the Siling Vandals in Baetica were wiped out. … The Alans … suffered such heavy losses … that, after the death of their king Addax, the few survivors, with no thought of their own kingdom, placed themselves under the protection of Gunderic, the king of the [Hasding] Vandals.

The need to settle the Visigoths in Aquitaine—economic quid for the Goths' military quo—brought a temporary halt to campaigning in 418, but a critical transformation had already been worked on the original coalition of 406. The losses not only changed the balance of power within, destroying the Alans' original dominance, but for most of its surviving personnel, much closer political confederation now replaced the originally looser alliance. The significance showed up dramatically when Romano-Gothic forces renewed their attacks. After initially successful operations in Gallaecia in 420 under Asterius, whose point was apparently to prevent the Hasding-led coalition from extending its domination over the still independent Suevi, imperial forces were decisively defeated in Baetica the following year. Apparently by detaching the Gothic element from its Roman alliance (our main source complains about the Visigoths' treachery), the new Vandal-Alan coalition won a stunning victory, which reportedly cost the Romans twenty thousand dead. At this point, a force directly ancestral to that which Belisarius's army would face in North Africa a century later had come properly into existence.[10]

Despite its victory, the Hasding-led coalition had every reason to suppose that the empire would soon return to the attack. The stakes were much too high for it not to, since Spain was a valuable source of the tax revenues on which the empire relied to support its military and political structures, and little revenue can have flowed from the peninsula into the centre since the Rhine invaders' entered it over a decade before. But the unexpected death of the current ruler of the West, Flavius Constantius, in September 421, followed by that of the Emperor Honorius in August 423, kick-started a lengthy process of usurpation and civil war, which ended in Eastern imperial forces putting the boy emperor Valentinian

III (Honorius's nephew) on the Western throne and an extended struggle for control of the minor's court. Political stability really returned to the West only in 432, when Aetius defeated the last of his rivals to claim pre-eminent authority.[11]

Back in Spain, the coalition initially used this respite to establish its domination over the cities of the south, but the accession of a new king, Geiseric, in 428, heralded a change of strategy. While maintaining the Visigothic alliance (Geiseric's son Huneric was married to a Visigothic princess) and after exploratory raids into the Mediterranean, in 429, Geiseric concentrated the entirety of his force at the port of Tarifa, near modern Gibraltar, and shipped it across the sea to Morocco. Writing a century later, Procopius claims that the coalition forces were invited to North Africa by its dissident Roman commander, the general Boniface, but this seems to be a baseless accusation. It does not appear in more-contemporary sources, many of which were hostile to Boniface. It was, in any case, a highly intelligent move on Geiseric's part and effectively killed two strategic birds with one stone. On the one hand, the wealth of Africa was legendary, but just as important given the coalition's defining experiences of 416–21, putting the sea between yourself and the main concentrations of the Western Empire's remaining military capacity made excellent sense.[12]

Landing close to modern Tangiers, Geiseric's forces quickly moved east towards the rich heartland provinces of Roman North Africa: Numidia, Proconsularis, and Byzacena. The immediate impact is vividly reflected in writings generated by the final moments of the life of Augustine of Hippo, one of the great Fathers of the Latin Church. By the winter of 429/30, the bishop's own city was under siege from both land and sea, and Augustine was having to rally his fellow bishops, panicked by the torturing of two of their peers, not to desert their flocks in their hour of need: 'Let no one dream of holding our ship so cheaply that the sailors, let alone the captain, should desert her in the time of peril.' The city was still under siege the following summer, when the bishop died at the age of seventy-five on 28 August, so that he didn't live to see the full denouement. But already the damage was done. As Augustine's biographer put it, 'an enormous band', 'overthrowers of the Roman world', had entered the

Western Empire's rich north African heartlands. 'The man of God saw whole cities sacked, country villas razed, their owners killed or scattered as refugees; the churches deprived of their bishops and clergy, and the holy virgins and ascetics dispersed.'[13]

The West's imperial centre was currently embroiled with a series of problems close to its Italian heartland, but military assistance was forthcoming from Constantinople which checked Geiseric sufficiently to make him accept a more peripheral and restricted settlement zone in the less rich hinterland of Hippo Regius in 435. He had not lost sight, however, of the prize. When, four years later, the West was stretched again by a massive Visigothic revolt in Gaul, Geiseric took full advantage of the opportunity to fight his way into Carthage and seize its economic hinterland, the richest of all Rome's North African territories in what is now Tunisia and western Algeria. This was not remotely acceptable to either half of the empire: a huge joint expeditionary force began to assemble in Sicily, with 1,100 merchant ships allocated for its transportation.[14] The East's troops had been drafted in from Constantinople's Danube frontier, however, and their absence was duly noted by Attila the Hun who launched the first of his mass attacks. As a result, the East's forces had to be recalled and the expedition cancelled. The Western Empire was left with no choice but to make a peace deal with Geiseric in 443, an entirely new type of treaty which acknowledged his sovereignty over Numidia, Byzacena, and Proconsularis. The Vandal kingdom had come into being, its starting point as far as its monarchs were concerned marked by the capture of Carthage in 439. It was the product of significant reorganization and violent self-assertion over two generations on the part of significant elements of an originally loose alliance of groups which had crossed into the empire in 406.[15]

What Geiseric did next ensured that it would also be the future descendants of essentially this group that Belisarius would have to face in the 530s. Having captured the richest provinces of the Roman west, the king's first priority was to reward his followers in line with their expectations. They had marched thousands of kilometres, fought countless engagements, large and small, and suffered enormous losses. Had he not done so, they would just have replaced him with someone who would. He had three provinces at his disposal—Numidia, Byzacena, and Proconsularis—and deployed these assets with care. He granted large estates to himself and other princes of the royal house in the first two provinces, but the bulk of his followers received land in Proconsularis. There were two reasons for this. Proconsularis was closest to Carthage, so that Geiseric was effectively concentrating his military forces around the seat of his government, where any future Roman military threat was likely to fall. Because of the dynamics of ancient Roman imperialism, when the initial conquest of Carthage in the second century BC was followed by land grabbing on the part of the Roman elite, Proconsularis also contained large amounts of land owned by absentee Roman senatorial aristocrats. This could be confiscated, therefore, without generating much internal political dissent within the coalition's North African kingdom. We do not have the full details, but a special legal category of Vandal settlement land—the *sortes Vandalorum*—was identified within Proconsularis and redistributed to Geiseric's followers. It was held hereditarily on a tax-free basis in return for continued military service. No doubt the same Romano-African tenant farmers and bailiffs continued to work the actual land, but Proconsularis found itself swapping a largely absentee Roman senatorial rentier class for a new and decidedly resident Vandal-Alan military elite. Elsewhere, the Romano-African landowners of Byzacena and Numidia were left largely undisturbed and continued to pay the normal taxes, via established Roman fiscal mechanisms, to their new Vandal ruler.[16]

Exactly how large was this new elite which spent the 440s establishing itself in Proconsularis? The one figure worth worrying about is provided by Victor of Vita, a North African bishop writing in 484. He reports that when the coalition crossed from Spain, Geiseric mustered its men, women, and children into seventy groups of notionally a thousand individuals each, but this was a ruse to hide that his following amounted to rather less than the implied seventy thousand. Victor was writing primarily for North African Catholics under Vandal rule and had a deeply serious purpose in mind. His account of the not very distant past had to be plausible, therefore, for an audience who had been living with the Vandals for a generation. There is a good chance, in short, that he gives us a reasonable order of magnitude: Geiseric brought with him several tens of thousands of people, therefore, but less than seventy thousand. Older estimates worked with a notional ratio of one warrior to five of total population, but thirty years on the road is likely to have been particularly tough, as in all migrant flows, on the old and the young, so that a total population of more like fifty thousand might imply around fifteen thousand warriors. Given the disastrous losses the Rhine invaders had suffered in Spain in the 410s and the fighting done since and the fact that the Suevi had remained in Spain, this seems a reasonable figure. Envisage, therefore, a new elite of some fifteen thousand households taking over various senatorial estates in Proconsularis as the settlement process unfolded in the 440s. Among other things, this helps explain why, after the settlement, the main North African export zones should have shifted southwards to Byzacena. Much of what had been the surplus produce of Proconsularis was now being consumed by a resident elite.[17]

There is every reason to think that the descendants of this landowning military elite were those that Belisarius had to fight in the 530s. The scale of the military problem seems about right, allowing for a not insignificant increase in Vandal-Alan numbers in the times of peace and plenty which followed, especially from the 470s. Procopius does not give a complete head count, but his conquest narratives do not suggest that Belisarius was facing an enemy numbering more than twenty to twenty-five thousand warriors.[18] There is also no sign in his narrative that Gelimer drew at all upon a newly militarized group of Romano-African landowners, recruited to supplement an original Vandal-Alan core. On the contrary, Belisarius worked overtime to keep indigenous Roman landowners from making any substantial contribution to the Vandal war effort. Their privileged legal position as holders of the *sortes Vandalorum* had kept the coalition's descendants recognizable and separate in the meantime (just as descendants of the conquering landowning elite of Norman England were perfectly recognizable a century after 1066), and Geiseric had taken one additional step to cement his followers' group identity.

Our knowledge here is again based on Victor of Vita, who composed his work to strengthen kingdom-wide Catholic solidarity in the face of a mass religious persecution launched by Geiseric's son Huneric in 484. At this point, Huneric was trying to make everyone within the kingdom subscribe to Arianism, an alternative form of Christianity which rejected the definition of faith adopted at the Council of Nicaea in 325. The Vandal elite seems to have adopted it originally from the Visigoths during their time in Spain. Victor presents Huneric's predecessor, Geiseric, as a persecutor of Nicene Catholic Christianity on the same scale as his son, but the reality suggested by the detailed measures Geiseric enacted is much more interesting. Geiseric took no action at all against Catholic Christians in Byzacena and Numidia, where there were no Vandal settlers. Instead, he confiscated church buildings and their landed endowments in Proconsularis, handing them over to the non-Nicenes; he also prevented episcopal vacancies from being filled in Proconsularis and eventually made it illegal to hold Catholic services in any of its localities where elements of the coalition had settled. Given that his followers can only have been exposed to Visigothic Christianity in Spain in the 410s and 420s and that, in all recorded cases, large-scale conversion is a lengthy process, Geiseric's policy looks very different to that of his son. Rather than try to win everyone in Africa over to non-Nicene Christianity, his measures were designed to give Arianism a free run at converting his own newly settled followers. Dispersed now much more widely than when they had been on the march and with the threat of Roman counterattack fading after the treaty of 443, there was a much greater danger that they might lose the hard-won coherence that had turned them into such an effective fighting force in southern Spain. In this context, giving their identity an extra cultural dimension made perfect sense.[19]

There were some further trials and tribulations to come for the Vandals after the 440s. Following the collapse of Hunnic power on Attila's death in 453, different imperial regimes returned to the offensive: the Western Emperor Majorian in 461 and Eastern Emperor Leo in 468. Thanks, however, to a new Vandal dominance of the sea, based on the maritime capacities of the North African ports that Geiseric controlled, the coalition was able to fend off these counterattacks until all hope of using restored African revenues to bolster a revivified Western Empire had disappeared. At this point, Constantinople was ready to sign a definitive peace agreement, and from 473 the kingdom was finally secure. Geiseric had also exploited the final collapse of the Roman west to add Tripolitania, Sardinia, and the westernmost promontory of Sicily to his domains. A decade later, Huneric's persecution generated a severe kingdom-wide religious crisis, but this was an internal matter. While certainly ferocious, it lasted only from February 484 until the king's death the following November.

None of these later events seem to have changed the basic nature of the task facing Belisarius and his army, which was largely set by the settlement of 443. The key to victory in the 530s lay in eliminating the militarized, colonial landowning Vandal-Alan elite, which had taken possession of the best agricultural assets of Proconsularis. The fact that this elite had adopted many elements of Roman elite lifestyles in the meantime and that the kingdom as a whole functioned on the back of Roman administrative structures did not change the basic military equation.[20]

THE DESTRUCTION OF THE VANDALS

In military terms, it is impossible to overestimate the importance of the fact that the Vandal fleet was absent in Sardinia. After Geiseric seized Carthage in 439, different imperial regimes of East and West made three serious attempts over the next thirty years to reconquer the Vandal kingdom. All ended in failure and two in disaster; the problem in each case was getting a large enough force safely onto North African soil. The expedition of 441/2 had been massing in Sicily when the first of Attila the Hun's campaigns into the Balkans had forced its abandonment, since its eastern contingents were required at home. In 461, the Emperor Majorian gathered forces in Spain to make the shorter crossing of the Straits of Gibraltar, but Geiseric got wind of the operation and destroyed the assembled Roman shipping while it was still in harbour—a disaster which led directly to Majorian's deposition and death. In 468, a huge East Roman armada had set sail from Constantinople but come to grief off the North African coast; nailed by hostile winds to a rocky shoreline on which it could not land, it was a sitting duck for Vandal fireships. The loss of life had been horrendous, and the expedition's failure—its cost in weight was a hundred thousand pounds of gold—bankrupted the Eastern regime of Leo I and marked the end of serious attempts to keep the Western

Empire afloat. In his account of the 533 expedition, Procopius makes much of Belisarius's ingenious signalling arrangements to keep his fleet of six hundred ships together even when sailing at night and of the skill of Antonina, the general's wife's, at keeping water fresh on long sea journeys. But he also notes that the troops were terrified of being at sea, which was only reasonable given the fate of the 468 expedition. In the end, the chance absence of the Vandal fleet rather than signalling arrangements or a plentiful supply of fresh water was what enabled Belisarius to land his army without any opposition at all.[21]

On the basis of Procopius's intelligence that the Vandal fleet had been despatched to Sardinia, Belisarius's armada could leave from Sicily with complete confidence. After brief stops at the intervening islands of Gozo and Malta, it arrived off the headland of Caput Vada (now Ras Kabudia) in the province of Byzacena more or less three months after leaving Constantinople. Never before had a Roman army—Western, Eastern, or combined—actually managed to land unmolested on the shores of the Vandal kingdom. Belisarius had a unique opportunity, and his task now was to make the most of it. At a hastily called council of war, various plans were put forward. Archaelaus, chief administrative officer to the expedition, urged that the expedition sail immediately for Carthage, since it was the only fortified harbour in the Vandal kingdom which could offer a safe base for both the fleet and the army. But Belisarius didn't want to take any further risks with the winds of the Mediterranean and ordered an immediate disembarkation, much to his soldiers' relief.[22]

A fortified camp was quickly constructed, and food obtained from the surrounding area. But time was of the essence, and the general moved fast. On the one hand, a hearts-and-minds campaign began in earnest. A nearby local community was approached and won over to the cause. To reassure local Romano-African farmers, there was a carefully publicized execution of looters who refused to pay for supplies, and the general also took every opportunity to claim that his army was there only to put Hilderic, rightful ruler of the Vandal kingdom, back on his throne.[23] At the same time, the army was readied for action. Within three days, perhaps just long enough to get over any lingering seasickness and bring the horses back into condition, the army began to move on Carthage, capital of the Vandal kingdom. An advance guard of three hundred regular cavalry was sent on about three miles ahead of the main body, and the six hundred Massagetae were deployed as a flanking force at about the same distance to the left. The infantry was in the middle, and Belisarius brought up the rear with the rest of the cavalry. His plan was to march north along the main, largely coastal road from Caput Vada to Carthage past Lepcis Minor, Hadrumentum, and Grasse, the fleet to keep pace in inshore waters as best it could.[24]

On the fourth day of the march, 13 September, the army arrived at the town of Ad Decimum, at the tenth mile post from Carthage, and battle began. Gelimer had been stunned by the sudden arrival of the enemy fleet, and his remaining forces, apart from the seven thousand men sent off to Sardinia, were widely dispersed. He himself was staying at a royal estate in southern Byzacena, so Belisarius had by chance landed between the king and his capital. Gelimer's response was to try to catch the Romans in a three-way pincer. His brother Ammatas was ordered south from Carthage with everyone he could muster. Ammatas also executed, on his brother's orders, the deposed king Hilderic—the likeliest response to Belisarius's claim that he had come to put the rightful Vandal king back on the throne and perhaps exactly what Justinian and his general had intended. Gelimer himself attempted to catch the Romans from the rear with his forces, while a third body of two thousand men, under the king's nephew Gibimundus, would attack from the western flank.[25]

A perfectly plausible plan on paper, but as always in a world without radio communications, coordinating dispersed forces proved extremely difficult, and so the first battle of the African campaign came in as a series of isolated skirmishes. First up, at around noon, Belisarius's three hundred screening cavalry encountered Ammatas and a Vandal advance guard moving south from Carthage, with the bulk of his men strung out behind him along the road in companies of twenty or thirty, not remotely in battle array. The Roman commander, John, went into immediate action and was lucky enough to kill Gelimer's brother almost immediately, at which point all the rest of the Vandal advance guard fled, but not before Ammatas had personally killed a dozen of Belisarius's elite guardsmen. Having no idea what was really going on and probably worried that they were wandering piecemeal into the main body of Belisarius's army in full battle order, the rest of Ammatas's force beat a hasty retreat to Carthage as remnants of Ammatas's advance guard fled through their ranks. John's force, mounted archers to a man, followed up and turned the retreat into a rout, driving their opponents all the way to Carthage.[26]

The next engagement occurred about five miles inland from Ad Decimum, where Gibimundus's force of two thousand ran into Belisarius's flank guard of six hundred Massagetae. Procopius preserves no details of what happened except that the Massagetae routed their opponents, who 'were all disgracefully destroyed'. Whether they were literally all killed is unclear, but they were certainly eliminated as an effective fighting force.[27] In the meantime, Belisarius, unaware of any of this, continued his advance and, finding a good place to camp, established a stockade for his infantry about four miles south of Ad Decimum, while he himself advanced with the rest of his cavalry to probe the Vandals' strength. The allied cavalry, presumably the four hundred Heruli, went forward first, followed by eight hundred of Belisarius's regulars under Uliaris, while the general himself brought up the rear with the remainder, the best part of three thousand men. Having learned about John's earlier encounter with Ammatas, the Heruli then ran slap bang into Gelimer's main body, which had advanced to Ad Decimum on a parallel route to Belisarius's main coast road. The Heruli were quickly routed and fled back to Uliaris's covering force, which also turned and ran until it reached Belisarius with the rest of the cavalry. Furious, Belisarius turned them all around and headed north with a combined force of four thousand cavalry to look for Gelimer. Procopius's opinion is that if the Vandal king had pressed his attack at this point, he could have won a famous victory, since he would have held a huge numerical advantage, but as it turned out, there was no battle at all. In the meantime, Gelimer had found his brother's corpse and presumably also discovered the fate of his nephew. Having no interest in further conflict for the moment, looking instead to mourn his losses, the king ordered a general retreat—not back towards Carthage, which would have allowed him at least to trap John's advance guard, but eastwards to the Plain of Boulla. When Belisarius's cavalry moved forward, therefore, they found not a Vandal army arranged for battle but an enemy in full retreat. At dusk, the Massagetae and John's advance guard returned, and Belisarius knew that the road to Carthage lay open. The Roman army had won its first major victory without really planning to. The infantry never left its camp.[28]

On September 14, the entire army moved up to the outskirts of Carthage but, since Belisarius was worried about a possible ambush, did not enter. The general also wanted to prevent his soldiers from taking advantage of fast approaching nightfall to start looting, although he was unable to prevent a few ships from slipping into harbour to engage in a little private pillage. But trap was there none, and the next day the Roman army entered the city in triumph, Belisarius's settling down in the Vandal royal palace, previously home to generations of Rome's proconsular governors, to enjoy a lunch originally prepared for Gelimer.[29] Within a week of the landing, Belisarius's soldiers were safely ensconced in the greatest city of North Africa. The contrast with the failed expeditions of 441, 461, and 468 could not be greater.

There then followed a period of phony war. Cautious as ever and conscious that the capture of Carthage was already a much bigger prize than Justinian's minimum requirement from the expedition, Belisarius carefully refortified the city, whose circuit wall the Vandals had allowed to degenerate. Apart from sending joyful messages back to Constantinople, along with some choice booty, the general concentrated on winning over the Romano-African provincial population. His soldiers were allotted quarters within the city's private housing according to due process, and all their supplies were scrupulously purchased at its markets. The looters from the fleet were also punished. Simultaneously, Belisarius rounded up all the Vandals he could get his hands on. Some had fled for sanctuary to various churches in the aftermath of Ad Decimum, and these were concentrated in Carthage along with all the prisoners that had so far been taken. Procopius does not describe this round-up in any detail but does portray Gelimer's fighting men, as they gathered to launch their eventual counterattack, complaining about how many of their women and children were now in Roman hands. It seems, therefore, that Belisarius's men were busy identifying and collecting Vandal dependents from among the many dispersed settlements of Proconsularis to the west of the city, which the capture of Carthage now allowed him to dominate, something which Gelimer, encamped to the east on the Plain of Boulla, was in no position to prevent.[30]

Away from the city, Gelimer licked his wounds and concentrated his surviving forces. Word was sent to Sardinia to summon the absent fleet and its seven thousand elite soldiers back to Africa. He also tried to organize outside assistance. Back in September, he had sent an embassy to Visigothic Spain, but such were the vagaries of ancient travel that it didn't arrive at the Gothic court until after an East Roman counterpart announcing Belisarius's capture of Carthage. Not surprisingly, this discouraged a positive Gothic response to Gelimer's request for help.[31] The king also tried to recruit Berbers from the desert fringes of his kingdom, but it had been a Berber revolt which had undermined Hilderic's rule in the first place, and few Berber allies turned up to fight. Nonetheless, in late autumn Gelimer felt ready to renew hostilities. Advancing towards Carthage, he cut one of the city's aqueducts and offered bounty to any Romano-African peasants who ambushed Belisarius's forage parties and brought him their heads. He also used his contacts within the city to sow dissent within Belisarius's ranks. The Massagetae were offered large rewards to swap sides, and at least one of Carthage's leading Roman citizens was caught red-handed. The general had him publicly impaled, to ram home the point that, while he would not allow his army to mistreat or pillage the indigenous population of North Africa, disloyalty would be punished as treason. And despite the Vandal advance, Gelimer had no wish to engage in siege warfare against the newly refortified city, so that tactical initiative remained with Belisarius.[32] The showdown would come when he was ready.

Three months after the battle of Ad Decimum, Belisarius opened the gates of Carthage and marched his army out in two divisions. The advance guard was composed of the bulk of the cavalry which had triumphed in the previous engagement, under the command of the same John whose screening force had killed Ammatas. Not far behind came the main body under Belisarius himself, comprising all the infantry and a smaller force of five hundred cavalry. In the evening, the advance guard located Gelimer and his army concentrated at Tricamarum, about thirty kilometres (18.6 miles) from Carthage. The Vandals had enclosed their camp with a fortified stockade to protect their women and children.

The day of battle began quietly; then around midday, the Vandals came out of their camp in full battle array and halted on one side of a small stream. John did the same with his forces on the other bank, but before fighting could begin, Belisarius arrived with his remaining cavalry, the infantry left to follow on as best it could. At Belisarius's command, the engagement opened with a series of skirmishes, always initiated by the Romans. John and a picked body of horsemen made two sorties against the Vandal centre but, when challenged, fell back on the Roman main body—a textbook example of the use of light and heavy cavalry as described in sixth-century military manuals (p. 53). The Vandals, however, refused to take the bait. Belisarius's next move was to initiate a general attack, crossing the stream with all of his cavalry. On all fronts, the Romans had the best of it, driving their opponents back to their stockade with the loss of fewer than fifty men, while the Vandals lost eight hundred. By now, the Roman infantry had arrived, and Belisarius set about preparing a full-scale assault timed for mid-afternoon. But it was not needed. At the arrival of the massed Roman infantry, Gelimer retreated in panic; seeing his departure, everyone else fled as well. Organized resistance collapsed, and the routed Vandals, many accompanied by their women and children, were cut down as they ran. But as the Vandal camp contained a huge amount of movable wealth, Belisarius's army, too, quickly lost its cohesion, turning from fighting to looting.[33]

In the end, the battle of Tricamarum became extremely messy, but it was no less decisive for that. Gelimer kept running westwards along the coastal cities of his former kingdom. Belisarius paused to restore discipline among his men and to round up any of the shattered Vandals left anywhere near the battlefield. The Romans then set off in pursuit of Gelimer and captured the Vandal royal treasure and a demoralized gaggle of leading Vandals at Hippo Regius. Gelimer himself fled for safety to some friendly Berbers high on the inaccessible Mount Papua on the borders of Numidia; he was safe enough, but he could do nothing to prevent Belisarius from rounding up the last remaining Vandals. By March 534, Gelimer had had enough and negotiated a surrender. Famously, he asked only for some bread to eat, a sponge to bathe his infected eye, and a lyre which he could use to lament the fall of his kingdom.[34]

At this point, the conquest of the Vandal kingdom had turned into a few mopping-up operations. Small expeditionary forces took possession of the Vandals' overseas possessions: Sardinia, the westernmost promontory of Sicily, and a run of coastal cities leading west to the Straits of Gibraltar. In the summer of 534, Belisarius himself was able to return to Constantinople to counter accusations of possible treason on his part, which jealous peers had been whispering in the imperial ear, with Gelimer and a host of Vandal prisoners in tow. He duly received, as was only appropriate, every honour that Justinian could find. Belisarius became the first non-emperor to be awarded a formal triumph in half a millennium. In Republican Rome such ceremonies, in which the victorious general rode through the streets in a four-horse chariot followed, in unarmed procession, by elements of his army, captives, and the spoils of his war, had been used to thank the gods and celebrate the general responsible for the victory, but no non-emperor had been granted such an honour since the time of Augustus, in line with the ideological claim that it was an emperor's legitimacy which really guaranteed victory whether he was present on the battlefield or not (p. 28). The breaking of this tradition emphasizes just how extraordinary and unexpected Belisarius's destruction of the Vandal kingdom was and just how politically important, too, to the regime of Justinian in its darkest hour. The citizens of Constantinople thus witnessed a great victory parade where Belisarius led through the city his soldiers, captured Vandals (above all, the captive Vandal royal family), and a host of captured treasures, although the ancient ceremony was carefully rechoreographed to underline Justinian's overarching dominance. At the climactic moment, when it all reached the Hippodrome, Belisarius doffed the garlands of victory and fell on his knees to kiss the emperor's feet in the royal box. But the general's success and loyalty was further rewarded with the consulship for 535, the greatest imperial honour of them all, and that brought its own parade. On 1 January 1 535, Belisarius was carried through the city, held aloft by Vandal captives, as a second reminder of the extraordinary service he had performed for his emperor.[35]

Belisarius's arrival in Constantinople with his prisoners marked the complete destruction of the descendants of the original Rhine coalition as an independent political force. When the East Roman army landed at Caput Veda, the passage of time had not fundamentally altered the character or composition of the Vandal kingdom's key political constituency, a numerically limited, landed military gentry cum aristocracy which had been generously rewarded with estates in the aftermath of Geiseric's seizure of Carthage in 439. Comprising at that point some ten to fifteen thousand warriors with their dependents, it was the descendants of this force that Belisarius had to defeat, and he not only overcame them in battle but destroyed them as a sociopolitical unit. On the most basic of levels, this was done on the battlefield. Even allowing for some increase thanks to the peace and prosperity it had been enjoying since the 470s, the Vandal military elite cannot have numbered more than twenty to twenty-five thousand soldiers. From this kind of total, the two thousand who fell with Gibimundus at Ad Decimum and another eight hundred at Tricamarum were far from insignificant losses. These are the only specific figures that Procopius gives, but many other elite warriors must have died in the headlong routs associated with both of those battles. Off the battlefield, Belisarius's forces also carefully rounded up all the members of the Vandal elite they could find (after Ad Decimum, in Carthage, after Tricamarum, and beyond into the spring of 534), and the younger males of military age were shipped off to the East. Gelimer and some of his royal relatives were granted consolatory estates in Asia Minor, but most of the surviving Vandal soldiery—something over two thousand men in total—found itself swapping baths, villas, and hunting for the much tougher life of Roman military auxiliaries, forming five new cavalry units which were dispersed across the Persian front. As might be expected, some individuals escaped Belisarius's net to find refuge among the various Berber groups of the African interior. About six hundred of them put in an appearance in later African events. But the East Roman army had ripped the heart out of the Vandal kingdom by battlefield victory and deportation. A more effective piece of political genocide would be difficult to find.[36]

Within ten astonishing months of the landing at Caput Veda, it was all over, and the bulk of Belisarius's army had not fought at all. As Procopius concluded:

> Whether such events as these ever took place before I am not able to say, wherein the fourth descendant of Geiseric, and his kingdom at the height of its wealth and military strength, was undone in so short a time by five thousand men coming in as invaders and having not a place to cast anchor. For such was the number of the horsemen who followed Belisarius and carried through the whole war against the Vandals.[37]

Two engagements in three months, in neither of which had Belisarius even begun to use his infantry, had been enough to overthrow a kingdom which had terrorized the Mediterranean world for much of the fifth century.

From hindsight, it is easy to take this astonishing victory for granted, but its nature is worth careful reflection, not least because of the role it went on to play in the broader development of policy within Justinian's regime. In part, Belisarius's success was due to the simple fact that, this time, the East Romans were able to land an army intact on North African shores, a feat which their predecessors had spectacularly failed to achieve on three separate occasions in the mid-fifth century. But there was more to Belisarius's victory than the fact that the Vandal fleet was not at home. By the fifth century, the Vandals had learned to fight effectively even against elite imperial field forces. The initial engagements of 416–18 were disastrous for the Rhine coalition, but by 421 greater political cohesion, allied with the experience gained from its previous defeats and a bit of help from the Visigoths, had created a force capable of inflicting heavy defeat on a full-scale Roman field army. Likewise in North Africa itself in the 430s, Geiseric's forces had fought effectively enough against a combined East-West Roman army to be initially allocated lands in Numidia and then to seize Carthage itself. Seaborne Vandal raiders subsequently spread terror across much of the Mediterranean for the next thirty years. The contrast between the Vandals' military record in the fifth century and their total military incapacity in the face of Belisarius's army in both smaller-scale fighting (the Massagetae's destruction of Gibimundus outside Ad Decimum) and set-piece battles (Tricamarum) is startling.

Procopius attributed this decline to Vandal decadence. By the time they had trekked from Slovakia to Carthage, suffered horrendous losses, and fought countless engagements, the surviving participants in the ancestral coalition must have become extraordinarily battle hardened. Yet subsequent generations born to peace and plenty would have found this impossible to emulate, particularly after the general peace with the Romans negotiated by Geiseric in 473. Gelimer's leadership also left something to be desired, at least as presented by Procopius. We can perhaps forgive the poetic self-indulgence of his surrender negotiations, since anyone would be clinically depressed after such a staggering run of disasters. But he does appear to have been very quick to withdraw at Ad Decimum on finding the body of his brother, when more resolute leadership could have wrapped up John's screening force, perhaps the Massagetae, too. This would at least have given Belisarius something to think about. Turning tail in the decisive engagement of the war at Tricamarum is also hardly the mark of effective leadership. But Gelimer was, we know, a hardened war leader who had performed effectively against the Berbers, and the Berbers would later pose plenty of problems for the East Romans, too. This suggests to me, as in fact do the details of Procopius's narrative, that the collapse of Gelimer's leadership was more effect than cause of the evident battlefield superiority of Belisarius's army, as emerges clearly in the destruction of Gibimundus's flanking force and the one-sided carnage at Tricamarum.

Still, Procopius's battle narratives for the Vandal campaign leave much to be desired. For Tricamarum, he gives page after page of invented exhortations from the mouth of Gelimer and his other surviving brother, Tatzon, leader of the returning Sardinian expedition, with only a few short paragraphs on the actual engagement.[38] Nowhere does he tell us why the Vandals lost eight hundred men to the Romans' fifty. But given that the action consisted entirely of cavalry attacks, it is overwhelmingly likely that mounted archery was responsible. In other words, the underlying key to Belisarius's success (apart from the sheer luck involved in landing intact) lies in the sixth-century transformation of the East Roman army. I am not generally a great believer in the broader explanatory powers of military technology in history; the opposition usually just get hold of it, too, or find ways to counter it. But just occasionally, if usually only for a short period, new military hardware can provide a crucial edge. A classic recent case in point is provided by the two Gulf wars. Saddam Hussein's armies had fought long and hard against Iran but basically with more advanced forms of World War II–type mid-twentieth-century equipment and tactics. Both proved utterly unable to live on the battlefield with the twenty-first-century hardware of the coalition forces, which won swift and utterly overwhelming victories on the battlefield in both 1991 and 2003.

In this case, Procopius's account of Vandal collapse is inexplicable without the flexible adoption of Hunnic-style mounted archery and revised tactical doctrines which allowed for far more effective combinations of lighter and heavier Roman cavalry units on the battlefield (see Chapter 2). For their part, the Vandals had learned to fight fifth-century Roman armies, which like their earlier counterparts had relied on the shock value of well-disciplined, well-handled heavy infantry, with cavalry there only to cover the flanks and engage in reconnaissance. Gelimer's Vandal army possessed plenty of cavalry, as demonstrated by the fact that the survivors were turned into Roman cavalry units on the eastern front, but there is no mention of a single horse archer among them, nor would the Vandals have had any prior exposure to the carefully drilled interactions of lighter and heavier cavalry units which was now central to East Roman war making.

So in large measure, the Vandals' defeat comes down to the fact that they were caught fighting a sixth-century war with a fifth-century army. The main focus of the intervening military restructuring was certainly its more traditional enemies in the Balkans and Mesopotamia, but the cavalry revolution also gave East Roman armies a shattering advantage over the now-outdated forces of the Vandal kingdom. The consequences of this revelation were about to be felt right across the Mediterranean world and much of the Near East.

6

ROME AND RAVENNA

BACK IN CONSTANTINOPLE, BELISARIUS'S victory restored the ideological and political credibility of Justinian's regime. The horrors of the Nika riot had given way to another kind of victory altogether. God's authority had been displayed, and though Belisarius commanded in the field, divine validation of Justinian's right to rule was manifest in an extraordinary triumph whose scale and ease went way beyond hope. The overall boost to the emperor's political prestige was incalculable. On the simplest level, the wealth and prisoners of victory, including much of the loot the Vandals had themselves taken from Rome and elsewhere across the Mediterranean in the fifth century, not least treasures from the Temple of Jerusalem (originally stolen by Titus four hundred years before) were no small matter. Of much greater significance, however, were the political benefits. God had spoken, and His word always carried most weight on the field of battle. The regime was now untouchable, and Justinian could afford to be magnanimous. The eighteen senators banished after Nika were pardoned, and the estates of Hypatius and Pompeius returned to their families.[1] Not only had the emperor's military gamble paid off, but the astonishing speed of Belisarius's victory kick-started new chains of thought in the upper reaches of Justinian's regime.

PETER THE PATRICIAN

The regime's first public comment on its victory in North Africa, in a law from early 534, explained the success in entirely religious terms. God had punished the Vandals for their many sins against the Catholic Church.[2]

There was no reference at all in this law to the fact that North Africa had previously belonged to the Roman Empire, and it carried no indication, implicit or explicit, that an aggressive conquest policy might be extended to other ex-Roman territories. Beneath the surface, however, the regime was already contemplating further military adventures.[3]

Having taken North Africa, the next target, should there be one, was obvious: the Italian kingdom of the Ostrogoths. Apart from the ideological attractions of the city of Rome for a self-styled Roman emperor, there was plenty of rich agricultural land under Gothic control which would fit nicely into an expanding imperial tax base. Taking control of the Italian peninsula also made excellent strategic sense. As Belisarius's route to Caput Veda—via Sicily, Gozo, and Malta—underlines, natural sea lanes, based on prevailing winds and currents, tied together the Italian mainland and the central North African provinces around Carthage. Getting to North Africa by sailing west, say, from Egypt was infinitely more difficult.[4] Controlling Italy as well as North Africa gave you absolute control of the central Mediterranean. It was also potentially possible for large armies to reach Italy overland, thus avoiding the kind of combined operations with the navy which had so terrified Belisarius's soldiers, even if it would involve pretty demanding marches through some of the more rugged corners of the Balkans. On the other hand, Ostrogothic Italy was an ostensibly friendly power whose material support for the Vandal expedition, above all the provision of horses, during the fleet's stay in Sicily had made the conquest of North Africa a viable proposition. Justinian trod very carefully, therefore, as his regime began to explore the possibility of elevating a one-off African adventure into stage one of a full-blown conquest policy.

An opportunity for working a political opening in Italy, which might ease the path for military intervention in due course, was immediately available in the form of that happiest of hunting grounds for political opportunism: succession. Its importance in the Constantinopolitan context is plain to see, but succession was just as significant in Italy, as indeed everywhere else. (If Bill Clinton had been a medieval historian, his aphorism would have been: 'It's about the succession, stupid.') No other issue had the same capacity for destabilizing all existing political relationships than thoughts of what might happen under a future ruler. The Ostrogothic kingdom had flourished under its founder, Theoderic the Great (493–526), but his succession plans went sadly awry (see Figure 6.1). To start with he had no son, and then, when he had successfully married off Amalasuentha, the daughter he had chosen to be the vessel of dynastic legitimacy, to a suitable son-in-law called Eutharic, the latter unfortunately predeceased him. The marriage had already produced a son, Athalaric, but he was only a boy at his grandfather's death. Could a minor inherit the Gothic kingship? Opinion was bitterly divided in the upper echelons of the kingdom, even though Athalaric was certainly his grandfather's choice. Our sources on this are all from the Ostrogothic kingdom, but they give unusually sharp insight into the political chaos resulting from untrammelled ambition, as important court factions identified the possible contenders and decided whom to rally around. There were at least two other serious contenders: Theoderic's nephew Theodahad, and a distinguished general called Tuluin, who had married into the royal Amal

FIGURE 6.1
The mausoleum of Theoderic the Great. Under his control, the Ostrogothic kingdom grew into a quasi-western empire.
Credit: ermess / Shutterstock

dynasty. The competition was intense enough to generate military unrest on Theoderic's death. In the end, Theodahad and Tuluin were bought off, but a nine-year-old cannot rule, so the ambitions unleashed by disputed succession simply mutated into a struggle for control of the young king's regency council.[5]

Procopius gives what followed a particular spin. Amalasuentha, he reports, wanted her son to have a Roman education, whereas three older Gothic male rivals on the council wanted him brought up as a 'proper' Goth, falling back on a supposed saying of the old king that if you make a boy fear the cane (ever the traditional accompaniment of learning Latin), he will never learn to despise sword and spear. The story cannot be taken at face value, not least since Theoderic had clearly given his own children classical educations, but controlling the young king's upbringing would certainly have been the key to immediate political power, and Procopius is explicit that her rivals were using the issue to try to force Amalasuentha into political retirement. Eventually, the rivalry took such a potentially lethal turn that Amalasuentha had a ship loaded with treasure and sent to Epidamnus, a port on the East Roman Adriatic, in case she needed to retreat to Constantinople. In the end, she got her three rivals away from court by appointing them to senior provincial commands and then had them murdered. Anonymous in Procopius, one of the three was probably Tuluin. To reinforce her position, the queen also publicly humiliated the other main contender for power, her cousin Theodahad, putting him on trial for land grabbing in Tuscany and making him return everything he had supposedly 'stolen'. The contest had been brutal, but by ruthless self-assertion, the queen had protected her regency.[6]

In the longer term, however, Amalasuentha's was a Pyrrhic victory. The murdered men had relations who, as Procopius puts it, were 'many and important', so that the queen managed to entrench a clearly identified and powerful political opposition. The true cost of her survival revealed itself when it became obvious that her son was dying. Procopius calls what finally killed Athalaric on 2 October 534 a 'wasting disease'. When exactly his declining health became apparent is unknown, but presumably it was in the spring or early summer of the same year; the results at the Ostrogothic court were what might be expected. Succession was back on the menu with a vengeance, and political stability evaporated as calculations about potential future benefits undermined, once again, all existing alliances. At this moment, before Athalaric's death but after Belisarius's success in North Africa, a first imperial embassy arrived in Ravenna. On the face of it, Justinian was pursuing two minor quarrels with the Gothic kingdom in the aftermath of victory. He wanted Amalasuentha to hand over a small portion of Sicily which had previously belonged to the Vandal kingdom and also ten renegade Massagetae who had taken ship for Italy. The emperor was perhaps already using these matters as pretexts to fish in troubled waters, but the response he got from Amalasuentha pushed a possible Italian intervention high up the agenda in Constantinople. Publicly, the queen denied Justinian's demands. Secretly, such was the toxicity of the Gothic court, she offered to resign her kingdom to the emperor's control if he would offer her a wealthy and safe retirement.[7]

Justinian responded by despatching a new ambassador plenipotentiary to the Gothic court, Peter the Patrician. From Dara in Mesopotamia, scene of Belisarius's first victory, he was renowned as a lawyer and scholar. He was also, according to Procopius in the *Wars*, clever, kindly and persuasive, while the *Anekdota* adds that he was the greatest thief alive. There is no doubting his cleverness and guile, however, nor the trust which he inspired in his emperor.[8] As one Victorian viceroy of India commented, it was the invention of the telegraph which ruined the diplomat's art. From that point on, difficult issues could just be referred back home. In the ancient world, ambassadors were on their own. They were briefed exhaustively, of course, but then had to exercise initiative, cut off from the practical possibility of further instruction—sometimes to live or die on the basis of decisions made on the hoof.

Peter's ostensible mission was to continue discussion of Sicily and the Massagetae, but his real job was to undermine resolve at the top of the Ostrogothic kingdom with a view to facilitating its handover to Constantinople. His key targets were Amalasuentha and her cousin Theodahad, the obvious pretender left standing after the triple assassination. In fact, Theodahad had himself made enquiries about retiring to Constantinople in the period when he was being publicly humiliated. Peter was briefed to attack their confidence and perhaps a lot more besides. In *Anekdota*, Procopius claims that he was given secret orders to organize Amalasuentha's assassination if nothing else would work. In the event, there was a delay before he could start. En route overland to Italy, he met Gothic ambassadors going in the other direction. Athalaric had just died, and Amalasuentha had associated Theodahad with her on the throne, trying to protect herself from a political opposition that was out for revenge. By the time that Justinian's new orders—to make the emperor's strong support for the queen explicit at every available opportunity—arrived and Peter finally made his way to Ravenna, the situation had changed again. In the winter of 534/5, Amalasuentha was removed from court and confined to the island of Marta in Lake Bolsena, where her murder, in the bath, was organized by those 'many and important' relatives of the assassinated trio. She was dead by April 535, conceivably a month or two before, and an entirely new situation confronted Constantinople's plenipotentiary when he finally arrived in Ravenna.[9]

Nothing daunted, Peter set to work to generate as much anxiety as possible. Stressing the emperor's declared support for the deposed and murdered queen, a rerun of the original pretext which had sent Belisarius to North Africa, Peter battered away at Theodahad's resolve, no doubt with lengthy and extensive reference to the dramatic outcome of the Vandal expedition. In the summer of 535, he shuttled back and forth to Constantinople, apparently taking Theodahad's messages that Amalasuentha's murder had not been his idea and returning with Justinian's response. In fact, Peter was sowing as much dissention as possible by stressing East Roman military superiority on the one hand while sorting out the details for Theodahad, in secret, of the same kind of deal that had been on the table for his murdered cousin: hand over the kingdom and enjoy a wealthy retirement in Constantinople.[10]

Pressure was ramped up by simultaneous, limited military operations on the fringes of the Gothic kingdom. At the same time Peter was whispering poison in Theodahad's ears, the commanding East Roman general in the western Balkans, Mundus, advanced northwards to take the Gothic-held city of Salona, on the Dalmatian coast. Belisarius was also despatched with a fleet, four thousand regulars, three thousand Isaurians, and few hundred others, including the general's own *bucellarii*.

His destination was given out as Carthage, but he had contingent orders again to test Gothic control of Sicily and if it could be easily overturned, to do so. At this point, Justinian was still not fully committed to an outright conquest policy. This is underlined by both the contingent nature of Belisarius's orders and the composition of this expeditionary force, which lacked much of the extensive cavalry arm that had destroyed the Vandal kingdom. The aim, if possible, was to force Theodahad into abdication and thus avoid total war. Belisarius duly landed close to Catania, which immediately surrendered, and the other cities of the island quickly followed suit, almost entirely without resistance, except at Panormus (modern Palermo). Its Gothic garrison held out until the general realized that archers posted in the masts of his ships could fire down on the walls' defenders, which was enough to prompt surrender. Syracuse was the last city to open its gates, and Belisarius entered it in triumph on 31 December 535, the final day of his consular year.[11]

Back in Ravenna, Peter went into overdrive, pressuring Theodahad with tales of the military juggernaut heading in his direction. Panicked, the king agreed to surrender his kingdom, and the ambassador thought he had his man. But then, around Easter 536, news arrived in Ravenna that a Gothic counterattack had thrown the Romans out of Salona. Theodahad did a complete volte-face, throwing his diplomatic tormentor in jail, where he would languish for the next four years. But it was now too late to show the kind of resolve which, a year earlier, might have discouraged a cautious emperor from rolling the dice of war. Peter had already sent the crucial letter to Belisarius in Sicily—which Justinian had ordered him to expect and respond to if ever it arrived—summoning general and army to Italy.[12] Imperial war making in the West was no longer dependent on favourable and highly contingent circumstances, as it had been when Belisarius left for North Africa. In 536, the Goths were already mobilized against Constantinople and had just won one round. But Justinian was now confident that his armies could topple the Gothic kingdom as quickly as they had that of the Vandals. There had been no abdication of power at the centre, and the Goths were ready to fight, but Justinian went to war anyway. Western conquest had finally become a fully fledged policy in its own right. Intervention in Africa had been a reactive response, born of desperation, to highly contingent circumstances beyond Justinian's control. When it came to Italy, the emperor had instead attempted to manufacture the right circumstances via his diplomatic agent provocateur and, even when they failed to materialize, was still ready to press the trigger. Was Justinian's regime correct in calculating that the Goths' Italian kingdom would fall as easily as its Vandal counterpart?

'A COPY OF THE ONLY EMPIRE'

It is certainly the case that by the mid-530s, the kingdom's most glorious days were behind it. About thirty years before, its founder, Theoderic the Great wrote a famous letter to Justinian's predecessor but one, the Emperor Anastasius:

> You [Anastasius] are the fairest ornament of all realms, you are the healthful defence of the whole world, to which all other rulers rightfully look up with reverence. We [Theoderic] above all, who by Divine help learned in Your Republic the art of governing Romans with equity ... Our royalty is an imitation of yours, modelled on your good purpose, a copy of the only Empire.[13]

The letter has often been cited to show barbarian deference to Roman ideals and the Eastern emperor in Constantinople. On the surface, Theoderic was laying it on with a trowel, praising Anastasius as a divinely appointed ruler, deliberately and explicitly employing the terms that Roman state ideology itself customarily used (Chapter 1). Read as a whole, however, the letter was doing much more.

The key phrase is 'by Divine help' (*auxilia ... divino*). In using it, Theoderic asserted that his ability to govern Italy as a fully fledged Roman ruler was the product not primarily of his own personal capacities honed by ten years' observation of Romanness in action as a child hostage in Constantinople (although this played its part) but, still more fundamentally, of God's direct intervention. In the context of Roman state ideology, this amounted to the direct assertion that Theoderic himself, together with the realm he governed, was just as legitimately 'Roman'—that is, divinely ordained—as the Eastern Empire itself. In appropriately aggressive vein, the substantive contents of the letter eventually turned into a demand note. The post-Roman west was in the midst of a major political convulsion as Theoderic wrote. The rise of Frankish power under Clovis threatened many of its neighbours, east and west of the Rhine, not least the Visigothic kingdom with which the Ostrogoths were in alliance. Anastasius supported the Franks and even organized coastal raids on the northern Adriatic coast of the Italian peninsula in 507 to prevent Theoderic from marching to the Visigoths' assistance. In this context, Theoderic's claim to independent, fully legitimate Romanness became the basis of reproach:

> we think you will not suffer that any discord should remain between two Republics [the Eastern and Western Roman states] which are declared to have ever formed one body under their ancient princes, and which ought not to be joined by a mere sentiment of love, but actively to aid one another with all their powers. Let there be always one will, one purpose in the Roman Kingdom. Therefore, while greeting you with our respectful salutations, we humbly beg that you will not remove from us the high honour of your Mildness's affection, which we have a right to hope for if it were never granted to any others.

Because, in other words, Theoderic runs the only other authentic, divinely guided Roman state in the world, Constantinople should be in alliance with him, not supporting the barbarian Franks who have no place in God's plan for the universe.[14]

Nor were Theoderic's quasi-imperial pretensions, which were recognized by his subjects, one of whom hailed him in an inscription as 'always Augustus' (*semper Augustus*), mere bombast. Clovis may have begun the crisis, but Theoderic emphatically ended it. If too late (just possibly deliberately so) to save his son-in-law, the Visigothic king Alaric II, who fell in battle against Clovis at Vouille in 507, Theoderic eventually intervened decisively north of the Alps. Throwing back Clovis's armies from the Mediterranean, he had united the Visigothic and Ostrogothic kingdoms under his own direct rule by 511 to create a vast Gothic power bloc in the western Mediterranean, running from the Adriatic coast of Dalmatia to the Atlantic coast of the Iberian peninsula. He also asserted hegemony over both the Burgundian and Vandal kingdoms, which were made part of this Gothic bloc by subordinating marriage alliances. The Vandal king was also forced to endure the public humiliation of having his gifts of apology refused and returned when he tried to stir up trouble for Theoderic in Spain and was caught in the act.[15]

At this point, Theoderic had reunited a solid chunk of the old Western Empire and in 517/18 was able to exploit the Emperor Justin's desire to end the Acacian schism (see Chapter 3) to extract effective East Roman recognition of the quasi-imperial structure he had industriously created. The reason why it took Justin's delegation so long to get to Rome in the second half of 518 is that all the key negotiations were actually conducted at Theoderic's court in Ravenna, and the end result was the healing of the schism on the one hand, matched on the other by full East Roman recognition of the king's choice as heir apparent. This was his son-in-law Eutharic, originally a Visigothic noble who, along with Theoderic's daughter Amalasuentha, was clearly destined to inherit both Italy and Spain. Justin adopted Eutharic as son-at-arms, a device which Constantinople regularly used to express its recognition of heirs to allied thrones, and granted him the utterly extraordinary honour of the consulship for 519, held jointly with the emperor himself.[16]

Everything the king touched had so far turned to gold, but the thorny issue of succession eventually derailed his master plan. Not only did Eutharic's early death generate lasting division at the court of Ravenna, which Justinian was still exploiting a decade later, but it also led the Visigothic and Ostrogothic kingdoms to separate, against Theoderic's wishes, after his death. This broke up the king's dominant, quasi-imperial Gothic power bloc, and it is no surprise to find Constantinople thoroughly implicated in the process. Justin refused to recognize the young Athalaric, Eutharic and Amalasuentha's son and Theoderic's next choice of heir, after his father's death, in what can only have been a calculated manoeuvre to help destabilize the situation at the Gothic court, while it simultaneously encouraged revolts against Ostrogothic hegemony in both the Burgundian and Vandal kingdoms. The chronology makes clear that both were designed to exploit the paralysing political effects within Ravenna of the early death of Theoderic's heir apparent and the fierce struggles over succession that this unleashed.[17]

They enjoyed mixed success. The new Vandal king, Hilderic, threw Theoderic's sister in jail, where she died, and eliminated her Gothic bodyguard, a process which inaugurated the good relations with Constantinople which later provided Justinian with his pretext for unleashing Belisarius against Gelimer. But the Vandals were protected by the sea, and the Burgundians paid a higher price for their disobedience, when the general Tuluin, one of those potential successors, led a punitive campaign against them before the king's death; it added to the Ostrogothic kingdom a substantial block of Burgundian territory north of the river Durance, the old boundary.[18] Despite this partial success in Gaul, the extended succession crisis and redivision of the Gothic kingdoms certainly dispelled the genuinely imperial aura surrounding the Ostrogothic kingdom in the 510s. So much so, in fact, that in the late 520s, Constantinople was happy to restore good relations, presumably based on Justinian's eventual recognition of Athalaric's accession. By 533, relations were even good enough for the Ostrogoths to provide important logistic support for Belisarius's African expedition.

Although the apogee of Ostrogothic power had past, the kingdom was not necessarily ripe for the taking. It was, as the name implies, an *Ostrogothic* kingdom but not in the sense that its population was largely or even substantially Gothic. The vast majority of its inhabitants were of provincial Italo-Roman stock, but the kingdom had been created and its boundaries were subsequently maintained by the power of the Ostrogothic army with which Theoderic had conquered Italy between 489 and 493. Really to understand the task awaiting Belisarius's second expeditionary force, therefore, we need to understand the nature of Theoderic's army and what had happened to it in the two political generations since it conquered Italy in the 490s.

Like the Vandals of North Africa, Theoderic's Ostrogoths were a new coalition put together on Roman soil, if East Roman soil this time, in the 470s and 480s. It had three main documented components, but the possibility cannot be ruled out that within or in addition to these groupings it had also swept up many of the smaller groups of human flotsam left loose in central and eastern Europe by the break-up of Attila's Hunnic Empire in the third-quarter of the fifth century. The first of the larger contingents was commanded initially by Theoderic's uncle Valamer, who united a series of separate Gothic warbands in the mid-450s. These had all previously lived under the domination of Attila's Hunnic Empire, and their unification was central to an assertion of political independence which allowed them to carve out their own domain in what is now Hungary in the late 450s. On his death, the kingship was inherited by Valamer's younger brother Thiudimer and his son Theoderic. After more than a decade in Hungary, in 472/3 this father and son combination, displaying heightened levels of ambition, shifted the group's centre of operations to Constantinople's Balkan provinces, with a view to extracting, by a dynamic mixture of alliance and protection racket, much more imperial financial support.

This inaugurated a decade of direct competition with the second documented component: a body of long-standing Gothic allies (*foederatii*) of the East Roman state, who had been settled in Thrace since perhaps the late 420s but were currently in rebellion under their own, rival Gothic dynasty. In the early 480s, his father having died, Theoderic won out, uniting the majority of both groups under his control. The extended narrative of competition between the two groups indicates that they must have originally been similar in terms of military manpower (or one would have swallowed up the other much more quickly), and precise figures in Roman sources suggest both could field something over ten thousand warriors. Once united, Theoderic's new following had become much too large for Constantinople to tolerate its autonomous existence on Roman soil. After a few failed agreements and assassination attempts, Gothic king and East Roman emperor agreed to resolve their differences at someone else's expense. The united Gothic force moved on to Italy in 488/9, picking up en route its third main component: a significant contingent of refugee Rugi from the Middle Danube region, where Odovacar had destroyed their independent kingdom in 487. The total size of Theoderic's armed forces by this stage, must have been some twenty-five to thirty thousand men. Within the ranks, there were probably many smaller groups (even apart from the Rugi) who would have defined themselves as something other than Goths in ethnic terms but subscribed all the same to an overall military-cum-political allegiance to Theoderic's leadership.[19]

In response to the evident fact that Theoderic's Ostrogoths were not an ancient people, one strand of recent scholarship has essentially flipped the old argument 180 degrees to suggest that Theoderic's following had no real group identity at all. It was just a ragbag collection of soldiery, much of it East Roman in origin, with few if any dependents, whose cohesion completely collapsed after the conquest of Italy. Once Theoderic had rewarded it, it disappeared into the Italian landscape to live the good life and was never seen again. To see that this is a perfectly realistic possibility in principle, you have only to look at the late phase of the East Roman war of conquest in the later 540s, when Totila (see Figure 6.2) managed to get large numbers of Justinian's troops, unpaid and cut off in isolated garrisons, to switch their allegiance to him on the promise of being treated just like the rest of his Gothic followers.[20]

Real life looks more interestingly complicated, however, than either the old 'people' or this replacement 'army' hypothesis might suggest. The presence of large numbers of wives and children (slaves, too) at the time of the move to Italy is alluded to unmistakably albeit briefly in a wide range of sources, including some from Theoderic's own court in Ravenna, so it really cannot be doubted. We also have a detailed narrative of events in the Balkans for the 470s which shows that prior to their unification, the two largest components of the new coalition were already called Goths and, much more important, were separate from the normal Roman army formations operating there. This does not mean, of course, that no Roman troops were picked up as stragglers; it does suggest that this was not the primary source of recruits. Overall, there may have been a greater degree of cultural unity among Theoderic's following than among the thoroughly multi-ethnic Vandal-Alan coalition. At least as important as any old cultural residues, however, as with the Hasding-led coalition, is what happened next. The shared experiences of marching thousands of kilometres, fighting countless engagements, and then being picked out as a privileged elite by a process of special reward—whatever the human

FIGURE 6.2
Totila, the architect of the Gothic revolt which delayed the conquest of Italy by a decade and a half.

diversity of a group's origins—will have generated a functioning political identity of some substance, even if not everyone shared the same folk dances, costumes, and marriage practices as the old model supposed.[21]

Quite clearly, Theoderic's following did anything but disappear into the Italian landscape after its successful conquest in 493. Once safely in power, the king rewarded his army with land grants concentrated in strategically chosen localities: the north-eastern and north-western approaches (Veneto, Liguria, and the Cottian and Julian Alps, which guarded all the key entry points to the Italian peninsula), around the court city of Ravenna on the north-east Adriatic coast. Highly defensible, because it was surrounded by marshes, Ravenna could also be easily supplied from the sea and was much better placed than Rome, situated much too far south, to function as a military and administrative capital as the final crisis of the Western Empire gathered momentum (p. 5). As a result, the city had grown massively in both size and importance in the fifth century, although the city of Rome retained considerable importance as both a cultural capital and the home of the Senate, mouthpiece for leading Italian landowner opinion. Aside from defending the key approaches, therefore, it was entirely natural that Theoderic settled additional elements of his army in the upland valleys of Picenum and Samnium, which provided the most direct route between Ravenna and Rome.[22] In return for these land grants, males and their male heirs of appropriate age continued to owe military service for which they received cash donatives, and Theoderic proceeded to deploy this army to great effect between 493 and 511 to create his ersatz Western Empire. As with the Vandal-Alan coalition, the evidence does not suggest that any further large-scale recruiting followed the initial settlement process of the 490s. Recruitment never shut down completely, but there is no sign that native Italo-Romans were ever drawn into the field forces deployed by Theoderic and his successors, although they had guard duties on the walls of their own towns. In tune with this evidence, Belisarius encountered an opposition Gothic army which in the 530s could muster around thirty thousand men, the vast majority of whom were descended from the force with which he had originally subdued the peninsula in the 490s.[23]

We know a little about its composition and internal workings. The settlement process seems to have respected pre-existing smaller subgroup identities, not least that of the Rugi, who were apparently settled together. Each local settlement cluster also had its own lower-level political leadership. This was chosen (in some way) locally but had to be recognized by the king. More generally, Procopius consistently identifies two grades of warrior within the Gothic army: a smaller elite comprising perhaps 20 to 25 per cent of total military manpower. This matches a broader run of evidence that two distinct grades of warrior were characteristic of many societies of the post-Roman west, and it may well be that in addition to horizontal ethnic ties (such as those within the Rugi), the different subgroupings were also bound together by vertical ties of patronage and control between individuals belonging to the two warrior grades.[24] Even if it was not a people and an important component of its manpower had certainly had a long previous history of Roman alliance between roughly 430 and 470, Theoderic's Ostrogothic following had internal structure and rules, and the terms of its settlement in Italy, not to mention an immediate history of shared conflict and victory, helped preserve its existence as a privileged colonial elite within the landscape of sixth-century Italy. How the second- and third-generation descendants of this originally improvised grouping of several tens of thousands of warriors and their families might respond to East Roman attack would fundamentally dictate the outcome of Justinian's new war.

Before turning to that war, one final issue demands attention. Thanks in no small measure to a magisterial paper by the great Arnaldo Momigliano, first delivered over fifty years ago, it is often supposed that the non-military but socially, administratively, and politically important Italo-Roman landowning elite of sixth-century Italy was fundamentally divided in its response to Gothic rule. Momigliano argued that, while a collaborator bureaucratic class of parvenus, which was personified in a man like Cassiodorus (who composed the letter of Theoderic quoted above) and whose activities focused on the new administrative capital of Ravenna, was happy enough with Gothic rule, the opinion of properly blue-blooded senators, whose lives still centred on the city of Rome, remained utterly unreconciled to Theoderic's dynasty and longed instead for the re-establishment of direct Roman rule from Constantinople. Two of the greatest advocates for direct rule were Symmachus and his son-in-law, the philosopher Boethius, who found themselves caught up in treasonable activities towards the end of Theoderic's reign and were put to death just before the king himself died. In one of Procopius's great stories, the king finds an omen of his own impending demise when he recognizes the face of the executed Symmachus in a fish being served for his dinner. Whether this suggests more about Theoderic's bad conscience or Symmachus's dashing good looks is obviously open to question. But if Momigliano's argument is correct, this would suggest that a major fault line ran through the middle of Italo-Roman political opinion, which Justinian and Belisarius might hope to exploit.[25]

The deaths of Boethius and Symmachus became part of the overall propaganda campaign by which Justinian's regime looked to defuse potential Italo-Roman resistance to its projected conquest, but such a stark divide between two tranches of the Italo-Roman elite did not and could not exist. Ties to court had become so central to senatorial status in the late Roman period (a pattern continued under Gothic rule) that it was not possible to be a major Roman senator without activating and exploiting a complex web of formal and informal connections to the court of Ravenna. From the late fourth century onwards, it had not been enough simply to be born into a senatorial family to take your place in the Roman Senate. That made you just a *clarissimus*. To sit in the Senate and speak there, you needed to acquire the higher rank of *illustris*, which could be done only either by holding actual office or through an honorary grant, both of which required all members of the Senate to become active at court in some way. The same kind of tax incentives for making high-level political connections which operated in the Roman world still survived in Gothic Italy (see Chapter 2).

All of this makes more sense of the detailed evidence that survives for the careers of Boethius and Symmachus prior to their fall in the 520s. Both apparently enjoyed good relations with Theoderic for the bulk of his reign before it all went horribly wrong at the end. The two feature in royal letters of the period 507–11 and are treated with honour and allocated significant tasks relating to the public life of the kingdom. They were also both involved in ending the Acacian schism, but this (contra Momigliano) was something that Theoderic himself orchestrated, extracting a very high price from Constantinople in return. Boethius also held high office at court in 522/3 immediately prior to his fall (something Momigliano always struggled to explain), with his two young sons being granted the unique honour of a joint consulship. What we are really looking at here is not so much a long-standing fault line as a variant of that common historical phenomenon: a king falling out with two of his great men. Since there is also good reason to link Boethius to Theodahad, one of the main alternative contenders for the throne after Eutharic's death, the smart money must be on Boethius and Symmachus having become compromised somehow in the struggle for power unleashed by the early death of Theoderic's chosen heir.[26] This does not make the Gothic kingdom any less divided at the top over the ever toxic issue of succession, but there is no evidence for a senatorial fifth column desperately wanting to be ruled from Constantinople. Nor did the executions of the two men generate any discernible crisis in the Ostrogothic kingdom, even among Italo-Roman landowning opinion. Boethius and Symmachus were eventually condemned by the Roman senate itself, and many of its members continued to serve Theoderic and then Athalaric and Amalasuentha after his death. In one of the lost mosaics of his palace, Theoderic portrayed Rome and Ravenna as the twin capitals of his kingdom.[27] There is no reason to suppose that Gothic rule generated any fundamental divide between the leading Roman lights of these two great cities.

VIA FLAMINIA

Not surprisingly, the war of conquest, when Justinian finally unleashed it, also focused precisely on these two capitals and the main road that linked them: the Via Flaminia, originally constructed by the censor Gaius Flaminius at the back end of the third century BC. Leaving Rome, it crossed the Tiber by the famous Milvian Bridge, site of Constantine's first great post-vision victory (see Chapter 1), before running north up the river valley and striking north-east into the Apennines at Castello delle Formiche. Much climbing and descending, not to mention several passes later, it reached Rimini on the Adriatic coast: a total distance of just over three hundred kilometres. From Rimini, it was a short hop of about another sixty kilometres up the coast road (which involved crossing the Rubicon, now a disappointing trickle) into Ravenna itself. Most of the Flaminia is now covered by the Strada Statale 3, but if you do follow it, and I utterly recommend the experience, you will be rewarded not only with some excellent lunches but with plenty of evidence of the astonishing Roman engineering which made it all possible. Highlights include a surviving arch of the largest Roman bridge ever built, at Narni over the Nera River (an improvement to the original route constructed under the Emperor Augustus), a replacement tunnel ordered by the Emperor Vespasian—the *Gola del Furlo*—which the modern road still uses, a beautifully preserved bridge at Cagli, and a terminus beneath the triumphal arch of the Emperor Augustus at Rimini itself.[28] It was precisely along the

Via Flaminia that Theoderic placed his settlement clusters in Samnium and Picenum, siting them strategically to hold the series of fortified hill towns which still dominate the route. Narni remains perhaps the most spectacular, with wonderful views over the Nera valley from its towering battlements, but Perugia, Spoleto, Urbino, and Ossimo are all old Roman foundations, and no army could move easily along any of the relevant stretches of road if they were held by hostile garrisons.

The difficulties and opportunities of fighting one's way along the Via Flaminia did not come into play immediately, however, because when the battle for Italy proper opened in earnest in the summer of 536, it began at Reggio Calabria, in the far south. Belisarius crossed from Sicily to the mainland with his numerically and tactically limited army of seven thousand men, then worked his way up the coast. Not until the army reached Naples, which had a Gothic garrison of eight hundred, was there any fighting, but here resistance was fierce, and for the first time the attitude of the non-Gothic population of the peninsula enters the action. The bulk of the city's population was unsure what to do, and Belisarius offered them the opportunity to switch their allegiance (and tax accounts) to Constantinople. The inhabitants were galvanized, however, by the arguments of two local notables, Asclepiodotus and Pastor, who emphasized all the benefits that they had received from the Goths and urged them to help the Gothic garrison by manning their designated sections of the wall. As a result, the East Romans were confronted with a well-defended city, and Belisarius's advance ground to a halt. The military problem was resolved by using the city's aqueduct as a route into the city for enough men to force open a gate, the clanking of their weapons as they crossed the line of the wall being covered by a carefully staged, shouted parley between one of Belisarius's officers and the Goths holding the relevant section.

Once that moment of tension passed off, there was a delay, which must have seemed interminable to Belisarius's men waiting outside. The aqueduct task force got inside the city but was unable to get out of it again until they were right in the centre, where it was finally unroofed. A difficult climb finally led them out through a derelict building—to the great surprise of its only inhabitant—but then they quickly overcame the garrison of two towers. Once a gate was open, the city fell quickly. Most of the citizens fled their stations in panic, the Goths surrendered, and the only serious resistance came from the Jewish section of the population holding the wall line nearest the sea. The Roman army turned to killing and looting, but Belisarius quickly brought it to a halt. He allowed his soldiers to keep all the looted goods, but freed the prisoners—men, women and children—in a well-calculated display of mercy, which managed at the same time to emphasize the likely fate of the inhabitants of any other Italian cities that helped the Goths resist the Roman advance. As for the advocates of resistance, Pastor died of a stroke, and Asclepiodotus was ripped to pieces by his fellow citizens.[29]

It is not known exactly when Naples fell, but it was in Belisarius's hands by November 536, and with it secured by a garrison of three hundred infantry, as was nearby Cumae, the other main strongpoint in Campania, the army prepared to move on to its next target: Rome. All through the siege of Naples, Theodahad, having mobilized some troops and moved south from Ravenna to Rome, did nothing, presumably hoping still to find a negotiated solution to the impending conflict. But the loss of Naples was too much for the rest of the Gothic leadership, who deposed and executed their hapless, indecisive monarch before the end of the year. Thus perished the last surviving male of the great Theoderic's Amal dynasty to rule the remnants of his empire, and in his place the leading Goths promoted Wittigis, who had an established reputation as a capable military leader. The Goths now had a regime that was as much committed to the war as that of Justinian. Assigning Rome a garrison of four thousand, the new king left the city in early December, returning to Ravenna to mobilize and equip the rest of the Gothic army. He also set about negotiating with the Franks to cede to them the Gallic territories which Theoderic had won in 508 and Tuluin extended in the 520s so as to secure the Goths' northern flank and free up further military forces for battle in Italy, forces which would otherwise have been stuck there on garrison duty.[30]

In the meantime, Belisarius's army, now not much more than six thousand men in total, advanced up the Via Appia. Faced with this impending threat, Rome's Gothic garrison decided to leave. Not only were they outnumbered, but Rome was not easy to defend. In Procopius's words,

> It cannot be supplied with provisions, since it is not on the sea, it is enclosed by a wall of so huge a circumference, and, above all, lying as it does in a very level plain, it is naturally exceedingly easy of access for its assailants.[31]

As the Goths were marching out of the Flaminian gate to the north, Belisarius's army was entering Rome by the Asinarian to the south. The city's inhabitants, initially confident that the general would soon be off after the Goths, quickly became agitated when, despite all the drawbacks, Belisarius started preparing for a siege. Small garrisons were pushed forward to hold some of the strongpoints along the southern stretches of the Via Flaminia: Narni, Perugia, and Spoleto. This was designed only to hold up an expected Gothic advance, not to prepare for Belisarius's own, but combined with what had happened in North Africa, it was enough to intimidate some of the local Gothic settlement clusters. A certain Pitzas and half the Goths of Samnium immediately surrendered to Belisarius rather than fight for Wittigis.[32] In the meantime, grain ships from Sicily stocked Rome's granaries, and local farmers were coerced into bringing all locally available food into the city. Belisarius not only did not have enough men to begin field operations against a fully mobilized Gothic army, but his infantry-heavy force currently lacked much of the offensive firepower which had brought down the Vandal kingdom. Justinian had promised reinforcements, but in the meantime Belisarius could do no more than take the city of Rome and look to hold it, much to the distress of its inhabitants, who had no desire to become the focus of the developing conflict. They would have been even more upset if they knew—such being the speed of ancient mobilization—that their city was going to remain at its epicentre for over a year.

By February 537, Wittigis had mobilized enough troops to advance in such huge numbers down the Via Flaminia that Belisarius's advance posts could do nothing to impede his approach. Belisarius himself made one attempt to delay the Gothic army, hoping to fight a delaying action at the Milvian Bridge which would buy the best part of a month for extra troops and provisions to arrive, but it nearly ended in disaster. The bridge was defended by a tower which Belisarius garrisoned to hamper the Goths' crossing, while he himself lay in wait with his entire force of cavalry, only around a thousand strong, to do as much damage as he could to Goths straggling over the bridge under its fire. Faced with Wittigis's fully mobilized Gothic army, however, the tower's garrison deserted in the night, some surrendering to the Goths while the rest did not stop running until they reached Campania; the next morning, the Goths were able to cross the bridge unimpeded. Belisarius's limited cavalry component was thus confronted with the full might of the Gothic army and, despite inflicting many casualties in well-drilled local stands, was soon driven back to the city walls. In the middle of the retreat, Belisarius became cut off and was saved only by his guardsmen forming a shield wall around him and shepherding him to safety. At the city walls, meanwhile, the same panic at the sight of the Gothic army which gripped the guards at the Milvian Bridge was raging with full force, and the defenders would not open the Salarian Gate to admit the retreating cavalry. As rumours ran wild that Goths were sweeping into the city from all sides, Belisarius and his troopers turned at bay, trapped between the walls and the moat. Seeing, however, that, both in numbers and formation, the advancing Goths were hampered by a log jam at the bridge and the heavy skirmishing that had followed, the general counterattacked to buy himself some time. This ground to a halt in the face of fresh, well-ordered Gothic infantry, but the Roman cavalry could at least conduct an ordered retreat this time, which was enough to convince the walls' defenders that it was safe to open the gate. The city had not fallen in a rush at the Goths' first onslaught, and now safe inside, Belisarius could coordinate its defence. As a first move, he kept reassuring bonfires burning throughout the first night of the siege.[33]

After the fierce skirmishing of that first day, things went ominously quiet as the Goths prepared their assault. They cut the city's aqueducts, which left the grumbling Romans no longer able to bathe, and Belisarius had to show them how to harness the power of the Tiber's flow to grind their corn. The Goths also tried to spread dissent in the city while they set about constructing siege towers and battering rams behind the five major camps they had established outside the gates of the northern arc of the city's walls. There is an inescapably *Monty Python*-esque vision here of the Romans hearing a great deal of distant hammering and sawing. After eighteen days of intensive woodwork, the anticipated blow fell.

Panic gripped the defenders as the massed Goths and their siege machinery came into view. Then Belisarius burst out laughing. Continuing the *Python* theme, siege towers and rams were all pulled by oxen, so it was child's play to kill them and leave the Goths' new toys stranded. In good heart, the defenders set about their work, and well-aimed barrages of arrows and ballista bolts (one of which pinned its Gothic victim to a tree in full view of the defenders), which combined with well-timed cavalry sorties, were enough to beat back the attackers with heavy losses. Procopius says that the Goths lost thirty thousand men in the attack out of a supposed total force of two hundred thousand, but these are both wildly inflated.[34] My own guess would be that both army and losses were about one-tenth of this, but it is impossible to be certain. Whatever the precise figure, the losses made it clear to both sides that Rome was not about to be stormed, and matters settled down into the more regular routines of protracted siege.

Belisarius immediately wrote to Justinian with renewed urgency to ask about the promised reinforcements. An initial tranche of 1,600 extra regular and allied cavalry under Martinus and Valerian had been sent before Christmas, but adverse winds had held it up in Greece, where men and horses were now overwintering, so nothing had so far arrived. He also evacuated all non-combatants from the city, sending them south to Naples, but this did not include males of military age who were retained, in return for promises of pay, to guard the walls. Perhaps in response to this flurry of activity, the Goths seized Rome's main port, the aptly named Portus, three days after their failed assault to cut off the easy flow of further supplies up the Tiber. The scene was now set for a long, hot summer of attritional warfare, as grain rations inside the city were steadily reduced, the only supplement, as famine really began to strike, being mule sausages, as Procopius recalls with evident disgust.[35]

This is not to say that there was no real fighting. Twenty days after the Goths captured Portus, Martinus and Valerian's cavalry finally arrived. From then on, Belisarius mounted regular sorties to unsettle the besiegers, using his cavalry in compact groups of a few hundred to deploy their missile-firing capacity to full effect and then withdrawing them with minimal losses. Like its Vandal counterpart in North Africa, the Ostrogothic army had plenty of cavalry, but again they were spearmen, not archers, and the Romans were able to hit them hard from a distance. The first sortie was made, the day after the reinforcements arrived, by Trajan, with two hundred of Belisarius's guardsmen. Occupying a hill, they rained arrows on their attackers before withdrawing under heavy covering fire from the walls, having inflicted, according to Procopius (with the usual hyperbole), another thousand casualties. Altogether sixty-nine engagements, mostly on this kind of scale, would be initiated by Belisarius in the months which followed.[36] Their very success tempted him into something more ambitious. On one occasion, he took out the entirety of his cavalry, now augmented by some of the infantry who had acquired their own horses in the course of the campaign, supported by a backing infantry phalanx, as recommended in the military manuals (p. 54), which was largely composed of Rome's citizen wall guards. If this was an attempt to break the deadlock, it failed. The cavalry was not strong enough to break up the Gothic counterattack, and instead of holding firm to cover the retreat and allow the horsemen to regroup, the improvised infantry phalanx turned tail and ran. If the Goths were not strong enough to storm the city, Belisarius was not strong enough to break out of it. The result was long months of stalemate, as the food stocks inside the city slowly ran out.[37]

Things began to change only slowly in the autumn of 537. As the food ran out, Belisarius sent his wife, Antonina, accompanied by Procopius, to secure new grain supplies in Campania and to dig out from there any extra reinforcements that could be gleaned from the garrisons left at Naples and Cumae. They had just obtained the necessary supplies and 500 more infantry for the beleaguered city when some real reinforcements finally arrived from the east: 3000 Isaurians, who landed at Naples. A separate contingent of 800 cavalry from the Thracian field army landed at Dryous under the command of John, nephew of that Vitalian who had revolted against Anastasius and had later been assassinated under Justin (see Chapter 3), along with another 1,500 horsemen, mostly from the praesental armies but supplemented by some allied mercenaries. Much heartened when the news reached him, Belisarius stepped up operations to the north of the city to allow the original 500 reinforcements and their wagons of grain to enter the city from the south.[38] This was enough to undermine the confidence of the thoroughly frustrated Goths, who came to Belisarius to ask for an armistice so that peace talks could be opened with Justinian in Constantinople. Wittigis put partition on the table, offering the emperor Sicily and southern Italy as far as Naples in return for peace. A three-month armistice was agreed, and Gothic ambassadors duly left for Constantinople, but the balance of power around Rome continued to shift away from the Goths. Around the winter solstice, the 3,000 Isaurians with another grain fleet arrived at Ostia, and as part of the armistice, the Goths evacuated Portus. The siege of Rome was effectively over, and Belisarius could prepare for future operations. His key move was to despatch a mixed force of 2,000 cavalry under the leadership of John, nephew of Vitalian, to winter quarters near the city of Alba. This was a hugely powerful, mobile force of elite horsemen, and Belisarius gave them contingent orders to create mayhem should the truce break down. Provincial Italo-Romans were to be left in peace, but it would be open season on all the Gothic settlement clusters stretched out along the Via Flaminia.[39]

According to Procopius's account, it was the Goths who broke the truce in the early spring of 538. No word had come back from Constantinople, and Wittigis, perhaps under pressure from hawks in his entourage, started to explore the possibility of using aqueducts to break into the city, as well as launching another surprise attack on the walls with scaling ladders. Both attempts were frustrated, however, and this gave Belisarius sufficient excuse to unleash his cavalry.[40]

The results were devastating. John's horsemen terrorized the Gothic settlement clusters stretched out along the Via Flaminia, treating women and children as slaves and destroying anything identified as 'Gothic' in their path. Wittigis's uncle, Ulitheus, attempted to intervene with a scratch force, but John was commanding the cream of Belisarius's army, and the result was further disaster: Ulitheus was killed along with 'almost the whole army of the enemy', although Procopius, who was not present, gives no sense of the scale of the fighting. Neither the composition of John's force nor his orders gave him any incentive to tackle the Gothic fortresses of Urbino and Ossimo. Instead, he pushed on north up the road and seized Rimini, about two days' journey from the Gothic capital at Ravenna. His reasoning was that on learning that a Roman army was so close to Ravenna, Wittigis would be bound to break up the siege of Rome, which was looking pretty much hopeless anyway, given all the extra food and reinforcements that had entered the city during the truce.[41] One year and nine days after it began, round about the spring equinox in March 538, the Goths left Rome and headed north back up the Via Flaminia towards Ravenna. Belisarius had given most of his cavalry to John but made one last sortie to harass the retreat. The whole balance of the war had shifted. Belisarius's initial, rather limited expeditionary force had managed—just—to take Rome and hold out long enough literally for the cavalry to arrive. Given the complications of ancient military logistics, it was only to be expected that the process of reinforcement had taken over a year to gather momentum. Now the Goths were in full retreat, and the strategic initiative had passed to Belisarius.

Wittigis's plans were straightforward. He needed to destroy John's raiding army, holed up in his rear behind the fortifications of Rimini, and remove the threat to Ravenna. Conscious that he would need time to accomplish this, he left powerful garrisons at key strongpoints along the Via Flaminia to delay Belisarius's advance. Two garrisons of a thousand men each were established at Clusium and Urvivento, and two more of four hundred each at Tudera and Petra. In the north, particularly powerful garrisons of four thousand men were established at Osimo and another two thousand at Urbino, backed up by two more of five hundred each at Caesena and Monteferetra.[42] These Gothic strongpoints along the road were interspersed with the East Roman–held outposts which Belisarius had established earlier at Narni, Spoleto, and Perugia, so that the whole route between Rome and Ravenna was bristling with garrison forces, making it difficult for either side to move along the road in safety.

Conscious of the impending threat to a key component of his army, Belisarius exploited the care with which Wittigis himself was having to move by sending another force of a thousand elite cavalry under Ildiger and Martinus, including many of his own guardsmen, by a different route to Rimini. Crossing the Apennines via Petra, whose surrender they forced, they reached Ancona, where, as clearly prearranged, a force of

East Roman infantry had been set ashore by the imperial navy. The plan was for some of this infantry to move up to Rimini and replace John's cavalry as the city's garrison. Infantry would require much less feeding in the event of a siege, and this would free up the cavalry again for mobile operations. Everything seemed set for a swift resolution of the entire campaign, because still more reinforcements were on their way, and local Italo-Roman communities could sense the changing tide. As he prepared to set off in pursuit of Wittigis, Belisarius despatched a small force by ship to Genoa. Overtures had been received inviting him to send troops to north-western Italy to take the surrender of Milan and other cities of Liguria, and he now felt able to respond.[43]

With well-laid plans in place, Belisarius moved off from Rome with his main body at around the summer solstice, in late June 538; the initial advance went smoothly enough. Tudera and Clusium quickly surrendered, their Gothic garrisons—eight hundred men—being shipped out to Naples and Sicily. But the apparent calm was deceptive. At the other end of the Via Flaminia, John refused to evacuate his cavalry from Rimini, even though Ildiger and Martinus arrived in good time with the infantry from Ancona. Procopius does not tell us why, implying only that he was stubborn and insubordinate. Perhaps horses and men were exhausted, but whatever the reason, John refused to move. He also insisted on retaining the infantry from Ancona, despite the extra pressure this put on his supplies. As a result and despite a relatively slow advance, Wittigis was still able to trap John's cavalry inside Rimini when the main Gothic army finally arrived. As the summer dragged on, John's forces beat off the Goths' assaults, even though their siege towers were not pulled by oxen this time, but supplies in the city were dwindling fast because Belisarius could advance only slowly and was eventually forced to move his army off the Via Flaminia proper. Wittigis had reinforced the garrison at Osimo, increasing it to some ten thousand men; this was much too powerful to force a way past in short order, so Belisarius took an alternative road eastwards to reach the Adriatic much further south at the city of Fermo.[44]

By now, the situation inside Rimini was critical. A messenger escaped the Gothic blockade to find the general and tell him that the city would have to surrender in a week. The entire campaign was back in the balance, because about half of Belisarius's elite cavalry was trapped inside. But there was some comfort, too. Belisarius had diverted off the Via Flaminia proper to Fermo, in part because yet more reinforcements, this time a large force of five thousand regulars and two thousand Herulian *foederatii* had been landed there by ship, again clearly by prearrangement. At the joint council of war which followed with the commanders of these reinforcements, Belisarius resisted the temptation to condemn John's stupidity, and instead devised an effective relief plan. A three-prong pincer move would break up the Gothic siege. One component returned to the ships to make straight for Rimini but was not to land until the siege was already broken. A second force was to march straight up the coast road, while Belisarius himself would take a third force round to the north, threatening to cut Wittigis off from Ravenna. A covering force of a thousand men would also be stationed about fifty kilometres from Osimo so that its powerful garrison would not be able to interfere. The triple threat proved sufficient, and in the late summer of 538, Wittigis's army gave up on Rimini and retreated to Ravenna.[45]

Not only had Rimini been saved, but on the face of it, the war was nearly over. The Ostrogothic army had suffered heavy casualties, and much of its remaining manpower was bottled up in various strongpoints: Ravenna itself, of course, but also Osimo and Urbino, at the top end of the Via Flaminia, and a few other strongpoints across central and northern Italy, such as Fiesole in Tuscany and Ticinum (modern Pavia) in Liguria. The Goths were also short of supplies; the heavy demands of supplying their concentrated army during the siege of Rome, plus the impact of John's raiding, meant that there were drastic food shortages all the way up the north-eastern Adriatic coastal hinterland; with the Roman navy controlling the sea, it was impossible to import extra supplies. Everything looked set for a coordinated endgame that would bring the Goths to a swift surrender. But wars tend not to run according to plan, and this was no exception.

First, Belisarius found his overall command of the campaign being disputed by Narses, one of Justinian's leading officials, who had brought the last tranche of seven thousand reinforcements to Italy. John, of Rimini fame, sided with Narses and claimed that half of the total now of just over twenty thousand East Roman troops in Italy were ready to follow him. Belisarius wanted to concentrate on reducing the two strongpoints, Urbino and Osimo, which protected Ravenna, since their garrisons could disrupt any attempt to besiege the Gothic capital. Narses, on the other hand, wanted to move substantial forces north-west towards Milan. Second—and this presumably underlay Narses's thinking although Procopius does not make an explicit connection—the Goths' Frankish alliance had borne fruit in the form of an army of ten thousand largely Burgundian warriors (their kingdom having just been conquered by the Franks), whose arrival enabled Wittigis's nephew Urais to counterattack in Liguria and besiege the small Roman force that had been sent to Milan. As Belisarius did not have enough forces both to fight in Liguria and pursue his Ravenna campaign, Milan paid the price. The small Roman garrison negotiated its own withdrawal, abandoning the city to be sacked.[46]

Unable to command unquestioning obedience, Belisarius was effectively hamstrung. His one major success at the back end of 538 was to capture Urbino, home to one of the two strongpoints making any formal siege of Ravenna impossible, and even that was a fluke. The town occupied another fortified hilltop, impregnable to assault, but quite suddenly, the spring on which its defenders relied ran dry, and Belisarius gratefully took their surrender. Otherwise, the campaign lost momentum through indecision and disputed command, which was resolved only at the end of the year when Justinian ruled unequivocally, after a series of exchanges, that Belisarius was to have undisputed command. But the intervening quarrels had certainly prolonged the war and affected the morale of most of those engaged in the action. Not least, the allied Heruli decided that they had had enough and set off home for the Balkans, selling all their prisoners and booty to the Goths as they left.

For his part, Wittigis, having come to the conclusion that he was no longer able to win the war alone, was casting around for allies. Apart from the Franco-Burgundians who had already arrived, he explored the possibility of securing Lombard assistance, but the Lombards were close allies of Constantinople, so he found a way, astonishingly, to make approaches to the Persian court. Picking two compliant Catholic clergy, he dispatched them overland through the Balkans; there they picked up some interpreters in Thrace and slowly wound their way through Asia Minor and Syria to Persian territory. In the meantime, Justinian, too, was starting to worry that the Persians were about to break the Eternal Peace and wanted to bring the war in Italy to a close. Towards the end of 539, therefore, the emperor finally decided to begin negotiations in earnest with Wittigis's ambassadors.[47]

The talks acquired still greater urgency because the Italian war had progressed only slowly during the previous campaigning season. Having regained undisputed command, Belisarius's first move was to invest the key fortress of Osimo with an army of eleven thousand. Trapped inside were the remnants of the ten thousand Goths Wittigis had allocated to the city. A second large Roman force was despatched to besiege the Gothic garrison holding the strategic hilltop town of Fiesole in Tuscany, and a third contingent was positioned to ensure that Wittigis's nephew Urais could not cross the Po from Liguria to intervene in the endgame unfolding around Ravenna. In broad terms, Belisarius's planning worked, but only just. A second, this time completely uninvited, Frankish army invaded Liguria, defeating both Urais and the remaining Roman forces occupying the southern confines of the province. This unexpected intervention threatened to overturn the balance that Belisarius had carefully swung in his own favour, but food was short, too, in war-torn Liguria, which had now endured a whole year of fighting, and the Frankish campaign quickly ran out of steam in the absence of readily available supplies. Instead of breaking out of Liguria and upsetting the entirety of Belisarius's plans, therefore, the Franks were forced to retreat.[48]

While the Franks came and went, the general refused to panic, continuing to press his two sieges. Fiesole was impossible to storm; to start with, its garrison was confident enough to make a series of sorties against their Roman opponents. Having sent a final message to Wittigis to ask for relief, however, they were forced back inside the city's walls to wait it out. The situation at Osimo was pretty much identical. Perched on its hilltop with only one steep access road, Belisarius found it impossible to get his forces close enough to mount any kind of serious assault, and the siege dragged on through most of 539. Unlike Fiesole, Procopius was clearly present for much of this, and his account is alive with detail.

The intensity of the skirmishes, where the Romans were trying to stop the Goths from gathering forage on the slopes of the hill, jump off the page. There is also a great account of the fighting around a cistern which caught the water from a stream flowing out of the mountain. The stream is still there, and it is easy to see how the Goths' height advantage made life impossible for the Roman attackers, who failed in attempts both to break up the cistern's masonry and to poison the water. What Belisarius did manage to do eventually was cut the garrison off from all further contact with Ravenna. Throughout the summer, Wittigis continued to reassure his trapped garrison that help was on its way. At length, the Romans worked out that messages were being passed back and forth by a soldier called Burcentius, whom the Goths managed to bribe when he was on solitary guard duty. Burcentius was solemnly burned alive in front of the city's walls.[49]

It was slow, frustrating work compared to the dramatic cavalry battles which had crushed Vandal resistance, but when at last the food ran out inside the two fortresses, there was nothing Wittigis could do. He lacked the necessary supplies to mount his own relief operations from Ravenna, and the Frankish wild card had prevented Urais from coming from the west. In due course, the surrenders came, first at Fiesole and in October/November 539 at Osimo, too. Even when the surrendered Gothic commanders from Fiesole were brought before the walls, however, and despite the crippling food shortages, the garrison of Osimo refused to capitulate. In the end, Belisarius had to sweeten the deal. The Goths at Fiesole had surrendered in return for just their lives, but at Osimo, the garrison was allowed to keep half its property and become fully fledged citizens of the empire.[50]

It was only right at the end of 539, therefore, that Belisarius was finally able to move his army forward to the walls of Ravenna. Inside, Wittigis had not yet given up hope, and with the Franks now gone from Liguria, Urais had become active again on his behalf. A fleet of grain ships was readied on the river Po to resupply the city, which lay on one of the branches through which it flowed to the sea. He was also mobilizing a mobile relief force from Liguria's many Gothic garrisons, not least those of the Cottian Alps. Belisarius, however, was alive to both threats and tightened the noose. The grain fleet was captured by his own men, and more or less simultaneously, fire broke out in some of the remaining grain stores inside Ravenna, which makes one think that the general had agents within the city. Urais's relief army also disappeared back home when the work of a Roman agent provocateur started to threaten their families.[51]

Wittigis was now shut inside his capital with no hope of relief. But the city itself was pretty much impregnable from land or sea, which is why it had become such an important centre of government as the *pax Romana* unwound in the fifth century. Procopius describes it succinctly:

> Ships cannot possibly put in . . . because the sea itself prevents them by forming shoals for not less than thirty stades (nearly five kilometres). . . . And a land army cannot approach it all; for the river Po . . . and other navigable rivers together with some marshes, encircle it on all sides.[52]

Storming the city was impossible, and anyway, Justinian, far from the action, was by this time getting serious about negotiations. He was ready to accept a modified version of the partition plan which Wittigis had put on the table late in 537. Under it, a truncated Gothic kingdom would be confined to lands north of the river Po: to Liguria and the Venetias, where the bulk of the Goths had been placed by Theoderic back in the 490s. On the ground in Italy, however, Belisarius considered that the extent of his military advantage justified pushing for imperial control of the whole of Italy. As he said to his commanders, the Roman army currently had an opportunity to win all of Italy for the empire. If spurned, it might never come again.

Wittigis, increasingly desperate, provided the opening. In secret contacts, the king tried to seduce the general away from his allegiance to Justinian, offering him 'rule of the West': a revival of the Western Empire based on a combination of Belisarius's army and Gothic military manpower. Belisarius eventually agreed—or so they thought. Thinking he had his man, Wittigis opened the gates of Ravenna in May 540, Gothic garrisons elsewhere submitted, and Belisarius allowed grain supplies into the city. But the Goths had been tricked. They surrendered thinking that Belisarius would declare himself emperor, but once the Romans were inside the city, nothing happened, and there was nothing that Wittigis could do.[53] Justinian's regime had scored a second colossal victory.

7

THE CULTURE OF VICTORY

THE GREATEST OF IMPERIAL Constantinople's thoroughfares, the Mese, culminated in a colonnaded square, the Augustaion, originally laid out under the Emperor Constantine, which was flanked on three sides by the cathedral Church of Holy Wisdom (Hagia Sophia), the Senate House, and the monumental baths of Zeuxippos. On its west side, in the early 540s, Justinian erected a seventy-metre column atop a seven-stepped marble pedestal. The column was made of brick but covered in brass plaques. On top was a colossal equestrian statue of the emperor himself, which stood until shortly after the Ottoman conquest, although the column itself was not dismantled until 1515, and odd fragments of the statue could still be found lying around the palace of Mehmet the Conqueror some time afterwards. Drawings survive of the statue but also a description by Procopius:

> [The emperor] wears a breastplate in the heroic fashion, a helmet covers his head … and a dazzling light flashes forth from it. … He looks toward the rising sun, directing his course, I suppose, against the Persians. And in his left hand he holds a globe, by which the sculptor signifies that the whole earth and sea are subject to him, yet he has neither sword nor spear nor any other weapon, but a cross stands upon the globe which he carries, the emblem by which alone he has obtained both his empire and his victory in war. And stretching forth his right hand toward the rising sun and spreading out his fingers, he commands the barbarians in that quarter to remain at home and to advance no further.[1]

With his usual humility, Justinian raised a monument to himself which would dominate the skyline of the city for nine hundred years. Portraying the emperor as Achilles, the statue emphasized that Justinian was a great conqueror and that his military victories, like his empire, came directly from God.

All imperial regimes needed to claim victory, to show that they were underwritten by the divinity (see Chapter 1), but after the capture of Carthage and fall of Ravenna, Justinian's could do it in spades and never missed an opportunity to underline the point. Nearly as prominent within the imperial city as his great column was the new entrance gate to the imperial palace—the famous Chalke, or Bronze Gate—that the emperor constructed, again just off the Augustaion.[2] This was a three-arched, roofed structure whose ceilings featured Justinian and Theodora in full majesty but also Belisarius and the conquests of Africa and Italy. Wherever you stood in the city, the great equestrian statue presented you with Justinian as triumphant conqueror, and the point was emphasized again when you entered his palace. The regime also referred to its victories pretty much ad nauseam in its written proclamations, on its coinage—for instance, the wonderful, commemorative gold medallion from just after the African conquest, now in the Louvre, which prefigures the Justinian of the equestrian statue (Figure 7.1)—and in a host of smaller images (such as the ivory covers of codicils of appointment) it generated in its everyday functioning.[3] Two great victories gave Justinian political capital to burn, and he proceeded to invest it liberally.

THE WHOLE BODY OF THE LAW

Aside from returning the family estates of Anastasius's two nephews executed in the aftermath of Nika and rehabilitating those senators who had been sent into exile at the same moment, victory in Africa renewed the regime's self-confidence to drive through to completion its second great project of legal reform: resolving the intractability of several hundred years' worth of jurisconsult opinion. To judge by the fact that the Hippodrome crowd had demanded the dismissal of Tribonian at the

FIGURE 7.1
Justinian depicted as the rightful, God-appointed ruler of the Roman world.
Credit: © RMN-Grand Palais / Art Resource, NY

same time as Justinian's chief financial officer (p. 110), ramming through the Fifty Decisions does seem to have generated considerable friction in well-connected legal circles in Constantinople. Probably more important than the detail of the decisions, though, was the more general point that written law was the great symbol of Rome's overarching claim to be a unique, God-guided civilization (see Chapter 1). Of and in itself, therefore, a successful resolution of the jurisconsult problem would have brought so much ideological kudos to Justinian's regime, that Tribonian, its key architect, was an obvious target for those seeking to use the Nika disturbances to undermine or at least curb its power, and the emperor was forced to dismiss him on that horrible Thursday in February 532. Strikingly, he did not feel able to bring him back into public office for over eighteen months, until November 533 (as *Magister Officiorum*, effectively chief of the imperial bureaucracy), by which time news of the victory at Ad Decimum and Belisarius's capture of Carthage had reached the imperial capital. There is every reason to think that Tribonian had been carrying on with the work in the meantime, however, since, just a month later, the finished Digest of jurisconsult opinion (or *Pandects*) was ready for publication.

On 16 December 533, Justinian confirmed its legal validity and linked the work's successful completion to victory in Africa:

> God has granted us, after Our peace with the Persians, Our triumph over the Vandals, Our taking of the whole of Libya, Our regaining of most famous Carthage, to fulfil the task of restoring the ancient laws—something which none of the emperors that reigned before Us never hoped even to conceive, nor would they have thought it humanly possible at all.[4]

Because the existence of its systems of written law was as much a sign of God's unique care for Roman civilization as military victory, it was entirely natural in ideological terms to link these two successes as proof of particular divine favour for the regime of Justinian. And when you go looking for it, there is plenty of evidence that resolving the jurisconsult problem was nearly as hard fought a victory as the capture of Carthage.

The overarching problem was not so much the quantity of material as its internal contradictions. Three centuries of trying to win cases for wealthy clients had generated not only millions of lines of legal commentary on highly significant matters of property law but conflicting opinions citing and using a variety of legal principles to construct highly complex arguments (p. 108). That the problem was there and needed resolution had long been recognized. Back in 429, the Emperor Theodosius II had announced two sequential legal projects. First, his commissioners were going to codify new imperial legislation generated between the time of Constantine and his own day, but then they proposed to combine that new law book with the two rescript codes produced in the time of the tetrarchy *and* all the rescript material to produce one universal uber-code of Roman law in which there would be no contradictions and all legal problems would be resolved once and for all. In the late 430s, when producing the initial law book had already taken the best part of a decade, the second project was quietly dropped (without explicit acknowledgement).[5] The best the Theodosian commissioners could offer on the jurisconsult problem was the so-called Law of Citations. This enshrined into a general principle—by dint of including it in the Theodosian Code—a method of resolving jurisconsult dispute which had originally been formulated for one particularly intractable case.

> When conflicting [jurisconsult] opinions are cited, the greater number of authors shall prevail, or if the numbers should be equal, the authority of that group shall take precedence in which the man of superior genius, Papinian [AD 142–121: a celebrated Roman jurist of the later second and early third century], shall tower above the rest, and as he defeats a single opponent, so he yields to two.

Among modern historians of law, this has long been seen as the 'low-water mark' of Roman jurisprudence, because it eschewed principled legal argumentation in favour of mathematics. In my view, such judgments miss the point that several hundred years of mutually competitive jurisconsult opinion giving had actually created the kind of confusion which was a paid lawyer's paradise. There is a strong sense that much of what apparent legal clarity there is in the Digest is actually a reflection of the work of Tribonian and his collaborators, not of that of the earlier jurisconsults on whom they were drawing.[6]

Against this backdrop, it is not remotely surprising to find clear evidence that Justinian and Tribonian had to work extremely hard on a whole series of levels to bring their jurisconsult project to a successful conclusion. For one thing, they took on a less ambitious form of the project than that envisaged by Theodosius II. His commissioners were going to combine imperial law and jurisconsult material into one unified law book. Justinian's reforms kept the two separate. Justinian's code of imperial law and his Digest of jurisconsult opinion remained two separate law books. Even if Tribonian surely was making his selections from jurisconsult material in the light of the detailed knowledge of current imperial law which he would build up while working on the code, not having to produce a single uber-code certainly speeded up the project. Equally important, Justinian's confirmatory edicts, which ratified the finished Digest, show signs of careful lobbying of the Eastern Empire's legal establishment. Representatives of its two most distinguished schools, Constantinople and Beirut, were brought on board in the reform process, sharing in the work and accepting its outcome. In return, on the Digest's publication Justinian officially suppressed the teaching of law at two competing schools, Caesarea and Alexandria. This was classic divide and rule. Consent from the most distinguished elements of the legal establishment for the reform package was won in part by ensuring that they would enjoy duopoly over law students, thereby securing higher fee incomes.[7]

Telltale signs of the difficulty of the project and the speed with which it had been pushed through are also visible in the text of the Digest itself. In announcing the project on 15 December 530, *Deo Auctore* had laid out the basic principles by which Tribonian and his fellow collaborators would approach the jurisconsult jungle:

> All legal writers will have equal weight and no superior authority will be reserved for any author, since not all are regarded as either better or worse in all respects, but only some in particular respects.

In contrast to the mathematical approach of the Law of Citations and its acceptance of the unique status of Papinian, Tribonian's commission was to weigh every individual jurisconsult opinion on its intellectual merits and remove superfluities, repetitions, and, above all, contradictions by applying consistent legal principles.[8] According to its own prefatory constitutions, the final Digest succeeded triumphantly. The Whole Body of the Law claimed without hesitation that 'everything has now been reformed and arranged'.

In practice, however, some loose ends had been left hanging to get the job finished within the desired time frame. On the matter of repetition, *Constitutio Tanta*, another prefatory constitution, has this to say:

> Should it chance that here and there, in so great a collection of legal rules, taken as it is from an immense number of books, some cases of repetition should occur, this no one must be severe upon; it should rather be ascribed first of all to human weakness, which is part of our nature. . . . It should also be borne in mind that there are some rules of exceeding brevity in which repetition may be admitted to good purpose.

It is essentially telling users not to be too critical if they find any repetitions, because a) there are not many and b) they were probably left in deliberately. Even funnier are *Tanta*'s comments on contradiction:

> As for any contradiction occurring in this book, none such has any claim to a place in it, nor will any be found, if we consider fully the grounds of diversity; some special differential feature will be discovered, however obscure, which does away with the imputation of inconsistency, puts a different complexion on the matter and keeps it safe from the imputation of discrepancy.[9]

So there are no contradictions in the book, and if readers think they have identified one, all they need do is consider the matter a little harder or from a different direction, and they will find a way of making it disappear. Not only was the reform pushed through by means of a political deal with some of the legal establishment, therefore, but even the commissioners realized that, in their haste, not everything had been fully resolved.

Both the timing of the Digest's publication and the less than perfect nature of its contents indicate the crucial role of victory in Africa to the regime's ability successfully to push through the greatest of its legal reforms. Victory made it possible to bring Tribonian formally back into public office and allowed Justinian to get away with publishing a summary reconciliation of jurisconsult opinion which was by no means perfect. Victory in Africa had made the regime politically untouchable so that, safe from the possibility of trenchant criticism and reinsured by the astute co-option of the legal prestige of the schools of Beirut and Constantinople, Justinian could go ahead and publish the Digest, possibly even before Tribonian wanted to. Perhaps Tribonian had finished everything he wanted to do and was ready to publish anyway, but the carefully worded apologies of *Constitutio Tanta* suggest not. The moment, however, was far too good to miss. With extraordinary news fresh in from Carthage, Justinian was not about to waste such a perfect opportunity. What Tribonian's commission had not fully achieved, of course, was a single, unified code of Roman law utterly free from all doubt. This was never to be achieved in Justinian's lifetime, not even with the publication of a second, revised version of his code of imperial law in 534, which amongst other things, now included many of the Fifty Decisions which had been central to the Digest project. For one thing, the emperor continued to issue his own new laws, to such an extent that in the Preface to New Law (*Novel*) 60 of 537, he even offered half an apology:

> For it is natural that some people will find fault with the mass of laws that are promulgated every day. Such people do not bear in mind that we are forced by pressing necessity to issue laws that are appropriate to the needs of government, since problems regularly arise unexpectedly which cannot be resolved by the existing body of laws.[10]

As Justinian himself admits here, an unchanging, entirely constant body of written law is fundamentally a chimera. New situations arise regularly, and if a body of written law is really being used to resolve matters of importance, it will continuously evolve. Even more, there were still contradictions aplenty when one compared older rulings in the code, new rulings in the *Novels*, and the Digest of jurisconsult material. When twelfth- and thirteenth-century academic Italian lawyers, taking the claims of *Constitutio Tanta* at face value, began working on the principle that there really were no contradictions in this material—if you argued long and well enough—it took them over a hundred years and two million lines of commentary to reduce the problem to just 122 small contradictions of little substance![11]

To focus on the inconsistencies of the Justinianic legal corpus, however, is fundamentally to miss the point. Almost no jurisconsult material now survives independently of the Digest; everything not included does seem to have been destroyed as Justinian's reform required. The same is true of the older imperial law codes of Hermogenianus, Gregorianus, and even (in the East) that of Theodosius as well. For all its problems, Justinian created a new working corpus of legal materials, with his own name stamped all over them, which completely superseded everything that had gone before. In due course, this secured his medieval reputation as a legislator, which is reflected in the highly exalted mercurial position he receives, as a protector of justice, in Dante's *Paradiso*. More immediately, the completed project added to the recent victory in Africa by demonstrating that Justinian fulfilled the civil side of the imperial job description equally triumphantly, where the protection of God-ordained Roman civilization, as enshrined in its written laws, held paramount importance. Unlike Theodosius II, whose legal reform project collapsed after the first stage, Justinian had completed an adequate enough version of a total legal reform package which was badly required. Trainee, first-year law students were now to be known as 'New Justinians', and the final element of the package was a new legal textbook—Justinian's Institutes—built around the revised curriculum that these trainees were now to follow.[12] The whole was powerful and coherent enough to act as the cornerstone of the *Ius Commune*, a legal system which was shared by Scotland, north of the Channel, and most of Latinate continental Europe to the south.[13] Riding the crest of the wave, by the end of 533 the regime had both conquered territories and reformed the law. It was not slow to express its overwhelming, divinely ordained legitimacy in other areas besides.

'SOLOMON, I HAVE SURPASSED THEE'

It is no accident that Procopius chose to devote an entire work to the building works of Justinian's reign. The emperor was a builder and wanted to be recognized as such. Some of the construction work was forced on him. In Constantinople, the devastation caused by the Nika riot at the ceremonial heart of the city left Justinian with no choice but to devote enormous resources to efforts at restoration. Some of his fortification away from the capital, likewise, was driven by urgent military necessity. But even without Nika, Justinian would have come down as a builder of ambition. In part this reflected an ancient classical tradition, which saw building as a generous act of benefaction to the recipient community, so beneficent emperors would always want to build.[14] Justinian's list of foundations goes way beyond the norm, however, and begins in the 520s, even before he became emperor. There was an immediate political purpose behind some of them, but many of his projects were driven by deeper ideological imperatives and reflected, too, a profound transformation which the nature of East Roman civilization was slowly undergoing.

At the heart of the imperial capital, the fires set by the Nika rioters destroyed two major churches—Hagia Sophia and nearby Hagia Irene—the entrance to the palace, the Senate House, and many of the colonnades around the Augustaion. This is equivalent to rioters having burnt down the entire area between Westminster Abbey and Horseguards Parade in modern London, and it was clearly imperative for any God-appointed emperor to clean up the mess. We sometimes do not know the exact chronology, but by the early 550s, all the damaged buildings had been replaced or repaired, and Justinian had taken the opportunity to celebrate the now victorious legitimacy of his regime. By the early 540s, his colossal equestrian statue towered over the skyline, reflecting the sun like a torch, and the new mosaics of the Chalke Gate reminded visitors of the conquests of Carthage and Rome. These were none too subtle reminders to anyone who might have entertained doubts when they contemplated the burnt-out rubble of central Constantinople in February 532 that phoenix-like, the regime had emerged triumphant from its time of tribulation. Who else but God could be behind such a staggering transformation?

First and foremost, however, Justinian built churches. Again, some of this was enforced. The destruction of Constantinople's cathedral Church of Holy Wisdom (Hagia Sophia) could not be left unremedied by an emperor who claimed to be appointed by God (see Figure 7.2). But Justinian had begun to build churches before he became emperor—at Blachernai, he remodelled a church dedicated to the Virgin during his

FIGURE 7.2
Justinian's magnificent cathedral Church of Hagia Sophia in Constantinople.
Credit: Erich Lessing / Art Resource, NY

uncle's reign—and altogether he would build thirty-three churches in Constantinople alone.[15] Not only is this a staggering record in purely numerical terms, but his construction work marked a major new phase in the development of Christian architecture.

When Constantine converted to Christianity, there basically was no Christian architecture. Local Christian communities met in converted houses, and especially in the face of periodic imperial persecution, the religion had developed no specific architectural forms of its own. In the fourth century, therefore, as imperial patronage and ongoing processes of conversion caused large numbers of specialist churches to be built for the first time, the religion took over an old form of public building from the Graeco-Roman world: the basilica. This was a rectangular, shallow-vaulted building, usually equipped with aisles around an elevated central nave and an apse at one end. It had long been used for town council buildings and audience chambers across the Mediterranean world, with the apse being occupied by the presiding figure of power (or indeed the emperor in the case of a palace audience chamber). For Christianity, the apse worked nicely for the sacred space of the altar, and the basilica was a building form essentially designed for meetings, which worked, too, as a space for church services.[16] It had, however, some distinct limitations if you wanted to move a large body of people around at all, and it was also difficult to get much sense of space or light into its relatively low roof spaces. By the beginning of the sixth century, Christianity had begun to experiment with other architectural forms which better suited its developing liturgical demands, and Justinian's constructions both reflected this ongoing transformation and materially advanced it.

He may have been encouraged along this path in the first instance by motives of immediate political rivalry. When he came to the throne in August 527, the largest church in the entire city of Constantinople was not an imperial construction at all, but the church of Saint Polyeuktos, recently completed by the female senatorial grandee Anicia Juliana. A granddaughter of the Western Emperor Valentinian III and great-granddaughter of the Eastern Emperor Theodosius II, she had always lived in Constantinople, not following her father to Rome when he briefly became Western emperor between April and November 472. What she built is known from some moderately extensive remains but also from its lengthy dedicatory inscription, which has come down to us in an anthology of Greek verse. This not only celebrated Anicia Juliana's decidedly imperial pedigree but made it explicit that she had modelled her church on the Temple of Solomon as described in the Bible, even to the extent, as archaeological investigation has confirmed, of basing its measurements on the royal cubit. Not only huge by contemporary standards—its basic ground plan was a fifty-two-metre square—Saint Polyeuktos may also have been revolutionary in being the first church in Constantinople to incorporate a dome, the significance of which we will return to. There is no explicit evidence to this effect, but the scale of some of the internal masonry supports strongly suggests it was all designed to support a dome. Either way, between 524 and 527, Anicia Juliana had laid down a kind of challenge by building the greatest church of contemporary Constantinople. Given her imperial pedigree and the fact that she had an adult male son (Olybrius, one of the senators exiled after Nika), it is hard not to see her church as a clear reminder, in Constantinople of the mid-520s, that there were alternative plausible candidates for divine appointment to the imperial throne other than the nephew of an elderly general from an obscure part of the Balkans.[17]

Justinian proved himself more than capable of a decisive response: initially in the Church of Saints Sergius and Bacchus, his first foundation as emperor, and then in his reconstruction of Hagia Sophia. Sergius and Bacchus was begun as soon as Justinian came to the throne in 527 and completed by 532. Sometimes called little Hagia Sophia, it utterly superseded the architectural form of the basilica by incorporating a three-story octagonal pillar (not solid) structure inside a solid two-story brick square. The octagon in turn supported a sixteen-sided pumpkin dome: the defining feature of the whole building. Hagia Sophia, as rebuilt by Justinian after Nika, took the same basic form, but exploded it onto a new and utterly unprecedented scale. Still standing in modern Istanbul, it boasts a nave that is about eighty metres long, and its dome soars fifty-five metres. This made it the largest open, vaulted interior known to the ancient or medieval worlds, and its real trick lay in achieving all the height of the dome via the innovative use of relatively slight internal arches, supported on massive ground floor masonry piers (see Figure 7.3). As a result, exterior walls, arches, and even the dome itself could be so slender in terms of their masonry construction and pierced by so many windows that the overall effect was to create a vast interior, reaching up to heaven and flooded with light. As Procopius put it:

> Its interior is not so much illuminated from without by the sun, but … the radiance comes into being within it, such an abundance of light bathes this shrine … and … [the dome] seems somehow to float in the air on no firm basis, but to be posed aloft. … The whole ceiling is overlaid with pure gold, which adds glory to the beauty, yet the light reflected from the stone walls prevails, shining out in rivalry with the gold.[18]

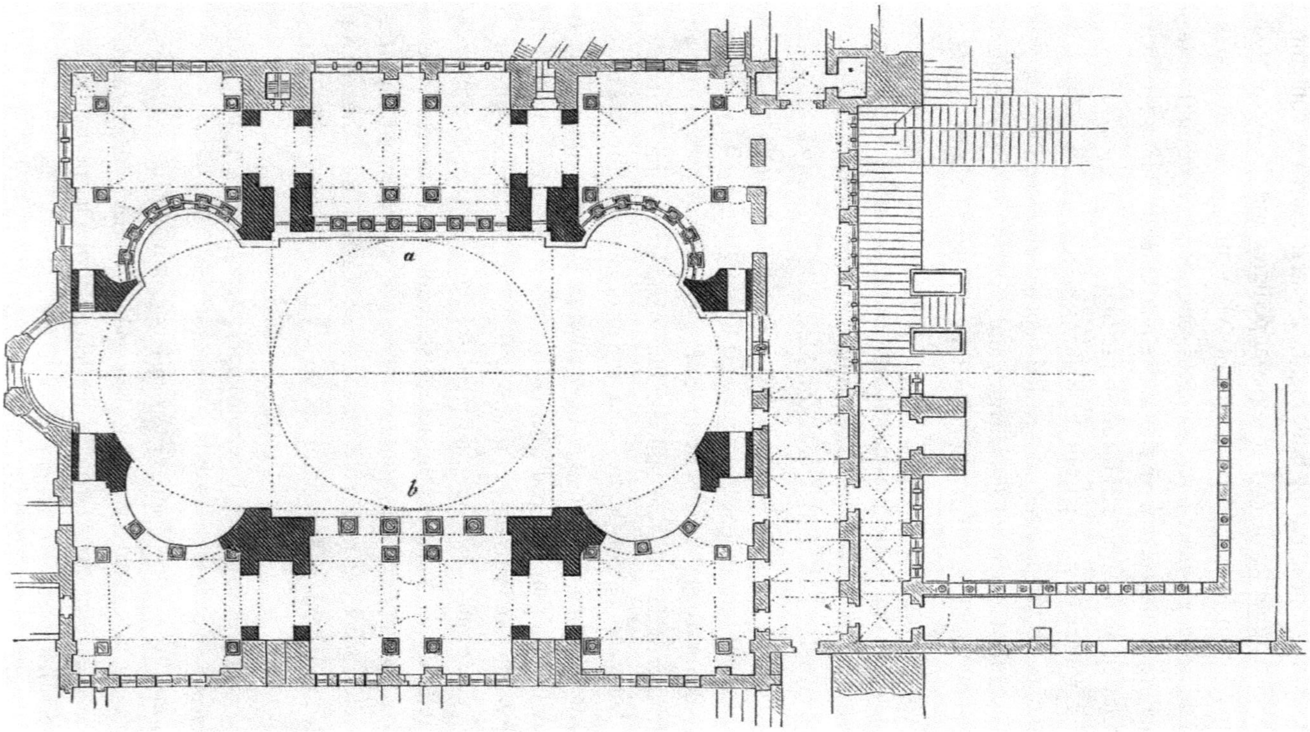

FIGURE 7.3

The four massive masonry pillars at the heart of Hagia Sophia held up its revolutionary dome which filled the interior with unprecedented light and space.

When he entered his new cathedral for the first time, an admittedly non-contemporary source records that Justinian declared, 'Solomon, I have surpassed thee.'[19] Given the explicit references to Solomon's temple engraved by Anicia Juliana into Saint Polyeuktos, it is tempting to think that Justinian might have had her challenge specifically in mind.

There is no doubt at all, however, about the political and ideological significance of Justinian's great exercise in church construction. Hagia Sophia was built at breakneck speed (especially if you compare it the extenuated histories of some of the great Renaissance cathedrals). The new church was dedicated on 27 December 537, having been constructed inside five years. Nothing could better illustrate the ideological imperative for the regime in rebuilding the religious prestige which had certainly been shattered when the great cathedral church of its capital city went up in smoke in February 532. At that point, divine protection must have seemed extremely distant, so that restoring a key physical reminder of the link between emperor and divinity was an urgent enough priority to command every available resource. Here again, I suspect, the extra prestige the regime had acquired from its astonishingly quick and total victory over the Vandals just a year later played a major role in quashing any potential resistance as it ransacked the empire for the resources it needed for this high-profile, wildly ambitious building project in the capital. We are also told that Justinian and Theodora decorated the interior of their new church with gifts of gold, silver, precious gems, and the richest possible textiles.[20] Some of this presumably also came directly from the liberated treasury of the Vandal kings of Carthage.

There was much more to Justinian's new-style church architecture, however, than an attempt to restore the credibility of the regime. The eclipse of the simple basilica was a general phenomenon of particularly the east Mediterranean world in the sixth century, and all the great religious buildings Justinian constructed across his empire reflected the trend. Like Constantine before him, Justinian rebuilt churches in all the great Christian centres of his empire: Jerusalem and Bethlehem in the Holy Land, Saint Catherine's monastery on Mount Sinai (see Figure 7.4), where mosaicists from Constantinople produced an astonishing representation

FIGURE 7.4
Saint Catherine's Monastery, Mount Sinai.
Credit: Sergey Novikov / Shutterstock

of the Transfiguration (the monastery's patronal feast), and the great Church of Saint John in Ephesus. None of these churches rivalled Hagia Sophia, but they all experimented in different ways with domes to create elevation and light. In part this responded to a new aesthetic of holiness. As Procopius put it in relation to Hagia Sophia, describing its overall effect upon the worshipper:

> Whenever anyone enters this church to pray, he understands at once that it is not by any human power or skill, but by the influence of God, that this work has been so finely turned. And so his mind is lifted up toward God, and exalted, feeling that He cannot be far away, but must especially love to dwell in this place which He has chosen.

In due course, this emerging Christian aesthetic developed into an accepted canon of church decoration which would see the figure of Christ as 'the ruler of all' (*Pantokrator*) portrayed only at the pinnacle of the dome with all the hierarchy of heaven—archangels, angels, evangelists, prophets, martyrs, and saints—appearing in their due places lower down in an overarching decorative scheme.[21]

At the same time, the availability of larger, more open, internal floor spaces was integral to new forms of Christian worship that were spreading simultaneously. Participatory liturgies, marked by processions not only of priests but sometimes of entire congregations, were becoming increasingly common, with worshippers encouraged not only to witness holy mysteries but actually to participate in them. This was done not just by the kind of movement which would have been extremely difficult in the traditional basilica but also by mobilizing the imagination, as in the work of Romanus Melodus, the famous hymnographer of the age of Justinian. His hymns, sometimes sung by congregations as well as priests, were designed to stimulate a heightened spirituality through individual reimaginings of sacred events, which Romanus framed in the present tense with a strong use of the first person, often for the vigils, which were another prominent feature of the new Christian piety of the sixth century—for example, in his hymn for Christmas eve:

> Today the Virgin gives birth to him who is above all being,
> And the earth offers a cave to him whom no one can approach.
> Angels with shepherds give glory,
> And magi journey with a star. . . .
> Bethlehem has opened Eden, come, let us see;
> We have found delight in secret, come, let us receive.[22]

Justinian's churches were not just buildings, in other words, but theatres designed to host a widening range of Christian public worship, which both encouraged the adoption of new building forms and themselves evolved to take full advantage of the new religious spaces opened up by Hagia Sophia, on the grandest scale, or more modestly in Saints Sergius and Bacchus.

The emperor himself, together with much of the citizenry of Constantinople, participated in these new religious dramas. The famous mosaic panels of Saint Vitale (see Figures 7.5a and 7.5b) in Ravenna portray Justinian and Theodora taking part in the offertory processions which now

(a)

FIGURE 7.5A AND 7.5B

Justinian, Theodora, and their courts, as presented in the mosaics of San Vitale in Ravenna. They are bringing offerings to the altar of God, whom the emperor credited for his conquests.

Credit: Art Resource, NY

became a standard feature of the Mass. The emperor was an enthusiastic participant, too, in the developing cult of the saints, with all its complex cycles of annual commemoration. In particular, he rebuilt the Church of Saints Cosmas and Damian on the waterfront at Constantinople, because

(b)

FIGURE 7.5A AND 7.5B
Continued

the saints had appeared to him in a dream to cure him when he was near death. Once again, Procopius's brief description of the renovation work stresses that the emperor flooded the building with light.[23]

The grandest religious dramas of all, however, were now being played out not in any building but on the streets of Constantinople, with the entire population of the city as at least potential participants. The dedication of the rebuilt Hagia Sophia in 537 began with a vast procession. The emperor proceeded on foot—the patriarch behind in a carriage—to give thanks to God for the completion of the project. He was followed by courtiers and guardsmen in their appropriate order according to staggeringly complex rules of status, and the entire route was decorated and full of citizens who played a full part in proceedings with chanted acclamations led, as usual, by well-prepared members of the factions. This was mimicked on 28 June 550, when a similar procession, with the patriarch entrusted this time with three caskets carrying the newly rediscovered remains of the Apostles Andrew, Luke, and Timothy, set off from the palace along the Mese for Justinian's newly rebuilt Church of the Holy Apostles, destined to be his own final resting place and home to the remains of his (fairly) recently deceased empress. By the sixth century, routes, stopping points, and acclamations were all laid down for a whole host of moments over the course of a defined ceremonial year: saints days, feast days, anniversaries of the dedications of churches, and great imperial victories, too, like the triumph Justinian celebrated over the defeated Gelimer in 534 (p. 143). In God's empire, ruled by God's personally appointed emperor, there could be no separation between religious affairs and affairs of state. In 528, the Empress Theodora and her accompanying coterie of four thousand attendants made a similarly sacred procession through the city on their way to visit a distant spa. Religion was the state's business, the state's business was religious, and the whole of Constantinople functioned, in a sense, as an open-air Hagia Sophia writ large: a theatre where key ceremonies of God's empire were regularly played out. Carefully orchestrated ceremonial to make the point that the emperor was God's chosen ruler for his own special society was as old as the Roman Empire itself, of course, but the scale, frequency, and concentration of such ceremonies—the product of over a century now of essentially permanent imperial residence within the city—had turned sixth-century Constantinople into an extraordinary showcase of Roman Christian imperium.[24]

This Christianization of the Roman culture of empire was not a new phenomenon. It had begun in the time of Constantine himself. But it certainly reached important new stages of development under Justinian.

Populations right across the social spectrum were affected by the spread of the new expressions of Christian piety now being played out in the developing church buildings of the empire. Bishops, priests, and monks formed more intense, two-way relationships with their congregations: they demanded more intimate engagement with the religion from their flocks and had to satisfy, in return, the demands for services and religious care that their own demands engendered.

In more elite circles, debate continued as to how much of traditional, classical Graeco-Roman culture was compatible with Christian teaching. Back in the fourth century, concern had focused on the education in classical literature, which was characteristic of the empire's landowning elites; but by the sixth, questions were being raised, too, about philosophy and science. Was Genesis's account of Creation compatible with the teachings of Aristotelian science, and what place was there now for the study of traditional Platonic philosophy? Famously, Justinian closed down the philosophical schools of Athens, but their counterparts in Alexandria continued to operate throughout the sixth century, and in terms of texts produced, traditional Greek philosophy actually flourished, so there were no simple, monolithic answers to such questions. But the increasingly intense and more widespread Christianity of the era was causing them to be asked, and Justinian was extremely happy to place his regime in the forefront of such developments.[25] Not only in church building and in the expression of due piety but also in the definition of appropriate cultural forms, God's chosen emperor was happy to guide God's chosen people and bask in the reflected glory of the divinity.

All of which was fine in moments of success. But by the same ideological token, setbacks and defeats of all kinds raised serious questions, which also had to be addressed somehow in the same highly charged theatrical arena of Christian empire. Droughts, famines, earthquakes (such as the shocking calamity of 557, which caused part of Hagia Sophia's magnificent new dome to collapse), and military defeats: these too had to be processed through the prism of the imperial capital's ceremonial life—and duly were, with yet more processions and solemn services giving thanks for eventual delivery from hardship and hoping to be spared further trials and tribulations.[26] Being in charge of God's empire was ultimately an extremely stressful job description. For if all success came from the Almighty, as all emperors proclaimed, then so too did every disaster, and these were not random occurrences. There had to be reasons why God was choosing to afflict his chosen people with earthquake, famine, or military defeat. Amidst all the legislation, campaigning, and building, therefore, it is no surprise to find that Justinian also devoted huge efforts to the unrelenting task of ensuring that the religious affairs of the empire were in tune with the divine will.

THE PEACE OF GOD

The fundamental religious problem confronting Justinian throughout his reign was exactly the same as that faced by his immediate predecessors, Justin and Anastasius. What response should his regime make to the deep divisions within the ranks of Eastern churchmen generated by the Council of Chalcedon and its use of 'two nature' language to describe the relationship of human and divine within the person of the Incarnate Christ? On the accession of his uncle, Justinian enthusiastically supported the policy reversal which restored full imperial support for Chalcedon, paving the way for reunion with Rome. He quickly showed himself to be more practical than doctrinaire, however, by trying to sell Pope Hormisdas on the idea that a watered-down version of Chalcedon might allow large numbers of currently disaffected Eastern churchmen to sign up to a broader ecclesiastical union, and that was even before he married Theodora, with her strong links to anti-Chalcedonian ecclesiastical networks. When the pope demurred, Justinian backed down.[27]

The same pragmatism is firmly in evidence in the early years of his own reign. While maintaining official support for Chalcedon, Theodora was used to build up contacts with anti-Chalcedonian circles, which manifested themselves openly in the conversations of 532. For Justinian, these discussions seem to have represented, in part at least, an alternative strategy for rebuilding his prestige in the aftermath of Nika; when the discussions failed to achieve any swift outcome, the emperor had brought them to a close, turning instead towards an African military adventure as a potential source of desperately needed success.[28] But the problem of a badly divided church did not go away, nor did Justinian's underlying interest in resolving it. As God's representative on earth, the overall state of the church was his responsibility, and for the ambitious Justinian, present divisions represented an opportunity for yet another great coup if only they could once be healed.

Throughout his reign Justinian clearly understood that, undiluted, the proceedings of Chalcedon could never provide the basis for Eastern church unity. Its definitions of faith enshrining 'two nature' language, and particularly its assertion of the fundamental orthodoxy of particular teachers stood in too stark a contrast to what the anti-Chalcedonians understood to be the central canons of Cyrillian orthodoxy. Somehow Chalcedon was going to have to be adjusted, but for another strand of church opinion, it was a fully ecumenical council whose teachings could not be questioned. Justinian was faced, therefore, with a delicate balancing act: maintain as much as possible of Chalcedon while jettisoning just enough of its proceedings to bring sufficient numbers of suspicious Eastern churchmen on board to be able to claim an effective restoration of church unity.

I do not suppose for a moment that Justinian thought he could fully convince *all* churchmen to unite around one position, but as previous major Christian disputes had shown, you did not need to do that to achieve effective success. Both the Arian and Donatist disputes of the fourth century, for instance, displayed similar long-term pathologies. While imperial policy vacillated, both sides thought they could win, and the disputes rumbled on in full vigour and with periodic viciousness. But what appeared to be distinct church parties turned out on closer inspection, like their modern political counterparts, to be coalitions forged between individuals holding a wider range of more precise opinions. This offered real opportunity. If a suitable compromise was found (as happened with both Arian and Donatist disputes), you could unite a majority, middle-range of contending churchmen, and isolate the extremes of both the original parties, so long as a run of (often short-lived) imperial regimes were consistently committed to supporting the same compromise position without vacillation. The marginalized points of view did not immediately disappear and sometimes still provided the basis for functioning religious networks. But faced with the full panoply of imperial ideological and legal authority confiscating their churches and threatening their richer supporters with complete loss of their property, the more extreme positions quickly declined to sect status and, as such, could be left to wither in peace, since they no longer represented a threat to mainstream church unity.[29]

It is with this kind of model in mind (and it is a model that has applied in many a successful peace process from Arianism to Northern Ireland) that we need to approach Justinian's religious policy initiatives. On the face of it, they can look like a bewildering series of volte-faces punctuated by lengthy periods of inaction, but underlying them all was the search for the silver bullet of compromise which would get enough contending Eastern churchmen into communion with one another. Very much in Justinian's favour, at least to start with, was the fact that leading churchmen on both sides did actually believe that the church *should* be united and did also accept, ideologically, that it was within the emperor's legitimate job description to broker a settlement. This gave him significant initial leverage, and Justinian proceeded to use it to the full.

Although not in the end successful, the conversations of 532 pointed towards possible compromise. Because Cyril of Alexandria had once himself used 'two nature' language (p. 79), it was just about possible to defend Chalcedon's definition of the person of Christ 'in two natures' to anti-Chalcedonians as a valuable formulation, so long as this did also not explicitly exclude the valid use, in other contexts, of the 'one nature' alternative formulation beloved of anti-Chalcedonians. Once this was admitted, the real sticking point with Chalcedon became its explicit defence of the orthodoxy of all or some of the works of three fifth-century church fathers—Theodore of Mopsuestia, Theodoret of Cyrrhus, and Ibas of Edessa—who, for anti-Chaledconians, were tainted with the heretical ideas of Cyril's arch-enemy, Nestorius. Slowly a compromise along these lines became Justinian's central strategy for restoring union within the Eastern church.

Already in 533 we find him taking initiatives pointing firmly in this direction. He issued two religious edicts, one of which, by asserting the fundamental 'hypostatic' unity of Christ's nature, made it impossible to read Chalcedon's 'two nature' language in a Nestorian sense (where the human and divine continued to be separable after the Incarnation), and a second which declared that 'one of the Trinity suffered'. This, again, made it impossible to understand Christ's nature in a Nestorian sense (Nestorius having questioned whether omnipotent, immortal divinity could really have suffered and died) and represented a resuscitation of the particular path to compromise that Justinian had tried to open up with Pope Hormisdas back in 520. This time, however, with imperial armies already in Sicily and a potential invasion of Italy in the air, the emperor managed to get Pope John II to accept what his predecessor had rejected. The same kind of compromise was also being tried out at a local level in Palestine by Bishop Leontius of Jerusalem, who attempted to convince moderate anti-Chalcedonians among his flock that by such means it was possible to rule out a Nestorian reading of the council's proceedings and hence win their acceptance, however grudging, of the council's validity.[30]

The way forward, of course, was not completely smooth. In 535, Severus of Antioch was invited back to the imperial capital from his Egyptian exile. For Justinian, this was presumably part of an attempt to win the support of as many anti-Chalcedonian leaders as possible for this developing compromise position. Whether Severus might have been willing to play ball or not is unclear, because the move backfired, sparking howls of protest among Chalcedonian monks who quickly mobilized the new Pope Agapetus to fire off letters of complaint. Perhaps because the protests made him realize that Severus's long track record of outright hostility to Chalcedon meant that it would not be possible to include him in the emerging compromise, Justinian not only sent him back to Egypt but also sacked the current patriarch of Constantinople, Anthimus, with whom Severus had been negotiating. This was enough to quieten the protests, and there were no more major moves for the rest of the decade. Possibly, events first in Africa and Italy and then in developing relations with Persia were consuming all of Justinian's energies, but I suspect, and there is some evidence to support such a view, that throughout, work continued on the religious front in the form of individual approaches to important anti-Chalcedonians. Not only did Severus arrive from Egypt in the mid-530s, but Justinian also invited to Constantinople at some point between 537 and 548 the influential abbot of the anti-Chalcedonian monastery of Pbow in upper Egypt. This makes perfect sense as an attempt to sign up as many influential opponents of Chalcedon as possible to Justinian's new approach for achieving church unity.[31]

By the mid-540s, the emperor was ready to move. In 543/4 he issued an edict, now surviving only in fragments, which condemned those sections of Chalcedon, the so-called Three Chapters, which had asserted the orthodoxy of the anti-Chalcedonians' arch-villains: Theodore of Mopsuestia, Theodoret of Cyrrhus, and Ibas of Edessa. After some more determined lobbying, a second edict, On the True Faith, followed in 551. This pulled together the different theological initiatives which the court had now put its money on as the basis for a possible settlement: above all, that Christ as God 'suffered in the flesh' and that after the Incarnation, the one fundamentally unified Christ was composed of two natures. Its substantive points were all supported by texts drawn from Cyril of Alexandria, and the document closed with thirteen anathemas: ten supporting its positive points and three, inevitably, condemning each of the Three Chapters.[32] Important in itself, the edict had still broader significance as the foundation document of a new ecumenical council: a gathering—supposedly—of representatives of the entire Christian Church, to be held in Constantinople in 553.

Only emperors could call ecumenical councils, and their remit was always to deal with matters of overarching significance to the Christian world as a whole. For Justinian, it was a high-risk strategy, and he surely had in mind the first Council of Constantinople, called by Theodosius I in 381, which had effectively ended the Arian dispute after fifty years of division within the Eastern church. His own council opened on 5 May 553 under the presidency of the Patriarch Eutychius of Constantinople. Present were 152 bishops, only 16 from the West, and on 2 June 553 the meeting came to a close. A full Greek text of its proceedings does not survive, but there is an extensive Latin summary, which was probably made for Pope Vigilius, who refused initially to attend the council but later declared himself in full agreement with its decisions.[33] Surprise: these precisely echoed On the True Faith. Justinian had identified his compromise, developed it, lobbied hard on its behalf for the best part of twenty years, and now had it rubber-stamped, according to proper late Roman tradition, by an ecumenical council. The script had been followed, and all was set for a triumphant restoration of ecclesiastical unity.

Except it was not. The outcome was not what Justinian wanted. For one thing, resistance to any tampering with Chalcedon remained strong among Latin churchmen of the western Mediterranean, although, as Chapter 10 will show, in areas under Justinian's direct rule protest soon died down. As this suggests, ideological acceptance of the emperor's overarching religious authority continued to exercise considerable force over the behaviour of many individual church leaders, and the emperor still had important levers at his disposal to twist the arms of particular individuals. Since the first Council of Constantinople had done its work in 381, however, the unfolding of two long-term and interrelated processes of structural religious development made the resolution of the division generated by Chalcedon a much more difficult proposition than solving the Arian problem two centuries before had been.

First, Justinian's dispute had gone on for longer: over a hundred years separated Chalcedon from Constantinople II, compared to the fifty-six between the councils of Nicaea and Constantinople I. One important consequence of the passage of so much time was that the positions of both sides had become much more entrenched, not only in terms of the amount of vituperative rhetoric they had fired off at each other but institutionally, too. For all his hostility to Chalcedon, Severus of Antioch had been extremely cautious in exile about ordaining separate bishops and priests of an anti-Chalcedonian persuasion. He was well aware of how much potential this had to complicate any future restoration of church unity, and it was always his aim to achieve, eventually, one unified church establishment again in the Roman east. Although the Emperor Justin had exiled some fifty-five anti-Chalcedonian bishops from the provinces of Syria and Palestine in the early 520s, this had not generated fifty-five pairs of rival bishops for the same sees, although one of Severus's colleagues, John of Tella, ordained a substantial number of priests. After Severus's death in 538, however, some of his successors showed much less caution. In 542, as one of his many bridge-building exercises, Justinian allowed the ordination of two anti-Chalcedonian bishops for the Arab allies of the frontier region: Jacob Baradeus and Theodore. To start with, they only ordained priests but, following the Second Council of Constantinople, extended their work to the higher levels of the church hierarchy as well, ordaining no less than twenty-seven anti-Chalcedonian bishops between 553 and 566. From then on, bringing the church back into unity meant finding a solution for what to do about all the many rival bishops.[34]

Even more important, the fact that despite their initial unwillingness, anti-Chalcedonian leaders eventually boxed themselves into this particular institutional corner directs our attention towards a deeper change which ties together the ongoing dispute over Chalcedon with some of the other key developments already observed in sixth-century East Roman Christianity. The pressure for all these ordinations, first for priests and eventually for bishops, too, came from below. When he entered Antioch as its bishop in 508, Severus was greeted with cries of 'We want to baptize our children.' In the 380s, as the Arian dispute was approaching resolution even in the third generation of the Christian empire, the new religion remained a minority. Cities like Antioch were then more or less evenly split between Christians and other believers, and Christianity had not yet made much impact in most rural areas. By the sixth century, pagan temples had been suppressed even in many country zones for the best part of a century, huge numbers of churches had been built, and bishops, priests, and monks had not only converted the population of the Roman world in large numbers but were introducing them to increasingly intense forms of participatory Christian worship.[35]

Chalcedonians and anti-Chalcedonians shared a basic religious culture, and both championed similar forms of piety in their particular areas of influence. The needs and demands of these congregations massively complicated the process of dispute resolution, by stimulating the growth of separate hierarchies, which was a problem in itself, but also by making it much more difficult for particular leaders to appear to change sides. Early in the next reign, Justin II managed to persuade some important anti-Chalcedonian leaders to come back into communion with his official ecclesiastical establishment, but the initiative broke down when those leaders were unable to sell the new compromise to their rank and file, especially monastic constituencies.[36] In many ways, therefore, the biggest obstacle to a successful restoration of church unity was the increasing intensity of Christianity itself, which made it much more difficult for church leaders to guide their congregations back into unity with those whom they had previously presented as deviant heretics, even if at some point they eventually wanted to.

Resolving division within the church was not, in my view, absolutely impossible by the 550s (although some commentators think so),[37] but Justinian certainly faced a much more difficult situation than Theodosius I had done 170 years before. His theological compromise could potentially win over anti-Chalcedonian leaders, as further stages of the dispute under Justinian's successor, Justin II, were to show, but selling the idea to religiously intense congregations and monasteries that they could now enter communion with the Chalcedonian enemy was bound to prove a difficult proposition, something that was hardly likely to happen quickly or smoothly. Ultimately, for all his efforts, Justinian was unable to pull it off. The rise of more widespread and more intensively Christian congregations was not always a positive development for a Christian emperor, therefore, and the signs are that Justinian became increasingly frustrated in the later years of his reign. As the struggle for compromise continued, he at one point saw potential merit in the teachings of Julian of Halicarnassus that Christ's body was divine and therefore incorruptible, and an air of possible heresy started to gather around the court.[38]

What all this emphasizes above all is that while prevailing religious ideologies offered a Christian Roman emperor many avenues of powerful support, which Justinian exploited to the maximum in rebuilding Constantinople and celebrating his cult of victory, they simultaneously posed serious challenges. Not only was it now increasingly difficult to generate in practice the unified Christian community that ought in theory to exist, but constant references to divine support also raised difficult questions should success give way to defeat.[39] After the respite provided by astonishing victories in Africa and Italy in the 530s, Justinian's regime found itself facing such questions for a second time, when its run of military success was checked by a series of setbacks, in the West but, above all, on the eastern front, against its traditional Persian enemy.

8

'OUR BROTHER IN GOD'

AMONG THE GREATEST ODDITIES to come down to us from medieval Byzantium are the various works of the Emperor Constantine VII Porphyrogenitus (905–959). His overall aim was to preserve the key elements of everything which made his society rational, superior, and in tune with God's plan for the universe (p. 20). His largest project collected extracts were to be made from the learning of classical antiquity, pagan and Christian, and arranged them in thematic volumes. As he himself puts it,

> Given the immensity of these writings, which is tiring even to think about and which seems generally overwhelming and heavy, [I] thought it a good idea to break it up and organize it in order to make more widely available everything it contains that is useful.

Fifty-three volumes were planned, but we know the titles only of twenty-three, and parts of just four have survived.[1] He also prepared another volume on formal imperial ceremonial—*De Ceremoniis*—which preserves a detailed account from the reign of Justinian of how to meet and greet ambassadors from the Persian king of kings. In what dusty corner of Constantinople this had been kept for the intervening four hundred years, and why, given that for three hundred of them the Persian Empire had not even existed, are questions that it is not possible to answer.

The volume is a fantastic step-by-step account of how to proceed, which may well have originally been penned by Peter the Patrician himself. It starts with who should be sent to the frontier to meet the embassy on its arrival and moves on to the details of its transportation to Constantinople.

Five post-horses and thirty mules are standard, but if the emperor is in a good mood (or hoping for a particularly good crop of diplomatic presents), more could be sent. Meanwhile back in Constantinople,

> [The ambassador's] lodging ... must be prepared in advance in accordance with the man's rank and the escort he brings with him: and there must be made ready in it beds, bedclothes, ovens, fireplaces, tables, and buckets to carry water and help with other hygienic services.

Many different bureaus lent a hand. The office of the *comes rei privatae* provided the mattresses; the city prefect, the beds, tables, pots and pans; and the weapons factories, the braziers. All of this is utterly fascinating, but the account of the formal diplomatic reception at court trumps it all. A good half a page is spent on who are to be present, what they are to wear, and where they should stand. Also dependent on whether the Persian presents include horses or not was the number of open doors into the audience chamber (presumably also the number of cleaners to hand). Then finally, once everyone is assembled and veiled behind silk curtains to echo the majesty of the Almighty hidden from us in heaven, it is time to get down to business:

> When the curtain is raised, the ambassador outside throws himself to the floor, where [there is] purple marble, does obeisance, and arises. And then he enters the gate, again he throws himself [down] and does obeisance on the floor and arises. Again in the middle of the *consistorium* (audience chamber) he does obeisance likewise, and then he comes and adores the feet [of the emperor] and stands in the middle; hands over the letter and declares the greeting of his king. The emperor should then ask, 'How fares our brother in God? We rejoice in his good health.'

Then the ambassador hands over the presents and is told to go back to his lodging to rest for a few days; at that point, all being well, the serious business of negotiation could begin.[2]

With so much formality and mutual flattery, expressed both ideologically and in practical care, one could be forgiven for thinking that the two great powers of the Near East generally conducted their affairs with mutual respect and with a strong sense of the responsibility that God had given them for the care of their millions of subjects. The reality could hardly have been further from the truth. Because each was the other's greatest neighbour, any success against the other ranked highest in the list of any ruler's achievements, and suspicions—fuelled by the fact that each claimed the support of mutually incompatible divinities: the Christian God on one side, the Zoroastrian on the other—about what the other might be planning were always in the air. It was only when both sides were facing huge outside threats from powerful nomad empires in the fifth century that new habits—of not seeking to exploit every opportunity for self-advancement at the expense of the other—actually took hold. When that threat was removed, older patterns of behaviour quickly returned. Justin and Justinian were quick to exploit Khavad's succession difficulties in the 520s, and it was only because Chosroes, a brand-new king of kings, had taken the throne and needed to deal with potential rivals that Justinian was able to negotiate the so-called Endless Peace. Otherwise, fresh from their great victory at Callinicum, the Persians would have been looking to ram home an evident advantage against a Roman emperor who had just seen half his imperial capital go up in flames in the Nika riot.[3] (See Figure 8.1.)

But if both parties had pressing reasons to opt for a peace agreement at the beginning of the 530s, by the end of the decade these had lost much of their force. To start with, Chosroes was now firmly in power. Not only that, but he was well aware of Justinian's successes in the West and of their potential for altering the balance of power between the two empires in the longer term by adding new territories and populations to the resource base of Constantinople. Already, after the conquest of the Vandals, Chosroes sent one embassy asking for a share of the loot, since it was his willingness to grant the Endless Peace which had made Belisarius's expedition possible. By the end of the decade, not only had the proverbially rich island of Sicily been added to the East Roman Empire with hardly an arrow fired, but the mainland Ostrogothic kingdom was on the point of collapse, too. Once Belisarius had broken up the siege of Rome in the spring of 538, the writing was on the wall, and the astonishing arrival of

FIGURE 8.1
Chosroes, Justinian's 'brother in God', who exploited the opportunities presented by the emperor's western commitments to wreak havoc in his rich eastern provinces.

Gothic ambassadors in Persia will have confirmed the point for Chosroes and his advisers that Justinian's power was only likely to increase in the medium term.

In the short term, however, Justinian's western adventurism presented the Persians with an attractive opportunity. Judging by the intensive improvement campaign that Justinian had to institute from the 540s, no money at all was spent on the military installations of the eastern front in the 530s, which is hardly surprising given all the resources that the emperor was having to find both to fund Belisarius's expeditions and to rebuild his burnt-out capital. Worse than that, Justinian's regime was also scrimping and saving on the pay of the eastern front's garrison troops, the *limitanei*. Procopius makes this general accusation in *Anekdota*, which it might be tempting to discount, were it not for a revolt in the garrison of the key fortress of Dara in 539 and the evident willingness of some troops, admittedly in small numbers, to shift to a Persian allegiance in the 540s.[4]

Chosroes had both positive and negative reasons to bring the Endless Peace to a premature conclusion by the late 530s, therefore, and this underlay an evident change in attitude. As Procopius reports, instead of minimizing the perennially destabilizing factors of frontier life—such as the endless squabbling of both sides' Arab allies and the attempt of local potentates in the Caucasus to recruit one empire or the other to their support—by 539 Chosroes was looking to pick a fight. The crux moment came when an embassy arrived in Constantinople in 539. Having enquired after the health of his brother in God, Justinian got an unlooked-for answer. Chosroes complained both that Constantinople was trying to buy off the Persians' main Arab ally, the Lakhmid Al-Mundhir, and looking to get steppe nomads to invade Persian territory through the Caucasus. At best, this was the preamble to a demand for serious damages, but it might also signal the start of a mobilization for actual hostilities. This embassy made Justinian start to take seriously Wittigis's offer to partition Italy in late 539 as a means of bringing the Gothic war to a close (p. 178) so that many of the over twenty thousand East Roman troops committed to the campaign could be returned to the East.[5] Before Justinian could extract them, however, Chosroes struck.

THE EAGLE HAS LANDED

On 22 May 330 BC, Seleucus I Nicator, one of Alexander the Great's generals who had picked up Syria in the post-mortem carve up of the great conqueror's domains, ritually prepared a piece of meat for an obliging eagle to carry off in its talons. It came to earth on Mount Silpius, next to a bend of the river Orontes, and there Seleucus built his capital, named for his son Antiochus (a creature of habit, Seleucus built no less than sixteen Antiochs). All in all, the eagle picked an excellent spot. Unlike many rivers of the Near East, the forty-metre-wide Orontes did not alternate between raging flood and barren trickle but flowed evenly all year round, making for plenty of water and a convenient avenue for trade, not least when it came to ferrying goods up from its port of Seleuceia a few miles downstream. There was also a highly fertile plain, and convenient space, varying between two and three kilometres in width, between river and mountain where a city could be built, not to mention a very nice island in the middle of the river, which was perfect for palaces and centres of administration.

Eight hundred seventy years later, Seleucus's foundation had grown into the capital of the Roman Near East, spreading now much further over the plain, especially towards the west, where about seven kilometres away lay the astonishingly beautiful woods and groves of its famous suburb of Daphne. Second city of the empire, Antioch—Antioch on the

Orontes, to be precise (to distinguish it from all the other Antiochs)—had a population numbering in the hundreds of thousands, if perhaps a little down from its first century AD peak of half a million. It was also no longer, as it had been in the fourth century, regularly home to reigning Roman emperors. With the growth of Constantinople and its immovable apparatus of bureaucratic government, emperors now rarely left the city, certainly not to travel as far as Antioch. But it was the political, administrative, and cultural capital of the Roman Near East, and along with Alexandria in Egypt, one of the twin-jewel regional capitals of the Eastern Empire. Home of the vicar of the Orient, it was responsible for raising taxation among the many rich agricultural cities of Syria and Palestine. It was also home to one of the oldest Christian communities in the world, founded, so the story went, by the preaching of Saint Peter long before he ever ventured west to Rome or, as reported in Acts, as part of the missionary efforts of Paul and Barnabas. It was where the name Christian was first coined, as a term of abuse amongst its extensive Jewish community, and the fourth century saw intense religious rivalries among Christian, Jewish, and traditional pagan leaderships for the loyalties of a population who were notoriously fond of religious festivals and would attend everyone's without fear or favour. But by the sixth century, its bishop was one of the five patriarchs of late Roman Christianity, and his religion had won the loyalty of everyone except the Jewish community, even if a love of festivals and worldly pleasures remained deeply entrenched in its collective psyche. A huge, bustling metropolis, it had many of the problems you would expect and some you would not. Its Christian population was sometimes deeply divided, there were extremes of poverty and wealth, and chariot racing in a hippodrome, which could hold an astonishing eighty thousand spectators, often sparked street violence. Close to the three-way junction of the African, Arabian, and Eurasian tectonic plates, it was also prone to earthquakes, the most recent of which, in 528, had devastated the city's magnificent octagonal cathedral, started under the Emperor Constantine and inaugurated in 341 in the presence of no less than two emperors, his sons Constans and Constantius II. Earthquakes were as nothing, however, compared to the devastation about to be visited upon the city by Justinian's brother in God.[6]

Having decided in the course of 539 to plunge the Near East back into warfare, Chosroes plans for 540 were unconventional. Avoiding Mesopotamia proper, studded with great fortresses such as Dara on the Roman side and Nisibis on the Persian, the Persian army, with the king himself at its head, advanced with the river Euphrates on its right, avoiding the Roman fortress of Callinicum on the far bank. The tone for the campaigning season as a whole was set by what followed at the fortified town of Sura, the first Roman strongpoint in Chosroes path. On the day of the Persians' arrival, the garrison fought gallantly, but its commander, an Armenian called Arsaces, was killed. The population decided that it would be best to surrender, therefore, and the next morning sent the bishop to abase himself before Chosroes and ask for pardon in return for a suitably enormous ransom. Chosroes received the bishop with apparent favour, but when escorting him back to the city with the good news, a Persian task force managed to wedge open the city gate, despite the flag of truce, and the Persian army stormed the city. The city was burnt to the ground, and all the survivors, twelve thousand souls altogether, were reduced to slavery.[7] The king of kings had made his point: resist at your peril.

The result was absolute panic right across the Roman Near East. The commander of the next city in Chosroes's path, Hierapolis, left only a small garrison for its walls, withdrawing the bulk of his soldiers on the grounds that they would be much more effectively employed in supporting the city's defenders by conducting harassing operations on the outside. They were never seen again, and the city quickly agreed to pay Chosroes a ransom of two thousand pounds in weight of silver. Next in line was Beroea, whose bishop happened to be in Antioch. After consulting with Justinian's cousin Germanus, who had been hurriedly sent from Constantinople, it was agreed that the bishop would go to the Persians under flag of truce and offer Chosroes the colossal sum of ten thousand pounds (in weight) of gold (its cost in 2017 would be about 160 million pounds sterling) to withdraw without doing further damage. Chosroes agreed, but Justinian had in the meantime sent more representatives, who refused to countenance the deal. The results were immediately felt at Beroea, whose inhabitants had fled to their highly defensible inner citadel while the Persians sacked and burned the outer city. All seemed set for a lengthy stand-off, but the Beroeans had made a rookie error. They took all their livestock with them, and so the water supply was quickly exhausted. Arriving just in time, their bishop managed to secure their lives but at the cost of all their valuables, and some of the unpaid *limitanei* signed up with the Persians.[8] Two days, march to the west of Beroea lay Antioch itself.

By the time Chosroes got there in May 540, the city had received reinforcements: six thousand *limitanei* from the Palestine command. Its inhabitants were in good cheer, taunting the Persian king and his army as they came into view. Given its general layout, the obvious way to attack the city was via the twin peaks of Mount Silpius, particularly the eastern peak, where the ground sloped more gently down into the city proper through vineyards. The city walls, about the only part of the Roman foundation still visible thanks to all the sediments deposited by the Orontes over the centuries, thus stretched up over the mountain, but there was a weak spot. Justinian's nephew Germanus had identified it a little before. Opposite the higher of the peaks, outside the wall, the rocky ground was relatively even and there was another high point which was virtually on the same level as the top of the walls: the perfect vantage point from which to bring down a weight of missile fire sufficient to clear a patch of wall of defenders and open it up to assault. This was the perfect place for an attack, but there was no time to rectify the problem before the Persians arrived, and to begin work without finishing would just draw attention to the trouble spot. All the defenders could do in the meantime was improvise an extra wooden fighting platform inside the walls at the weak point so that more defenders could mass there to hold off an assault by weight of firepower.

Not being stupid and outraged by the insults hurled in his direction, Chosroes marched his army up the slopes of Mount Silpius and launched a massive attack. Disaster struck. The fighting platform collapsed under the weight of defenders, and there was insufficient counterfire to keep the Persians from the walls. Realizing that the city was bound to fall, since the Persians would break through up above and swarm down on the city below, the Roman commanders withdrew the garrison troops that had just arrived. As the Persians were breaking in up on Mount Silpius, the six thousand Palestinian *limitanei* were marching out of the western gate that led to Daphne. The local faction members held up the Persian advance in some vicious street fighting, but the end was inevitable. Part of the population escaped, but many more were captured, and by the time a new Roman embassy got to the scene, it was too late. Not only was the city sacked and looted, but deliberate fires were set to destroy everything except the cathedral, which had just been rebuilt after the earthquake of 528. The ambassadors also found that the price of peace had gone up. To withdraw, Chosroes now wanted fifty thousand pounds of gold and subsequent annual payments to the tune of a further five thousand pounds. Leaving the ambassadors to take this message back to Justinian, Chosroes admired Daphne, which he left intact apart from the shrine to Saint Michael, because of a fatal incident of stone throwing, on his way to Seleuceia, where the thankful and profoundly victorious king bathed in the waters of the Mediterranean and sacrificed to his God.[9]

These formalities complete, the Persian army proceeded south along the Orontes to Apamea. Since no one was about to resist him, Chosroes held fake chariot races there, supporting (and making to win) the Greens over Justinian's favourite Blues. He also extracted another thousand pounds of silver from the city but was convinced, supposedly by a miracle, not to take with him its prize relic, a portion of the True Cross which glowed through the dark wood of the box in which it was kept. At that point, the king struck for home, presumably satisfied with all the cash and kudos he had extracted and before any major supply issues could develop, but he continued to treat the Roman communities of Syria as a convenient set of ATMs. Chalcis was next in line, and from there he took out another two thousand pounds weight, this time of gold. Carrhae and Constantia also paid him off in unspecified amounts, and the final act of the campaign was a siege of the forward Roman military base at Dara. This was unsuccessful, but it still netted him another thousand pounds of silver as a going-away present.

Chosroes also intended to make more money by ransoming off all his prisoners from Antioch, in the same way he later allowed the bishop of Sergiopolis to ransom the twelve thousand from Sura, but Justinian's officials prevented this, so the poor unfortunates were dragged a further seven hundred kilometres back to his capital Ctesiphon and the new city of Veh-Antioch-Khusro—'The Better Antioch of Chosroes'—which he had constructed just to its south. According to the ninth-century Arab chronicler Tabari,

> [Chosroes] ordered that a plan be drawn up for him of this city of Antioch, taking account of its dimensions, of the number of its dwellings and roads, and of everything that was in it. ... When the people of Antioch entered the gate of their city, each resident proceeded to a house which so resembled his own in Antioch it was as though he had never left it.

This, it goes without saying, is purest fantasy. The reality was a forced march on which many will surely have died, especially the young and old, and the brutality of continued subjection in a settlement which was being created from scratch, no doubt at least in part by the labour of the surviving captives.[10] That image captures much of what Chosroes astonishing campaign of 540 meant from a Roman perspective, both for the general population and for the imperial regime. Justinian's brother in God extracted seven thousand pounds of silver, another two thousand of gold, and a huge number of prisoners and burned down three cities, including the regional capital of Roman Syria. It was an utter disaster, one that must be reckoned a further, if indirect, cost of Justinian's western adventurism. Not only had Justinian's new acquisitions stirred up Chosroes paranoid (though entirely well-placed) jealousies, but the necessary transfers of twenty-thousand-plus Roman troops to allow Belisarius to complete the conquest of Italy, combined with some scrimping and scraping on defence spending in the east, had provided the Persian king with a unique opportunity. The result was a campaign of ransack and disaster on a scale not seen since the dark days of the third century.

News of all this arrived in Constantinople at pretty much the same moment as Belisarius and the first of the Gothic prisoners from the fall of Ravenna, so it is hardly surprising that, this time, there was no extravagant victory parade. Justinian instead created a private museum of Ostrogothic treasures to show off to favoured guests to the palace[11] while he contemplated how to respond to the shocking collapse of Roman Syria. Desperate for any kind of success, Belisarius was sent east for the campaigning season of 541 with whatever extra troops the regime could scrape together. There were not many, because it took so much preparation to pull forces back from Italy, but they did include Belisarius's *bucellarii*, perhaps now including some Gothic cavalrymen, who found themselves, like their defeated Vandal peers, posted to the eastern front. In addition, Belisarius had Arethas and his Arab allies and a two-month loan of six thousand Palestinian *limitanei*, who could be spared during the Arab holy months when Al-Mundhir's Lakhmids would not be launching any raids. It was an improvised scratch force, and Procopius stresses that Belisarius spent much of his time rearming and training what was a far cry from the elite army he had led to victory in North Africa. The one point of comfort was that intelligence reports put Chosroes far from Mesopotamia, on the other side of the Caspian Sea, facing up to a further invasion of his particular brand of nomad nemesis: the Hephthalite Huns (p. 76).

As spring made the grass green again, Belisarius's army made a military demonstration outside the Persian forward base of Nisibis, which was enough to make its garrison retreat behind the walls. With no hope of taking such a powerful fortress, the Romans pushed on to Sisauranon. Intelligence reports told Belisarius that its garrison of eight hundred elite cavalrymen were out of provisions—one effect perhaps of Chosroes having mounted such a massive and prolonged operation the previous year—and they were duly persuaded to surrender. They were immediately despatched to Constantinople and the fortress's walls razed to the ground. At this point, Belisarius himself decided to withdraw, sending his Arab auxiliaries and the *limitanei* on an extended booty raid through the adjacent Persian provinces. In *Anekdota*, Procopius claims that the general was so desperate to join his wife, Antonina, at Callinicum that he neglected his duty and curtailed the campaign. The reality was surely that his scratch force had already achieved the requisite face-saving success and was not powerful enough to do anything more substantial than a little raiding, especially given the time limit attached to the *limitanei*.[12]

The Persian cat, however, was not away for long. In 542, Chosroes returned to Mesopotamia with his field army, another major operation in mind. His plan was similar to the campaign of 540, his forces advancing again with the river Euphrates on their right. This time, however, his booty raid had in mind the rich cities of Roman Palestine, above all Jerusalem with its massively endowed Christian shrines, since he had just stripped out much of the wealth of Syria. The obvious route for a conventional Persian army was to turn left at the ruins of Sura, wrecked in 540, and follow the Strata Diocletiana south-westwards. First in line was the city of Sergiopolis, with whose bishop the king had a bone to pick. The bishop had intervened in 540 to ransom the Persians' twelve thousand prisoners from neighbouring Sura, but the money was never paid. Chosroes therefore sent six thousand soldiers to attack the city, but its garrison held out, even though there were only two hundred of them, no doubt greatly assisted as usual by the male citizenry of military age. At this point, Procopius's account starts to look more than a little unconvincing. Belisarius was again assigned to the eastern front and gathered his forces at Europeum, further up the Euphrates. It is noticeable that he never made any move actually to interfere with the Persian army (unlike Dara and Callinicum in 530 and 531; see Chapter 4), but Procopius suggests, nonetheless, that the general's implicit threat to Chosroes's lines of communication was enough to force a retreat. In particular, Belisarius arranged an interview with a Persian envoy where he surrounded himself with six thousand of the biggest, toughest-looking hombres available: a mix of Thracians, Illyrians, Goths, Heruli, Vandals, and Moors, all of whom were briefed to look utterly relaxed. According to Procopius, this convinced the envoy to tell his king that he had better retreat immediately.[13] We have no alternative account, but it is worth noting that there was another potentially major factor in play: 542 was the year when the Justinianic plague hit the Near East in full force. While Procopius does not mention it until after Chosroes decided to retreat, the outbreak of disease, potentially devastating to concentrated bodies of men, may well have forced his hand. Either way, the campaign quickly fizzled out, with the Persians just capturing a large number of prisoners near the city of Callinicum, which the Romans were currently in the middle of refortifying and hence chose not to defend. It is noticeable, again, that Belisarius did not directly intervene.[14]

This pattern of Roman non-interference repeated itself the next year, when Chosroes launched another major expedition. This was a much shorter incursion, perhaps because the king did not want to offer his opponents extended supply lines to hit. His main target was the rich city of Edessa. Chosroes seems to have extracted a small sum from it in 540 but realized that there was much more to be had. The defenders knew what was coming and were ready to fight. The result, a two-month siege, is related by Procopius with some vigour. The action opened with a battle for the heights above the city, where the inhabitants had left all their sheep. After a lengthy struggle, the Persians were repulsed, and the sheep, as in all the best nursery rhymes, found their own way home. On the eighth day, it got much more serious: the Persians started to build an artificial hill next to the walls to serve when the time was ripe as a fighting platform from which they could bring enough firepower to bear to clear defenders from the neighbouring section of wall so that it could be stormed. For the next few weeks, this was the focus of all the serious action. The Persians built away using tree trunks, uncut stone, and many tons of earth. The defenders used sorties to break up the work and, when that option was cut off, tried to undermine it until the Persians heard the diggers and sank their own countermine. Since mines could potentially offer the attackers a way into the city, the Romans had to stop. Eventually, the defenders covertly undermined just one corner of the mound, closest to the city wall, and filled the hole they made with flammable materials. When the Persians were ready to attack, the fires were lit and continuously fed, all the time with fighting going on above; the Persians tried to douse them until it became clear that the fire was too well established. They were forced to abandon the enterprise. According to Procopius, the flames became so fierce that the smoke could be seen at Carrhae, the best part of fifty kilometres to the south-east. Six days later, Chosroes ordered one last assault but, when that failed, accepted that the city was not going to fall. Negotiations began, and the Persians departed, enriched to the tune of five hundred pounds in weight of gold.[15]

By this point, Chosroes's renewal of war in Mesopotamia had pretty much run its course. The Romans had still not deployed enough field forces in the region to meet him in open battle. Even when Edessa faced its two-month ordeal, no direct help had been sent. But in reality, the

Romans did not need to take that risk. The refortification programme, which had found Callinicum so vulnerable in 542, was advancing apace. The defences of Dara, Singara, Sergiopolis, and a series of other fortified centres were substantially strengthened. On a slightly less military note, Justinian also poured five thousand pounds in weight of gold into rebuilding Antioch.[16] There were now also enough Roman forces in the theatre for it to be impossible for Chosroes to risk the kind of extensive booty raid that had worked well in 540. Let Chosroes expend his cash and soldiers on lengthy sieges of the well-defended cities of Mesopotamia if he wanted to. In fact, the king of kings was well aware of the point and clearly drew the conclusion from Edessa that it was time to call a halt. He had scored astonishing victories in 540, Justinian's prestige was reeling from the destruction of the second city of the empire, and his treasury had been enriched by colossal booty and ransom payments. Both sides were willing, in 545 therefore, to agree a truce to halt the fighting in Mesopotamia; it held, more or less intact, for the next seventeen years until a general peace agreement followed. There were clearly some nervous moments in between. The Arab allies of both sides continued their squabbles all through the 540s and into the 550s as well, until Harith scored a substantial victory over his Lakhmid rival in 554, offering a foretaste of the power of the desert nomad that would find full expression in the seventh century (see Chapter 11). There was also a mass panic in the Roman city of Amida in the winter of 559/60, when rumours of renewed Persian invasion did the rounds. To all intents and purposes, however, the war was over in Mesopotamia by the mid-540s. To understand why it took so long to negotiate a full peace agreement, we need to look elsewhere.[17]

THE GATES OF ALEXANDER

In the medieval *Alexander Romance*, a story whose roots can be traced to the time of Justinian, Alexander the Great chases his enemies north through the Caucasus to a pass between twin peaks known as the Breasts of the World. To keep civilization safe for the future, he decides to imprison the unclean nations of the north, including Gog and Magog of book of Revelation fame, behind a wall of adamantine built between the two mountains.[18] Gog and Magog did not feature much in Roman-Persian relations in the late antique period, but fortifications in the Caucasus certainly did after 395, when a huge Hunnic raid underlined the importance to both empires of securing the potential access routes from the steppes to the north through this mountainous region between the Black and Caspian seas. There were two main routes, but a dozen more in fact that were reasonably easy to cross. Close to the south-western shores of the Caspian lay the city of Derbent, set in a three-kilometre plain. The Persian state constructed mud-brick fortifications here in the fifth century, but Chosroes's father, Khavad, replaced them with twenty-metre high walls, studded with thirty north-facing towers, at the beginning of the sixth. Further west, in the heart of the mountains, lay the Darial Pass. Here the eastern base of Mount Kazbek is pierced through for about thirteen kilometres by the gorge of the river Terek, and it was possible for large forces to get south through the mountains into what is now Georgia and eastern Turkey: the Armenia of antiquity. These routes had become a significant irritant in Roman-Persian relations from the end of the fifth century, with Khavad attempting to force his brother in God, Anastasius, to help pay for the fortifications and garrisons which kept both empires safe.[19]

Aside from issues of strategic defence, Armenia as a whole had become a zone of broader competition between the two empires with the rise of the Sassanian dynasty in the early third century. Geography again dictated its nature in two important ways. First, the mountain chains of Armenia are folded broadly east–west. The valleys between, therefore, provided a number of possible invasion routes for Persian armies looking to break into Asia Minor and the Roman heartlands of Cappadocia. Second, the whole region was mountainous, with populous, fertile valleys often cut off from one another by winter snows. This created a particular political landscape. On the one hand, it was possible for client kings in the region consistently to play one empire off against the other to maximize their own independence. Time and again in the late Roman period, when one of the two great powers tried to establish firmer control over allied territories, local leaders responded by appealing to the other. At the same time, reflecting the region's intense geographical fragmentation, even the client kingships, when looked at under the microscope, proved to be loose, confederative alliances, not centralized polities, so that it was quite possible for subgroups within a notional client state suddenly to seize opportunities for political agency, with a tendency to complicate immediate political relations.

The great-power tension which had flared periodically across Armenia in the third and fourth centuries was defused by a partition agreement in 387, when Theodosius I, hard pressed by Goths, Huns, and western rivals, accepted a division into spheres of influence which massively favoured Persia—Persarmenia encompassing about three-quarters of the whole—and this set the scene, as in Mesopotamia and its desert fringes, for broadly peaceful relations between the two empires for the next century and more. As soon as both sides began to feel less constrained by dangers from the north, however, imperial rivalry was bound to be expressed once again in this region as well. In the reign of Justin and the first bout of hostilities with Persia in the reign of Justinian, the Romans had gained a slight advantage in Armenia, despite the devastating defeat at Callinicum which prompted the Eternal Peace. Following the lead taken by the regime of Anastasius, all Persian demands for annual payments for the upkeep of the garrison and fort at Derbent were firmly resisted. And when Khavad tried to enforce the Zoroastrian religion on the ruling elites of Lazica and Iberia, at the eastern end of the Black Sea, both leaderships—Kings Tzath in 521/2 and Gourgones in 524, respectively—defected to Constantinople as textbook examples of what happens in borderlands where one power can be played off against the other.

Iberia was quickly constrained back into a Persian allegiance, but Lazica remained Roman, an advantage which Justinian had duly consolidated by creating an independent regional military command for Roman Armenia.[20] The different fates of the two regions reflects a basic fact of geographical life. Whereas Iberia could be easily accessed from the main Persian heartlands, Lazica, to the north, was on the other side of the Surami Ridge, a southern extension of the Caucasus range. There were only two passes across it—guarded in antiquity by the Shurapani and Scanda fortresses—and it was a four-day trek by wagon train.[21] As

Chosroes already had some axes to grind in the north anyway, by the late 530s the troop transfers to the west and reduced Roman military spending in the east put war back on his agenda. Then another attractive offer came in from the Caucasus.

Its root cause was the arrogant behaviour of some of the Roman military who had been despatched to Lazica to help maintain its independence against any future Persian intervention. Justinian had caused a stronghold to be built and a garrison established at Petra, at the south-western coastal tip of Lazica. By the 530s, it was under the command of a Roman general named Peter. But he used his position first to establish a nice little monopoly over the grain and salt imports, on which the Lazi depended, and then to rack up prices far beyond the norm. By the late 530s, the Lazi had had enough, and their king, Gubazes, sent encouraging messages of promised support to Chosroes, should he choose to intervene. Where Roman intelligence was reporting, after the disasters of 540, that the king of kings had disappeared from Mesopotamia to deal with an attack of the Hephthalites, he had actually moved a substantial army north to Persarmenia. While Belisarius was making his token demonstration in front of Nisibis in 541, therefore, Chosroes was crossing the Surami ridge north into Lazica, where he received obeisance from Gubazes. His target was the Roman fortress at Petra, which quickly felt the full force of Persian assault. Its garrison put up stout resistance, making one vigorous sortie to destroy a ram, which led to its Persian commander being impaled *pour encourager les autres*. The defenders also beat back an attempt to storm the wall, inflicting considerable losses on their attackers, but in that melee their own commander was killed. At this point the Persians turned to less direct means, employing the same trick that the Edessans would use against the Persian mound two years later. Tunnelling under one of the two key defensive towers, they filled the space with combustible materials and set the whole conflagration roaring. The tower came tumbling down and the Roman garrison asked for quarter. This was granted, but Chosroes could now place a Persian garrison right on the Black Sea. Stung into action, Justinian's commanders responded in 542 with a large expedition directed towards the capital of Persarmenia at Dvin, but a much smaller Persian force exploited the landscape to spring a well-calculated ambush, which sent their opponents running for home.[22]

No further action is then reported in the Caucasus for five years. In part this reflects Chosroes's renewed focus on Mesopotamia and the negotiation of a truce there. It is generally reckoned, too, surely with a great deal of truth, that this must also reflect the impact of the plague. With the truce coming into force in the other theatres of Roman-Persian conflict in 545, however, and the first ferocity of the plague perhaps dying down, Chosroes was ready to return to the offensive in the north by 547. He did so with plans that reached utterly unprecedented levels of strategic ambition and set off a string of complex twists and turns which would make Lazica the centre of great power competition for a decade.

Justinian's brother in God had clearly spent the intervening five years contemplating the new strategic possibilities laid open to him by possession of the fort at Petra. Two related lines of thought emerged. First, at the other end of the Black Sea from Petra lay Constantinople. Constructing a Persian fleet to operate in the Black Sea offered hugely attractive opportunities for ruffling Justinian's imperial feathers. But second, the Lazi, like other client powers of the Caucasus, could not be relied on. As soon as you pressed your authority over them, they immediately made overtures to the other side, and by 547, the Lazi were already feeling restive about the economic effects of being cut off from their normal Black Sea trade networks. The result was a huge campaign for 547, designed to assassinate Gubazes, deport enough of the Lazi to ensure the region's Persian loyalties, and install a much larger Persian garrison in Petra with all the necessary lumber to start constructing ships.[23]

Massively overambitious, Chosroes's plans came to nothing. According to Procopius, lightning struck the assembled timber and set it ablaze, but this sounds so unlikely that you have to wonder if it was sabotage. It was certainly sabotage which ruined the assassination plot. The Persians were planning to use one of Gubazes's enemies among the Lazi, a noble by the name of Pharsanes, to entice the king to Petra where a picked force of three hundred men would eliminate him and his entourage. Sensing that an even better opportunity lay elsewhere, Pharsanes used the information to get back into his king's good books, and the results were utterly predictable. Gubazes switched sides again, calling in Roman assistance.[24] In 548 a Roman army of seven thousand men entered Lazica under Dagistheus, the commanding general in Armenia, tasked with capturing Petra, while a Persian relief force of thirty thousand came in the other direction. Dagistheus was unable to take the fortress and retired in the face of superior opposition, but Petra had become the central focus of the action, and it rapidly became clear that the whole campaign was going to turn on the issue of supply. Lazica relied on food imports anyway, so that additional large armies could not live off the land there, and fighting in Lazica meant massively overextended, overland supply chains for Persian forces. A reinforced Persian garrison of three thousand men, deposited inside the walls of Petra with as many supplies as could be carried, proceeded to strengthen its fortification. Otherwise, all the expedition's commander could do, given the supplies available, was leave behind a minimal covering force of five thousand to overwinter in Lazica and provide further support for the fortress and its garrison. Most of his army then withdrew south over the Surami ridge for the winter, while both sides made preparations for the next year's fighting.[25]

Operating with much shorter supply lines, a combined Roman and Lazi army of fourteen thousand went quickly into action in the spring of 549, long before the snows had cleared to allow the Persian main body to trek back over the Surami ridge from Persarmenia; it decisively defeated the Persian covering force. The Romans then turned back to besiege Petra, but the fort's position and defences, mostly built on solid bedrock, made it extremely difficult to capture. The attackers were also blissfully unaware that the Persians had laid three water courses, one on top of the other, so that when they thought they had cut off the city's main water supply, they had not. Chosroes was also by no means ready to surrender his strategic ambitions, and as the siege dragged on into the summer, another large Persian army moved north from Persarmenia. One element of it was ambushed and defeated by Roman and Lazi forces operating in combination again, but a second force got as far as Petra to break up the siege and resupply the garrison. This was all very well, but the costs of maintaining Petra in the current political-cum-strategic climate were proving colossal: two expeditions were required annually, one of which had to be thrown to the wolves.[26]

To make Petra viable in anything but the short term, therefore, it was necessary to facilitate resupply; the Persians attempted to do this by undermining Gubazes. In 549/50, their diplomacy concentrated on and for a while succeeded in exploiting long-standing tensions to subvert the loyalty of two subordinate allied peoples of the Lazi: the Abasgi and the Apsili. But here too the Persians were operating at the limits of their supply chain, and even this was not enough to prevent the slow shift of the tide of the campaign against Chosroes's interests, despite all the resources he was willing to commit to the war. In the course of 550, new Roman forces and commanders succeeded in bringing the Abasgi and Apsili back on board by a mix of violence and diplomacy. The scene was set for the final extinction of Chosroes's Petra gambit in the following campaign season.[27]

Command of the vital operation went to Bessas, now commanding general of the Armenian field army and an old warhorse of the East Roman military, who received heavy criticism from Procopius for his avaricious and overly cautious command of the defence of Rome in the later 540s (p. 260). By 551, he was over seventy and a bit past his prime, being, as Procopius tells us, rather on the heavy side. At one point he lost his footing in the middle of an attempted assault and because of the weight of his armour could not get up. His guards had to form a shield wall over him while they literally dragged him off the battlefield. Having been helped to his feet again, however, Bessas immediately charged back into the action and hoisted himself up another scaling ladder; there was nothing wrong with his fighting spirit.[28] The task he faced, however, was not an easy one. He was commanding a force of 6,000 Romans up against now 2,300 Persian defenders. The defenders had plenty of water, contrary to what the Romans believed, and they were also powerfully supplied with both weaponry and foodstuffs. When the fortress finally fell, the Romans were astounded to find enough equipment to resupply all of them many times over and enough food for several years: such was Chosroes's commitment to the position. Starving the Persians out just was not an option. But trying to storm Petra posed serious problems. The garrison, an elite Persian force, would not easily capitulate. Most of the fortress's walls rested on solid bedrock, so that tunnelling was not possible, and the ground also sloped uphill towards the walls to such an extent that it was impossible to bring conventional rams to bear with any force. In the end, new lightweight rams were constructed. Not on wheels (to take the slope out of the equation), they could be carried by men hidden inside a protective layer of hides; each ram itself was mounted on chains to be swung with maximum velocity against the walls. Men in heavy protective armour with long poles topped with vicious hooks accompanied each of the rams to help pull down weakened masonry.

When the Roman attack was pressed home, the Persians responded by constructing a projecting wooden tower on top of the walls, which allowed them to drop incendiary bombs on top of the rams. The poles with their hooks then showed a second dimension of usefulness, since they could be used to pull off the fire bombs before they did serious damage. At the same time, Bessas also attacked other parts of the walls with scaling ladders, and some of his men worked their way up the precipitous cliffs overlooking the battlements. In the end, though, it was a freak of nature which turned the tide. High winds caused some of the fire bombs to set the wooden projecting tower alight, and the Romans forced a way into the city in the resulting confusion. By this stage, nearly half of the Persians were already dead: 730 of the survivors were taken prisoner, but another 500 fled to the fort's small acropolis, which the Romans burnt to the ground. There were no survivors. Petra had been taken, and Chosroes's plans to challenge Roman control of the Black Sea went up in the flames.[29]

Not that the king of kings was ready yet to admit defeat. If he could not have the Black Sea coast, then at least he would have the lion's share of Lazica. The focus of the action switched, therefore, to the eastern part of the kingdom and two of its other satellite dependencies: Suania and Scymnia. These had all fallen under Persian control in 551, when the commander of a supposed relief expedition for Petra realized that he was not going to get there in time and changed the direction of his operations. This set the tone for the next five years, which was occupied in a series of sieges of key strongpoints and diplomatic manoeuvres designed to win over—for one side or the other—the loyalties of Lazica's various micro-regions. The fighting was fierce at times, and tensions ran high. By the middle of the decade, Gubazes was so fed up with what he saw as incompetence and lack of resolve that he demanded that Justinian remove most of the Roman commanders. This made two of the generals so angry that they arranged the king's assassination, in September or October 555. In other contexts, this would have immediately sent the Lazi running to Chosroes, but the sides were far too set, and they contented themselves with a temporary refusal to cooperate while complaining to Constantinople, from where Gubazes's younger brother, Tzath, was quickly despatched as a replacement.[30]

The Persians girded their loins for one last major effort. For 556, Chosroes gave his commander, the nakhveragan, a grand total (according to Agathias, whose much less precise narrative we are now following) of sixty thousand men. The Romans and Lazi, supported by a contingent of nomadic Sabir auxiliaries, were commanded by the general Martinus, who had served with Belisarius in Italy. The Persian army advanced down the line of the river Phasis, looking to trap their opponents into a decisive engagement and to detach more micro-regions (particularly Misimia and Apsilia) from existing alliances. The key battle was fought at Phasis (named for the river), the fortress and political centre of the kingdom. The Persians received intelligence that it could be captured easily, but the Romans got there first. Not only did the Persians find Phasis bristling for a siege, but Martinus was able to make a surprise attack with a detached cavalry force of five thousand men, which pushed them into full-scale withdrawal. Once again, there were only enough supplies for the Persians to leave behind part of their army over the winter, and the numerically smaller Roman force was able to reconsolidate control, bringing the micro-regions back onside and recapturing some of the key fortresses which guarded the main route from Persarmenia.[31] This failure was followed by the negotiation of a new armistice in 557, which now included the northern front as well as Mesopotamia. Fundamentally, Chosroes had been beaten by geography. If the Lazi did not willingly adopt a Persian allegiance, then it was not possible for Chosroes to maintain large enough armies in the region for long enough to prevent smaller Roman-Lazi forces from overturning the small gains that could be made in the course of a summer with the limited supplies that the Persians could carry with them over the ridge each spring. The king of kings had devoted huge resources to the task but had not been able to overturn this basic fact of logistics, and his belated acceptance of the inevitable now opened the path to a full-scale peace deal.

PEACE IN OUR TIME

By this stage, the truce had held in Mesopotamia for well over a decade. Negotiated originally for five years in 545, it had been renewed again in 551, but by 557, Chosroes had realized that the returns on his Caucasian adventures were never going to be worth the expenditures they required. Both sides were ready to make a deal, but it took a long time for a full-scale resolution of the complex problems generated by a full fifteen years of conflict to emerge, not least because the solutions necessarily involved so many third parties: from Arabs in the south to the various micro-regions of Greater Armenia in the north. There was also the political problem of selling the deal to home audiences who were used to regarding the opposition not so much as a brother in God as the Great Satan. In 551, the population of Constantinople (or elements within it) was outraged when the Persian embassy to renew the armistice was treated with the kind of diplomatic honours earlier described. Indeed, there is a good chance that it was at this moment that these practices were first adopted. Even the armistice came at a price: two thousand pounds in weight of gold. The Persians were willing to take four hundred a year for the five years of the armistice, but Justinian eventually decided on a one-off payment so that it would not look like tribute.[32]

It was not until 562, therefore, that a full, final, and comprehensive peace agreement, officially to last for fifty years, was ratified. Luckily, a full summary of the terms and conditions survive in the fragments of Menander Protector. The outlines of the deal were straightforward. Clause 1 proclaimed:

> Through the pass at the place called Tzon [the Darial pass] and through the Caspian Gates the Persians shall not allow the Huns or Alans or other barbarians access to the Roman Empire, nor shall the Romans either in

> this area or on any other Persian borderlands send an army against the Persians.

Alexander's adamantine gates had been slammed shut, and in return the Romans paid up, to the tune of just over four hundred pounds weight of gold per annum—not that anyone thought the peace would necessarily last the full fifty years, which made the Persians want as much of the money up front as possible. The Romans were therefore to pay for the first seven years in one lump sum, the next three in another, and only after that revert to annual payments. In terms of borders and spheres of influence, each side agreed to return to the status quo ante bellum, the only disputed zone being the micro-region of Suania, where it could not be resolved whether it really owed allegiance to the kingdom of Lazica or not. The agreements particularly specified that discipline was to return to the desert zone, where the Arab allies of both sides were to be kept firmly in line. The Persians promised to stop complaining about the fortress of Dara—they had been doing so since the time of Anastasius—so long as it was not made the main base of the commanding Roman general in Mesopotamia. With everything now in place, both rulers ratified the treaty, and sacred letters were exchanged.[33]

Taking the long view, Justinian's regime had successfully restabilized all three main sectors of the Persian frontier after the disasters of 540 and 541. The cost, however, was colossal. The destruction of Antioch and huge sums in protection money paid out by the cities of Roman Syria were only one item in an expenditure list, which included the costs of subsequent campaigning, particularly in Lazica, where war carried on for a decade and a half, and of revamping the defences of Mesopotamia, not to mention the new—admittedly only small—cost now of the annual payment for the Persian defences in the Caucasus. Most of this has to be added to the expenditure involved in the actual wars in any attempt to calculate the full cost of Justinian's policy of western conquest. The Endless Peace would surely have come to an end at some point anyway, but Justinian's western adventurism fed longer-term Persian paranoia, in terms of what the new acquisitions might do to Constantinople's tax revenues, while providing an immediate opportunity for a quick advantage by reducing both Roman troop numbers committed to the East's defence and overall military spending there. The fact that war with Persia came when it did and in circumstances which allowed the Persians such substantial immediate gains absolutely must be reckoned a further cost of the western wars, one borne substantially by the local communities in Syria and Armenia, who found themselves both at the centre of the storm of battle and then saddled with the subsequent financial burden of military restoration. These were not the only parts of the empire, however, whose history needs more careful exploration if we are to arrive at anything like an accurate appreciation of the full costs of Justinian's military adventurism.

9

INSURGENTS

BELISARIUS'S CAVALRY CHARGE SWEPT away Vandal rule in just a few months, but when he left Carthage with Gelimer, much remained to be done. Justinian's new North African provinces in Tunisia and Algeria had never been ruled from Constantinople, and their existing governmental system was based on a resident Vandal monarch and manned by functionaries who had prospered through their connections to his court. Justinian sent one highly experienced administrator with the expedition, the patrician Archelaus, who had already filled the posts of chief administrative officer (prefect) both regionally in Illyricum and centrally for the city of Constantinople. His knowledge of taxation, law, and bureaucratic functioning was substantial, but his job was to keep track of the expedition's finances.[1] Resetting governmental structures for the whole of North Africa was a much more difficult task altogether. Besides, when the fleet left Constantinople, neither emperor nor administrator had any real idea of what exactly, if anything, was about to be conquered.

In just a few months, the world turned. Once Gelimer had surrendered and the scale of Justinian's new acquisitions became clear, setting the administration of Constantinople's new provinces properly in order assumed the highest priority. Even before Belisarius's return, detailed regulations were enacted by Justinian on the ides of April 534, which laid out a new set of civilian and military structures. East Roman North Africa became a self-standing administrative unit headed by its own Praetorian Prefect, answerable only to the imperial centre. The prefect was to be equipped with an office staff of 396, comprising everything from lawyers to messengers. Answerable to the prefect but again appointed from the centre, were seven provincial governors, each with a staff of 50. Day-to-day defence was to be handled by six province-level military commanders (*duces*), each with his own *limitanei*.[2] As Western coalitions have found in Afghanistan and Iraq in recent years, however, it is much easier to use advanced military technology to destroy a regime than to erect a functioning alternative. Effective government is not just about putting a workable administrative design in place. The resulting structure will work only if it is based on a set of functioning political relationships with all or at least a critical mass of key constituencies within its domain.

IMPERATOR FOR TEN YEARS

In practice, the new administrative structure itself went some way towards massaging relationships with one key African constituency: the secular Roman landowners, particularly of Byzacena and Numidia, who had been left largely untouched by Vandal settlement in Proconsularis and who had continued to operate their estates within existing Roman legal frameworks under Vandal rule. Belisarius had been willing to execute looters within his own army to ensure that local Roman landowning opinion was not alienated, and the conquest narrative throws up only two examples of Romano-Africans willing to fight tooth and nail for the Vandal cause. Boniface, Gelimer's treasurer, did his best to round up Visigothic support for his embattled king, and Belisarius had to impale a certain Laurus, who tried to suborn his Bulgar mercenaries. Otherwise, the Romano-African landowners seem to have been generally neutral, and the chance was certainly there to win them over to full Constantinopolitan allegiance.[3] For these men, East Roman conquest raised three important issues: security, of course, but also taxation and the distribution of patronage.

This is where Justinian's administrative structures come in. Late Roman bureaucracy did administer things, particularly justice and taxation, but it was also a patronage network, distributing advantage and access to power, at a variety of levels, to a broad range of local landowners (see Chapter 2). Top-ranking officials for the new African administration would come from Constantinople for the foreseeable future, but most of the lower- and mid-level posts were filled by locals. These men and the wide range of more local connections that came with them could all be tied effectively into the new governmental systems of East Roman North Africa by well-judged appointments.[4]

Relations with a second powerful Romano-African constituency, the Nicene Catholic Church, presented, in the first instance, much more of a problem. Here the most pressing issue was what to do about the rival, non-Nicene 'Arian' Church which had prospered under Vandal rule. Geiseric and his successors had fostered it to provide extra internal coherence to their mixed bag of Vandal, Alan, and other followers, particularly once the latter were dispersed across the landscape of Proconsularis in the 440s. Some of the biggest Catholic churches in Carthage were handed over to it, along with churches and their supporting landed endowments in every locality of Proconsularis where Vandals settled. This rapidly turned the Arian Church of North Africa into a rich, property-owning corporation whose congregation was not just limited to the descendants of Geiseric's original following. Even if Huneric's ambitious religious programme of the 480s, to bring the entirety of his subjects—Roman and Vandal-Alan—to a non-Nicene religious persuasion did not work, there were many switches of allegiance, even among bishops, so that by the time of the conquest, the Arian Church was a powerful force within the Vandal kingdom.

Justinian's initial response was cautious. His first edict, which has not survived in the codes (having been made redundant by subsequent developments), ruled out any immediate confiscation of Arian Church properties and ordered that existing Arian priests could be rebaptized as Catholic clergy and retain their existing ranks and dignities. The North African Catholic Church establishment, however, would have none of it. In the first half of 535, it held a church council under the presidency of Reparatus, the new primate of Proconsularis, in the Basilica Fausti in Carthage, symbolically, where Huneric had launched his religious persecution. The council demanded the immediate return of all confiscated Nicene Church properties, refused to absorb rebaptized Arian clergy seamlessly into their own Catholic hierarchies, and demanded a total ban on Arian church services. In the face of this pressure, which was reinforced by the pope to whom the council turned for support, Justinian gave way. Without Vandal military-political backing, the Arian Church was not really a powerful constituency at all, and Justinian quickly jettisoned it. In the summer of 535, he ordered the immediate return of all confiscated church properties to the Catholic hierarchy, denied the rights of rebaptised Arian clergy to hold clerical office, and upheld a total ban on Arian church services.[5]

Unfortunately for Justinian, however, this decision quickly spilled over into a different and much more damaging dispute. The religious enthusiasm of North African Catholic clergy proved too much for about one thousand members of the East Roman army left around Carthage who were themselves Arian and who found themselves on the wrong end of the ban on Arian church services at Easter 536. Easter was the most important festival of the Christian year, when all rites of baptism took place, so the refusal of the African Catholic establishment to allow any Arian services whatsoever prompted intense resentment in an army which was already feeling restive because its pay had fallen substantially into arrears.[6]

Procopius makes no explicit link, but already by the spring of 535, the emperor was preparing his Sicilian and possible Italian expeditions, and Mundus was mobilizing his men to test out Ostrogothic resolve in Dalmatia (see Chapter 6). These preparations involved substantial expenditure, and paying the new garrison of an already-conquered Africa was not high priority. The African army, some of it at least, also had a second financial axe to grind. Most surviving Vandal males of military age had already been shipped off to the eastern front, but many of their women were left behind, most of them falling as booty and captives into the hands of different members of the victorious Roman army. This generated a further financial grievance, because the new governor of East Roman North Africa, the first of its new prefects, Solomon (one of Belisarius's subordinate commanders on the original expedition), refused to treat any of the estates that had previously belonged to Vandal males—the land originally confiscated by Geiseric plus anything acquired subsequently—as anything other than imperial property. With an initial batch of military reinforcements had come two tax specialists, Tryphon and Eustratius, whose task it was to set the fiscal structures of the new prefecture in order; the most important item on their list would have been what exactly to do about all the *sortes Vandalorum* in Proconsularis, which had not been taxed since the 440s and were also now ownerless in legal terms. Having evidently recovered a little from the original shock of defeat, some at least of leftover Vandal women were pushing the new men in their lives to lay claim to their old properties (whether just later acquisitions or also Geiseric's original distributions Procopius does not make clear), but Solomon and his officials were having none of it.[7] By the spring of 536, these financial grievances combined with the ban on Arian services to cause serious disaffection in an army which, despite the initial destruction of the Vandals, which saw Belisarius swanning off to his glorious triumph in Constantinople, had continued to see hard fighting.

The origins of continued fighting lay in a particular feature of the geography of Roman North Africa. Thanks to relief rainfall generated by the Atlas Mountain range, the highly populous and agriculturally rich heartlands of eastern Numidia, Proconsularis, and Byzacena lay in close proximity to an alien world of desert fringes, grassy steppe lands, and more barren uplands that were home to nomadic Berber populations, called Moors in late Roman texts, with economies were much more focused on stock rearing than agriculture. The natural sociopolitical structure of this world, which required a larger area to support a given size of population, took the form of numerous small groupings—tribes, for want of a better word. When the Roman general John Troglita faced a large force of Berbers in 548 on the evocatively named Plains of Cato, it was led by no less than seventeen different chiefs. Given the disparity in wealth but close geographic proximity between agricultural and nomad populations, there had always been endemic low-level raiding throughout the imperial Roman period, but for the most part, relations between nomads and farmers were 'managed' rather than being a source of constant or even large-scale conflict. Berbers came in units too small to pose much of a threat, and anyway, the underlying economic relationship was symbiotic. The nomads needed to exchange the products of their herds for the produce of nearby farmers. The main job of the small-scale forces that the high empire maintained in North Africa, therefore, was to minimize raiding and generally organize necessary exchanges with the minimum of fuss between two worlds that would often intersect through transhumance; for instance, when the nomads were cycling their animals round between blocks of seasonal grazing land.[8]

When the Vandal-Alan coalition captured Carthage in 439, it inherited a network of established relations with these nomads and soon exploited them in new ways. Contingents of Berbers participated in Geiseric's famous sack of Rome in 457 and in the wave of Vandal piracy which hit coastal communities right across the Mediterranean until a comprehensive peace settlement was negotiated between Constantinople and Carthage in the early 470s. After Geiseric's death (25 January 477), however, his successors found it increasingly difficult to exercise the same level of control over at least some of their Berber neighbours. Already in 483/4, Huneric lost control of the Berbers of the Aures plateau region of southern Numidia, which has produced a fascinating inscription:

> I, Masties, *dux* for sixty-seven years and *imperator* for ten years, never perjured myself nor broke faith with either the Romans or the Moors, and was prepared in both war and peace, and my deeds were such that God supported me well.

In an entirely Roman idiom, the inscription expresses Masties's assertion of an independent political authority (*imperator*), based on the will of the Christian God, after a long period as a subordinate *dux*.

There is, as has recently been argued, an extremely good chance—although the inscription lacks a precise date—that this change of status directly reflects the overthrow of Huneric's control over the Aures region (perhaps prompted, given Masties's evident Christianity, by the anti-Nicene persecution that the king had just unleashed). Nor was Masties alone. Right across North Africa in the later fifth century, Berber nomad rulers were showing greater levels of ambition and assembling larger power bases than anything they had previously controlled. Another famous inscription from Altava, far to the west of the Vandal kingdom but dating from the same era, commemorates a 'king of the Moors and the Romans', and a third self-assertive inscription is also known from the Little Kabylia, just beyond the eastern fringes of Vandal Numidia. King Thrasamund (496–523) had to fight campaigns against Moors in Tripolitania in the east in the 510s, and Hilderic's regime ran into serious political trouble when it failed to combat other Berber groupings in southern Byzacena (see Chapter 4). The Vandal crown clearly had not lost complete control of its nomad neighbours by the 530s. As soon as Belisarius entered Carthage, he was greeted by a posse of Moorish chieftains looking for confirmation of the gifts and honours they had already been granted by Gelimer; some Berbers at least pretended that they were going to turn up and fight for the Vandals, even if in practice they stood aside to see who was going to win. But there is no doubting the overall pattern. From the 480s onwards, the Vandals found nomad management an increasingly daunting task.[9]

Why this was so, none of our sources tell us (always supposing that they knew). It is plain, however, that a Vandal monarch sitting in Carthage, with just a few provinces to his name, cut a much less impressive figure to neighbouring nomads than the distant imperial ruler of a global empire. Vandal monarchs also had to guard against their Mediterranean neighbours in a way that had not been an issue for older Roman provincial governors, so that their military assets were necessarily more dispersed. I also suspect that there was an additional factor at play. In many analogous contexts, the injection of new cash flows into a politically fractured world of small-scale groupings has intensely destabilizing effects. One group or another will usually benefit disproportionately from the new wealth—having deliberately positioned itself to do so—and will then use it further to entrench their dominance. This model of political restructuring recurs alarmingly often in the earlier (and sometimes later) phases of recorded human political history. My strong suspicion, therefore, is that in addition to the Vandal monarchs' relative lack of overall impressiveness and evident inexperience in the task of nomad management, the flow of cash which came to Berber participants in the Vandals' military adventures had revolutionary effects. Those who benefited would have employed it at home subsequently to expand their formal and informal political networks, and when these adventures ceased in the 470s, the prime beneficiaries will have needed to replace the cash flow from home-grown sources.[10] Alongside the immediate problems naturally generated by Belisarius's conquest—religious revenge and an army convinced it was not getting its fair share of the spoils—the establishment of East Roman rule in Carthage ran head-on into the more structural problem of a nomad world that had increased massively in political ambition. All of these originally separate problems came together to generate a damaging insurgency of potentially lethal proportions for Justinian's new domains.

As soon as Belisarius left Carthage for Constantinople in the late spring or early summer of 534, serious trouble broke out in the nomad-dominated fringes of Byzacena. Four Berber chieftains went into coalition, and the result was a substantial escalation in raiding through the subsequent winter. Solomon, the new Praetorian Prefect, sent messages to all four reminding them that he held their children hostage. They supposedly replied that they had lots of wives and dozens of children, though this is perhaps Procopius's attempt to underline just how far beyond the civilized pale nomads actually were. Solomon responded in the following spring, but not before his own forces suffered serious losses. Two detached cavalry commands, led by two of Belisarius's most trusted *bucellarii*, Aigan and Rufinus, and totalling around five hundred men, had been deployed to ambush Berber raiding parties in the hope of freeing prisoners and recapturing booty. But they themselves were cut off and exterminated by much larger Berber forces. Rufinus—from Thrace (modern Bulgaria)—was originally taken prisoner, but his captor was so taken by his unusually large head, complete with luxuriant beard and hair, that he cut it off to show his wife.[11]

It was with some trepidation, therefore, that Solomon's forces advanced south from Carthage, and their anxiety was not lessened when they went into action for the first time. Tens of thousands of Berbers (according to Procopius, the confederation could put fifty thousand men in the field) had pulled their camels into a circle, twelve deep, inside which were women and children whom the Berbers (again according to Procopius) customarily brought along on military expeditions to prepare food and weapons. The Berbers themselves were armed with two throwing javelins, a small shield, and swords but wore no defensive armour. Thinking about the fate of Aigan and Rufinus, Solomon's troopers were hesitant, and their horses could not stand the smell of the camels. The Roman ranks fell into disorder as the horses plunged and reared, but Solomon got a grip. Dismounting his cavalry, he ordered most of his army to hold position with locked shields so that the enemy's hail of javelins would have little effect. He himself led five hundred heavily armed and armoured men to attack the rear of the circle. Two hundred dead camels later—this is not a tale for naturalists—they had cut their way inside the circle from behind and the Roman main body advanced. The lightly armed Berbers found themselves trapped between two bodies of heavily armed men with catastrophic results. Procopius says ten thousand died and the rest ran away, leaving women and children and the remaining camels to be taken in triumph back to Carthage.

The campaign, however, continued. Solomon eventually cornered his surviving opponents halfway up the slope of the eastern peak of Mount Bourgaon, separated from its western partner by a substantial ravine. It looked like a stand-off, with the Romans not wanting to fight their way uphill, but overnight Solomon infiltrated a thousand men to the top of the same eastern peak. At dawn, the Berbers found themselves again trapped between two heavily armed bodies of Roman soldiery and ran for it. Their only escape, however, was via the ravine and the western peak of the mountain, which was precipitous enough by itself to cause many deaths among the panicking Berbers and of course slowed them up so much that they were exposed for much longer to the arrows and javelins of their Roman opponents. Again, there was carnage. In the aftermath of the battle, one of the four chieftains, Esdilasas, made his submission to Solomon's authority. The other three fled with their surviving followers to the Aures region in the south of Numidia. For the moment, peace returned to Byzacena, as the other substantial Berber confederation on the fringes of the province, led by Antalas, had remained loyal throughout.[12]

Without respite, Solomon's hard-worked army then shifted its operations eastwards, but this time without the same success. Their destination was the Aures plateau region of modern Algeria. An eastern extension of the High Atlas of Morocco, this rugged stretch of territory comprises a series of peaks more than two thousand metres high, deep valleys, terraced hillsides, and some reasonable upland grazing. Not bad for nomads but highly inaccessible for anyone else, it was the first Berber locality to break free from the Vandals (much more recently it was where the Algerian war of independence began against the French). By the mid-530s, the dominant chieftain here was a certain Iaudas, with a reported following of thirty thousand men. He had already been raiding the excellent adjacent farmlands to the north even before he was reinforced by the surviving rebels from Byzacena. With the assistance of more Berbers, whom he did not really trust, Solomon knew his troops needed to travel light and fast to catch their opponents in upland regions they knew well. Taking only field rations for themselves and their horses, Solomon led his soldiers upwards. Ten days later, the food was pretty much gone, and they had not so much as seen a hostile Berber. All the effort had been for nothing, and it was an exhausted, dispirited Roman army which trekked back to winter quarters in Carthage at the end of 535.[13]

Underpaid and overworked, a thousand of its members deeply resentful at being denied church services and another group simmering with hostility over the land issue, it was an increasingly mutinous body of soldiery now overwintering in the city. Plots formed, even among Solomon's elite guardsmen, and it was decided to kill him in the cathedral on the first day of Easter, 23 March 536. When it came to it, as beautifully described by Procopius, no one could quite bring himself to strike the first blow on either Easter Sunday or Monday. Five days later, however, the mutineers gathered in the hippodrome, and this time there was a big enough crowd to work itself up to a killing spree. After murdering the officers sent to calm them, the soldiers rampaged through the streets of Carthage killing at will, while Solomon, with Procopius and five others in tow, ran for cover. There was a ship in the harbour, but the tide was not right, so they stopped to eat even though Solomon did not want to. Later the same night, the party got itself safely on board and headed for Sicily, where the headquarters for Belisarius's expeditionary force was already installed in Syracuse, awaiting the fateful message from Peter the Patrician (p. 153). Grabbing some cash and a hundred of his most reliable men, Belisarius rushed back to Carthage.

Utter chaos greeted him. About eight thousand mutineers had gathered outside the city, reinforced by a thousand leftover Vandals, including an extraordinarily enterprising party of four hundred who, on their way to the eastern front, had hijacked their ships at Lesbos and returned home. Numerous slaves had also joined in the mayhem. The rebellion now had a leader: Stotzas, originally a guardsman of Belisarius's general Martinus. The rebels were expecting Carthage to surrender the next day, but Belisarius, landing at dusk, arrived just in time. Distributing cash generously—funds, presumably, that had been destined for the projected Italian expedition—the general put together a force of two thousand reliable men from the soldiers still inside the city. At Membresa, about fifty kilometres from Carthage, the two forces came together; after some not very lethal skirmishing, in which only a few of the Vandals seem to have died, the rebels broke and ran. They headed as fast as they could for Numidia and left behind them many of the Vandal women who had been one fundamental cause of the trouble.[14]

That, however, was not the end of the story. As Belisarius was needed for the Italian campaign and there were rumours of possible mutiny among his own men, he could not stay to finish the job. Carthage itself was now safe, but it was to be another year—reflecting the standard reaction time imposed by ancient logistics—before a proper surge could be organized to stamp out the insurgency. It was headed by the emperor's cousin, Germanus, who arrived in North Africa in 537 with few men but plenty of cash. In the meantime, Stotzas had recruited the support of the Berber chief Iaudas and suborned much of the garrison of Numidia, but Germanus had well-laid plans. When he arrived, about two-thirds of the Roman army of Africa was in open revolt. Germanus immediately started distributing back pay, letting mutineers know that, if they returned to the colours, not only would no questions be asked but they would also be paid. Enough trickled back to alarm Stotzas, who decided that he had better have a showdown now, before his army disappeared. The result was the battle of Scala Veteres, about six kilometres from Carthage. Iaudas's Berbers were also present, but they sat on the side again to see who would win. What followed was deeply confusing.

> Neither side could be distinguished either by their own comrades or by their opponents. For all used one language and the same equipment of

arms, and they differed neither in figure nor in dress nor in any other thing whatever.

But it was decisive. Procopius, who was not present, gives us no casualty figures and little detail, but at its conclusion Stotzas fled to Mauretania, far to the west, with only about a hundred followers, the vast majority of them Vandals. The mutineers were either killed or re-enrolled in the army, and all their booty lost.[15]

Germanus had put the Roman army back into some kind of order, and his work was continued by Solomon, when he returned to Carthage as prefect again in 539. On the one hand, there was leeway now to attend to details. The last Vandal women were rounded up and shipped, like their menfolk, out of North Africa. Solomon was also able to tidy up after the mutiny, transferring potentially disloyal soldiers either to Belisarius in Italy or to Constantinople and finding more loyal replacements. Procopius is not explicit, but the implication is that this was being done at least partly by local recruitment. Solomon also began a programme of refortification to protect the agricultural towns which dotted the rich farmlands of the coastal hinterland. Inscriptions and archaeological evidence confirm the reality of Procopius's report, and the whole enterprise was given extra impetus by the prefect's successful pacification of the upland Aures region in 540, a task that had proved beyond him five years before. Procopius does not report that Iaudas had been raiding the adjacent lowlands in the meantime, but Iaudas's control certainly extended over some of the good farming country in its foothills, such as the old Roman legionary colony of Timgad, and Solomon was determined to restore it to imperial control. Faced with the Roman advance, Iaudas withdrew most of his following, not wanting to risk battle, and attempted instead to delay the Roman advance and cause the same kind of difficulties which marred the 535 campaign. This time, however, Solomon was better prepared, probably better informed, too. He confronted and defeated the twenty thousand warriors, at least according to Procopius, that Iaudas had kept with him. Having taken a javelin in the thigh, Iaudas retreated, like Stotzas, to Mauretania, and Solomon established a chain of fortified posts across the Aures to prevent its hostile reoccupation. His men also stumbled across a fortified tower containing all of Iaudas's treasure (and some of his wives), which helped fund the rebuilding of urban defences.[16]

With the successful conclusion of the Aures operation, matters in Africa finally seemed back on track. The chaos of regime change was giving way to regularized governmental structures, deliveries of pay had restored army loyalty, and both bureaucracy and defence forces had begun to recruit locally. The most dangerous Berber confederations had also been restrained. Not only was the Aures region brought back under Roman control, but Procopius notes that a series of submissions on the part of local dynasts meant that the province of Mauretania I was restored to the empire, too. But here, as in other insurgencies, however, just when the fires of rebellion seemed to have died down, a new spark appeared to rekindle the flames of war.

This time, the trouble began in the easternmost provinces of the prefecture, Tripoli and Cyrenaica, governed by Solomon's nephew Sergius, when a further bout of Berber management spun wildly out of control. The local nomads of Tripolitania had turned up in force outside the city of Lepcis Magna in 543/4, to receive, they said, their usual diplomatic gifts. Sergius gave oaths for their safety and invited eighty of the leaders inside the city for a banquet, where he promptly murdered them. Eliminating potentially threatening barbarian leaderships at dinner parties, either by murder or kidnap, was an old Roman habit, so perhaps Sergius did not really believe they had come in peace, but we have no way of knowing the truth. The result, unsurprisingly, was a massive revolt, which was given added impetus when Antalus, leading Berber chieftain in Byzacena, quickly joined in, claiming that his brother had been killed for no reason and that his normal annual diplomatic gifts, too, had been suddenly rescinded. These measures, if Procopius's reporting is accurate, suggest that the good relations which had prevailed between Antalus and the Roman administration in Carthage since 534 were beginning to break down, quite possibly because Antalus's power began to be perceived as a threat.

Solomon gathered his forces but, after some initial success, was defeated and killed at the battle of Cillium, in which the assembled Roman forces lost most of their standards. Procopius was not present, and his account of the action is completely lacking in detail, but that of Corippus blames it on the cowardice of a certain Guntharis, whose desertion caused the entire army to flee, Solomon being surrounded and killed when his horse lost its footing in a ravine. As Guntharis launched a usurpation shortly afterwards, he makes a hugely convenient scapegoat. The catastrophic nature of the Roman defeat is clear enough, however, and the result was a complete lack of any coherent response for the best part of eighteen months, as the situation was reported back to Constantinople and a series of ad hoc improvisations were tried locally. Initially, overall command in Africa devolved to Solomon's nephew Sergius, whose deadly banquet had sparked the revolt. Sergius is reported to have been young, lecherous, and a braggart, and he certainly failed to secure the full cooperation of the battered military. Sensing the power vacuum, everyone with an issue came back to join in the insurrection, not least Iaudas and Stotzas from the depths of Mauretania, the latter followed by the last few tens of Vandals now left in North Africa. This generated a further Roman defeat, although Stotzas himself was killed in the fighting. In due course Justinian sent out the high-ranking Ariobindus, who was married to the daughter of his sister, to Carthage. But he proved no more effective, and Guntharis, one of the remaining senior Roman commanders, responded to the chaos by making his own bid for power. Plan A was for Ariobindus to be frightened out of Carthage, but when he would not go, Guntharis murdered him instead and offered Antalas a deal. Antalas could have Byzacena with fully recognized control of its 1,500-strong Roman garrison, while he would control the remaining provinces himself. Antalas was highly suspicious of the offer, however, and after thirty-six chaotic days Guntharis was himself murdered in turn.[17]

Only with the arrival of John Troglita in the second half of 546 was effective leadership restored. John, a veteran of Belisarius's original expedition, had served as *dux* of either Byzacena or Triploitania down to 540/1, at which point he was transferred to the eastern front, ending up as *dux* in Mesopotamia.[18] In 546, Justinian transferred him back to Africa with promotion to commanding general (*Magister Militum*), and before the end of the year, he had scored one victory in Byzacena, defeating and killing the Berber chief Ierna, with strong support from other Berbers, particularly Cutzinas, whose centre of operations was further west in Numidia and who perhaps was not best pleased to see the return of Iaudas to his old stomping grounds. In the next spring, however, the Berbers of Tripolitania massed again under the leadership of their pre-eminent chieftain, Carcasan; in a first engagement, John was defeated. Corippus trots out the same lame excuses for a defeated hero as Procopius did for Belisarius at Callinicum: the general did not want to fight, but the troops' enthusiasm forced his hand (p. 107).[19] Whether any of it is true is impossible to know, but in the meantime, Carcasan and Antalas had control of rural Byzacena. In 548, however, John came out in force and confronted the full might of Carcasan's coalition on the Plains of Cato. The result was decisive. Carcasan himself and sixteen other Berber chieftains died in action, and their following was routed. With John's great victory, the immediate post-conquest cycle of military mutiny, Vandal rebellion, and Berber insurgency was broken.[20] It had taken little more than six months to destroy the Vandal monarchy but the best part of fifteen years to erect a functioning East Roman regime in its new North African prefecture.

TOTILA THE GOTH

The situation in Italy when Wittigis opened the gates of Ravenna to Belisarius in May 540 bore only a superficial resemblance to North Africa at the time of Gelimer's surrender. In North Africa, a series of bloody defeats had eroded Vandal military manpower, and the Berbers had shown no willingness to take part in the struggle. Belisarius's military dominance was pretty much complete, therefore, certainly over the Vandals, whose effective genocide was completed by the deportation of most remaining males of military age, of whom only about a thousand (including the enterprising four hundred returnees) remained to feature in the extended insurgency which followed Belisarius's departure. The surrender of Wittigis and the Goths of Italy, by contrast, was the result of deception. Belisarius knew that forcing his way into Ravenna would be long and difficult and also, with renewed war against Persia in the offing, that his emperor needed a quick resolution to the Italian campaign. Wanting more than the partition deal that Justinian himself was willing to accept, the general jumped—apparently—at the offer of the crown of Italy to get through the gates of Ravenna.

This solved his immediate problem, but left a much bigger one, as Procopius himself realized, giving us an arresting vignette of Gothic women spitting at their menfolk in disgust as they watched the Roman army march into the city:

> For although the Goths were greatly superior to their opponents in number and in power, and had neither fought a decisive battle since they had entered Ravenna nor been humbled in spirit by any other disaster, still they were being made captives by the weaker army and were regarding the name of slavery as no insult.[21]

In strategic terms, Belisarius had achieved nothing like the same destruction of Gothic military capacity as he had of its Vandal counterpart at the moment of royal surrender. Some Goths had already been deported to the east, where they were about to find themselves fighting Persia, but only a limited number of surrendered garrison forces. Otherwise, not only was Wittigis's main body intact inside Ravenna (far outnumbering the Roman forces Belisarius brought into the city), but other substantial Gothic forces were still at large, too. The king's nephew Urais had one concentrated force in Liguria, the garrisons of the Cottian Alps represented another significant body of fighting men, and there were still more Gothic soldiers to the north-east of Ravenna, in the Venetias.[22]

The situation was delicate in the extreme. The Goths had surrendered only because they thought that Belisarius had agreed to become king of Italy and putative Western emperor. Large-scale conflict—the exact opposite of what the emperor wanted—could easily break out again if Belisarius's opponents realized that they had been tricked. Through the second half of 540, therefore, the general did his best to minimize the chances of renewed fighting. As a first priority, he distributed Roman garrisons to a whole series of cities and fortresses south of the river Po. This not only secured Roman control of the landscape but allowed him to disperse those elements of Wittigis's army of Ravenna whose homes were in the same regions, defusing the situation inside Ravenna, where his own forces were now no longer outnumbered by Goths. He also continued to receive formal surrenders from various local Gothic communities, presumably made by the kind of local leaderships met in Cassiodorus's *Variae* (p. 161).[23] To stabilize the situation fully, he needed to spread a web of Roman garrisons north of the Po as well, both in Liguria and the Venetias. But he did not have enough men and could send only a token force north to Treviso. And since the Persian war had kicked off again (Antioch was being sacked by Chosroes as Belisarius's men were marching through the gates of Ravenna), not only could no further reinforcements be expected from Constantinople but the demands for his own return, along with some of his troops, increased to fever pitch as the months wore on. By December 540, Belisarius had done what he could, and Justinian's demand notes brooked no further delay. Loading up his ships with Wittigis, much of the Gothic court, and his own *bucellarii*, he left Ravenna for Constantinople.

As soon as his departure became known, the remaining Goths realized that they had been tricked, and the embers of potential revolt burst into flames. In the Venetian provinces, Ildebad, with a force of a thousand Goths, quickly defeated the one Roman force north-east of the Po at Treviso, a body of Heruli under Vitalis, in an engagement for which Procopius provides no detail whatsoever.[24] The overall strategic position of the Roman military within Italy had deteriorated to a much greater extent than this one-off reverse might suggest. To start with, Belisarius had taken his *bucellarii* with him to Constantinople, presumably in response to Justinian's desperate demands for troops. Procopius tells us that this force numbered seven thousand men at its maximum but does not tell us when this was.[25] Even if those serving on the Italian campaign had not been so numerous (and the narrative indicates pretty firmly that they were not), they certainly represented an elite element within Belisarius's overall expeditionary force. Both in Africa and Italy, relatively small numbers of elite cavalry made the difference on the battlefield, so that the withdrawal of Belisarius's guardsmen immediately swung the underlying military balance back in the favour of the largely undefeated

Goths, now dispersed in large numbers across the landscapes of central and northern Italy.

Equally important, Roman morale was falling rapidly. As in North Africa, Justinian had quickly dispatched administrators in the aftermath of conquest, this time an individual known as Alexander 'Snips' for his legendary parsimony, as expressed in trimming precious metal from the edges of coins, and particularly in anything to do with the military budget. His central concern, of course, was to get a flow of Italian tax revenues running into Justinian's coffers both to repay the costs of conquest and to make up for some of the horrifying financial losses and necessary military expansion occasioned by the disastrous opening year of the new Persian war.[26] Paying the remnants of Belisarius's conquering army, many now dispersed in penny-packet garrisons across Italy, was only a low priority, with the same basic effect on morale and loyalty that we have already encountered in post-conquest North Africa.

Before an incipient Gothic insurgency could take advantage of the rapidly changing situation, the power vacuum left by Wittigis's departure needed to be filled. There were two obvious contenders: the ex-king's nephew, Urais, who was commander in Liguria, in the north-east, before Wittigis's surrender, and Ildebadus, who had become the focal point for resistance in the north-east, refusing to surrender formally to Belisarius in the summer of 540. His refusal was the reason the general had pushed that small force of Heruli north to Treviso. Initially, Urais deferred to Ildebadus. But power-sharing proved difficult, and when the two fell out, Ildebadus engineered Urais's death. This alienated a significant body of the Goths, who organized Ildebadus's death in return. As Procopius tells it, they hired as hitman one Velas, a Gepid whose Gothic lover had been married off to a third party by Ildebadus during Velas's absence in a Roman prison camp. He cut off Ildebadus's head so suddenly at dinner that his hand was still holding the food as his head hit the ground. For the next five months the kingship was held by Eraric, current leader of the Rugi, who had joined Theoderic's Italian expedition at the last minute (p. 158). Eraric's official platform was to reopen negotiations with Justinian on the basis of reviving the partition deal that had been on the table before Wittigis's surrender. In secret, however (at least according to Procopius), he was ready, à la Theodahad, to surrender the entire kingdom for a comfortable retirement in Constantinople. As suspicions to this effect circulated among the surviving Gothic leadership, they approached Ildebadus's nephew Totila, who agreed in principle to take power, but only if someone else removed Eraric. Eraric was duly killed and Totila declared king of the Goths, probably right at the end of 541.[27]

As the nephew of Ildebadus, Totila was clearly from the network of leading noble Gothic families who had surrounded and occasionally even challenged Theoderic's Amal dynasty. He was also related to Theudis, whom Theoderic had originally sent as his agent to Spain but who had married into enough old Hispano-Roman money to defy his king and play a leading role in negotiating the separation of the Visigothic kingdom from Theoderic's united Gothic realm in 526 (p. 156). After the death of Amalric in 531, he also ended up as the Visigoths' new king, so that the promotion of Totila carried some hope of securing Visigothic assistance in due course. But Totila had more personal attractions, too. Not least, he was a warrior through and through. Before the battle of Busta Gallorum he gave a virtuoso display in gilded armour between the battle lines which held its Roman observers spellbound:

> He wheeled his horse round in a circle and then turned him again to the other side and so made him run round and around. And as he rode he hurled his javelin into the air and caught it again as it quivered above him, then passed it rapidly from hand to hand, shifting it with consummate skill, and he gloried in his practice in such matters, falling back on his shoulders, spreading his legs and leaning from side to side, like one who has been instructed with precision in the art of dancing from childhood.[28]

Clearly he would have made one hell of a polo player, but even more important, he was energetic and highly intelligent and had the distinct advantage of being held in high regard by a broad cross-section of leading Gothic opinion. His stock was set for a rapid increase as the new campaigning season opened in the spring of 542.

Having kept a close watch on all this internal Gothic politicking, the Roman military command in Italy realized that the murder of Eraric meant that those who favoured war over negotiation had returned to power. To nip matters in the bud, an expeditionary force of twelve thousand men was mobilized, advancing north from Ravenna to Verona, where a local sympathizer let an advance party into the city which secured and then opened the southern gates. Its small Gothic garrison initially fled but then observed that the main Roman army had not moved into the city, halting some distance away. According to Procopius, its eleven different unit commanders (perhaps reflecting the effects of unpaid salaries) were too busy arguing over how to divide all the booty that was coming their way. The Goths returned, shut the gates, and trapped the Roman advance party, who were forced to jump from the walls. With Verona's gates now firmly shut, the Romans retreated back towards Faenza, where they camped south of the river Senio. Totila came after them with five thousand men, everyone he could currently muster. Crossing the river, he gave battle but then sprang his surprise. He had sent three hundred cavalry on a longer route to hit the Romans in the rear. The battle quickly became a rout, with heavy Roman casualties, lots of prisoners, and the loss of nearly all the standards:

> As for the [eleven] commanders, each one of them as he could fled with only a few men, and finding safety in whatever cities they happened to reach, they continued to guard them.[29]

The dose was repeated shortly afterwards just outside Florence, which Totila's army had put under close siege, drawing out another large Roman relief force. In the resulting battle, rumours that the Roman commander (Belisarius's old nemesis, John the nephew of Vitalian) had been killed spread enough panic to cause the entire army to run. Once again, it fragmented into its constituent units, dispersing under individual commanders to a series of fortified strongholds.[30] By inflicting two substantial initial defeats on the only kind of field armies that the Romans could now assemble, Totila set a pattern for his insurgency, which held for the rest of the decade.

In essence, Totila's early victories reversed the strategic situation which had prevailed in Italy since the moment Belisarius unleashed his cavalry reinforcements to break up the Gothic siege of Rome (p. 171). At that point, Wittigis still controlled many thousands of mobilized Gothic warriors but was forced to disperse so many of them as garrison forces, in the face of the mobile hitting power of the elite Roman horse troopers, that he lost the military initiative, being largely relegated subsequently to responding to whatever moves Belisarius chose to make. After the defeat and dispersal of the last viable Roman field forces available in the peninsula in 542, Totila's forces had freedom to conduct whatever offensive operations they wished, reinforced, not surprisingly, by a large flow of recruits after the huge boost to Gothic morale of two victories in the field: the first won by any Gothic army since the war began in earnest in 536.

To exploit this freedom of manoeuvre fully, Totila's strategy encompassed several related lines of action. First, pressure was progressively brought to bear on the isolated Roman garrisons which now dotted the Italian countryside south of the Po. Those on the coast could sometimes be supplied from the sea, but inland forces relied on surrounding farmlands and were vulnerable to siege.[31] In these cases, Totila consistently offered generous surrender terms, often allowing Roman garrisons under pressure to set a future date when they would capitulate if not resupplied in the meantime. Desperate as he was for military manpower, Totila also generally offered surrendering garrisons, as well as prisoners taken in his first two battlefield successes, the opportunity to join his Gothic army on equal terms to its current manpower. Many took this path, but Totila also allowed those who did not want to join him to depart in safety, sometimes even providing them with the necessary supplies.[32] Simultaneously—the lines of action overlapped—he looked to bring ever larger tracts of Italy under his administrative control, so that their tax revenues could fund his war effort. This meant, of course, eliminating the major Roman bases and garrison forces that stood in his path.

The strongholds of Caesena, Urbinus, Mons Feretris, and Petra Pertusa quickly fell to Totila in the aftermath of his two initial victories in 542, at which point he moved south of the Tiber into Campania and Samnium, where he captured Beneventum and put Naples under siege. At the same time, other forces spread out to capture Cumae and the remaining strongholds of Campania and bring all of southern Italy (Lucania, Bruttium, Apulia, and Calabria) back under Gothic control. At Naples, Totila's aim was twofold: secure southern Italy in general, but also win control of an important naval base from which he could cut off the maritime supply line from Sicily to Rome. The city's garrison consisted of a thousand Thracians and Isaurians but quickly ran short of supplies. Two relief fleets were organized, but the first, carrying mostly grain from Sicily, was wrecked by a storm, and so much of it fell into the hands of the Goths. The second, which came from the east with both supplies and extra troops, arrived off the Italian coast after substantial initial delays but put into Rome. There it remained, until Demetrius, the governor of Naples, sailed single-handed to Rome to persuade its commander to move on to Naples. Unfortunately, this effort came to grief, too, when it tried to land, ambushed by the Gothic besiegers who were keeping tight watch on the city. This was particularly unfortunate for the brave Demetrius. He had been very free with his insults of Totila from the walls of Naples, so the king took his revenge: cutting off his hands and tongue before turning him loose. Back inside the walls, the food was fast running out, and in the absence of any relief, its garrison surrendered in the spring of 543. Totila sent those who wanted to off to Rome, supplying them from his own stores, and then tore down the city's walls so that it could not be used against him again. On the Gothic side, the rest of 543 was spent tightening the king's grip on the south by besieging the few remaining Roman garrisons, such as that of Hydruntum (Otranto), and in starting to build pressure around Rome itself. At the same time as a large Gothic force moved up towards the city and laid siege to nearby Tibur (modern Tivoli), Totila made written overtures to the Senate, looking to win support for a restoration of Gothic rule. These were rebuffed and all the Arian clergy in the city expelled in response, for fear that they might become a Gothic fifth column.[33]

As news of these defeats filtered back to Constantinople, Justinian decided, the initial ferocity of Persian attack having subsided, to send Belisarius back to Italy at the end of 543, but he would not allow him to take his *bucellarii*. General and emperor did cobble together four thousand reinforcements, Belisarius even using some of his own money. But this was a scratch force, neither sufficiently numerous nor of high enough quality to allow the Romans to contest Totila's control of the initiative. All Belisarius could do was deploy it piecemeal over the next year to reinforce threatened positions. A thousand men were initially sent to Auximum at the head of the Via Flaminia but quickly withdrawn again, since all they were likely to do was use up the garrison's limited supplies more quickly. Belisarius also sent an extra five hundred men to Portus but could not get them into Rome itself as its commander, Bessas, was unwilling to risk the necessary diversionary sortie. Hydruntum, at least, highly accessible by sea, was successfully reinforced, but an attempt to retake Bologna proved unsuccessful when an underpaid contingent of Illyrian troops, hearing of large-scale raids on their Balkan homelands (see Chapter 10), simply upped sticks and left. Belisarius found the whole experience deeply frustrating. Throughout 544 and the following year, too, he was constantly asking Justinian at least to release his guardsmen from the eastern front.[34]

The emperor wanted no repetition of the disasters of 540, however, and the troops stayed put. In consequence, Totila's freedom of manoeuvre could not be contested, and the middle years of the decade saw Gothic forces strengthen their hold on key strongpoints on and around the Via Flaminia. By the end of 545, Firmum, Asculum, Assisi, Clusium, Spoleto, and Auximum were all in Gothic hands. All except Auximum had been starved into surrender, and many of the garrisons switched allegiance to Totila. Only Perugia held out. Tibur, too, by this point had fallen under Totila's control, and the naval patrols he had established at Naples and in the Aeolian islands had intercepted at least one large grain fleet en route from Sicily to Rome.[35] By late 545, therefore, the scene was now set for another siege of Rome.

Procopius was by now writing his histories in Constantinople, not peering over the battlements at hordes of besieging Goths. Nonetheless, his account of this second siege is not only clear but contains some wonderful flashes of life. The basic situation was straightforward. Rome contained a reasonably large garrison of over three thousand men, but the Goths had held Tibur for over a year now, which, combined with the naval patrols from Naples, meant that they had been able to block most attempts to resupply the city, and provisions were running short. To start with, the garrison itself had plenty of food in the military storehouses, and for a while a busy black market enriched the soldiers (especially, Procopius says, their commander, Bessas). But soon even the military storehouses started to empty. Most of the civilian population was expelled, and the garrison itself started to go hungry.[36] Desperate times call for desperate measures, and Belisarius had a plan.

One Sicilian grain fleet had made it as far as Portus, where the general was now based. The trick was how to get the food its final twenty-five kilometres up the river Tiber and into Rome. To carry it, Belisarius had a fleet of two hundred river transports, which he equipped with fire ports for his archers. In the way were Gothic pickets, a great iron chain laid across the river, and the biggest obstacle of all, a fortified bridge with towers from which Gothic bowmen could rake anything trying to force a passage. To deal with this, Belisarius lashed together two more boats, constructed on top of them a higher tower than those on the bridge and added a small boat full of highly flammable material. His one concern was that the Goths would take advantage of the armada's departure to break into Portus, cutting the Romans off not only from the one stronghold they still held in the region (apart, of course, from Rome itself) but also from their lifeline to the sea: complete catastrophe. The operation began well. The fleet and its covering forces on both banks fought their way upstream against the current; they drove off the Gothic pickets and even managed to haul the chain out of the river. Even better, the napalm dinghy then did its job on the fortified bridge, setting off a conflagration which consumed its garrison of two hundred Goths. Then disaster struck. Reports came in to Belisarius that Isaac, the lieutenant he had left in charge at Portus, had been defeated. Supposing that the Goths might be cutting him off as he feared, Belisarius turned the whole armada round and retreated downstream. In fact, they were not. Isaac had been defeated, but only in a small, unauthorized sortie of his own. Roman Portus was intact. But by now the Gothic army was fully mobilized, and it was not possible to restart the relief operation.[37] The chance was lost, and no supplies could be got into the city. Garrison morale began to plummet, and Totila set to work on a small group of Isaurians who controlled the Asinarian gate. On 17 December 546, they opened it and let the Goths into the city. Most of the garrison left by the opposite gate, and there was little fighting. Twenty-six soldiers and sixty civilians lost their lives, but by now there were only five hundred of the latter in the city anyway.[38]

Having finally taken Rome, Totila made a fateful choice. Deciding not to hold it, he dismantled about a third of its wall circuit and destroyed the gates to render it indefensible. This was all about manpower. Rome required a much larger garrison than Totila could spare, and despite his many successes, the king was feeling the pinch. While the siege of Rome was in progress, he had decided to hand over his Venetian provinces to the Frankish king Theudebert to free up more Goths for Italy from garrison duties there. After it was over, he sent ambassadors to Constantinople to start peace negotiations.[39] Totila clearly grasped the realities of his position. His run of success, astonishing as it was, was largely dependent on what was happening out in the east. Many thousands of East Roman troops remained in Italy, and if Justinian could only reinforce them once more with an effective field army, the delicate military balance would swing decisively back against the Goths, just as quickly as it had in the spring of 538. For Totila, the fall of Rome was not an overture to total victory but a means to bring Justinian to the negotiating table.

In response, Belisarius enjoyed the best moments of his second Italian tour of duty. In April 547 his forces reoccupied Rome and spent twenty-five days repairing the walls. Alarmed, Totila hurried south to find the battlements serviceable but, as yet, no gates. A series of hard fights then followed with Belisarius's troops deploying the *munitiones* recommended in the military manuals (p. 55) to help keep Gothic cavalry away from the unbarred gate openings. Once replacements were fitted, Rome was securely (East) Roman once more. The loss to Totila, apart from the men killed in trying to force a passage back inside the city, was mainly one of prestige rather than strategic position, although it is reported that this failure to hold on to the city counted against him later, when he was trying to secure a Frankish marriage alliance. Once he had accepted that Rome was definitively lost, Totila spent the rest of the year in relatively minor operations. Tibur was refortified to ensure against any offensive operations on the part of Rome's new garrison, and he took as many senators as he could round up under guard to Campania. For his part, Belisarius continued to badger Justinian for reinforcements.[40]

In December, Belisarius finally received a message that the first serious East Roman reinforcements in four years were on the way: over two thousand men, including a thousand *bucellarii* of Valerian, the commanding general in Armenia. Taking nine hundred of his own best men, Belisarius sailed to meet them at Taranto but was blown off course to Crotone, where three thousand Gothic cavalry lay in wait to destroy part of his command. But while heavy fighting still continued in Lazica at this point, Justinian was increasingly confident that the current truce was going to hold firm in Mesopotamia and, as a result, found more reinforcements. Early in 548, two thousand infantry arrived in Sicily, in addition to Valerian's command. For the moment, this was still not enough for a field army which could win the war and for which Belisarius continued to press, sending his wife, Antonina, back to Constantinople in the summer to use her considerable influence with her old friend the Empress Theodora. So while certainly encouraging, the renewed flow of reinforcements still had to be used to fight whatever fires Totila chose to light. In 548, this meant properly securing Rome, whose garrison received substantial reinforcement, and trying to relieve the hard-pressed garrison of the port city of Rusciane. Here, too, Belisarius's efforts ended in frustration and failure. His relief fleet was first scattered by a storm and then prevented even from landing by Gothic counteraction. In the end, towards the end of the year, the unsupported garrison had to capitulate, and Belisarius, seemingly at his own request, was recalled to Constantinople. As he left Italy, in the winter of 548/9, Perugia, last Roman bastion along the Via Flaminia, surrendered.[41]

Worse was to follow. In the summer of 549, Totila returned to Rome. The Franks had now taken possession of the Venetian provinces, and its former Gothic garrisons reinforced his army. This time, Portus fell quickly to the Goths so there was no hope of maritime resupply. Again an Isaurian contingent within the city's garrison proved unreliable, allowing Totila this time through the gate of Paul the Apostle on 16 January 550 (See Figure 9.1), even though there were by now so few people in the city that the garrison could support itself by growing grain inside the walls. Some of

FIGURE 9.1
The Porta San Paolo, one of the southern gates in Rome's Aurelian Walls; unpaid Isaurian soldiers opened them to Totila in 549.
Credit: Art Resource, NY

the defeated, unpaid garrison switched sides, as apparently did the garrisons of Taranto and Rimini, both of which surrendered shortly after (and perhaps because of) the loss of Rome. The Gothic king also increased his naval capacity through captured East Roman shipping. As the siege of Rome had dragged on in the summer and autumn of 549, he was able to deploy a raiding fleet, commanded by Indulf, a deserter from the East Roman army, to ravage the coast of Roman Dalmatia. After Rome's latest fall, however, these naval assets were redeployed, in a dramatic escalation of the war, to transport substantial Gothic forces to Sicily, which they happily ransacked for booty and supplies through most of 550.[42]

This was the high-water mark of Totila's insurgency, but despite enjoying much greater success than Wittigis, he never lost sight of the fact that absolute military victory was impossible. Immediately after his second capture of Rome, therefore, Totila sent a third embassy to Justinian, offering to cede Dalmatia and Sicily, to pay an annual tribute, and to provide Constantinople with military support.[43] Totila understood that without face-saving gains, Justinian would never be persuaded to end the war, and it was overwhelmingly in the Goths' interest to persuade him to do so. The renewed flow of (some) better quality East Roman reinforcements into the peninsula from 548 must have acted as one reminder of underlying strategic realities, but he was already aware of another, much more ominous development.

As news filtered through to Constantinople in the spring of 550 that war had spread to Sicily, Justinian responded in two ways. A fleet and relief force were to sail there directly. Given the usual limitations on the speed of information flows and logistic response in the ancient world, it was pretty good going that the fleet was ready to leave by the end of the year. Much more important, the emperor also appointed his cousin Germanus, another nephew of the Emperor Justin, to mobilize a much larger expeditionary force. This was a significant choice. It was Germanus who had commanded the successful North African surge of 537 which had quashed Stotzas's mutiny (p. 247). At the moment of appointment, Justinian still did not have many spare troops, but he did supply Germanus with a great deal of cash, which, as in Africa, was deployed to good effect. Raising his banner in the Dalmatian coastal city of Salona, Germanus began to assemble an army: some regulars to start with, along with a thousand Lombard mercenaries, but numerous recruits soon flocked in. Procopius claims that prior to Germanus's appointment—through the 540s in other words—Justinian had simply not been interested in what was happening in Italy. This is palpably unfair. It was not a lack of interest which prevented him from responding to Totila but the Persian war, and it was the slow easing of the situation in the east that now made it possible to devote more resources to Italy. By 550, negotiations to extend the truce in Mesopotamia were already under way; the huge costs to the Persians of continued warfare in Lazica had become clear. As far as Justinian was concerned, Chosroes could wear himself out on the Surami ridge for as long as he liked. This made any renewal of large-scale campaigning in Syria impossible and gave the emperor a chance to pay serious attention to Italy. Procopius reports that Germanus's appointment quickly became known to those Roman units in Italy who had swapped sides to the Goths on surrendering their forts for lack of pay and supplies. As with the mutineers in Africa, Germanus let it be known that those who swapped sides again would be paid off, no questions asked, and he received several approaches from individual units. If this was known to Roman soldiers in Italy, you can be sure that Totila, too, was aware of what was unfolding at Salona which explains why, even at the height of his military success, the king redoubled his efforts to negotiate peace.[44]

Justinian rejected all the Goth's diplomatic overtures, however, even when events did not quite work out as planned. Germanus died in harness at Salona before the end of the year. By April 551, after some indecision, Justinian gave control of the expedition to the eunuch Narses, long a trusted confidant of both the emperor and his (now-deceased) wife. It was this same Narses who had gone into the Hippodrome to pay off the Blues at the height of the Nika riot, so there was no doubting his courage. And where Germanus had just received money, Narses was given both money and soldiers. As 551 was the year in which Bessas finally captured the Persian fortress of Petra in Lazica (p. 230), Persia could make no more than minor tactical gains in the Caucasus, so Justinian felt much more confident again about shuffling substantial forces back to Italy. Hence Narses was allocated East Roman regulars from the Thracian, Illyrian, and central praesental field armies, together with an enormous force of 5,500 Lombard mercenaries and another 3,000 Heruli *foederatii*. In the face of this build-up, Totila tried to up the ante. In 551, his raiding fleet, now comprising three hundred ships, was unleashed first on Corfu and the Sybota islands and then hit the Balkan coastal cities of Nicopolis and Anchialos. Back in Italy, the main action of the year was a Gothic siege of the East Roman base at Ancona, which came to nothing. Worse, when a Gothic fleet of forty-seven ships tried to intercept a Roman naval force, thirty-six of them were destroyed with all hands. Procopius notes that since Totila had manned the fleet with a large number of his elite warriors, its destruction hit Gothic morale hard.[45]

Nor was this the only reason for fading Gothic morale. There was always plenty of maritime traffic back and forth across the Adriatic, and just as the significance of Germanus's appointment had quickly become known in Italy, the Goths must have soon become aware of the military juggernaut that Narses was preparing to lead in their direction. Since Justinian was showing not the slightest inclination to negotiate, Totila had no choice but to fight it as best he could. Probably in April 552, Narses's advance began. En route, he learned that the Goths' Frankish allies, who held the Venetias, were not willing to allow his army passage. Totila's trusted lieutenant Teias had also blocked the main roads and was ready to harass and ambush the Roman army at will. Renewed Roman naval supremacy (the result of the Goths' defeat off Ancona) made it possible to bypass both impediments, however, by moving the army along the Adriatic coast all the way to Ravenna, since the ships could quickly form pontoon bridges to get the army across the many river mouths. It took a while, but Narses entered Ravenna on 6 June and, after a nine-day halt, continued his advance. The first armed encounter of the campaign occurred on the bridge at Rimini, which the Goths had damaged to restrict the number of opponents who could cross at any one time. The stratagem worked for a while, but once the garrison's commander was killed, Narses's men successfully forced it and entered the city.[46]

Totila, who had been mobilizing and preparing his forces, advanced to Tadinum on the Via Flaminia. Because the Goths now held Petra at its northern end, Narses took the coast road further south before turning west into the mountains. He camped in the Apennines near Busta Gallorum, about twenty kilometres from the Goths. The next day the two armies came together, and battle could begin but not immediately. First, Totila showed off his horsemanship (p. 255). He was playing for time so that a final detachment of two thousand Goths could arrive. Then the Goths disappeared for lunch (Narses's men ate in formation), and finally all was set. The Roman army was arranged with the dismounted Heruli and Lombards forming a strong centre, and the regular cavalry in a crescent on each flank, fronted on each side by groups of four thousand foot archers. The key moment in the battle was a full-on charge by the Gothic cavalry, the elite of Totila's army:

> Orders had been given to the entire Gothic army that they should use neither bow nor any other weapon in this battle except their spears.

The idea, presumably, was to close quickly on the Roman line and break it in one fell swoop. The result was disastrous:

> In making their charge against their enemy's centre, the [Gothic cavalry] placed themselves in between the eight thousand [Roman] infantry, and [were] raked by their bowshots from either side.

The cavalry charge was broken up before it could inflict serious damage on the Roman line, and its retreat prompted a general rout, since, as Procopius gloats, the Goths were not used to integrating cavalry and infantry on the battlefield, and the return of the routed horsemen just made the infantry run, too. He also reports that the Goths left six thousand dead on the battlefield, a casualty count which quickly mounted with the subsequent execution of all prisoners. Totila himself died in the fighting, being mortally wounded either on the battlefield itself or, in the story Procopius prefers, while running away afterwards. In this account, his bodyguards buried him quietly but were being watched by an old woman who told his Roman pursuers where Totila lay. They dug up his corpse to make sure.[47]

In the aftermath of his devastating victory, Narses quickly occupied Rome, subduing all the remaining Gothic garrisons both along the Via Flaminia and in Tuscany. Many of these were actually unpaid, ex-Roman soldiers who were happy to return to the colours. But still the insurgency had not quite run its course. Teias, offered the crown by the surviving Gothic leadership, gathered as many of the remaining Goths as he could at Pavia. The new king realized that he had not a hope without outside help, since the Goths on their own no longer possessed sufficient military manpower to challenge Justinian's armies. The obvious potential allies were the Franks, but they would fight only for cash, and Totila had left most of his treasury inside the coastal fortress of Cumae in Campania, together with most of the senatorial and other high-status Roman hostages whom Teias had killed. The scene of the action quickly switched to the south, therefore, with Teias manoeuvring his available forces to avoid Narses's army around Rome and get in position to harass any attempt to besiege Cumae. If he could only hold on until the Franks arrived to collect their payment, then some kind of a Gothic kingdom might still be saved.

When Narses finally caught up with the Goths, the confrontation developed into a stand-off on either side of the river Dracon on the slopes of Mount Vesuvius. For two months, the Goths continued to receive supplies by sea, but when this was cut off and still the Franks had not come, they realized that they had to fight. This time it was an infantry battle with Teias at the front. His opponents recognized him and looked to bring him down. But surrounded by his bodyguards, he was a formidable opponent. Eventually there were twelve javelins in his shield, and he could not move it. Just as he was swapping it, an unlucky thirteenth hit him in the chest, killing him instantly. The Romans stuck his head on a pole and paraded it up and down the battle line. But the Goths kept on fighting until dusk on that day and all through the next. Only then were they ready to negotiate, and Narses was willing to offer an armistice.[48] Organized Gothic resistance had finally been broken. With the Ostrogoths destroyed as a coherent military and political force like the Vandals before them, never again would the East Romans face a Gothic army on an Italian field of battle. The task that was apparently complete with Belisarius's coup de théâtre had been finished the hard way. Nearly twenty years after the bloodless seizure of Sicily, imperial domination had finally been established over the Ostrogothic kingdom.

10

THE WESTERN EMPIRE OF JUSTINIAN

THE EMPEROR JUSTINIAN OUTLIVED the final two kings of Ostrogothic Italy by over a decade and died on the night of 14/15 November 565 at the extraordinary age of eighty-three. Belisarius, his great general, had died the previous March, and Peter the Patrician, the East Roman 007 charged with optimizing conditions for the fateful invasion of the Italian mainland, passed over the following winter. Within the space of just a few months, three key architects of the western conquest policy—emperor, general, and diplomat—all departed the Constantinopolitan stage, power there passing to Justinian's nephew Justin II, the middle-aged son of Justinian's sister Vigilantia. Justin in turn had married Aelia Sophia, the niece of Justinian's wife, Theodora.

The new regime organized a suitable send-off. Justinian's body was embalmed with costly spices, so that it would 'last forever', as the poet Corippus tells us, and wrapped in a gorgeous embroidered robe which recorded all his great achievements, although the only image specifically mentioned is one of him treading the Vandal king Gelimer underfoot. After lying in state in the palace, the coffin lid was finally closed but not before Justin kissed his uncle goodbye with the words (again as reported by Corippus), 'You my venerable father, you are joyful far off in the ranks of angels; having now left your body you see God.' Then in solemn procession, the entire court—royal family, dignitaries, bureaucrats, soldiers, and senators—drawn up in their jealously guarded rank order by status, followed the bier out of the palace to Justinian's great Cathedral of Hagia Sophia. Women tore their hair, choirs sang, and the emperor was eventually laid to rest in the golden tomb that Justinian had himself prepared as his final resting place. At the funeral banquet which followed, the gold and silver plate again depicted the emperor's victories, and the imperial robe worn by his successor was fastened with a brooch festooned with jewels looted from the royal treasuries of the Vandals and Ostrogoths.[1]

Constantinople had given the self-proclaimed 'conqueror of many nations' an appropriately grandiose funeral, entirely in tune with the image the emperor had fought hard to sustain throughout his long and eventful reign. Leaving aside all the dramatic twists and turns of these epic campaigns and the splendour of the imperial capital that rose from the ashes of the Nika riot, is it possible to come to some kind of summary judgment on the overall impact of Justinian's extraordinary reign on the course of Roman imperial history? If so, what should it be? Did the emperor's western conquests stretch Constantinopolitan resources so thin that they actually paved the way for disastrous imperial collapse in the early seventh century?[2]

Procopius's overall judgment on the expansionary wars of the Emperor Justinian could not be clearer. The final sentence of the *Vandal Wars* is unequivocal:

> Thus it came to pass that those of the Libyans who survived, few as they were in number and exceedingly poor, at last and after great toil found some peace.

This comes in the *Histories*, which were published openly, so that it is no surprise to find a still more damning (or perhaps just fuller) exploration of the same theme in *Anekdota*. It begins with an overview:

> To state exactly the number of those who were destroyed by him would never be possible, I think, for anyone whomsoever, or for God. One might more quickly, I think, count all the grains of sand than the vast number whom this emperor destroyed.

And then it moves on to a quick survey of different parts of the empire, beginning with Justinian's two main additions to it. North Africa, we are told, 'has been so thoroughly ruined that for the traveller who makes a long journey [there] it is no easy matter ... to meet a human being.' As to what followed in Italy, '[I]t has become everywhere even more destitute of men than North Africa.'[3] Justinian's conquest policy may have added new territories to the empire, but the sustained violence which made them Roman had also left them so utterly devastated that they constituted no worthwhile addition to the portfolio of territories ruled from Constantinople.

Viewed from a human perspective, it is impossible to disagree with Procopius. Historians have sometimes approached Justinian as one of history's great romantics, desperate to return the Roman Empire to its glorious apogee. The reality is more prosaic. Western expansion began as a desperate gamble to save Justinian's imperial skin, only slowly evolving into an actual policy when the degree of immediate battlefield advantage enjoyed by the new model East Roman field army of the sixth century became clear. All the many thousands of human beings who died, as these processes unfolded, were killed to satisfy the short-term political agendas of an autocratic ruler who cared not one jot for the fate of anybody outside his immediate circle. Of course, this phenomenon has not disappeared from the modern world, and there is a nasty way in which the tragic realities of human loss—which really should be the perspective of paramount importance—become lost as soon as any other levels of analysis are introduced.

Does Procopius's condemnation have validity at the level of the East Roman state, as well as that of individual humans? Did Justinian leave his successors a poisoned chalice: an enlarged but structurally weakened empire that was ripe for collapse? As a historian of the late Roman period, it is my task to think systematically about these questions and Justinian's conquest policies.

THREE CHAPTERS

In North Africa, the apparently swift victory of 533/4 proved illusory. Teething troubles with the Catholic Church, leftover Vandals, and Roman soldiers short of pay had quickly given way to the main event: confrontation with the Berbers, amongst whom the dislocations of Vandal rule had stimulated a new capacity for large-scale predatory ambition towards the agricultural assets at the heart of Justinian's new prefecture. All this had taken the best part of a decade and a half to resolve and had involved huge numbers of casualties until the victories of John Troglita stabilized the situation. The Vandal-Alan elite of maybe fifteen to twenty thousand households had ceased to exist, extinguished either on the battlefield or by forced deportation, which started with males but was soon extended to women as well, most of the latter reduced to slavery. Most of the children of these families presumably also ended up as slaves, although Procopius does not tell us much about them. He does tell us rather more about the Berbers, and if his figures can be believed, several tens of thousands of Berber males were killed between 534 and 548, with, again, many women and children being reduced to slavery. And then there is the settled agricultural population of indigenous Romano-Africans.

> The wretched ploughmen wept as they fled, to see the enemy unyoke their cattle and drive them away, and all their houses were destroyed with all they contained. The poor were not the only victims of this disaster for they sank beneath it with the wealthy beside them. . . . On all sides, in a frenzied rage, the bandits set fire to cities and fields.[4]

Corippus is obviously giving us a few poetic images to be getting on with here, but the nasty realities of raiding have to be taken seriously. Even though the African insurgency generated nothing like the sustained intensity of the Gothic war, many people were dead by 548 who would have lived still had Justinian not decided to save his political skin by sending Belisarius to North Africa. What, however, about the longer term? Did the North African prefecture become a useful, productive contributor to the balance sheet of empire?

On the negative side, the Berber problem did not and could not disappear. Detailed narrative sources give out with the victories of John Troglita, but briefer chronicle sources give us one interesting final vignette to think about. In January 563, Troglita's greater Berber ally, Cutzinas, celebrated by Corippus for his great loyalty to the Roman cause, went to

Carthage to collect his usual annual gifts from the current prefect, John Rogathinus. The prefect refused to pay and murdered him instead, at which point Cutzinas's children rebelled.[5] The source says nothing more, making it impossible to know exactly what happened, but the Berbers were only the latest variant in a long-standing Roman game of frontier client management, and this suggests some important lines of thought. The perfect frontier client from a Roman perspective was a loyal keeper of the peace. But the financial rewards of such loyalty—the kinds of annual payments that Cutzinas had been receiving since the 540s—were always redeployed by the clients for their own political purposes, which generally meant strengthening their own position among home constituencies. This always had at least the potential to be in tension with a second pressing Roman concern, however, which was to prevent the build-up of dangerously large confederations, which could easily develop inflated ambitions and disturb frontier peace on a much larger scale. Client management was an art, not a science, a question of deciding when a long-standing client was about to become just that bit too powerful and taking the appropriate step, whether kidnap, murder, or switching support to a rival.[6] Against this backdrop, uninterrupted, long-term peace with the chiefs of the nomadic Berbers was not possible, but then, it never had been. Incidents like the Cutzinas volte-face (whatever its precise circumstances) and, slightly earlier, Antalus's sudden transformation from ally to enemy in the 540s (p. 249) were bound to recur periodically on the frontiers of Justinian's new prefecture. The key question is not, did such events occur, therefore, but did levels of nomad disturbance after John Troglita's campaigns make sustained agricultural productivity noticeably more difficult?

On one level, the silence of the sources about North Africa for the rest of the sixth century is suggestive. If there had been large-scale conflict with the Berbers within the new prefecture, then we really do have enough narrative historical coverage for the sixth-century Eastern Empire overall to think that this would have been picked up. This general, if negative, perspective finds some positive support in a range of more specific archaeological evidence, although by its nature this tends to illuminate the history only of particular localities rather than broader patterns of gain and loss right across the region. But there is no doubt, at least, that general measures were taken to increase the level of protection available to settled agriculturalists.

Procopius refers to Solomon's fortification programme in the *Histories*, and no less than twenty-three inscriptions have been found with the prefect's name on them. Fourteen of these certainly commemorated building work, and the other nine probably did (they are too fragmentary for absolute certainty). East Roman North Africa clearly sprouted huge numbers of different types of fortification. Geiseric had ordered city walls torn down in the Vandal period to minimize the possibilities of Roman resistance. At least some of these depredations were made good and more, probably from a mix of central and local initiative and central and local funding.

The city walls of Carthage itself were generally strengthened and its defences brought up to date by the addition of a moat. Inside the city, too, the governmental centre on Byrsa hill, now home to the prefect's palace, received its own fortifications as an inner redoubt. The cities of Sabratha and Lepcis Magna, likewise, received brand-new wall circuits, while in many other towns disused monumental structures—forums, bath complexes, amphitheatres, old pagan temples—were recycled to create fortified strongpoints at the heart of urban complexes. In the countryside, too, defence was a high priority. Spread across the hinterland of Numidia and Byzacena (most numerous in the latter) were large numbers of fortified guard posts. Ain Tounga (see Figure 10.1) is utterly typical. Barrack block, granary, and cistern: everything a watch unit of *limitanei* might need. As a whole, the evidence strongly indicates that Procopius could hardly be further from the mark in suggesting, as he does in the *Buildings* (p. 27), that the ancient patterns of Greco-Roman city life were re-established within the province. Too many of the old communal spaces required for its public rhythms—everything from law courts, to baths and theatres—were turned into forts of one kind or another. On the other hand, we are clearly looking at a population that was well provided with defences against nomadic raiders.[7]

There is plenty of archaeological evidence, too, that within this well-defended prefectural fabric a reasonable degree of prosperity was being

FIGURE 10.1
One of the fortified posts from which the reconstituted *limitanei* of Justinian's North African prefecture sought to manage the movements and limit the potential depredations of the nomads.
Credit: © Vanni Archive / Art Resource, NY

sustained. From urban contexts, the evidence is specific but suggestive. Within Carthage itself, the commercial port was redeveloped after the conquest: given a ceremonial inner arcade and equipped with a pair of cisterns. The great Antonine baths in the city were also put back into operation, the pottery business that had operated in its caldarium in the Vandal period being summarily expelled. Aside from Carthage, the one other town that has been subject to extensive modern study is the port city of Leptiminus. Here a combination of excavation and survey has again produced a great deal of evidence for commercial activity. This material matches the available rural survey evidence which likewise suggests that if the countryside was not as populous and productive as it had been in the third and fourth centuries, then neither, as the second half of the sixth century unfolded, was it anywhere near as empty of people as Procopius's rhetoric might imply. All in all, everything indicates that the North African prefecture quickly became a well-integrated contributor to the life of the empire. By the early seventh century it was important enough to provide the base from which Heraclius père et fils could launch a successful bid for the imperial throne in Constantinople.[8]

The most impressive body of archaeological evidence from post-conquest Africa, however, is actually for religious architecture. In some ways, this is not surprising. The initial justification for Belisarius's campaign was a religious one, and a whole portfolio of former Catholic churches had been held by the Vandal-Alan Arian Church for the best part of a century after 439; so you might expect the conquest to have found religious expression. Within Carthage itself, no less than eight churches, two monasteries, and a martyr complex were either extensively remodelled or built from scratch, and this pattern repeats itself across the prefecture. At Lepcis Magna the old judicial basilica was redeveloped into a huge and richly decorated church dedicated to Mary Theotokos (i.e. the 'God bearer'), and the list could go on.[9] This archaeological dossier is not only striking but also in some ways surprising, because the church is the one North African political constituency for which we have substantial evidence for resistance to the new patterns of life and belonging that were generated by enforced membership of Justinian's empire. One spat between emperor and North African churchmen was generated in the immediate aftermath of conquest over how exactly to dismantle the Arian Church of the Vandal monarchy. That was resolved pretty quickly, however, and with little actual conflict (p. 240).

Much more significant was the Three Chapters dispute. It gathered momentum in the 530s and 540s out of an attempt to heal divisions within the Eastern church by finding an unambiguously anti-Nestorian way to read the Council of Chalcedon. Matters came to a head when Justinian published his official edict of 543/4, which condemned Theodore of Mopsuestia, Theodoret of Cyrus, and Ibas of Edessa (see Chapter 7).

In Justinian's new Western Empire, the edict was greeted with howls of disapproval. Its consistent opposition to all the earlier Eastern attempts to revise the decisions of Chalcedon had been triumphantly vindicated—or so it seemed—by the triumphantly pro-Chalcedonian termination of the Acacian schism (see Chapter 3). Suddenly to find that all this was now under threat not surprisingly generated determined opposition.

One strand of resistance came from Pope Vigilius, but the most ferocious opposition to the emperor's ecclesiastical initiative was North African. To a man, African churchmen refused to sign (i.e. show their assent to) the letter that came round with Justinian's edict. A deacon of the Carthaginian church, Facundus, wrote a fiercely worded condemnation of it, and when Vigilius showed signs of wavering, Patriarch Reparatus called a council of the whole North African church in Carthage, which proceeded to excommunicate him. Fresh from their triumphant resistant to the imposed Arian Christianity of the Vandal monarchy, North African Catholic churchmen were much more ready than most to resist state-based religious initiatives and much less impressed by imperial claims to religious authority.[10]

What happened subsequently, however, is extremely instructive. Justinian upped the pressure on all dissenters by calling another ecumenical council to meet in Constantinople in 553. Vigilius refused to attend but was subsequently 'persuaded' to accept its validation of the emperor's condemnation of the Three Chapters. This then became the springboard for a general approach to the council's enforcement in the West, which combined blandishment and oppression in more or less equal measure. Called to Constantinople, Reparatus of Carthage was deposed, and a royal agent called Mocianus (said to have been a former Arian by the pro-Chalcedonian opposition) set about selling the deal to North African churchmen. New church councils in Numidia and Proconsularis quickly endorsed the Council of Constantinople and its condemnation of the Three Chapters, and that was pretty much that. With hindsight and from the perspective of the later Middle Ages, the Three Chapters dispute can be held up as a striking example of church resistance to imperial claims to religious authority. At the time, exactly the opposite was true. After an initial outburst of resistance, which surely does reflect a century of separation from the imperial system, the church in North Africa quickly came into line with an imperially sponsored solution to the broader problem of church unity.[11]

Strikingly, the same broad conclusion jumps out from the archaeological evidence for North African church architecture. Both the reconstructions and new building followed distinctive idioms. Remodelled churches were all reoriented in an east–west direction or, where they were already on that line, acquired an apse in the east. This was a new element in North African church architecture, one which followed now well-established East Roman norms. The post-conquest era also saw the construction of North Africa's first pilgrimage churches, such as Damous El Karita and Bir Ftouha, specifically designed to allow large numbers of people to express their faith in mass processions. This again was utterly typical of what has been labelled the 'tactile' nature of East Roman Christianity of the sixth century. The later sixth century also saw the sudden influx and popularity of some important Eastern saints previously unknown to African Christians: Tryphon, Theodore, Pantaleon, and Menas.[12] What all this demonstrates, in other words, is that the new prefecture of North Africa, after the early chaos and heavy loss of life associated with violent regime change, quickly became fully integrated ideologically and religiously, as well as politically, into the East Roman imperial oikumene. Add to that the evidence for agricultural prosperity, and it is hard not to conclude that from the perspective of Constantinople, if none other, the costs of conquest soon came to be viewed as money well spent. Before we can assess whether the same was true of the Italian territories acquired from the Goths, it is necessary first to explore the impact of Justinian's reign upon the East Roman Balkans.

GEOPOLITICS AND THE BALKANS

The Balkans was not a major theatre of warfare for Justinian, although the conquest of Italy did begin with the seizure of Salona and Gothic Dalmatia. Nonetheless, its history plays a major role in any overall understanding of the impact of the emperor's conquest policies on two levels. Not least important, we need to take proper account of the incidental damage suffered by the Roman provincial communities of the Balkans as larger-scale conflicts unfolded on other fronts. As Procopius puts it in *Anekdota*, the Roman Balkans

> was overrun practically every year by Huns [meaning Bulgars], Sclaveni and Antae, from the time when Justinian took over the Roman Empire, and they wrought frightful havoc among the inhabitants of that region. For in each invasion more than twenty myriads [a myriad equals ten thousand] of Romans, I think, were destroyed or enslaved there.

Apart from its *limitanei*, the region was protected by two field armies, one in the eastern Balkans, in Thrace, the second further west in Illyricum. Particularly for the conquest of Italy, the emperor regularly drew upon these Balkan troops. It was the *Magister Militum per Illyricum*, Mundus, who fired its opening shots at Salona, and transfers of Balkan troops to Italy occurred regularly afterwards. One of Belisarius's main reinforcements in 538/9 consisted of troops from Thrace and Illyricum; others followed in the hard times of the mid-540s. The great military build-up under Germanus and Narses also drew on Balkan military assets, both officially, in the form of whole units reassigned to the campaign, and unofficially, in terms of volunteers attracted by the liberal pay suddenly available; many of these latter, Procopius implies, slipped away from their existing regiments.[13]

It is hard not to link the noticeable increase in the scale and frequency of Slav and Bulgar raiding into the Balkans in this period to such troop transfers. Roman frontiers had always leaked information like a sieve as a whole range of merchants and other individuals travelled back and forth across them, and adjacent non-Roman populations had long learned to watch Roman troop movements carefully, both for their own well-being in case of Roman assault and to assess likely raiding opportunities (or potentially threatening troop concentrations). It cannot be an accident, therefore, that the first really large Cutrigur Bulgar raid of Justinian's reign hit the Balkans in 539, just after the emperor had sent extra troops from both Balkan field armies to Belisarius in Italy. The Cutrigurs were a grouping of steppe nomads who operated in large, coherent blocks, with a central authority structure in the form of a khagan. In 539, the Cutrigurs enjoyed huge freedom of movement, breaking through the defences on the Lower Danube in large numbers to range far and wide—as far as the suburbs of Constantinople in one direction, but also west into the Chersonese peninsula and further south-west into Greece, even penetrating the passes at Thermopylae. All told, the Cutrigurs captured thirty-two fortified centres, briefly crossed over to Asia Minor from the Chersonese, and carried home reportedly 120,000 prisoners.[14] What is really striking about Procopius's narrative is the complete absence of any Balkans field army intervention capable of containing the attack.

The Slavs of the Carpathian uplands and its immediate hinterlands, by contrast, were organized in numerous small-scale chieftainships and had been raiding the Balkans in small groups off and on since the 510s. They generally lacked the capacity to take fortified towns and cities, keeping off the main roads and preying instead on isolated rural communities. Hence they posed an entirely different kind of problem to the Cutrigurs, one equally difficult to counter if for different reasons. Because they could travel cross-country, even through the difficult interior landscapes of the Balkans, conventional Roman armies found them very difficult to chase down—as in 548, when a mobilized Illyrian field army of 15,000 men could not bring a Slavic raiding force to book. In the late 540s, however, Slavic raiding began to demonstrate a distinct increase in scale and ambition. Raiding groups—probably improvised from more than one north

Danubian chieftainship—started to number (a few) thousands, not hundreds, and started to take on larger Roman targets. En route to Salona in 549, Germanus was held up by an (at that point) unusually large concentration of 3,000 Slav raiders. These eventually split up into separate groups of 1,200 and 1,800, but some of their targets were substantial. The larger managed to lure the garrison of Topirus in Thrace out from behind its protective walls, defeat it, and sack the city afterwards. They also crucified all their prisoners. In the next year Narses was likewise forced into an extended stay at Philippopolis (modern Plovdiv), because an even larger force of Slavs had its eyes on Thessalonica, the largest Roman city of the Balkans. This was surely not a realistic target, and the force again split up into three groups, but these overwintered for the first time in Thrace and wreaked considerable havoc.[15] Again, it can hardly be a coincidence that all of this came at the end of a decade in which Justinian had been slowly eroding the rosters of the Balkans military to feed reinforcements into the Italian campaign.

This is not to say that Justinian took no thought at all for his Balkan provincials. By the start of his reign, the messy political complexity generated by collapse of Attila's empire, which spawned the best part of two political generations of warfare and large-scale population movement in and around the Balkans (of which the arrival of Theoderic's Ostrogoths in the Balkans was just one episode: p. 158), had given way to a situation of greater stability. The middle Danubian region west of the Carpathians (roughly modern Hungary and western Romania) was divided between two kingdoms dominated by Germanic-speaking elites: the Lombards in the west and the Gepids further east. The lands north of the Black Sea, likewise, were divided between two Turkish-speaking Bulgar nomadic groupings: the Utigurs and the Cutrigurs. In between were the multiple smaller Slavic chiefdoms.[16] If, like Justinian, you were playing the great game of diplomacy from the imperial palace in Constantinople, overall strategy was clear enough: play Lombards off against Gepids at one end of your northern frontier and Utigurs against Cutrigurs at the other while seeking to minimize the raiding damage Slavs might do in the middle. In overall terms and from his own perspective, Justinian achieved a certain degree of success, keeping Lombards and Gepids consistently hostile to one another while switching imperial support between them at carefully chosen intervals. He also recruited Utigur assistance after the disasters of 539 to prevent the Cutrigurs from deploying their full military capacities against the Roman Balkans in any future raiding. But Slavic raiding could not be controlled by diplomacy, and the Utigur ploy was too late to prevent the heavy losses of 539.

Justinian's other approach to Balkans security in the absence of sufficient field forces was to strengthen the physical defences available to its provincial populations. Imperial initiatives on this front are given a whole book in Procopius's *Buildings*, and as laid out there, the plan was straightforward: defend the Danube frontier line to the hilt while providing interior communities with their own improved fortified refuges in case any raiders managed to break through. Procopius records Justinianic building work at literally hundreds of sites, many of which cannot be identified: so many, in fact, that in order that his account might not become 'utterly irksome', *Buildings* casts aside prose description at several points, resorting to bare lists of forts that Justinian 'built' or 'repaired'. There is much panegyric and exaggeration in this work, but the tendency to discount any substantial Justinianic component to the evolution of Balkan defences, which was marked in the 1980s, has now given way to a more balanced scepticism.

As with the defences of Roman Mesopotamia, some of the reported improvements show up in narratives of subsequent events. The Cutrigur raid of 539 clearly came as a horrible shock, and some specific improvements were made subsequently to restrict the possibility of any recurrence, particularly at key interior choke points: the famous Long Walls which protected the rich Thracian suburbs of Constantinople, a second set of Long Walls which protected the Chersonese Peninsula, and the passes of Thermopylae. When the Cutrigurs came again in 559, adopting broadly the same strategy, Thermopylae was held against them, as were the Long Walls of the Chersonesus. In 539 they had walked through the shallow water round the edge of the existing fortifications. By 559 (as recorded by Agathias, note, not Procopius), this avenue had been closed off. Despite their improvement (also lovingly described by Procopius), the Long Walls of Constantinople were again breached, and Agathias gives us a full account of Belisarius's last hurrah. At this point, the general had not commanded in the field for a decade, but with just three hundred regulars and a scratch force of volunteer civilians, he managed to win a morale-boosting victory over the Cutrigurs (which cost them one-fifth of a force of two thousand men and cost the Romans precisely nobody) and drive them, by ruse and stratagem, away from the capital's outskirts. But the attempt to strengthen the Long Walls after 539 had clearly been genuine, and the blow to imperial prestige substantial. In the aftermath of the raid, Justinian made a rare pilgrimage outside his capital to express his solidarity with those who had suffered and find out what had gone wrong: a sure sign that imperial prestige had been invested in the claim that these walls had been made impregnable.[17]

Where Procopius is specific, in other words, there is good reason to suppose that what he says was done actually was done. But at the same time, Justinian's building work clearly rested on the back of major efforts on the part of his predecessors. For his part, Anastasius devoted massive efforts to re-establish Danubian security after the catastrophic damage inflicted in the Hunnic heyday of the 440s. If you read Procopius's lists closely, then, in the vast majority of places Justinian is credited with repairs (which might mean no more than a little repointing) rather than building from scratch. Only in the far south, in Old and New Epirus, did new building outnumber repairs, which suggests that the Justinianic building programme was fundamentally an extension of well-established strategies for Balkan defence.[18] Justinian did not callously ignore his Balkan subjects, but he did make them a lower priority than his expansionary wars of conquest, which drew field forces away from their defence and left them more vulnerable. Diplomatic manoeuvring and strengthened defences could make up some of this shortfall but not all, and the Roman population of the Balkans certainly suffered greater damage because of the war in Italy at the hands of Cutrigurs and Slavs than would otherwise have been the case. For this reason alone, the Balkans have a place in our discussion, though they are a relative sideshow in the reign of Justinian. There is another level entirely, however, where its developing history has a direct impact upon overall assessments of the gains and losses of Justinian's expansionary wars.

In 558, at a moment when the war in the East was running down towards comprehensive peace negotiations and North Africa had been more or less at peace for a decade, a new nomadic steppe power announced itself:

> One Kandikh ... was chosen to be the first envoy of the Avars, and when he came to the palace he told the emperor [Justinian] of the arrival of the greatest and most powerful of the tribes. The Avars were invincible and could easily crush and destroy all who stood in their path. The emperor should make an alliance with them and enjoy their efficient protection. But they would only be well disposed to the Roman state in exchange for the most valuable gifts, yearly payments, and very fertile lands to inhabit.

This was the kind of diplomatic bluster which seems to have been a specialty of first-millennium nomads. As with the second-level Hunnic chieftain Uldin, who announced to East Roman ambassadors that he ruled all the territory from where the sun rises to where it sets—he actually controlled one captured Roman fortress—the reality was rather more prosaic. The Avars were refugees looking to get out of the way of the western Turks. Whereas the Avars controlled just one small corner of the western steppe in 558, the western Turks were rapidly building the first nomad superpower known to history. Within a decade, their power would straddle Eurasia, stretching from China to the eastern approaches to Europe.[19]

From Justinian's perspective, perhaps not overly impressed by their ambassador's rhetoric, the Avars looked like a useful addition to the network of interlocking diplomatic checks and balances, which had been playing such an important role in the emperor's strategic approach to Balkan defence. Menander Protector records the eventual response:

> He sent an ambassador Valentinus, one of the imperial bodyguard, and he urged the tribe to make an alliance with the Romans and take up arms against their enemies. This ... was a very wise move, since whether the Avars prevailed or were defeated, both eventualities would be to the Romans' advantage.[20]

This was particularly true after the Cutrigurs' devastating raid of 559, when Justinian had paid the Utigurs to attack their fellow Bulgars, scoring a devastating victory over their neighbours while the main Cutrigur army was still on Roman soil.[21] This was satisfactory enough as a form of revenge, but the scale of the Utigur victory was so great—essentially leading to the destruction of Cutrigur independence—that their power was now unchallenged north of the Black Sea, which is where the Avars could come in as a new balancing force to keep the Utigurs in line. And come in they did. By 562, Avar might extended right across the northern shores of the Black Sea, a series of undocumented campaigns having swallowed up both Utigurs and any remaining Cutrigurs. The speed and scale of this victory would have been worrying from a Constantinopolitan perspective, but lacking any obvious alternative, Justinian maintained the alliance down to his own death in November 565, fortifying their increasing strength with a substantial subsidy paid annually to their khagan.

At that point, the new imperial regime reversed policy. When the next Avar embassy arrived in Constantinople to collect its annual gifts, the new emperor, Justinian's nephew Justin II, announced:

> Never again shall you be loaded at the expense of this empire, and go your way without doing us any service: from me you shall receive nothing.

According to Menander, this left the ambassadors 'thunderstruck': extremely hesitant about returning home empty-handed, though they eventually did so.[22] The removal of East Roman subsidies actually threatened the stability of the Avar confederation. Like the Huns before them, the Avars lacked the capacity, perhaps even the desire, to rule subordinate members of their confederation (like the recently conquered Cutrigurs and Utigurs) directly; they exercised control through compliant native chieftains and princes. Thus it was easy to add new components to the confederation, but the resulting political structures were fragile, since existing patterns of loyalty among the subject peoples could easily reassert themselves in bids for independence. In context, the characteristic bluster of first-millennium nomads was deeply functional. What held confederations together were its current leader's prestige, based on actual or perceived military dominance, and his distribution of the kinds of rich gifts which were its most effective expression.[23]

In 582, when the Avars were besieging the important Danubian fortress of Sirmium but realized that they were not going to capture it, its Roman commander received an extraordinary message. The Avars were willing to withdraw if the Romans would hand over a large gift which the khagan could use to conceal his defeat. In 626, likewise, as soon as the reality of the Avars' spectacular failure to capture Constantinople became apparent, contingents from the subject peoples immediately deserted in such numbers that the Avar core of the army had to start killing them.[24] Any loss of prestige could spark off challenges to Avar domination, so that the khagan had little choice but to respond decisively to Justin's rebuff. It is no coincidence that in the same year, 566, the Avars inflicted a major defeat on the easternmost of the Frankish kings, Sigibert, who afterwards 'immediately sent to the Avars wheat flour, vegetables, sheep, and cattle'.[25] It is this heightened Avar interest in stretching their power towards the west in the later 560s that eventually ties together Balkan geopolitics and the fate of Justinian's conquests in Italy.

As Justin dismissed the Avar ambassadors, yet another quarrel was breaking out between the Gepids and Lombards. In 566 the Gepids won a victory with some Roman military assistance but then refused to keep their promise to return the city of Sirmium to imperial control. The Romans saw no reason to intervene again in 567, therefore, when the Lombards secured Avar help at high economic cost and with it smashed Gepid independence forever. This was no doubt highly satisfactory to the king of the Lombards, who proceeded to turn the skull of his defeated enemy, the Gepid king Cunimund, into a drinking cup.[26] But it also had serious drawbacks. The defeat of Sigibert in 566, followed by the destruction of the Gepids in 567, made it clear both that the Avar star was rapidly in the ascendant and that its direction of travel was increasingly westwards. There was now no buffer at all between Lombard territories and those of their dangerous nomad neighbours. Early the next year, reportedly on 2 April 568, the Lombards left the middle Danube in a large body. At least several tens of thousands strong—a ragbag of

Lombards proper and many others besides: nobles, freeman, and slaves—this human procession left the middle Danube forever. Its destination was northern Italy.

EXARCHATE

On 13 August 554, nearly two years after the death of Teias, Justinian issued a Pragmatic Sanction: a set of regulations for his new Italian provinces. Like North Africa, Italy was to constitute its own prefecture (*exarchate* in Greek), with a series of subordinate governors. The central thrust of this legislation was to clean up the messy aftermath of Totila's insurgency. Much thought was given to issues of property and ownership. All the grants and gifts of Gothic kings up to and including Theodahad (i.e. not those of Wittigis and Totila) retained full legal validity, and the Sanction sensibly recognized that an awful lot of legal documentation might have gone up in smoke in the chaos of war, setting out alternative mechanisms to prove title. It also championed the rights of returning refugees to reclaim property and set out the principle that individuals who had been intimidated into damaging economic arrangements in the time of Totila, especially during the siege of Rome, might petition to have those arrangements overturned. These rules applied both to fixed and movable property and must have opened the door to countless lawsuits, of which some reflection survives.[27] The emperor was also concerned that taxation structures should get back up and running but did allow that collection should be in the hands of local Italian communities themselves rather than outsiders from Constantinople. This was an important concession: it imposed important informal limits on the severity of exaction. Other regulations dealt with matters as general as which laws and coins were now valid and to others as specific as nuns who had been dragged out of monasteries and forced into marriage (the point being, seemingly, not just true love but also to claim their dowries). The concerns of the great and good (already implicitly covered in the laws about valid property grants and restoring lost and/or stolen property, of course) likewise received specific mention. Senators were free to come and go from Constantinople, and the fate of one particularly large grant which Theodahad had originally made from the property of Marcianus was singled out. The Gothic king had originally given it all to the senator Maximus, but half of it was now to go to Liberius.

In fact, the emperor was getting ahead of himself. Another piece of legislation from the following year admitted, as the Pragmatic Sanction had not, that peace was not yet fully established and so set out particular protections for Sicilian debtors who could not, because of prevailing conditions, repay their loans. In the summer of 554, as the Sanction was being drafted, Narses still had his hands full fighting a Frankish army that had invaded the Italian peninsula in 553. Led by two brothers, Butilinus and Leutharis, it consisted mostly of Alamanni and, according to Agathias, numbered seventy-five thousand men. It crossed the river Po in the summer of 553 and occupied Parma, defeating a force of Herulian *foederatii* who attempted to intervene. Having overwintered at Parma, the two brothers then moved as far south as Samnium in the first half of 554, where the force divided. Leutharis invaded Apulia and Calabria, causing much destruction and taking many prisoners. It was now summer, and Leutharis wanted to return home with the booty, but Butilinus had been offered the kingship of the Goths and wanted to stay with his (larger) portion of the army, having carried on down the west coast of Italy through Campania, Lucania, and Brutium as far as the Straits of Messina. He then returned to Campania, camping near Capua, on the banks of the river Casilinum, with the express intention of fighting it out with Narses.[28]

According to Agathias, Narses had eighteen thousand men to Butilinus's thirty thousand, but the Frankish-Alamannic army consisted mostly of lightly equipped infantry, conspicuously lacking in defensive armour. On the morning of the battle, Narses encountered a hitch with his Heruli. He was forced to execute one of their officers for murder, at which point the rest threatened not to fight. They eventually changed their minds but arrived late on the battlefield, and Narses had had to leave a gap in the line for them. As per normal, Narses had placed his cavalry on each flank, some of it on the left concealed in heavy woods, with the infantry in the middle. Before the Heruli could move into position, however, Butilinus's forces made a massed, wedge-shaped charge straight at the Roman infantry. Its weight pushed through Narses's light vanguard, with some going straight through the gap in the line where the Heruli should have been. For these men, it felt like victory, especially when they saw the Roman camp straight ahead and thoughts of booty instantly took hold. But the bulk of the lightly equipped Alamanni had actually been held up by Narses's main battle line of heavy infantry, and in reality Butilinus had lost all control of his now-disordered forces. It was easy enough, therefore, for Narses to spring a trap. His cavalry closed in from the flanks, launching volleys of arrows into the rear and flanks of the opposition while the advancing Heruli, with the lighter infantry archers held in reserve behind the main battle line, mopped up those who had broken through to the rear. The result was the complete destruction of Butilinus's force. According to Agathias, only five of the enemy survived, while the Romans lost a grand total of eighty men. You do not have to believe these casualty figures to realize that, once again, the tactical superiority of an East Roman field army had prevailed over larger numbers of opponents.[29]

Leutharis's force did not fare much better. It retreated north along the east coast road as far as the port of Fanum, but at Pisaurum Leutharis's advance guard was ambushed and routed, and in the chaos most of his prisoners escaped, taking with them much of the booty. After this setback, the retreat continued directly northwards to the Po, at which point Leutharis's men re-entered territory controlled by the Franks and made camp for the winter at Ceneta (modern Vittorio Veneto). Here the army was struck by disease, and Agathias takes great pleasure in telling us (*a*) that Leutharis himself had insane fits and died miserably and (*b*) that his entire army—pretty much—died as well. Again, Agathias's propensity for hyperbole is determinedly on display, but the defeat of the Frankish army did mark the end of large-scale warfare for control of Justinian's new exarchate.[30]

It also snuffed out, pretty much, the last embers of concerted Gothic resistance. Butilinus and Leutharis had come to Italy in response to Teias's appeals for help in the second half of 552. He knew they were coming, which is why he had struggled so hard to defend Totila's treasury at Cumae (p. 268). And though too late for Teias, the Franks' arrival managed to rekindle some fires of Gothic resistance, because Justinian had adopted a substantially different policy towards the Goths than he had towards the Vandals.

In North Africa, the Vandals were utterly exterminated as a group. Any males not killed on the battlefield were deported, to be followed eventually, after their role in the mutiny, by Vandal women; all the landed property distributed to them by Geiseric or acquired subsequently was confiscated by the Roman state. In Italy many Gothic males died on the battlefield and some were deported to the East: early garrisons wrapped up by Belisarius, together with some of those trapped with Wittigis inside Ravenna in 540. This potent combination of death and deportation certainly meant that no serious Gothic army could be put in the field after the defeats of Totila and Teias in 552. On the other hand, Goths who surrendered (apart from the prisoners reportedly butchered after Busta Gallorum) were normally sent back to their homes. Belisarius did this in 540 with all of Wittigis's army who lived south of the Po, and Narses did the same with all the remaining Goths who negotiated a ceasefire after Teias's death at Mons Lactarius. By recognizing as valid all the grants of the Gothic rulers of Italy down to and including Theodahad, the Pragmatic Sanction also implicitly promoted the same policy.[31]

When the Franks arrived in the spring of 553, therefore, they could draw support from militant Goths who had returned to their homes after Mons Lactarius but were ready to renew the fight and from three points of continued resistance, which Narses was currently trying to snuff out. Behind the walls of Cumae, with Totila's treasury at his back, Teias's brother Aligern was fighting on with determination. Agathias provides a compelling account of the action which combined full-on Roman assaults intermixed with attempted underminings of the fortress walls and every other move in the sixth-century siege playbook. Indulf—a man of non-Roman origins but one of Belisarius's guardsmen who had deserted to the Goths on his general's recall to Constantinople in 548/9 (p. 262)—had retreated north to Pavia with a thousand men. Still in the south, a third group led by Moras and a Bittigur Hun by the name of Ragnaris was holding out at Acheruntia (modern Acerenza in Basilicata).[32] Many in these groups threw in their lot with Butilinus in a final roll of the Gothic dice; they were even ready to offer him the kingship of the Goths if Narses could be defeated. For all of these groups, the battle of Casilinum destroyed any lingering hopes of restoring an independent Gothic kingdom in Italy.

Some had decided that the game was up even before this. Faced with the news that Butilinus might become the Goths' king, Aligern negotiated Cumae's surrender. As Agathias puts it, with characteristic verbal economy,

> A careful assessment of the situation ... led him to realize that the Franks had indeed come in response to an appeal for help, but were in reality availing themselves of an empty formula of alliance in order to mask what, in the event, would prove to be very different intentions. Assuming they did get the better of the Romans they would certainly have no intention of letting the Goths have Italy, but would in actual fact begin by enslaving the very people whose cause they were supposed to be championing.[33]

After surrender, Aligern was even ready to fight against Butilinus, putting his men in the field on the Roman side. What this demonstrates is a reality that the Franks' arrival could not conceal. East Roman military action had worn down effective Gothic numbers to such an extent that the group was no longer capable of maintaining the independent domination of the Italian peninsula that it had established under Theoderic. Totila had tried to hide this by recruiting underpaid and disaffected Roman garrisons, but most of these had swapped sides again when a Roman field army finally re-entered the arena. Teias tried the alternative tack of recruiting Frankish assistance, but by the time it arrived, another major Gothic defeat had intervened, eroding numbers to such an extent that surviving Gothic leaders were split over whether there could be any real Gothic future at all.

Butilinus's defeat was followed by no further large-scale Gothic rebellions, therefore, although there was certainly some mopping up to do. After Casilinum, Ragnaris and a force of seven thousand men—quite likely survivors (along with the other five mentioned by Agathias) of the battle—ended up in the fortress of Conza della Campania. Narses besieged them over the winter of 554/5, but the fortress was well supplied, and the two leaders met face to face in the spring of 555 to discuss surrender terms. The discussion got nowhere, and Ragnaris shot at Narses as the meeting broke up. He missed, but Narses's bodyguard mortally wounded him in return. After his death, two days later, the garrison surrendered, and all seven thousand were shipped out of Italy.[34] That brought to an end all resistance in the south, and slowly Narses extended his control northwards. By 560, East Roman dominance had been securely established in Liguria, Histria, and most of Venetia. Only eastern Venetia was left unsubdued, and it was this region which witnessed the last dim flicker of revolt. In 561, a Gothic count called Widin rebelled in Brescia and called again for Frankish help. The manoeuvre failed.[35] Widin's defeat marked the final extinction of Gothic resistance to Justinian's conquest of Italy, and in November 562 Narses formally reported to Constantinople the capture of Verona and Brescia.

The fact that despite all the intervening defeats, Widin had nonetheless decided to chance his arm in revolt strongly suggests that formal imperial control in the north was not yet strong, as equally does the sudden rebellion there of Sindual, the leader of the Heruli *foederatii*, on Justinian's death in 565. Sindual had come to Italy with Narses in the 550s and had been appointed the Heruli's commander by Narses himself in the winter of 553/4, receiving the rank of field army commander (*Magister Militum*) with *illustris* status as a result. But on Justinian's death, his followers, up in the mountains of the north-east at Trento, suddenly proclaimed him king: a declaration of political independence. Narses deposed and killed him, but the fact that after more than a decade of loyal service, Sindual suddenly chose to display such an increased level of political ambition strongly suggests that the situation in the north must have remained pretty chaotic into the mid-560s.[36]

Before matters could even begin to stabilize, northern and central Italy were thrown into further chaos by the arrival of the Lombards in the spring of 568. One year later, King Alboin, having already swallowed up many cities further east, led his army into the north-western city of Milan (3 September 569). In 572, after a lengthy siege Pavia, too, fell to him; by that date most of northern Italy was under Lombard control. Although our narrative accounts become sketchy, within a very few years, probably by the mid-570s, two additional Lombard duchies had been established in upland central and southern Italy: one based in Spoleto, close to the crucial axis of the Via Flaminia, and a second at Benevento. East Roman control within the old Ostrogothic kingdom was quickly reduced, therefore, to Sicily, the far south of Italy proper, and reasonably large blocks of territory around the cities of Rome in the west and Ravenna, seat of the exarch, in the north-east.[37]

The main observation that follows is straightforward. The Italian territories lost in the 560s and 570s were never recovered. The arrival of the Lombards overturned any possibility of establishing an Italian prefecture encompassing the entirety of the old Ostrogothic kingdom. In that sense, Justinian's conquest policy, as it applied to Italy, was a failure.

Whether this was the fault of Justinian himself, however, is more questionable. First, since it was in large measure the arrival of the Lombards which made it impossible for the new exarchs of Ravenna to consolidate East Roman control right across the peninsula, much of the overall 'blame' has to be attributed to the rise of Avar power. A source written over two hundred years after the event reports that the Lombards were 'invited' to move into Italy by Narses himself, due to an ongoing quarrel with the Empress Sophia, wife of Justinian's successor, Justin II. Given his past career and the fact that he soon retired to live quietly in the city of Rome, which remained firmly under Constantinopolitan rule, this is completely implausible. In reality, the Lombards came to Italy on their own initiative, and the operation of both positive 'pull' and negative 'push' factors is obvious. On the positive side, Italy remained an attractive, richer landscape to occupy than the Lombards' middle Danubian territories, and as the Widin and Sindual incidents show, imperial control of the north was far from firmly established. That much was Justinian's fault. His eventual determination to pursue the war to such a hard-fought conclusion opened a door to the Lombards by creating chaos in northern Italy.

Yet it must be doubted that the Lombards would ever have left the middle Danube at all without the sudden explosion of Avar power which arrived on their doorstep after the destruction of the Gepids in 567. Steppe nomadic empires were expansionary by nature, and Avar power had just reinforced itself by adding the surviving Gepids to a list of subject peoples that now included Cutrigurs, Utigurs, and a range of smaller

Slav groupings. In strategic terms, the Lombards were no more powerful in overall military terms than the Gepids (as the repeated draws they fought to over the previous half century make clear), so that their chances of surviving an attempted Avar conquest were not good if they did remain in the middle Danube region. Lombard contingents had also been involved in the Gothic war, witnessing at first hand the firepower of Roman field armies. They would have been equally aware of the destruction of Butilinus and Leutharis, so that they cannot have thought that conquering a piece of East Roman territory was going to be easy. Like several other late fourth- and early fifth-century Germanic groups faced with the analogous rise of Hunnic power, however, the Lombard leadership decided—and managed to sell that decision to a critical mass among their following—that organized retreat (even if it did mean fighting Romans) was the best method of dealing with rampant nomad neighbours. There is a direct causal link, in other words, between the rise of Avar power in central Europe and the arrival of the Lombards in Italy.[38] In the short term, it was less imperial overstretch which caused the loss of such a substantial chunk of Justinian's new Italian prefecture than the sudden assertion of Avar hegemony in central and eastern Europe. This, it seems to me, is hard to blame on the emperor, since it had been a hundred years since the collapse of Attila's empire and there was no obvious reason to suppose that a new steppe empire was on the rise.

Overall, the Lombard invasion divided the Italian peninsula between Constantinople and a second, Germanic-dominated power. In effect, the longer-term outcome of Justinian's conquest strongly resembled the partition deal which Wittigis had put on the table late in 538 and which the emperor himself was moved to accept by December 539. The reason why it had not come to fruition was Belisarius's conviction that the military situation, as it stood at the back end of 539, offered him a possibly unique opportunity to win control of the whole peninsula, so he took a series of military and diplomatic initiatives which made the negotiations redundant (p. 178). If he had not, much the same overall outcome would have been achieved in territorial terms but with much less cost to all interested parties: the Goths themselves, of course, but also the empire, and above all the population of Italy, which would not have had to suffer the repeated traumas of Totila's insurgency, Frankish intervention, and Lombard invasion. The imperial territories in the peninsula would also have been better protected from any new chaos in central Europe, such as that generated by the Avars, by a stronger, more resilient Gothic buffer state. A strong case can be made, therefore, that Belisarius's miscalculation on the ground rather than Justinian's policymaking back in Constantinople was the fundamental cause of the element of chaotic imperial overstretch which partly underlay the Lombards' decision to invade.[39]

Without the Lombards, there is no reason to think that East Roman rule would not have been consolidated eventually, as it was in North Africa. The new prefecture's administrative structures built on a long-established Roman-Gothic heritage, which surely would have worked effectively enough. No doubt, as in North Africa, there would have been an initial and intrusive influx of top officials from Constantinople (as was already happening in the early 540s: p. 238), but the Pragmatic Sanction was seeking to involve local elites in the politically sensitive task of tax raising, and there were plenty of returning Italian exiles who were already tied into East Roman social and governmental networks. In due course, too, East Roman forces in Italy were sustained by local recruitment.[40]

Ideologically, all the evidence indicates that the process of integration was fundamentally unproblematic. In the long term, the medieval papacy developed into a centre of political and religious authority independent of the empire; Pope Vigilius was originally hostile to Justinian's initiatives for resolving the problems of the divided Eastern church. Historians have often supposed, therefore, that the papacy's period of independence under Gothic rule would have forestalled fully re-reintegration into a Roman imperial system whose ruler had not the slightest doubt about his own overarching religious authority (see Chapter 1). To judge by the Three Chapters dispute, however, the problem should not be overstated. Pope Vigilius held out to start with, issuing a formal refutation of Justinian's initiative (the pope's *First Constitutum*), and refused to participate in the emperor's fifth ecumenical council of 553. But after repeated badgering by high-level delegations, in which Belisarius himself sometimes figured, Vigilius's *Second Constitutum* of 26 February 554 entirely accepted the full validity of the council and its condemnation of the disputed Three Chapters. This was the price Vigilius had to pay to be allowed to return to Italy, but sadly, he died en route. His successors, however, continued to support the imperial position. Pope Pelagius I (556–61) simply maintained, lying through his teeth, that the condemnation did not represent any policy change at all. Gregory the Great (590–604) more truthfully acknowledged that there had been a change but justified it on the grounds that new information, not available to Pope Leo when he composed his famous *Tome* for the council of Chalcedon (p. 79), had come to light subsequently. By the late sixth century, only two Italian ecclesiastical provinces, Milan and Aquileia, continued to hold out against the decisions of II Constantinople, and both, significantly, now fell outside of imperial control. This pattern strongly suggests that the emperor's religious authority, even in the later sixth century, was more than strong enough to overpower any local centrifugal tendencies among Italian ecclesiastics, just as it had proved to be in North Africa (p. 277). Again, as in North Africa both Sicily and Rome came quickly into line with the norms of East Roman sixth-century Christianity, whether they concern church building or actual piety. In the seventh century the papacy itself came to be dominated by a string of Greek-speaking churchmen.[41]

Economically, too, the picture which emerges from a comparison of the historical narrative with recent archaeological evidence is extremely striking. Narrative sources imply that the assertion of East Roman rule inflicted much greater losses on many provincial populations of the Italian peninsula than their North African counterparts suffered, even given the mutiny and subsequent Berber insurgency. Being subjected to an entire political generation's worth of large-scale warfare punctuated by bouts of occasionally intense violence must have led to huge losses for the population of Italy. Particular sacks, such as those of Naples and Milan early on in the war and Tibur later, are vividly described by Procopius, The dislocations of army supply and raiding also generated regionally serious famines. Through it all runs a subtheme of warfare centring on cities and disrupted agricultural production, punctuated by moments of social rupture, such as Totila's desperate arming of Roman slaves towards the final stages of the war. It is impossible to reach any kind of quantitative judgment on the effects of the fighting in terms of numbers of people killed, but the archaeology of Italy was permanently altered.

Northern Italy in particular, the area taken over by the Lombards, completely failed to recover from the dislocating effects of the warfare, in the sense that there is almost no evidence for complex exchange systems there in the later sixth and seventh centuries; the admittedly incomplete settlement evidence is highly suggestive of considerable population decline. No figure can be put on the latter, but a region which had been a great hub of the late Roman world both declined in demographic terms and saw its economy move decisively towards patterns of only local exchange. The pattern in areas that remained under Constantinople's control is markedly different. Southern Italy retained commercial pottery industries which sold their wares across reasonably wide areas, which suggests that more general patterns of exchange retained greater complexity. The city of Rome also recovered from its various sieges to become, again, a centre of wealth; it was importing goods in considerable quantities by the seventh century. All this was on nothing like the scale of the late Roman period, and it is widely reckoned that the city's population dropped by a factor of ten, from a few hundred thousand people in the early fifth century to just a few tens of thousands two hundred years later. Nonetheless, despite this evident decline, southern Italy was probably richer than any other part of the old Roman west in the seventh and early eighth centuries. Whether or how much of this economic decline would have been avoided had Justinian's armies not been set loose in the region is difficult to estimate. Cassiodorus's *Variae* give the impression that everything in the Ostrogothic kingdom was running as normal prior to 536, but this is only a facade, and it is certainly true that the same kind of economic simplification we observe in Lombard Italy affected every other region of the post-Roman west as well, once the *pax Romana* was removed. So I have no doubt that Justinian's wars caused a lot of damage and killed many people unnecessarily in the Italian peninsula, but the chances are that the Italian economy, even under Ostrogothic rule, would have moved more towards the simpler patterns of the early medieval north in any case.[42]

CASTLES IN SPAIN

At first sight, there is a strong sense of the ephemeral about Justinian's Western Empire: the effect, above all, of losing much of the Italian peninsula to the Lombards within a decade of the Goths' final pacification. This is only reinforced by the last of the emperor's adventures, in Spain, which is not even reported by Procopius. In 551 the Visigothic noble Athanagild rebelled against the reigning king, Agila, and sent to Constantinople for support. It arrived in the form of a fleet and some soldiers led by the patrician Liberius. No narrative details survive of what happened next, but Athanagild ended up as king and the East Romans did not leave. Scholarly opinion has gone back and forth over the geographical size of Justinian's final addition to his Western Empire, but a pretty conservative answer looks the most convincing. The fleet occupied a limited string of southern coastal towns, without, as far as we can tell, an arrow being fired in anger. Cartagena, Malaga, Sagunto, and Assidonia, together with their rural territories, now belonged to Constantinople and remained under East Roman control for just over fifty years until a restructured Visigothic monarchy reasserted its control. King Sisebut (612–21) took back everything except the Algarve, and Suinthila completed the job in 624.[43] An initial impression, very difficult to shift, is that the whole Spanish episode provides an appropriate metaphor for Justinian's entire enterprise: an intense bout of jousting at windmills, which generated a huge amount of human misery, cost a huge amount of cash, and achieved precisely nothing of lasting value. Before signing up completely to that judgment, however, it is important to analyse Justinian's activities with both geographical and chronological precision.

The Hispanic gains were extremely ephemeral in chronological terms, and even though they apparently cost little in terms of effort, it is hard to see that they gained much either. Their main benefit would have been to add to the string of port cities in the western Mediterranean that had come under Constantinopolitan control after the conquest of the Vandal kingdom (p. 148); they would presumably have assisted East Roman merchants in selling into Hispanic markets, even if their military and fiscal value can only have been limited.

If we leave aside the human cost of the enterprise (though we should not), the same judgment clearly does not hold true of Justinian's conquests in Sicily and North Africa. We have to adopt a qualitative, not quantitative, approach, as imperial tax returns do not survive to give us precise figures. Nonetheless, from a centrist Constantinopolitan perspective, the conquest of Sicily was undoubtedly worth the costs incurred. In the ancient and medieval worlds, Sicily was a great prize. Its agricultural productivity had attracted Greek settlers early in the first millennium BC and made it an initial target for Roman expansion, too. Centuries later, Henry III of England virtually bankrupted himself and plunged his realm into political crisis to make good on his convoluted claim to its crown. Justinian, by contrast, picked Sicily up at virtually no cost and with little disruption to either its inhabitants or its economy, apart from when Totila ransacked it for supplies (550). Subsequently, Constantinople held it without trouble down to the 650s, when the first Islamic Arab raids began, and then at rather greater expense until the ninth century. By that date, the island must have paid for the costs of its conquest and garrisoning many times over; its economic and cultural importance finds confirmation in the written sources generated by later sixth- and seventh-century bishops of Rome. The same holds true of the North African prefecture. There, the initial costs of conquest and pacification were much higher, and Berber management remained a perennial issue. Constantinople's African prefecture also fell much more quickly into Arab hands, the loss of Carthage in the 690s marking the effective end of East Roman rule. Nonetheless, even by 690, the bulk of the conquered North African territory had been in East Roman hands for the best part of 150 years. Time periods become easily compressed when dealing with the distant past. The mid-sixth and late seventh centuries are both so long ago that they feel pretty much adjacent. But 150 years is many lifetimes, especially when people generally died younger, and there is more than enough archaeological evidence now for solid African agricultural productivity—complemented by the evidence for its political importance in the time of Heraclius and after—to prompt the conclusion that the costs of acquisition had been repaid many times over by the time it fell to Islam.

Constructing a similar balance sheet for Italy is more complicated than might be supposed. Surprisingly large parts of Italy remained under Constantinopolitan control for a very long time, and as we have just seen, those that did show more signs of economic prosperity than those that did not. A substantial enclave around Ravenna, together with Rome and most of southern Italy, were ruled directly from Constantinople until the third and fourth decades of the eighth century. At that point Ravenna was lost to Lombard conquest, and Rome declared itself independent: the Republic of Saint Peter under the control of the papacy. The southern reaches of the Italian peninsula remained solidly East Roman for another two hundred years after that, however, and isolated communities for longer still. The campaigns of Belisarius and Narses thus inaugurated well over 150 years, again, of East Roman rule along the diagonal axis of the Via Flaminia between Rome and Ravenna and more like half a millennium of Constantinopolitan control in southern Italy. Certainly in the south, the costs of conquest and pacification must have been long since repaid by the tenth century, and even Rome and Ravenna probably represented a reasonable return on Justinian's original investments.[44]

The same was not true, of course, of northern Italy, and it bears re-emphasis that the terms of analysis applied in the last few pages are of economic, not human, cost. Measured in human terms, none of Justinian's conquests were worth it, but if you accept the validity of an economic approach, then North Africa, Sicily, and just about enough of Italy were all held on to for just about long enough by Constantinople to repay Justinian's investment. Another important point to make about the subsequent losses of territory in this new Western Empire is that the vast bulk of the losses, whether directly or indirectly, had their origins in events unfolding much further east, in the Near and Middle East heartlands of the East Roman Empire: Egypt, Palestine, Syria, and Asia Minor.

The loss of the Hispanic coastal enclaves in the 610s and early 620s and the largely ineffectual response to the Lombard invasion of northern Italy (see Chapter 11) had their roots in an intense preoccupation within Constantinople with a renewed outbreak—really a sequence of outbreaks—of large-scale warfare with Persia, which directly threatened the key heartlands of the East at intervals from the early 570s through the late 620s. This meant that there were no military resources, particularly in terms of a field army, available to inflict the same kind of military annihilation on the Lombards that Narses had effected on the intrusive Frankish armies of Butilinus and Leutharis.[45] The later losses of North Africa to Islamic conquest in the 690s, of Ravenna to Lombard conquest in 730s, and of Rome to republican independence were all—again, directly or indirectly—the products of a second wave of Islamic expansion, which unfolded ca. 690 after a lull following the first Arab conquests (ca. 630–60). North Africa was a direct casualty, of course, but Rome revolted in response to large tax rises that Constantinople imposed on the West to try to meet the costs of the desperate struggle for survival against the Umayyad Caliphate in the early eighth century (including a year-long siege of the capital itself in 717/18). So, too, there were no resources to spare when the Lombards sensed the opportunity to wrap up Ravenna and add the missing piece of the north Italian jigsaw to their own burgeoning kingdom.[46]

Even the definitive loss of much of the Balkans arguably had its roots in the East. At first sight, the Avars look primarily responsible for what happened. Not only did they conquer parts of the north-western Balkans for themselves, but they also facilitated a more general Slavic intrusion into the region as a whole. Major Avar campaigns in the 580s and especially the 610s blew huge holes in Justinian's defensive arrangements for the Balkans and precipitated large-scale slavicization in the region. When you take a close look at the overall pattern of triangular Roman, Slav, and Avar relations, it is striking that in the 590s, after the first wave of Avar-Slav intrusion, during a lull in the empire's sequence of eastern conflicts, the Balkan situation was brought substantially back under control by sustained Roman counterattack.[47] The dose could not be repeated in the seventh century, because by then the deteriorating situation in the all-important East meant that the necessary military resources could never again be made available for the Balkans.

This final observation helps define the final question we need to ask. Since the fate of Justinian's Western Empire was ultimately defined by what happened in the East, its losses all being the product of losses there, did Justinian's western conquests cause the disastrous sequence of seventh-century losses in the East that in turn undermined the stability of the new empire those conquests had brought into being?

11

THE FALL OF THE EASTERN EMPIRE

GIVEN EVERYTHING THAT PROCOPIUS has to say about the destruction that Justinian's conquests generated in the West, it is no surprise that for him the policy had equally devastating effects in Constantinople's eastern heartlands:

> The Persians under Chosroes four times made inroads into the rest of the Roman domain and dismantled the cities, and as for the people whom they found in the captured cities and in each country district, they slew a part and led some away with them, leaving the land bare of inhabitants wherever they chanced to descend.

In all, Procopius reckons that 'a myriad myriads of myriads'—that is, ten thousand cubed, or a hundred billion people—died because of Justinian's demonic reign.[1] This is poetic license, but since most of the tax revenue–generating heartlands of the East Roman Empire—Syria, Palestine, and Egypt—fell first to Persian and then to Islamic Arab conquest in the first half of the seventh century, it has proved seductively easy to generate a causal link between the two sequences of events. Justinian's conquests overstretched and exhausted the Eastern Empire in the mid-sixth century, leaving its heartlands open to outside conquest in the early seventh. A perfectly plausible argument, but is it correct?

ISLAMIC (SATELLITE) STATE

Justinian's western campaigns certainly caused serious losses in the East. In 540 in particular, as we saw, the Persian king of kings launched a huge assault on the rich cities of Roman Syria in direct response to those campaigns, worried, it is said, by the extent of the emperor's success in Africa and Italy but also to take full advantage of the opportunity left open in the East by close to a decade of troop transfers and general neglect. His attack was met by no Roman field army, some of the cities' fortifications were in a state of disrepair, and morale among some underpaid garrison forces was low. The results were catastrophic. Apart from the huge sums of money Chosroes extracted from Hierapolis, Beroea, Apamea, Chalcis, and Dara, Antioch, capital of Justinian's eastern prefecture, was destroyed with much of its population dragged off into Persian captivity. There were further losses, too, in 542/3, and all of these have to be seen as direct effects of Justinian's western adventures.[2]

It is also inconceivable that Justinian was not spending much more per annum on the military budget from 527 until at least the mid-550s—from the moment he began his first aggressive war against Persia until Italy and Lazica finally fell quiet—than Anastasius and Justin. Armies cost far more on campaign. Muster rolls were filled only for battle, and all the extra pay, equipment, food, supplies, transport, and pack animals cost a small fortune, not to mention wear and tear on the navy plus the cost of hiring in the merchant ships used as troop transports: not just the five hundred that transported Belisarius's original army to Caput Veda but the many others busy landing different contingents at various Italian ports during the 540s. The bills for all his different wars must have been extraordinary, and Justinian clearly struggled to pay them.[3]

When putting together the western expeditionary forces, corners were cut with more routine military payments. Pay arrears played a major role in the African mutiny of the mid-530s, when the second army was being gathered for Italy, as they did in the willingness of Italian garrisons to sign up to the insurgency of Totila in the period when all the cash and energy was being absorbed by war with Persia in the east. Justinian also found it impossible to mount more than one major offensive at a time.

Few reinforcements could be found for Italy in the 540s, when the Persian war was at its height, and for a long period Lazica, too, was starved of resources. Only when the Persian war had largely run out of steam did Justinian find it possible to make the necessary resources available to Narses for the decisive Italian surge of the early 550s.[4]

Merchants involved in military supply will have made enormous profits from all this, but most of the Eastern Empire's population saw only the resulting tax bills, and the evidence is unequivocal that these increased substantially. One of the themes running through *Anekdota* is Justinian's voracity for other people's money, the text combining rebarbative general condemnation with specific examples of rich individuals who fell foul of the emperor's greed. Emperors always had a strong interest in the affairs of their richest subjects, and it was their overarching capacity potentially to raise or ruin which meant that the aristocracy simply had to engage with the politics of the court.[5] More generally, the rich and well-connected of the Roman world had many and varied devices for engaging with the system in order to minimize the amount of tax they paid, and Justinian's regime specifically targeted this group in structural terms. The year after Gelimer's humiliation in Constantinople saw no less than nine separate measures going region by region round the Eastern Empire, with the express intention of ratcheting up the overall tax take by getting more out of the wealthy. And this was before the costs of fighting Goths and Persians simultaneously in the 540s began to bite. Victory in Africa not only made Justinian politically untouchable; it also emboldened him to take on his richer taxpayers, and the resulting anger still burns through Procopius's writings (he was himself from at least a gentry-level family).[6] Is Procopius's anger proof that the Eastern Empire as a whole was overtaxed?

There are two forms of overtaxation: political and economic. Political overtaxation prompts huge amounts of protest, avoidance, and evasion among taxpayers either because they consider current levels too high or because the money is being spent badly. Economic overtaxation is straightforwardly about numbers. In an industrial economy, if high taxes increase production costs to the point where too many purchasers stop buying, output declines; the result is serious economic damage.

In an agricultural economy like the East Roman Empire's, overtaxation shows up not just in peasants hiding production and making uncoordinated protests against landlords or state but at worst in peasant families not being left with enough to sustain themselves properly. This generates chronic if not usually immediately fatal levels of malnutrition, and lack of food reserves make the population more prone to disease. Then normal, unavoidable crop failures will generate bursts of high mortality, so that, in the longer term, population and the area under cultivation both gradually decline.[7] Against this kind of framework for a qualitative judgment, because no figures survive, does it look like Justinian overtaxed the eastern heartlands, politically or economically, to pay for his western conquests?

He clearly did overtax his landowners politically. Procopius's diatribe is one indication, but there is a better one. After Justinian's death, his nephew Justin II immediately rescinded his uncle's policies—or some of them—on taxing the rich.[8] One of the easiest ways for any new regime to gain quick political capital is to reverse the least popular policies of its predecessor. But there is no sign, however, that levels were high enough to cause serious political damage. East Roman landowning elites showed no interest in seeking a Persian or other alternative allegiance, and structures of political consent within the Eastern Empire remained solid enough.

Nor is there much sign, either, of economic overtaxation in Justinian's reign either at elite or peasant level, although discussion is complicated by a serious outbreak of plague. The Justinianic pandemic, alongside the Black Death and another of the late nineteenth century, is one of the three great outbreaks known from documented human history. In 541, disease spread up the Red Sea coastline and through Egypt to Alexandria, from where it quickly reached the rest of the Eastern Empire and beyond. It arrived in Constantinople in the spring of 542 and in the cities of Syria, Palestine, and North Africa by the end of the year. By 543 it had infected Armenia, Italy, and Gaul before arriving in Britain. Huge controversy, however, surrounds its effects.

That it killed on a terrifying scale in Constantinople is beyond doubt. The contemporary accounts of Procopius and John of Ephesus agree that at least tens of thousands of people died in the city. As it cut a swathe through the population, the authorities resorted to the same kind of desperate measures for getting rid of the corpses that are reported during the Black Death: mass graves on the outskirts of the city, filling up the lower, unused levels of the towers. In economic terms, however, the really important thing is what happened in the countryside. The Eastern Empire's economy was overwhelmingly agricultural, and the health or otherwise of that sector of the economy dictated Constantinople's fiscal fate. Again, the Justinianic plague certainly killed in the countryside, as the sources report, and there is some evidence for a consequent shortage of agricultural labour. Egyptian contracts from the later sixth century show land workers able to demand higher price wages, and some of Justinian's legislation of the 540s complains about workers overcharging.

But there is little convincing archaeological evidence for any major disruption to the fabric of the East Roman agricultural economy in the mid- to late sixth century due either to plague or to Justinianic overtaxation. Attempts to date what clear archaeological evidence there is for more general East Roman economic decline in the sixth and seventh centuries as early as ca. AD 550 do not convince; most of it is certainly later. Excavations at particular sites, such as Apamea in Roman Syria or Gerasa in Palestine, likewise suggest that prosperity continued throughout the sixth century, as do a number of rural surveys which show that exchange networks—not just in pottery but in the olive oil and wine that ceramics often contained—continued to function substantially as normal. And Justinian's regime was also able to find sufficient funds to rebuild both the ceremonial centre of Constantinople on a grandiose scale and Antioch, too. There, the continued flooding of the Orontes makes it difficult to be sure exactly what happened, and some have taken a minimalist view. But in the *Buildings*, Procopius devotes a lengthy, specific section to restoration after the sack of 540, and what archaeological evidence there is confirms the picture. Both the cities and countryside of the Eastern Empire show every sign of continued prosperity into the late sixth century, with no evidence for a major economic downturn.[9]

The hard evidence for both large-scale fiscal and economic disruption in the Eastern Empire is actually seventh-century and is so geographically specific that it looks like effect and not cause of the Persian and

Islamic conquests of that era. By 640, Egypt, Syria, and Palestine had all fallen definitively to Arab conquest, after briefer periods under Persian domination. Equally important, western Asia Minor, another region of great agricultural productivity, became a battleground, and archaeological investigation has revealed just what that meant for two of its ancient metropolises, Sardis and Ephesus.

Sardis suffered a sudden decline from great urban centre to fortified military stronghold. Until the end of the sixth century, the city continued to prosper, maintaining its great monuments. Its commercial life, too, continued to bustle; excavators uncovered outside the main bathhouse a colonnade of shops—a sign of vitality. The very wealthiest houses display, just possibly, a little decline in maintenance standards, but that is about it. Then the Persians sacked the city in 610. Not many of the inhabitants seem to have been killed, at least in the streets, but the refugees took few of their goods with them from the shops, and the city never recovered. On the old main site, all that excavators have ever found dating to the seventh century are a few clusters of poor houses; the main centre of activity shifted to a nearby hilltop. But this was a fortress, constructed out of reused materials from the old city, not a centre of population and economic activity. As a proper city, Sardis ceased to exist.

The situation was nearly as bad at nearby Ephesus. Here, too, straightforward continuity in the old city centre was broken. Habitation shifted to two new walled enclosures: one a small area, about a kilometre square, within the old site, the other marking off a smaller area around what had been the extramural Church of Saint John. The seventh-century population within these two sets of walls was larger than at Sardis, and its economic life more diverse. A great fair was still held there on a regular basis. Even so, post-AD 600 Ephesus was a shadow of its former self in size, wealth, and grandeur. The archaeological picture from the other old Roman cities of western Asia Minor is similar.[10]

Fundamentally the same picture emerges from Egypt in the papyri. We met the Apion family, with substantial landed estates (perhaps alongside others unknown) in the Oxyrhynchite nome, in Chapter 2. The family's estate records are substantial, though not without their methodological issues, throughout the century ca. AD 520–620. These suggest no major disruption to the estate's operations at any point in the sixth century, despite Justinian's heavier than average taxation demands and the impact of plague. The records continue into the early years of the Persian occupation but then stop in the year 626, and there is no sign that the estate or the fortune of the distinguished aristocratic family it used to help support was ever reconstituted subsequently, despite the return of Egypt, if briefly, to Constantinople's control in the 630s.[11]

Even the city of Constantinople itself did not escape the cull. Its population declined drastically in the seventh century, probably by as much as 90 per cent from its maximum half a million. It remained a large community in early medieval west European terms, but its late seventh- and eighth-century manifestation saw relatively few people living among the grandiose remains of its late Roman past. The Arab conquest terminated the Egyptian grain fleets which had supported the city's enormous late Roman population, and the more restricted resources available from the mid-seventh century could sustain only much smaller numbers. Using figures from the sixteenth-century Ottoman Empire, which had much the same shape as Justinian's Eastern Empire, the Muslim conquests of Egypt and the Middle East, combined with evident economic collapse in western Asia Minor, would have cost the seventh-century emperors of Constantinople somewhere between two-thirds and three-quarters of the annual tax revenues enjoyed by their sixth-century predecessors.[12] The economic devastation experienced by the citizens of Ephesus and Sardis at the micro level had its fiscal counterpart at the macro level of the imperial system as a whole, and the effects were catastrophic.

As its tax base shrank, the entire administrative structure of the empire had to be recast. The main job of imperial government remained, as ever, making war, but all the pre-existing parameters had been overturned. The seventh-century empire still needed to maintain substantial armies because the Arab threat to what was left of its territories remained potentially overwhelming, but only a fraction of its previous revenues was available. As in the earlier crisis generated by the Persians in the third century, the rump East Roman Empire emerged from the disasters of the seventh with a brand-new fiscal-military structure which was able to sustain what remained in the new era of fiscal impoverishment. Taxing the empire to finance the army along the lines which had crystallized under the tetrarchs (see Chapter 2) could no longer support large enough military forces, given the losses of tax base, to fend off continued Arab attack. Some monetary taxes continued, and soldiers continued to receive some cash payments, but these were both smaller and less frequent (also now in silver rather than gold), and the basic remuneration of the military instead took the form of land grants. Under the so-called theme system, the troops received land in return for a hereditary military obligation, which had to be passed on to another member of the household when the original individual was no longer able to serve. This was a much simpler system than raising and moving about vast sums of cash, as had formerly happened. Again, as in the third-century analogue, the whole administrative structure of the empire adjusted to this new fiscal-military spine. Whereas the old system had required large numbers of bureaucrats, pursuing many and varied tasks, the new one did not. The end result, one appropriate to the scale of its fiscal losses, was a much simpler small-state structure for what remained of Justinian's empire.[13]

So great were these losses that they even generated an ideological recasting of the empire's cosmological self-understanding. Claiming to be a unique, divinely guided state, destined by the Almighty to bring Christian civilization to the entire globe lost most of its force once two-thirds of the empire had been swallowed up by the standard-bearers of the alternative Islamic religion. Fortunately, Judaeo-Christian tradition offered another, more appropriate model. Emperors increasingly drew on the Old Testament to style themselves the leaders of a much more restricted Chosen People, riding a Constantinopolitan ark of salvation through desperate adversity towards a final triumph at the end of time.[14]

In general terms, the losses to rampant Islam relegated what had been an East Roman global empire, capable of exerting power and influence all the way from Spain to central Asia in the time of Justinian, to a regional power, largely confined to the eastern Mediterranean by the end of the seventh century: it was as much of a successor state, in reality, to the Roman Empire (despite its own persistent claims to the contrary) as its counterparts in the early medieval West. In practice, what remained of the East Roman Empire at this point became an unwilling strategic satellite of the Islamic world. All subsequent periods of Constantinopolitan expansion, even that led by the famous Macedonian emperors of the tenth and early eleventh centuries, came when the Islamic world was fragmented. Correspondingly, whenever a substantial portion of the Islamic world formed a united bloc, the area of Constantinopolitan rule contracted. Macedonian prosperity was quickly curtailed when Seljuk dominance unified much of the fragmented post-Abbasid Islamic world in the later eleventh century, and the pattern applied earlier, too. It was a second period of early Islamic unity under the Umayyads (see Chapter 10) which generated the loss, directly or indirectly, of much of Justinian's new Western imperial holdings in Africa and Italy in the later seventh and early eighth centuries.[15]

Bringing these intersecting patterns of political, economic, and administrative development clearly into focus allows us to refine the central question that needs to be asked. Justinian's conquest policies generated a great deal of immediate economic loss, combined with huge administrative and political strain within Eastern imperial heartlands. But these were not enough to derail or even fundamentally transform the structures of the Eastern Empire in the sixth century. The real changes that mark the demotion of Constantinople from world to regional power all belong to the seventh century, following the high drama of Persian and Arab Islamic conquest. In the current state of knowledge at least, attributing Eastern imperial collapse in any simple way to Justinian's conquests policies, therefore, does not convince. There is too big a time gap and too much evidence for intervening agricultural prosperity in too much of the eastern heartland. To understand if there might, nonetheless, be some kind of more complex relationship between Justinian's conquests and subsequent East Roman collapse, we need to take a closer look at the processes which led to the initial Persian and, above all, the Arab conquests of the imperial heartland.

LOSS OF THE HEARTLAND

Two substantially separate processes came together to undermine Constantinople's control of its traditional economic heartlands. The first was a long-term transformation of the Arab-dominated world of the desert fringes of both the East Roman and Sassanian empires which culminated in the creation of a force capable of overcoming, in an astonishingly brief moment in the seventh century, both the great powers of antiquity. The underlying intellectual problem in understanding the rise of Islam, which played such a fundamental role in the final stages of this transformation, is the lack of any early historical material from within the Islamic tradition itself. No narratives of the life of the Prophet Muhammad now survive from earlier than the ninth century. By then, Islam had been through two major revolutions: a first crisis, which generated the original divide between Sunni and Shia in the seventh century, and then the Abbasid revolution in the mid-eighth. Given his overwhelming importance to the religion, these narratives naturally give an account of the Prophet's life which legitimizes Islam as it had evolved by the later ninth century; what relationship this may bear to the realities of the early seventh century is uncertain.[16] Nonetheless, it is crystal clear that the backstory to the rise of Islam is firmly rooted in the interstices of superpower conflict between Rome and Persia.

The Arabs of the desert fringe were the critical protagonists of the southern, desert conflict zone between the two great powers. Large conventional armies could not operate there, but the desert front offered many opportunities for profitable raiding and for distracting your opponent's attention from the heavily contested Armenian and Syrian fronts to the north, as practiced by Khavad in 531 and Belisarius a decade later. Hence both sides recruited, paid, and armed Arab allies to protect their own provinces from desert raiders and to cause as much trouble as possible for the other side. If you piece together the information available in late Roman sources from the fourth century to the sixth, one central fact emerges. Thanks at least in part to the wealth and weaponry with which both sides supported them, the political-military networks of their Arab allies increased markedly in size and power over this three-hundred-year period. In the fourth and fifth centuries, the Romans maintained a series of separate allied Arab chiefdoms on the fringes of the Palestinian and Syrian deserts. By the sixth century, Rome and Persia supported single allied networks: the Ghassanids and Lakhmids, respectively. The increased power of these groups is distinctly visible in the fact that they—sometimes at least—had their own seat at the negotiating table during peace talks and regularly pursued their own agendas independent of their imperial patrons. Caught between two superpowers, the world of these Arab clients went through a similar kind of transformation to that well documented in the case of Rome's largely Germanic-speaking clients on its European frontiers. This is no accident. The range of relationships, both positive and negative, that imperial powers tend to establish with their neighbours has the long-run effect of generating larger and more cohesive political entities on the fringes of empire, and the Arab world, of course, was being catalyzed by the interference of, not one, but two imperial powers.[17]

Viewed from this perspective, the political side of Muhammad's career, marking the final culmination of a long-running process of political unification in an imperial periphery, bears a striking resemblance to that of Attila the Hun. Attila generated unity among a whole series of Rome's former European frontier clients and some of their neighbours from the deeper interior. All these groups had previously been just as likely to quarrel among themselves as fight the empire, although—as was observable in the Arab world, too—long-term exposure to imperial interference meant that Rome's clients of the fourth century were larger and more solid entities than their counterparts of the first. United, however unwillingly, under Attila in the fifth century, they created a power bloc large enough to confront the empire directly and sometimes even win. Muhammad's career has close parallels. He united Arab groupings both from the frontier zone and the deeper interior who, over the previous centuries, had grown accustomed to operating in larger military and political networks without ever threatening to unify sufficiently to confront the might of Rome and Persia directly. Muhammad, however, added a religious element to his political authority, which proved powerful enough (just about) to hold his new confederation together after the death of its charismatic leader. After Attila's death, by contrast, so many of his subjects, like the Goths led to Italy by Theoderic (see Chapter 6), took the opportunity to re-establish their independence that the Hunnic empire ceased to exist within a generation. After Muhammad's death, the so-called *Ridda* ('Apostasy') wars saw a similar attempted breakaway, but a critical mass of the Prophet's supporters maintained overall unity by preventing those who were less committed to the enterprise from destroying it. Instead of rising and falling again with more or less equal rapidity, therefore, as its Hunnic counterpart did in Central Europe, Muhammad's unification of two empires' Arab clients, together with other groups from deeper within the interior of Arabia, not only endured but swiftly conquered virtually the whole of the Roman orient and all of the Sassanian Empire.[18]

Apart from the role of religion, there is one other fundamental difference between the emergence of seventh-century Arab unity and the earlier unification process operating among Rome's European clients. Many contingent factors, not least the Huns themselves, came together to bring down the western half of the Roman Empire in the fifth century, but the process was one dimension of much broader processes of strategic development which meant—whatever precise contingences might have unfolded—that the empire could not have survived in its original form. In origin, Rome was a Mediterranean-based empire which used its regional resources to conquer and/or dominate large parts of non-Mediterranean Europe in the century on either side of the birth of Christ. At this point, non-Mediterranean Europe was home only to relatively small populations due to its own internal underdevelopment, above all in agricultural production. By the mid-first millennium, however, new agricultural techniques had begun to unlock the vast potential of this landscape, populations grew accordingly, and northern Europe started to eclipse the Mediterranean as the centre of imperial power in the western Eurasian landscape. By the time that Charlemagne was crowned emperor on Christmas Day 800, northern Europe was predatory on its Mediterranean neighbours rather than vice versa, large states were emerging in northern and eastern Europe, and the balance of strategic power had shifted decisively northwards. It is not impossible to imagine other sequences of events in which a reshaped Roman Empire responded to these underlying shifts by moving its own centre of gravity much more to the north-east. Arguably it had already begun to do so by the fourth century, when Trier, on the Rhine frontier, had become the functioning capital of the Western Empire. But in overall terms, the fall of the Western Empire and the Hunnic unification of many of Rome's European clients were part of a momentous shift in overall balances of power across western Eurasia.[19]

The Arab conquest of Sassanian Persia and of most of the East Roman Empire in the seventh century, by contrast, marked no similar shift in the Near East. The rise of Islam certainly reshuffled control of the vital revenue-generating regions of the region—Egypt, Syria, Palestine, Iraq, and Iran—into new hands, but it did not see the rise of entirely new centres of population, revenue, and political domination. Before Muhammad, these centres were divided between two empires, afterwards only the one, but they, and not Arabia itself, remained the key centres of wealth and political power. The Umayyad Caliphate of the seventh and earlier eighth centuries was based in Syria, its Abbasid successor in Iraq; only for the briefest period was the new Islamic world actually run from Arabia. This contrast strongly suggests that while Arab unification was clearly important to the extraordinary transformations of the seventh-century Near East, it did not represent the same kind of fundamental shift in prevailing strategic balances of regional power that worked itself out in first-millennium Europe. Wealth and power continued to be located in broadly the *same* places before and after the Arab takeover, and direct rule from Arabia itself represented only the briefest break in long-standing historical patterns.[20] This draws our attention to the second major factor in the loss of Constantinople's traditional heartlands: a complete breakdown in its relations with Persia.

Justinian's immediate legacy here was peace on all three sectors of the Persian front. At the time of his death on 14 November 565, Mesopotamia had been quiet for twenty years and the Caucasus for a decade and a half. Raiding seems to have continued on the desert fringes to the south but not on a large scale. The peace of 562 was supposed to last for fifty years but never got close. War began again within a decade of Justinian's death and culminated in twenty-five years of total war between 602 and 627 which left both empires much weaker than when it began.

Two factors kick-started this vicious cycle of destabilization; one was a perennial feature of Roman-Persian relations, the other was entirely new. The old favourite was succession: the arrival on the throne of a new emperor facing the usual desperate imperative to establish himself securely in power. Apart from his calculated rebuff to the early Avar ambassadors (p. 285), the new emperor, Justin II, like his uncle Justinian before he slid into a policy of western expansion, had a firm eye on establishing his ruling credentials at the expense of Persia—always the East Roman enemy of choice.

The problem, of course, was that while they were the target of first choice against whom any kind of victory could generate great political capital, the Persians were also a dangerous opponent, as many Roman emperors had found to their cost. What prompted Justin nonetheless to seek to define his reign at Persian expense was a second, entirely new factor: the growing power of the western Turks, who had pushed Avars westwards in the late 550s (p. 284). By the later 560s, western Turkish hegemony had reached the northern fringes of the Aral, Caspian, and even Black seas, so that its armies could now potentially intervene in Roman-Persian relations by direct attack through the Caucasus. Justin II's strategy for success centred on mobilizing the western Turks against the Persians, and a succession of embassies and gifts left Constantinople for the steppe. It was eventually agreed that a joint campaign would be launched by East Roman and western Turkish armies in the year 573. The Romans would attack Nisibis, lost 210 years before, while the Turks prevented any Persian response by launching their own attack from the east.

Justin's armies duly moved on Nisibis, but the Turks never appeared. In the resulting disaster, its garrison held out amidst ferocious assault, while the undistracted Persian field armies mounted a well-calculated counterattack. One division struck into Syria, but Chosroes (still the same Chosroes, amazingly, that Justin had refused to adopt) led his main body against Dara: cornerstone of the defence of Roman Mesopotamia. After a six-month siege, the Persians stormed the city and enslaved its population. Distraught, Justin II suffered such a complete mental collapse that power devolved to a regency council. Why the Turks failed to show is unclear, but Justin had destabilized relations with Persia only to suffer catastrophic defeat.[21]

For the next decade, war dragged on, and despite a few successes—in 576, the Romans captured the shah's wife, extinguishing the holy flame that he brought on campaign—the non-stop and highly expensive warfare in Mesopotamia gradually told against them. By the later 580s, the new Emperor Maurice was running out of money. In 588, the unpaid garrison of Martyropolis simply handed over their important frontier fortress to the Persians, and much of the imperial field army, stationed near Edessa, rebelled on the news that their pay had been cut by 25 per cent. Then, in the depths of Roman despair, the inherent weakness of the Persian system intervened. Chosroes himself had finally died in the meantime (579), and in 590, a leading Persian general, Bahram, deposed and killed his successor, Hormisdas IV. Hormisdas's son and designated heir, Chosroes II, fled to Constantinople, offering a huge advance to the Roman position in the Caucasus in return for Maurice's support. By 591, Chosroes II was established back on the Persian throne, and in return, Maurice received most of Armenia, giving the Romans strategic control of the top end of the passes through the Zagros Mountains which led straight to the Persian Empire's economic heartland between the Tigris and the Euphrates: a knife over the Persian jugular. Peace returned after eighteen solid years of warfare, but the scale of the triumph was so great, however, that it was a destabilizing factor in itself. One recent study has labelled it the Eastern Empire's 'Versailles moment'. The treaty gave the Romans such a strategic advantage that any shah was bound to go to war again to redress the balance whenever a suitable opportunity presented itself.[22]

It was not long in coming. With his armies freed from the Persian front by the peace of 591, Maurice set them to work in the Balkans to overturn the Avar successes of the 580s. After considerable gains, his generals concluded that real victory required large-scale campaigning early in the year, before grass was growing for the Avars' horses. Late in 602, therefore, the field army was ordered not to return south for winter quarters but to stay in the field; on the back of long-simmering resentments generated by the pay cuts of the 580s, it rebelled. By late November, under the leadership of Phocas, it approached Constantinople. Phocas was crowned emperor on 24 November, Maurice being executed three days later with four of his five sons. The fifth son, Theodosius, died a little later, along with many of the former emperor's chief ministers. Or did he? The head of Theodosius, unlike those of the rest of Maurice's unfortunate family, was never displayed in Constantinople, and shortly thereafter, an individual claiming to be Theodosius was fighting alongside Persian armies, who said they had come to avenge the deposed Maurice. We do not really know if Theodosius escaped or not, but if he did, Chosroes quickly eliminated him. The end result was a second bout of knock-down, cataclysmic warfare between the two empires in quick succession.[23]

While Roman imperial politics degenerated into coups and rebellions, Chosroes II proceeded to roll up virtually the whole of the Roman east. Even the arrival in October 619 of the new emperor, Heraclius, from North Africa initially made no difference. By the end of that year, Persian forces had systematically reduced all the Roman fortresses guarding the Mesopotamian front, opening the door to still grander ambitions. By 607, too, Maurice's Armenian gains from the 591 treaty had been lost. In 611, Chosroes's commander, Shahvaraz, struck deep into Roman Syria, capturing Apamea, Antioch, and Emesa. Unlike 540, this was no raid. The Persians also pushed north onto the Anatolian plateau, capturing Caesarea. In the south, Damascus soon followed, leading to the loss of all Palestine, including Jerusalem and the True Cross in 614. Further north, a scorched-earth policy was unleashed; Ephesus was stormed, its centre reduced to dust and ashes. Chosroes refused all peace offers from an increasingly desperate Constantinopolitan political establishment, including an extraordinarily abject embassy in 616 ostensibly from the Senate (since the shah refused to acknowledge Heraclius) which offered to recognize Chosroes as 'supreme emperor' and style the Romans his 'slaves'. A successful invasion of Egypt was then completed by 621, sea raids simultaneously hitting Cyprus and the island chains of the Aegean. The nadir came in late July 626, when the imperial capital was faced with a Persian army on the other side of the Bosporus and an Avar army camped outside the great Theodosian land walls.

In the end, however, the great assault on Constantinople foundered on a combination of the city's impregnable land walls, which beat off a week of Avar assaults, and the imperial navy's control of the Bosporus. The crunch moment came when a fleet of Slav canoes tried to break into the city from the water, only to be utterly massacred, a setback which made the Avars' composite army fall apart. Astonishingly, Heraclius himself had not been in the city during the siege, so great was his confidence in its defences. He was retraining and organizing his field forces further east. Critically he also managed, finally, to negotiate a functioning alliance with the western Turks, that chimera which had led Justin II to go to war.

In 627 a huge Turkish army stormed through the Caucasus into the Persian-dominated kingdom of Iberia. They killed its Persian client king and handed over to Heraclius forty thousand men for further operations. This combined army marched over the Zagros Mountains and down the line of the Tigris into the Iranian heartland of the Sassanian Empire, defeating a Persian army just outside Nineveh in December. Rather than take on the walls of Ctesiphon, Heraclius employed scorched-earth tactics to batter the economic engine of the Persian Empire. Then he sat back and watched the Persian polity implode. Chosroes II was deposed by coup d'état in early 628, and a sequence of short-lived regimes followed. Eventually Heraclius got the deal he wanted. The Persians withdrew from the conquered Roman provinces, most of whose administration they had not touched, and Heraclius returned to Constantinople in triumph, the True Cross safely back in Roman hands.

Though perfectly natural, any thoughts of victory he may have had proved utterly misplaced. Persia had been beaten back and the empire's boundaries restored, but it was not actually a victory. The new peace deal did not reassert the advanced frontier line of 591 but reverted to the old one from the time of Justinian. The final outcome was actually a draw. Heraclius had not so much won a great victory as fought his way back from the brink of defeat; the overall situation remained fragile. Parts of the rich lands of western Asia Minor had been ravaged—witness the fates of Sardis and Ephesus—and loyalties in Syria, Palestine, and Egypt had been muddled by a decade and a half, in some cases, of Persian rule. The situation in the Balkans, too, was utterly out of hand. With all available troops needed south of the Bosporus, Avars and Slavs had run wild, the settlements of the latter increasing apace. Worst of all, the imperial treasury was exhausted. In the depths of crisis, Heraclius had forced through extraordinary measures. Military pay was halved, free bread within the capital ended, the treasuries of the churches emptied of their precious metals. It had been enough, if only just, to pay off the Turks and launch the great counterstrike into Iran.[24]

Left to its own devices, there is no reason why the East Roman imperial system could not have resurrected itself in due course. The nightmares of the previous twenty-five years had not involved greater losses than the depths of the third-century crisis, when, again, large tracts of the East fell out of Roman rule. Then, for a decade and a half after the defeat and capture of Valerian, the city of Palmyra had become the centre of a successor state which defeated both Persians and Romans and ran an arc of territory from Egypt through to Asia Minor. Yet the empire had bounced back successfully, restoring its control under Aurelian in the mid-270s, and eventually refilled its treasuries from the cities' taxation flows. Three political generations later, in the mid-fourth century, loyalty to the empire was once more second nature, and the Near East was in the middle of a three-hundred-year patch as Constantinople's heartland.[25] In principle, there is no reason why a similar rebuilding job could not have been undertaken by Heraclius and his successors.

They were not, however, to be afforded the same luxury. It is impossible to know exactly what went on in the desert during the quarter-century of total war between the two old superpowers of the Near East. But it cannot be a coincidence that it was in this period that Muhammad was able to build his new coalition. Both Rome and Persia normally kept a close eye on their Arab clients and would intervene if political developments took a dangerous turn. The Emperor Maurice dismantled the Ghassanid phylarchate in the 580s, when its independence was becoming far too marked. Complete fixation on total war between 603 and 628 left Muhammad free of the early imperial intervention which would at least have made his task much more difficult and possibly even impossible. Starting the process of confederation building in the Hijaz, well away from either imperial frontier, represented extra insurance against early, decisive imperial intervention.[26] It is also the case that twenty-five years of total war bankrupted both protagonists, putting enormous strains on their imperial systems. The actual outcome was a draw of exhaustion. A bit like the modern self-declared caliphate, Muhammad's original exploded into and exploited, if to much greater effect, a looming power vacuum.

Temporarily, Arabia's human resources, or the large chunk of them united by Muhammad, could provide a large enough power base to conquer most of the two empires exhausted by an unparalleled fifty years of more or less continuous warfare. But longer-term patterns do emphasize that imperial exhaustion was crucial to the story. Unlike non-Roman Europe further north, Arabia did not become the permanent site of a new Islamic empire based on the rise of new and unstoppable economic and demographic forces in human history. Rather, Muhammad's religion provided a new unifying system which realigned the existing centres of wealth and population into a new political order, which continued to be run, after a very brief period (ca. 630–60) from one or other of the old imperial centres for the foreseeable future. Arabia itself, apart from its importance as the centre of religious ritual, retreated once more into the background.

This strongly suggests that while Arab unification played a central role in the story, it would never have been enough by itself to conquer the East Roman and Sassanian empires without the mutual exhaustion brought on by large-scale warfare between the two in no less than forty-three of the fifty-five years between 573 and 628. The Arab conquests across the Near East demonstrate the effects of a momentary possibility opened up by self-inflicted devastation in the old imperial heartlands, not a permanent relocation in regional centres of strategic power. This, in turn, limits the amount of direct responsibility that can be placed at the door of Justinian for the loss of Constantinople's eastern heartlands.

At most, the emperor can be ascribed only a marginal role in the emergence of greater Arab unity. He did promote an unprecedented degree of unity among East Rome's Arab federates, recognizing the then-Ghassanid leader Arethas as the first supreme phylarch (overall leader) ca. 529. But he did so only reactively and unwillingly. The Persians had already united their federates under Lakhmid control and were able, as a result, to launch a damaging raid through Rome's desert fringes in 529; it was too powerful for Constantinople's not-yet-united Arab allies to oppose. In response, Justinian created a larger network of allied Arabs, but that network was dismantled again by the Emperor Maurice in the 580s, and it was not a direct ancestor of the coalition put together by Muhammad in the 620s.[27]

Nor is there a direct line of cause and effect leading from Justinian to the utter financial exhaustion which made the Near East of the 630s so ripe for a takeover at the hands of Muhammad's newly united Arabs. Justinian's wars created acute financial strains within his empire and caused it substantial direct losses, but nothing on the scale generated by the wars of the later sixth and early seventh centuries. In other words, it was the political decisions of Justin II and Maurice—the one to start world war, the other to enforce a punitive peace—and the appearance of the western Turks which were fundamentally responsible for creating the conditions in which the forces of Islam could conquer the Roman orient, not the sporadic and generally limited spats with Persia which distinguish the reign of Justinian.

JUSTINIAN AND THE STRATEGY OF EMPIRE

There has been periodic debate about whether Rome pursued any rational underlying strategy for imperial defence and, if so, what form or forms it may have taken in the different eras of empire.[28] In the policies of Justinian's reign, it is possible to detect some recognizable elements of strategic military and diplomatic calculation. Because an effective defence of the Balkans was consistently hampered by troop shortages, divide-and-rule diplomacy—setting Lombards against Gepids and Utigurs against Cutrigurs—and intensive fortification were employed in compensation. A developed understanding of landscape also shows itself in the attention given to particular choke points where a strong defensive line could protect a geographically isolatable area within: the two Long Walls—one protecting the Chersonese, the other the suburbs of Constantinople—or the passes of Thermopylae. The regime clearly also took a strategic approach to prioritizing its different theatres of warfare, even if its calculations did not always work out as planned. The eastern front, above all Mesopotamia, which protected the key revenue-generating heartlands of empire, consistently received the highest priority in men and materiel; only when that was secure were sufficient reinforcements sent to Italy to complete the subjugation of the Goths. A rational, analytic approach is also visible in the conduct of individual campaigns, not least in Lazica. There, the logistic problems faced by Persian forces, who could not provide for large armies off the land but had to get huge quantities of supplies over the Surami Ridge, meant that smaller Roman armies could use the spring to isolate and defeat in detail the limited Persian forces able to overwinter there before reinforcements could arrive. For all its administrative limitations and structural corruption, the post-third-century fiscal-military skeleton of empire functioned well enough to allow Justinian and his chief advisers to balance income against expenditure with enough accuracy to deploy forces across a number of theatres of war and maintain balance between those deployments, which reflected fairly accurately the regime's priorities. Justinian's failure to close hostilities in Italy in 539 did concede an important (and costly) military advantage to his Persian rival at one point, but only for a limited period. Otherwise the regime was just about able to hold its position on secondary fronts while pursuing more active warfare in the areas of priority.[29] Maintaining such a balance certainly involved costs and losses for many of those caught in the theatres temporarily put on hold (e.g. Italy for most of the 540s). But from the regime's own perspective at least, strategic control was maintained well enough apart from the disastrous period between 540 and 543, when the initiative in the East was seized by Chosroes.

It is nonetheless utterly impossible to conclude, in my view, that Justinian's reign is marked by anything like a rationally framed strategy of empire overall. His conquest policy was not based on careful calculation of the potential long-term strategic gains to be had from acquiring North Africa, Italy, and southern Spain versus the costs, direct and indirect, of their acquisition any more than it was the result of some romantic notion about restoring old Roman boundaries. On the contrary, it was driven by a potent mixture of the demands of internal political agendas and immediate opportunism. Justinian found himself in a catastrophic political mess after the failure of his aggressive Persian war and the destruction of central Constantinople in the Nika riot. At that point, his regime had lost all ideological legitimacy, and the dissentions within the Vandal kingdom offered him a chance for restoring lost political capital. Past disasters made him tread carefully in preparing and launching the expedition, but that is not remotely the same thing as saying that it was the result of careful calculation of potential strategic gains measured against inherent costs. Justinian was interested only in the gain to himself; he did not really care about what the effect would be on the overall strategic position of the empire. Indeed, Belisarius was originally dispatched with complete license to make up precise policy—in terms of how much was to be attempted militarily—on the hoof.[30] Only after the full extent of the current battlefield advantage enjoyed by the elite field forces of the remodelled East Roman army sank in did opportunistic one-off improvisation transform itself into a full-on conquest policy with its own internal logic and momentum, as predatory diplomatic manoeuvring was used to create an opening in Ostrogothic Italy. Even then, immediate circumstances and internal politics continued to drive decision-making. The realization that East Roman forces enjoyed a significant battlefield advantage just generated its own kind of more ambitious opportunism, and when that window of opportunity began to close in the face of Persian response, Justinian himself was willing to settle for a partial Italian victory in 539/40—until, that is, Belisarius took control of events on the front line to trick Wittigis into surrendering Ravenna. From that point on, prestige would not allow the emperor to return to a compromise peace based on partitioning Italy, even when Totila's insurgency and war with Persia were making huge, simultaneous demands on the resources of the empire.[31]

The constant in all this was emphatically not rational strategic calculation focused on the good of the empire as a whole. As the Nika riot in particular demonstrates, along with many other incidents in Justinian's long reign (such as the refusal to negotiate Chosroes's retreat in 540 when there was no Roman army of substance available to protect the cities of Mesopotamia), Justinian cared not a jot for the good of his subjects (or anyone else for that matter). His priority throughout was nothing more than maintaining his regime's political control of the empire. His subjects and opponents could die in their tens of thousands, as far as the emperor was concerned, so long as Justinian sat securely on his throne (whatever his propaganda might declare). In that sense, the conquest policy cannot be considered any more strategic than the rushed job the emperor did on legal reform in the 520s and early 530s or his determined if ultimately unsuccessful attempts to heal division within the Eastern church. Not only do all betray the same hallmarks of momentary improvised opportunism, utterly subordinated to the immediate political imperatives of the regime, but foreign policy, legal policy, and religious policy were interchangeable, sometimes interconnected, avenues for Justinian to win political capital, all ranking more or less equally in his mind. The failure of the conversations of 532 with anti-Chalcedonian church leaders was a further stimulus behind the decision to attack North Africa. The success of that expedition was used to drive through his legal reforms; Justinian returned to a more ambitious religious policy in the early 540s as military success lost momentum in the face of reverses in both Italy and the East.[32] Fundamentally, Justinian's drive for western expansion was not about some kind of modern-style, strategic foreign policy at all.

This is not to say that the calculations behind it were not rational, just that they were overwhelmingly driven by internal political agendas rather than any kind of overarching strategic foreign policy. Internal political agendas always intrude into foreign policy discussions and decisions about whether or not to go to war. Sometimes, even in the modern day, it is much harder to tell where one begins and the other ends than governments like to pretend. But contemporary Western states at least have to sell their foreign policy decision-making as plausible to a large audience of voters, in the face of the direct scrutiny of semi-independent press agencies. The Emperor Justinian ran a very different kind of political entity. On the one hand, he did not have to answer to voters, and independent scrutiny did not exist. As Procopius tells us in *Anekdota* and many incidents recorded in a whole run of late Roman histories confirm, criticism of a God-appointed ruler was essentially treasonable and punishable by death. The later Roman Empire was a one-party state in its public political culture, and this afforded a sitting regime considerable advantages.[33] On the other hand, if the politically enfranchised elements within the system were limited in number, this did not make the political game any less intense or lower the stakes involved. If anything, it increased both. The Emperor Maurice may have won the greatest victory over the Persians that anyone could remember in 591, but this did not stop him being executed with probably all five of his sons just eleven years later. The Emperor Zeno held onto power successfully, in one sense, for a decade and a half but spent two years in exile and had to fight off the best part of half a dozen plots as he struggled to keep control in Constantinople. The price of failure at any point, as it was for all his challengers, would have been some unpleasant form of death. Both winning and subsequently holding onto power in the late Roman world were extremely difficult political tasks, with death the price of failure, so it was utterly rational to frame all your policies with that end in mind.

The key constituencies in the violent and profoundly turbulent political process at the heart of the late Roman world, as Chapter 1 showed, are easy enough to identify. The broader run of minor royals was always a source of potential contenders for the throne, as were the senior ranks of the military and senior court dignitaries and high officials. The latter two categories tended to overlap with each other and with a potentially separate third category: the very richest landowners within the empire. However, the demands of maintaining substantial landed fortunes pretty much obliged you to be part of some kind of senatorial or court network, even if you did not formally hold office. There have been attempts recently to identify the broader ranks of the imperial bureaucracy as a further power bloc, particularly in Justinian's reign, not least to argue that Procopius's *Anekdota* had an extremely serious political purpose to sway opinion among it.[34] But while the bureaucracy was full of well-educated and certainly opinionated individuals, largely deriving from the social level of the gentry and above, there is not the slightest sign that the bureaucracy was capable of functioning as a coherent political bloc. From the age of Justinian, the evidence of John Lydus strongly demonstrates that this was a group much too riven with departmental rivalries ever to function as a single force in the shaping of imperial politics, although individual members of it (like John himself) were certainly tied vertically to much grander patrons who were, so that they would have been watching what happened higher up with the greatest of interest and would have had opinions on it. In two hundred years of quite detailed, political narrative history—from the fourth century, when it first came into existence, onwards—there is not a single recorded occasion where the bureaucracy functioned as an effective power bloc responsible for the rise and fall of any imperial regime, even for exercising a collective veto. It is probably most accurate to view it in much the same light as the Christian church establishment: an important body of opinion but one incapable of enough unity actually to shape overall religious affairs. As also emerges clearly from Justinian's reign (and this is the same throughout late antiquity), all real initiative at the macro level, even in religious affairs, remained with the emperor, even if he could not always get everyone to do precisely what he wanted.[35]

In practice, certainly, it was from these traditional political constituencies, whose influence is equally well evidenced in other reigns, that we see all the potential and actual challenges to Justinian's rule. The nephews of Anastasius I, two of them, at least, from the extended reaches of one imperial family, posed the most direct threat at the start of Justinian's reign. In a sense, the emperor's high-risk strategies in both provoking Persia and taking on the difficult, high-profile project of legal reform were about proving his ruling credentials in the face of these potential alternative contenders for the throne, especially as Hypatius seems to have been associated with a more conciliatory line towards Khavad. But from an older royal family, Anicius Olybrius was also lurking in the wings, his mother's great Church of Saint Polyeuktos dominating the religious landscape of the capital at the moment of Justinian's accession. Justinian seems to have exiled him after Nika, only bringing him back into the fold when victory in Africa rescued his position.[36] But even that security was only provisional. As soon as Belisarius had decisively defeated Gelimer at Ad Decimum, rumours started that the general himself was intending to make a move on the purple. These were plausible enough that he returned to Constantinople as soon as possible to scotch them. A popular and successful general with a core of his own loyal *bucellarii* was an obvious threat to a sitting emperor; in 540 the whispers began again, as the general took possession of Ravenna and much of the Ostrogothic leadership. Belisarius remained consistently loyal and was celebrated both with a triumph (although that involved self-abasement in front of Justinian's majesty at the vital moment) and on the mosaics of the Chalke Gate, but the potential threat from the upper reaches of the military was real enough.[37]

Absolutely typical of late Roman power politics were the final two plots against Justinian reported in the sources. Although victory in North Africa and initial success in Italy gave the emperor a period of untouchability, the destruction of Antioch, Totila's insurgency, and even the setbacks in Lazica once again raised the usual question marks against Justinian's divinely chosen legitimacy, as military reverses always did. In 548/9, after the death of Theodora, two Armenian princelings approached a senior East Roman military officer called Artabanes, also of Armenian origins, who thought the moment might be ripe for regime change. He in turn made overtures to the son of Justinian's cousin Germanus, who was not only politically prominent but had a decent military record. In the end, Germanus decided not to take the risk, perhaps not least because he was a plausible heir to the throne anyway, and who knew when the emperor might die?[38]

The final plot unfolded in November 562, when a cabal of wealthy bankers and medium-level functionaries were caught red-handed in the act of attempted imperial assassination, one of the plotters killing himself to avoid capture. The web of suspicion in this case led towards Belisarius on the one hand (some of the plotters belonged to his household) and to the Quaestor Constantine and a senior bureaucrat called Julian on the other. By this stage, the childless Justinian was eighty, so questions of succession were everywhere, and the regime's prestige had taken a heavy recent blow when the Bulgars broke through the Long Walls of Constantinople in force, an action which also saw Belisarius's last hurrah as he took command of the counterattack (p. 283). Whether the plotters wanted to put one of these senior connections directly on the throne, perhaps trying to tempt Belisarius to exploit all the prestige he had just won against the Bulgars, or were trying to affect the process of choosing an heir among the potential contenders, is unclear, as is the degree of guilt to be attached to the chief protagonists. But it was enough for Belisarius to suffer a period of disgrace from November 562 through to the following June, although the later story that Justinian had his great general blinded and forced him to beg in the streets is nothing more than medieval legend.[39]

Both incidents are typical, however, of the way in which major defeats or setbacks tended to generate plotting and of the kind of circles—senior officers or high officials and fringe members of the imperial family—on which the plotting usually coalesced. In such a fiercely competitive environment, all power was highly contingent, and there was no such thing as abdication followed by a peaceful retirement. The only way off the imperial throne was in a coffin or via the gibbet, as Maurice's family found to its cost. Even if we do not want, from a modern perspective, to approve of the kind of tactics that were required to hold on to power, we can certainly understand why it was rational for those who were engaged in this competition to subordinate all policy and everybody else's interests to this task. Against this standard, if none other, Justinian succeeded triumphantly. Holding on to power for the best part of forty years to die in your bed, as an active emperor, too—not merely a figurehead—was no small achievement, since holding on to power did not get easier the longer you held the throne. Unlike his uncle Justin I, the emperor did not formally designate and advance the interests of a chosen heir; the sources suggest that in the emperor's last years, his favour was more or less evenly distributed between two contenders, both called Justin: one a senior palace official and the son of his sister Vigilantia; the second the son of Justinian's cousin Germanus, who had led the surge in Africa and resisted the overtures of plotters in 548/9. In the end, the nephew seized the throne and had his rival executed, despite an earlier agreement that they would effectively share power. But even the refusal to name an heir outright can be understood as a mechanism to hold on to power on Justinian's part. Were an eighty-plus-year-old incumbent unambiguously to name an heir who got his hands fully on the reins of power, then influence and control would inevitably pass to that heir, as is reported to have happened in Justinian's own case in the later years of Justin I.[40]

But if it is impossible to see Justinian's policy of western expansion as the product, in any real sense, of rational strategic calculation, neither is there any strong evidence that it undermined the overall security of his empire. The economies of both the new African and particularly the Italian provinces suffered substantial dislocation in the process of pacification, not so much in the initial wars of conquest as in the suppression of subsequent insurgencies. Nonetheless, enough of both territories was held for long enough to repay the costs of initial conquest and cover the costs, too, of their subsequent defence. Even the loss of northern Italy to the Lombards and the failure to recover it subsequently was due to the intrusion of third-party forces—the Avars and above all the Arabs—whose rise to prominence cannot really be blamed on the emperor. The western conquests obviously had direct and indirect costs for the East, too: everything from the destruction of Antioch in 540 to appreciably higher tax bills throughout the reign. But even with the impact of pandemic on top, there is no clear evidence that any of this caused any major dislocation in the agricultural prosperity of the beating economic heartlands of Constantinople's empire in western Asia Minor, Syria, Palestine, and Egypt. On the contrary, the available archaeological evidence strongly suggests that normal levels of prosperity—despite all the extra tax bills—continued here throughout the sixth century. However deplorable they were in humanitarian terms (I have no doubt that they were utterly deplorable), Justinian's policies did not undermine the overall strategic security of the empire as a whole. Rather, the loss of these East Roman heartlands (not to mention the complete eclipse of Sassanian Persia) must be ascribed to specific political decisions taken in the next two generations. It was the highly aggressive decision-making and overly ambitious responses of Justin II, Maurice, and Chosroes II which plunged the two great powers of antiquity into virtually fifty years of head-on, full-scale conflict and made it temporarily possible for an Arabian-based power decisively to remake political and cultural boundaries across the Near East as a whole.

The conclusion that it was the political decision-making of the next two generations of Roman and Persian leaders which fundamentally unhinged the strategic position of both empires does, however, suggest one final line of thought by which Justinian can be held at least partly responsible for what happened after his death. The events of Justinian's reign bequeathed his Roman successors a very particular political inheritance. As his own propaganda proclaimed, he was the 'conqueror of many nations'. By the time of his death, Constantinople was full of monuments emphasizing the fact. His triumphant equestrian statue presided over the city, stunning mosaics reminded you of the conquests of Africa and Italy as you entered the palace, and his astonishing thirty-three churches proclaimed his special relationship with the Almighty that made it all possible. Given the ideological importance within the Roman imperial system of military victory as the ultimate guarantor of divinely appointed legitimacy, you can see why these victories were placed at the forefront on every possible occasion where the regime celebrated itself.

But the victories also represented a highly toxic political legacy for his immediate successors. If the mark of a divinely appointed emperor, hence the route to political security, had now become victory on the scale of a Justinian, it was extremely difficult to return to the cautious policies of an Anastasius or a Justin I and expect to hold on to power. Within six days of Justinian's death, as we have seen, Justin II was telling the ambassadors of the Avars that there would be no more diplomatic presents. Corippus's careful treatment of this incident in his account of the transfer of power from Justinian to Justin makes it clear that this was a consciously taken decision on the part of the new regime to show that it was even tougher on barbarians than its predecessor in the defence of divinely ordained Roman civilization.[41] There is every chance that the need to outdo, even somehow to match, Justinian also played a similar role in Justin's fateful decision to forge an alliance with the Turks in a rather desperate attempt to win a great victory over Persia. If so, then Justinian's poisonously successful legacy of military victory played a major role in kick-starting the fifty-year cycle of world war which led inexorably to Constantinople's eventual demotion to regional power status.

TIMELINE

406	Vandals, Alans, and others crosses the Rhine.
416–18	Visigothic coalition settled in Aquitaine; joint campaigns with Roman armies destroy Siling Vandals and independence of Alans in Spain, leading to the creation of the Hasding-led Vandal-Alan coalition.
429	Vandal-Alan coalition crosses to Morocco.
438	Theodosian Code published after nine years work.
439	Geiseric seizes Carthage.
451	Council of Chalcedon defines the Incarnate Christ as 'in two natures'.
468	Defeat of Basiliscus's expedition; final attempt to reconquer North Africa from the Vandals.
469–74	Campaigns of Euric, which spread power of the Visigothic kingdom from the Loire to the Straits of Gibraltar.
ca. 470	Justin recruited into the imperial guards.
473–4	Amal-led Goths enter East Roman Balkans.
474	Zeno becomes emperor.
476	Deposition of Romulus Augustulus and sending of Western imperial regalia to Constantinople.
482	Zeno publishes *Henotikon*; start of Acacian schism.
482/3	Birth of Justinian.
484	Huneric's persecution of Catholic North Africans.

489–93	Theoderic the Amal conquers Italy after having united the Thracian *foederatii* to his inherited Amal power base; he recruits Rugi besides.
491	Anastasius becomes emperor.
500?	Birth of Procopius.
ca. 503	Birth of Theodora.
502–4	Anastasius's Persian war.
511	Severus becomes patriarch of Antioch; Anastasius's humiliation in the Hippodrome.
511–15	Revolt of Vitalian.
518	Justin becomes emperor.
519	End of the Acacian schism.
	Theoderic's heir, Eutharic, co-consul with Justin I.
520	Murder of Vitalian; rehabilitation of Hypatius; Justinian becomes *Magister Militum Praesentalis* and consul designate.
521/2	Baptism of King Tzath of Lazica in Constantinople.
	Marriage law changed to allow Justinian to marry Theodora.
523	Accession of Hilderic in North Africa; end to religious persecutions there.
525	Justinian becomes Caesar.
	Khavad's embassy requests Justin to adopt Chosroes; Justin rejects the request.
526	Death of Theoderic.
527	1 April: Justinian made co-Augustus, Theodora crowned empress.
	August: death of Justin I.
	Construction of Church of Saints Sergius and Bacchus begins.
529	7 April: First edition of the *Code of Justinian*.
530	January: Belisarius defeats Persians at Dara.
	May: Gelimer overthrows Hilderic to become ruler of Carthage.

531	Belisarius humiliated at Callinicum.
532	11–18 January: Nika riot; death of Hypatius, exile of eighteen senators. 'Endless Peace' with Chosroes; 'Conversations' with the Orthodox.
533	June: Fleet sails for North Africa. 15 September: Belisarius captures Carthage. 15 December: Battle of Tricamarum and destruction of Vandal military. 16 December: *Digest* and *Institutes* published.
534	March: Gelimer surrenders. Belisarius returns to Constantinople in triumph. Second edition of the *Code* published. October: Death of Athalaric.
534–5	Solomon campaigns against the Berbers. Theodahad deposes Amalasuentha; Peter the Patrician dispatched to Ravenna.
535	Belisarius takes Sicily. Revolt of Berber Godas in North Africa.
536	Easter: Stotzas's mutiny in Carthage. Autumn: Belisarius takes Naples and Rome.
537	27 December: Dedication of rebuilt Hagia Sophia.
537–8	March–March: Goths besiege Belisarius in Rome.
537–40	Germanus's surge and the initial pacification of the Berbers.
538	Death of Severus of Antioch.
538–9	Belisarius resumes mobile operations and traps Wittigis in Ravenna.
539	Cutrigurs raid Balkans and return with 200,000 prisoners.
540	May: Wittigis tricked into surrendering; Chosroes sacks Antioch and ransacks Roman Syria. December: Belisarius returns to Constantinople with his *bucellarii*.

541	Belisarius takes Sisauranon; Chosroes takes Petra in Lazica.
	Totila becomes king of the Goths.
542	Totila's initial victories at Verona and Faenza.
542–3	Chosroes returns to Mesopotamian front; plague hits with full force.
543–8	Second Berber revolt in North Africa and eventual victory of John Troglita.
544–8	Belisarius's second Italian period.
545	Truce with Chosroes on the Mesopotamian front.
547–56	Persian campaigns in Lazica.
548–9	Plot against Justinian in favour of Germanus.
550	Totila creates raiding fleet and ransacks Sicily.
551	Edict *On the True Faith.*
	Bessas recaptures Petra; destruction of Gothic raiding fleet.
552	Narses defeats and kills first Totila, then Teias.
	Liberius's expedition seizes southern coastal cities of Visigothic kingdom.
553	May–June: Second Council of Constantinople (ecumenical council).
553–4	Narses defeats Butilinus and Leutharis.
555	Death of Ragnaris, surrender of Gothic treasure.
557	New truce with Chosroes covers both Mesopotamia and Lazica.
558	First Avar embassy.
559	Cutrigurs raid Balkans; break through Long Walls of Contantinople.
562	Avar conquest of Cutrigurs and Utigurs.
	Plot of the bankers against Justinian.
565	Death of Belisarius; death of Justinian.
567	Avars destroy Gepids.
568	Lombards leave middle Danube for the Balkans.
573	Justin II reopens Persian war.
590	Bahram's coup.

591	Peace with Persia gives Maurice control of most of Armenia.
602	November: Deposition of Maurice.
614	Persian capture of Palestine and Jerusalem.
624	Suinthila recaptures last Constantinopolitan outposts in Spain.
626	Avar–Persian siege of Constantinople.
628	Deposition of Chosroes II.
636	Battle of Yarmouk.
642	Arab conquest of Egypt.
651	Death of last Persian king, Yazdgerd III.

GLOSSARY

Acacian schism (484–519): The formal split between the bishop of Rome and the patriarch of Constantinople occasioned by Pope Felix's excommunication of the Patriarch Acacius over the latter's acceptance of Zeno's *Henotikon* (q.v.).

***Adventus*:** The orchestrated formal imperial ceremonial of entry into a major city; involved the court and population lined up by grouping and status order.

Agathias: Poet and historian who 'completes' Procopius's account of Justinian's wars; he describes the final campaigns of the mid-550s in Italy and Lazica.

***agri deserti*:** In English, 'deserted fields'; used to describe farmland abandoned in late antiquity. Latter-day archaeological evidence of continuing rural prosperity in that era suggests that a better translation might be 'land paying no tax', with no necessary implication that it had ever paid tax.

Amal-led Goths: A group of Goths united in Pannonia (modern Hungary) after Attila's death (453) by Valamer, the uncle of Theoderic, the Ostrogothic king of Italy (489–526). They moved onto East Roman territory ca. 473.

Augustaion: A colonnaded square at the heart of Constantinople, flanked by the cathedral Church of Holy Wisdom (Hagia Sophia), the Senate House, the monumental baths of Zeuxippos, and the Chalke Gate to the imperial palace.

Augustus: Exclusive title of the senior reigning Roman emperor.

***bucellarii*:** In the sixth century AD, elite guardsmen who were attached personally to senior field army generals (*Magistri Militum*), were paid largely from public funds, and took an oath of allegiance to the emperor as well as the general.

Byzantine Empire: The post-seventh-century successor to the East Roman Empire; specifically, the rump state that survived the loss to Islam of two-thirds of the old empire's heartland territories in Egypt, North Africa, and the Near East.

Caesar: A title sometimes used of the junior partner in an imperial college. Justinian, for example, from 525 was a Caesar during the reign of his uncle Justin.

Chalcedon: Site of an important ecumenical council (451) summoned to heal the breach generated in the Eastern church by alternative responses to the teachings of Patriarch Nestorius of Constantinople.

Chalke (or Bronze Gate): A three-arched, roofed structure giving entrance to the imperial palace; Justinian reconstructed it after the Nika riots to show himself and Theodora in full majesty and to celebrate Belisarius and the conquests of Africa and Italy.

***Chronicon Paschale*:** An important world chronicle produced in Constantinople; its contemporary accounts for the years 600–627 are particularly full.

***civilitas*:** In imperial ideology, the supreme, divinely ordained form of human civilization which God brought the Roman Empire into existence to establish, particularly via the operation of written law.

***civitas* (plur. *civitates*):** In English, 'city': The basic unit of local government in the Roman Empire. Besides the urban centre, it consisted diagnostically of an extensive dependent rural territory which it administered. In the early empire, cities were run by curials, a council of landowners from this dependent territory.

***clarissimus*:** The most junior of three senatorial statuses in the late empire.

***Codex Justinianus* (Code of Justinian):** The first of Justinian's legal reforms, promulgated on 7 April 529; a collection of new imperial law from 439 to Justinian's own day, integrating material from three earlier collections of imperial rulings: the Codes of Hermogenianus, Gregorianus, and Theodosius.

comes rei militaris: A senior field army commander, second in rank only to the *Magistri Militum*.

comes rei privatae: A senior financial official in charge of the administration of directly owned imperial estates.

comitatenses: The higher-status field army troops of the later Roman Empire, collected in both regional and central (or 'praesental') army groups (see also *palatini*).

consulship: The most coveted dignity of the Roman world. There were two consuls annually and the years were officially charted in imperial and legal documents by the consular sequence, as they had been in the era of the Roman Republic.

Conversations of 532: Justinian's first attempt to negotiate reunification within the Eastern church, which was bitterly divided in its response to the Council of Chalcedon (451).

Corippus, Flavius Cresconius: Latin epic poet from North Africa who chronicled in particular the campaigns of John Troglita, which subdued the Berber rebellion of the late 540s. He also wrote and a highly legimitisiizing account of the accession of Justin II after Justinian's death, which wherein also he describes the latter's funeral arrangements.

curials: Members of the town councils, qualifying by landownership, who ran the *civitates*.

Cutrigurs: A Bulgar steppe nomadic grouping established north-east of the Danube frontier in the sixth century; they were responsible for two huge incursions (539 and 559) into the Balkans in the reign of Justinian.

Cyril, patriarch of Alexandria (412–44): Avowed enemy of Nestorius and chief advocate of the one, indivisible, divine and human nature of the Incarnate Christ (see also Formula of Union and nature language).

defensores: Heavily armoured cavalry element, wielding bows, lances, and sabres, of the new model East Roman field armies of the sixth century.

denarii: Standard silver coins of the early empire in which the army was customarily paid. Military expansion in the third century left insufficient silver available to pay the expanded troop complements and led first to inflation, as the currency was debased, then to the new military pay regime (see donatives) of the fourth century.

Digest (*Corpus Iuris Civilis*): Second tranche of Justinian's legal reform, hastily published after Belisarius's capture of Carthage on 16 December 533. It was a massively abbreviated selection from ancient jurisconsult writings designed to remove all repetition and contradiction.

donatives: The periodic payments in gold—on recruitment, retirement, and intervening imperial anniversaries—which supplemented the rations (delivered sometimes in kind, sometimes as a cash equivalent) that were the basis of military pay from the fourth century.

***duces*:** Commanders of provincial-level concentrations of lower status garrison troops (see *limitanei*).

Eastern Roman Empire: The territory ruled from Constantinople from ca. AD 400 until the Islamic conquests of the seventh century: central and eastern Balkans, Asia Minor, Syria, Palestine, Egypt, and Libya, with the addition, under Justinian, of the western Balkans, Italy, and North African provinces encompassing what is now Tunisia and Algeria.

ecumenical council: One of a sequence of councils notionally of bishops representing the entire Christian community (Greek, *oikumene*); an ecumenical council was the most important decision-making body of the Christian Church in late antiquity. The earliest post-Apostolic council was held in Nicaea in 325.

Endless Peace: The agreements which brought Justinian's first Persian war to an end in spring 532.

***excubitores*:** One of the two palace guard units (see *scholarii*), whose senior officers often played a major rule in succession.

Evagrius Scholasticus: Author of a six-volume church history covering the period from the first council of Ephesus (431) to the 490s.

Fifty Decisions: The key resolutions of famous jurisconsult disagreements. Tribonian and Justinian forced them through between 1 August 530 and 30 April 531 to prepare the way for the publication of the Digest.

Fine Rolls: Royal records of who owed what to the crown in thirteenth-century England; they were used as a tool of political management, in the same way that imperial fiscal records were from the fourth through the sixth century AD.

***foederatii* ('federates'):** In Justinian's era the name given to bodies of foreign manpower; federates, who were sometimes settled on imperial territory under privileged terms, owed the emperor military service and were commanded on campaign by their own leaders.

Formula of Union: An early attempt (433) to resolve the doctrinal quarrel between Cyril of Alexandria and his opponents. Cyril alone said that it was legitimate to use 'two nature' language of how the human and divine were united in Christ. The formula was an important precedent for Justinian's attempts to restore church unity.

Ghassanids: The favoured Arab dynasty at the head of Constantinople's alliance system; the Ghassanids protected the southern, desert end of the Persian frontier.

Hephthalite ('White' Huns): A Hunnic group that expanded from north-western Afghanistan to conquer Sogdia and Khurasan in the early fifth century; it became a dangerous and aggressive neighbour on Persia's eastern frontier.

***Henotikon* (482):** The Emperor Zeno's attempt to restore Christian unity in the East by downgrading the disputed Council of Chalcedon (451). It stated that the faith had been defined once and for all at Nicaea (325) and I Constantinople (382). Enforced in the East, it was not accepted by Rome and generated the Acacian schism.

Iberia: Transcaucasian kingdom firmly under Persian control from the agreement of 380s that disavowed Roman claims to the bulk of greater Armenia. It was the base for the Lazican campaigns of Chosroes in the time of Justinian.

***illustris*:** A senior senatorial rank in the later empire; it could be attained only by actual or virtual imperial service.

Institutes: The third element in Justinian's legal reform, promulgated simultaneously with the Digest in December 533. It was an introductory textbook which set out a revised curriculum for students of law enrolled at the two official remaining schools of Constantinople and Beirut.

***iugera* (sing. *iugum*):** Tax units by which the agricultural wealth of the *civitates* of the empire was assessed, with each city having an assigned number. A *iugum* was a unit of value, so that *iugera* of more valuable land would be smaller than those areas of lower or less valuable productivity.

John of Ephesus: Church historian whose work originally covered the period from Julius Caesar to 588; only the sixth-century portions survive.

jurisconsults: Up to the third century AD, officially recognized legal experts responsible for authoritative opinions which, in practice, advanced and extended existing law into new areas.

***koursoures*:** A lighter cavalry element, armed with bows and other weaponry, of the new model East Roman field armies of the sixth century.

Lakhmids: The chief Arab allies of the Persian Empire, responsible for military alliance systems protecting the Persian side of the southern, desert frontier.

Latin Anthology: A ninth-century Carolingian manuscript of Latin poetry. Amongst much else, it preserves a great deal of material written at the court of the Vandal kings of North Africa.

Lazica: Transcaucasian kingdom at the south-east corner of the Black Sea which tended to swap allegiance between East Rome and Persia in the fifth century. In reality, it was a confederation whose ruler exercised hegemony over a number of autonomous subregions, including Abasgia, Apsilia, and Misimia.

***limitanei*:** Lower-status frontier garrison troops under the command at provincial level of *duces*. These troops were occasionally mobilized for field army operations, as they were by Belisarius for his Palestinian campaign of 541.

***Magistri Militum* (*Praesentalis*):** A senior field army commander, whether of one of the regional concentrations (Thrace, Illyricum, the East, and, under Justinian, Armenia) or, with even greater seniority, of one of the two central (praesental) field armies.

***Magister Officiorum*:** A senior bureaucratic functionary of the later Roman world.

Malalas, John: A chronicler whose eighteen books cover sixth-century events down to 563 in some detail (the end is lost). He at first focuses on Antioch, then on Constantinople.

Mauretania: Westernmost region of old Roman North Africa (modern Morocco and Algeria). It did not form part of the Vandal kingdom and was not restored to Roman rule by Belisarius's victories.

Menander Protector: A classicizing historical continuator of Procopius; his work survives in extensive fragments covering the years 558 to 582 in great detail.

***munitiones*:** Portable anti-cavalry barricades employed by the infantry of the new model East Roman field armies of the sixth century.

nature language: A mode of discussing how the human and divine were combined in the Incarnate Christ; specifically, as one nature or two. The radical two-nature approach of Nestorius made much of the Eastern church, under the influence of Cyril of Alexandria, hostile to anything other than an explicit one-nature approach from the mid-fifth century onwards.

Nestorius, patriarch of Constantinople (428–31): His views that the human and the divine elements in the nature of Christ were still discernible after the Incarnation and that the immortal divine element could not have suffered and died on the Cross generated huge division in the Eastern church. The Council of Chalcedon (451) was summoned to heal the rift.

Nika riot: An extended sequence of disturbances (11–18 January 532) which nearly toppled Justinian's regime and destroyed much of the ceremonial centre of Constantinople.

non-Nicene (Arian) Christianity: An older theological formulation which placed the persons of the Trinity in a hierarchical relationship, with the Father at the head, as opposed to the strict equality laid down at Nicaea (325). Originally a variant of Roman Christianity, it became associated in the fifth century with the ruling dynasties of the western successor states (Vandals, Visigoths, Burgundians, and Ostrogoths).

***Notitia Dignitatum*:** A ceremonial but comprehensive listing of the military forces and bureaucratic officers of the two halves of the Roman Empire as they stood ca. 395 but with some Western additions down to the 420s.

***numerus* (Greek, *arithmos*):** The standard term for an army 'unit'; in the late imperial Roman army, the *numerus* replaced the legion of the Republican and early imperial periods.

Ostrogothic Italy: A kingdom founded by Theoderic the Amal in 489; it included Italy, Dalmatia, parts of the middle Danube, Sicily, and after 511, southern Gaul and Spain.

***palatini*:** The most senior (i.e. best equipped and highest paid) units of the late Roman field army (*comitatenses*); these units were found exclusively in the two central, praesental concentrations.

patriarchs: The five bishops of Rome, Alexandria, Antioch, Jerusalem, and Constantinople—the senior Christian Church leaders of the late Roman world. All except Constantinople could claim to have been founded by one of Christ's Apostles, and Constantinople claimed an equal dignity because it was in formal and legal terms the New Rome.

patrician: From Republican times, the highly exclusive senior dignity awarded the great and good of the Roman world. Justin granted it to Justinian in 523 as part of the latter's rise to power.

Persarmenia: The larger portion of Armenia recognized by Theodosius I as belonging to the Persian sphere of influence in 387.

***phylarch*:** Title of Arab princes commanding the alliance systems which dominated the southern, desert frontier between Persia and Rome.

***Praepositus Sacri Cubiculi*:** Chief of the palace eunuchs, who was often a trusted imperial adviser exercising great immediate influence but one highly vulnerable to the vagaries and perils of regime change.

praesental field armies: See *Magistri Militum*.

Praetorian Prefect: The chief administrative officer responsible for fiscal and legal operations of the empire at the regional level. Justinian's empire had prefects of Illyricum and the East; his conquests added two new prefectures, in North Africa and Italy, to the empire.

Pragmatic Sanction: Justinian's order of 13 August 554 designed to settle affairs in newly conquered Africa.

Procopius: Historian of the reign of Justinian; he published eight volumes of *Histories of the Wars*, the first seven in one instalment (550) and the eighth probably in 554, He also composed the *Anekdota*, or *Secret History* (also in 550) and the *Buildings* at a later date.

quaestor: Chief legal officer of the late Roman bureaucracy.

***scholarii*:** see *excubitores*.

***silentarius*:** Senior court functionary within the palace; it was the position occupied by Anastasius before marriage to Ariadne elevated him to the purple.

***sortes Vandalorum*:** The landed estates in Proconsularis transferred by Geiseric to the ownership of his chief Vandal-Alan supporters after his conquest of Carthage (439).

tetrarchic emperors: The imperial college, established by the senior Emperor Diocletian (284–305), responsible for important fiscal and legal restructuring of the empire.

Theodosian Code: The important collection of imperial regulations issued between ca. AD 300 and 438.

Thracian Gothic *Foederatii*: large body of Gothic soldiery established in the Balkans in the mid-fifth century; these *foederatii* served under their own leaders in East Roman armies. Most later threw in their lot with the Amal-led Goths to create the Ostrogothic coalition used by Theoderic to conquer his Italian kingdom.

Three Chapters: Three clauses of the acts of the Council of Chalcedon which explicitly declared orthodox some or all of the works of Theodore of Mopsuestia, Theodoret of Cyrrhus, and Ibas of Edessa. Justinian's attempted compromise involved striking out these clauses to appease anti-Chalcedonian opinion in the East. The policy was enforced at II Constantinople (553) but generated great hostility in the Latin West, where Chalcedon was considered an untouchable cornerstone of orthodoxy.

***Tome of Leo*:** A letter of Pope Leo I inscribed into the published acts of the Council of Chalcedon. The *Tome* made Rome hostile to any strategy of downgrading the council's status as part of reunifying eastern Christian opinion.

urban prefect: Senior bureaucrat responsible for affairs within the imperial capital of Constantinople. The position was modelled on a counterpart who ran the city of Rome.

Utigurs: A Bulgar steppe nomadic grouping established north of the Black Sea and to the east of the Cutrigurs. They supplied contingents of *foederatii* for Justinian's wars.

Vandal Africa: The kingdom established by Geiseric after his conquest of Carthage (439) and comprising the old Roman provinces of Proconsularis, Byzacena, and Numidia (modern Tunisia and Algeria), with Tripolitania, in western Libya, added later as the Western Empire unravelled.

Vandal-Alan coalition: The force led by Geiseric across the Straits of Gibraltar in 429; it was built up from a much looser, albeit much larger, alliance of many groups which had forced their way across the Rhine on 31 December 406 and then moved into Spain three years later.

Via Flaminia: The main Roman road between the Eternal City and Ravenna, it emerged as a key military and political administrative centre in the fifth century. Most of the key battles of the Gothic war were fought up and down its length. Its line is now followed by Italy's Strada Statale 3.

Vicar of the Orient: The subordinate of the Praetorian Prefect of the East who was responsible for financial and legal affairs of the provinces of Roman Syria and Palestine.

Victor of Vita: Writer of an important contemporary account of Huneric's persecution of Nicene Christians in North Africa (484). It is prefaced with an introduction covering the reign of Geiseric (439–477).

Zachariah of Mitylene: A church historian whose work, which survives only in the Syriac language, covers the period 451–91.

NOTES

INTRODUCTION

1. Bavant (2007) is a recent summary of the findings.

2. Malalas 18. 1 (trans. Jeffreys et al., 1986, 245); *Chron. Pasch.* ad a. 566 is similar.

3. The revisionist case really started with two works of Walter Goffart. Goffart (1980) and (1981) argue, respectively, that the new deals between provincial Roman elites and barbarian kings did not involve any financial losses and that the Western Empire had ended peacefully and by choice. Heather (1996), (2005), and (2009) lay out an alternative view, but see also the highly important collection of Porena et al. (2012), which emphasizes that even the best of the new deals involved significant financial loss for provincial Roman elites.

4. Another significant element of the Goffart thesis—see esp. Goffart (1981)—is the attempt to argue that the Eastern and Western Roman Empires essentially functioned as separate states by ca. AD 400, but this ignores their unified legal system in the fifth century (on the development of which see p. 99) and the East's respectable record of assistance to the struggling West in the same era (see Heather 2016).

5. This process is examined in more detail in ch. 11.

6. Procopius *Wars* 7. 1. 6.

7. For full references, see nn. 24 and 25 in ch. 4.

8. Corippus *Iohannes* (ed. Teurfs et al., 2007; trans. Shea, 1998) provides important narrative information on the later stages of the African Wars. *In Praise of Justin II* (ed. and trans. Antès, 1981) provides fascinating insight into the self-presentation of Justinian's immediate successor.

9. Justinian's legal and religious policies are explored in detail in later chapters.

10. A good place to start on the still developing sixth-century chronicle tradition is Scott (2012), with references to the extensive scholarly literature. Three ecclesiastical histories have particular relevance for the reign of Justinian: Zachariah of Mitylene (trans. Hamilton and Brooks, 1899), Evagrius Scholasticus (trans. Whitby, 2000), and John of Ephesus, which survives in fragmentary form (ed. and trans. Harrak, 1999, pt. 2; Brooks, 1952, pt. 3; trans. Smith, 1860).

11. On the Greek tradition in late antiquity, see generally Blockley (1981), (1985); Matthews (1989) looks at the main surviving Latin representative.

12. A. M. Cameron (1970) is an excellent introduction to Agathias. Blockley (1985) provides both introduction and text and translation of the surviving fragments of Menander Protector.

13. The bibliography on Procopius is enormous, but good (if contrasting) introductions in English are provided by A. M. Cameron (1985) and Kaldellis (2004).

14. 'Autopsy'—literally witnessing something yourself—was considered the strongest guarantor of veracity; so the ancient world liked historians who had been part of the events they described. The same conventions applied to those working in Greek and Latin, although their stranglehold was not so strong as to prevent very different authorial voices from coming through.

15. Dara and Callinicum, pp. 103–7; Bessas, p. 54.

16. Gothic number problem, p. 158; African and Italian expeditions, chapters 5 and 6.

17. *Buildings* can be read in the English translation of Dewing (1940). The attack on its veracity was led by Croke and Crow (1983), but see, e.g. Whitby (1986a), (1986b), (1988), ch. 3; Curta (2001), ch. 4.

18. *SH* 1. 3 (trans. Dewing, 1935).

19. *SH* 8. 22–33 (Justinian's general character); *SH* 9. 10–30 (Theodora); with the demoniacal character and alliances of the pair being laid clear at *SH* 12. 14–32.

20. *SH* 1. 10–15. 33, with p. 107 on the importance of the battle of Callinicum.

21. Bury (1889, vol. 1, 355ff.) at first argued that the *Secret History* could not be by Procopius but later came to think it genuine (no one now doubts it); Bury (1923), vol. 2, 417. A. M. Cameron (1985, ch. 4) makes the case unanswerable and underlines the correlation between it and the darkening tone of the *Wars*.

22. The date of *Buildings* has seen a fair amount of discussion between those favouring the early to mid-550s (e.g. A. M. Cameron, 1985, ch. 6; Greatrex, 1994)—and an alternative dating to c. 560 (Whitby, 1985). The issue remains open in my view. A. M. Cameron (1985), esp. chs. 1, 6, and 14 makes a case for *Buildings* containing part of what Procopius really thought about Justinian. See Kaldellis (2004), 51ff., with references, for the view opposed to the one I generally subscribe to.

23. A. M. Cameron (1985), ch. 5, is excellent on Procopius's carefully drawn inversion of what Theodora should have been. Potter (2015), ch. 2, develops the case further, identifying the relevant classical sources.

24. *SH* 8. 12–22 for Justinian's supposed resemblance to Domitian. The late fourth- and early fifth-century poetical satirist Claudian, working for the great Western generalissimo Stilicho, used sexuality to lampoon one of his employer's East Roman enemies (Eutropius) and demonize another (Rufinus): A. D. E. Cameron (1970), chs. 4 and 6. In reading the demonization of Justinian as a constructed piece of rhetorical artifice just like the tarting up of Theodora, rather than as Procopius's genuine belief, my account is closer to that of Kaldellis (2004), esp. 150–9, than to A. M. Cameron (1985), 56–9. But Kaldellis in the end sees a directly political intent behind the strategy, in terms of using the text to prompt a potential coup, on which I am less convinced; see further pp. 326–7.

1. 'IN THIS SIGN CONQUER'

1. Lactantius *On the deaths of the Persecutors* 44. 5–6.

2. *Buildings* 1. 2. 11.

3. Matthew 5:39; Luke 6:29.

4. For a fuller introduction to the classical ideology of civilization (among many possibilities), see Dvornik (1966), with Dauge (1981) on the counterimage of the barbarian. Kaster (1988) is excellent on the importance of grammar and education in general.

5. E.g. Sorabji (1983), esp. chs. 13, 20.

6. Dvornik (1966), ch. 8 on the role this gave to the Roman state. Excellent examples of these idea sets being applied to celebrate the general character and specific policies of a succession of late Roman regimes are provided by surviving speeches produced for ceremonial occasions, such as the orations of Themistius—translation and commentary in Heather and Moncur (2001) and Swain (2013)—and the Latin prose panegyrics, trans. Nixon and Rogers (1994).

7. Whether they were being taught in Latin in the Western Empire or Greek in the East: Kaster (1988), esp. chs. 1–2.

8. Eusebius: Dvornik (1966), ch. 8. An excellent introduction to imperial ceremonial is MacCormack (1981).

9. Athaulf: Orosius 7. 43. Roman merchant turned Hun: Priscus fr. 11.2 (trans. Blockley 1983, 269ff.). The preface to the *Bavarian Code*, trans. Rivers (1977), best captures the overall ideological significance of written law in the early middle ages, but it is very broadly present: see e.g. Heather (1994a).

10. McLynn (2004).

11. Athanasius of Alexandria was highly critical of the Emperor Constantius II—Barnes (1993)—but only behind his back. Daniel the Stylite is presented as castigating the usurper Basiliscus for his rejection of Chalcedon; *Life of Daniel* 71–85. A convenient English translation of Gelasius's letter is online: sourcebooks.fordham.edu/source/gelasius1.asp.

12. Claim to papal authority: *Nov. Val. III* 17, with discussion of the broader context in Heather (2013), chs. 7–8. Five patriarchates: Herrin (1987), ch. 3; cf. Brown (2013), ch. 2. It is sometimes claimed that Justinian claimed to exercise a new type of religious authority in the sixth century—e.g. most recently Leppin (2011); cf. Pazdernik—but I find nothing in Justinian's ideological claims that is not fully prefigured in fourth-century materials. What really changes, Chapter 7 will argue, is the context in which the emperor was trying to make these same claims stick.

13. *Philanthropia* is thoroughly explored in its different dimensions in the speeches of Themistius: Heather and Moncur (2001), ch. 1. On the actual imperial domination of lawmaking from the third century onwards, see Honore (1994), (1998). The claim to be *nomos empsychos* is sometimes said to be an innovation of Justinian himself—e.g. Pazdernik (2005), 202—but was already a fully developed theme in official fourth-century propaganda imperial such as the speeches of Themistius; Heather and Moncur (2001), ch. 1.

14. On the reality of regime building, see Heather (1994b). The importance of an emperor's 'friends' is a theme of several of Themistius's speeches (for different regimes); Heather and Moncur (2001).

15. Procopius *Buildings* 6. 4. 15–16. Though fiscal restructuring in the third and fourth centuries had in many ways emasculated local self-government at the level of the polis in practice; see pp. 61–4.

16. *VI Cons. Hon.*

17. Continued doctrinal quarrels after 325; Hanson (1988).

18. McCormick (1986).

19. Discussion of victory titles in theory and practice occupies many pages in Barnes (1981).

20. Town council minutes: Wilcken (1912), 45, with Jones (1964), 722–3. *Adventus*: MacCormack (1981), ch. 3. On the *basilikos logos* of Menander rhetor, see Russell and Wilson (1981). About half the Latin prose panegyrics follow this speech form; Nixon and Rogers (1991). Themistius deliberate avoids it but always works in a reference to imperial success in warfare anyway; Heather and Moncur (2001), ch. 1.

21. Calo Levi (1952).

22. *Gesta Senatus Urbis Romae* 5; cf. Matthews (2000), ch. 3.

23. Matthews (1974), (1986).

24. Brooks (1893) remains an excellent introduction.

25. Not to mention failed mid-fourth-century examples like Magnentius or Silvanus from the same elevated military circles.

26. Ammianus 25. 5 provides a vivid account of the attempt to recruit Salutius Secundus.

27. Julian: Heather (forthcoming). Gallus: Ammianus 14. 1, 7, 9, 11 with the superb commentary of Matthews (1989), ch. 3. Lydus: Kelly (2004), chs. 1–2; Germanus: see p. 328.

28. Heather (1994b). For an introduction to Synesius in Cyrene, see Bregman (1982), chs. 7–8 (who concentrates more on the writings than political fixing).

29. Sudden death of Valentinian is particularly well reported thanks to Ammianus 30. 5–6. The normal age at death for Carolingian males was also ca. 50.

30. The sources for the fall of Crispus are collected at *PLRE* 1, 233.

31. Matthews (1975), ch. 3.

32. Ammianus 29. 1 is the fullest account, but there are others; *PLRE* 1, 898.

33. Themistius *Orr.* 5 and 6 with Heather and Moncur (2001), ch. 3.

34. Carolingian regimes: Goldberg (2006), esp. introduction (1–11) and epilogue (335–46).

35. Valens: Lenski (2002). Usurpation patterns more generally: Matthews (1976).

36. Gratian: sources as *PLRE* 1, 401. Fl. Constantius: Matthews (1976), chs. 12–14.

37. Majorian: *PLRE* 2, 702–3. Stilicho: Matthews (1976), chs. 10–11.

38. Constantius: Themistius *Or.* 1, trans. Heather and Moncur (2001), ch. 1. Valens: Themistius *Or.* 10, trans. Heather and Matthews (1991), ch. 2. Theodosius I: *Orr.* 16 and 34, trans. Heather and Moncur (2001), ch. 4.

39. Ammianus 16. 12. 67–70; cf. Matthews (1989), 378–9 (with ibid. 87–93 on the background).

40. Drinkwater (2007), 289–93 (the fortress building Valentinian I staged to reassure a senatorial fact-finding mission; 267–70 (unilateral lowering of the value of the annual gifts). Drinkwater's broader argument that the Alamanni were *never* aggressive is less convincing; Heather (forthcoming).

41. Themistius *Or.* 5 with translation and commentary in Heather and Moncur (2001), ch. 3.

2. THE MILITARY- FISCAL COMPLEX

1. An excellent introduction is Campbell (1984).

2. Losses at Hadrianople: Hoffmann (1969), 450–8, with Heather (1991), 146–7, on the overall level of loss this implies. On Isaurian recruitment, Thompson (1946); Brooks (1893).

3. Frontier garrison troops could also be promoted to the intermediate category of *Pseudocomitatenses*; Jones (1964), 609–10.

4. Jones (1964), app. II, remains indispensable on the different chronological layers of the *Notitia*, as does his ch. 17 on the late Roman army. Excellent supplementary discussions of various aspects of the late Roman army are Elton (1996), Whitby (2002), and Lee (2007). See also Synesius *Catastasis* II on the demoted Unnigardae.

5. Trans. Dodgeon and Lieu (1991), 343–6, 50, 57.

6. Whitby (2002).

7. For discussion of military numbers with full references, Campbell (2005). For fourth-century Roman/Persian relations, Dodgeon and Lieu (1991).

8. Elton (1996), 245.

9. Germanic confederations of the late Roman period: Heather (2009), ch. 2.

10. Issues of supply emerge clearly from Julian's campaigns on the Rhine in the 350s: Heather (forthcoming); cf. Elton (1996), 237ff.

11. General introduction: Jones (1964), 665–7. Belisarius's 7,000: Procopius *Wars* 7. 1. 18–20 (according to Procopius the largest force of *bucellarii* ever known). But he didn't have that many in Africa or seemingly in Italy either: see chs 5 and 6. When transferred to Italy, the Armenian *MVM* Valerian brought a thousand guardsmen with him: Procopius *Wars* 7. 27. 3.

12. Heather (1995), (2005).

13. Maechen-Helfen (1973), 94ff., remains the best narrative reconstruction of Attila's campaigns.

14. Heather (1995), (2005), ch. 6.

15. See references for n. 2.

16. Thracian Goths: Heather (1991), 251–63, with 108–13 on the evolution of the term *foederatii* in the late Roman period; also see p. 158. In the sixth century, Heruli served on similar terms and feature in many of Justinian's campaigns; Agathias *Histories* 1. 11. 3 (Fulcaris succeeds Philemuth); 1. 20. 8 (Sindual succeeds Fulcaris).

17. Massagetae (Bulgars), see ch. 5 on the African campaign. For Lombards and Narses final pacification of Italy, see ch. 9.

18. On the Hunnic bow, see Heather (2005), 154–8, with full references. My understanding of the new battlefield tactics employed by the revamped sixth-century East Roman army is substantially based on Janniard (2015).

19. Solomon, John Troglita, Martinus. and Valerianus, for example, all served under Belisarius in the conquest of Africa and all rose to the rank of field army general subsequently. Aigan and Rufinus were on course for similarly distinguished careers until the Berbers intervened; p. 244.

20. Janniard (2015) with full references.

21. Discussions of military finance: Jones (1964), ch. 17; Elton (1996), ch. 4 (but note also ch. 6 on fortifications).

22. Heather (1994a) with references.

23. Excellent accounts of the third-century fiscal crisis and various dimensions of state response can be found in Whittaker (1976) and the relevant chapters of *CAH* 12, esp. Carrie (2005) and Corbier (2005a), (2005b).

24. Jones (1964), chs. 13, 20, remains the basic account, but see also the works cited in n. 23.

25. *CTh* 7. 6. 3. In the sixth century, the Oxyrhyncite estate of the Apions customarily disbursed large amounts of wine as part of what look like its tax liabilities; Hickey (2012), ch. 4, esp. 111–29.

26. Crown gold and supertaxes: Jones (1964), 462–9. Liebeschuetz (1972), 104–11, 161–6, is an excellent exploration of one violent local response to the imposition of a supertax.

27. See the consensus view deployed across the relevant chapters of the first editions of the Cambridge Medieval (Gwatkin and Whitney 1911, esp. Reid and Vinogradoff) and Ancient Histories (Cook et al. 1939, esp. Ennsslin and Oertel); cf. Rostovtzeff (1926).

28. Which incidentally made fifth-century Western imperial political collapse easy to explain.

29. For overviews, with full references to the more detailed studies on which they are based, see e.g. Lewit (1991); Ward Perkins (2000a), (2000b); Wickham (2005), pt. 3.

30. The *PPO. Or.* Auxonius's organization of Valens's first Gothic war (367–9): Zosimus 4. 10. 4.

31. Julian: Heather (forthcoming). Riot of the Statues: see n. 26.

32. For a virtually complete text of the standard municipal constitution, see Gonzalez (1986); cf. Liebeschuetz (2001), pt. 1, and Woolf (1998) on the standard patterns of local political life that it quickly generated.

33. I once did a sample head count for the letters *P* and *T* in *PLRE* 1, which covers the fourth century AD: about a third of known individuals appear in Libanius's correspondence. On the Apions, see most recently Hickey (2012), esp. 8–18.

34. Old orthodoxy: references as in n. 26. For a general account of bureaucratic expansion, Jones (1964), chs. 12, 15, and 16, remain basic, supplemented now by a series of individual studies of specific bureaus; Delmaire (1989), (1995); Teitler (1985); Vogler (1979).

35. Heather (1994a) lays out this model in more detail.

36. Fake rosters: Jones (1964), 623–6; Africa: Ammianus 28. 5; cf. Symmachus *Relatio* 23 on bureaucratic obstruction and disappearing cash. MacMullen (1988) lovingly catalogues all the different types of corruption associated with this flow of wealth.

37. Heather (1994a) explores some of this in more detail but by no means exhaustively. On the Apions, see Hickey (2012), 8ff. (taxation jobs in the fifth century). The sixth-century situation is controversial. Sarris (2006) considers that the relevant documents define the size of the Apions' own holdings, but see Hickey (2012), esp. chs. 1–2, for a convincing counter.

38. Jones (1964), ch. 13, assembles the evidence for the practical mechanics of taxation. I find myself in broad agreement, therefore, with Gascou (1972) that the tax system provided a fundamental stimulus for landowners at all levels to engage appropriately with the imperial political system as a whole and that their position is best understood as one of constructive engagement in that they accepted its basic outlines while attempting, of course, always to minimize their individual tax bills.

39. The fine rolls project can be consulted at www.finerollshenry3.org.uk. I thank my colleague Professor David Carpenter and all his MA students for this insight derived from many happy hours of reading their work.

3. REGIME CHANGE IN CONSTANTINOPLE

1. *De Cer* I. 92, with ch. 1 n. 22 for the Theodosian Code ceremony; cf. MacCormack (1981) on imperial ceremonial in general.

2. On the factions in general, see Cameron, A.D.E. (1976), with Dagron (2011) on Constantinople in particular.

3. The evidence for Longinus's career is assembled at *PLRE* 2, 689–90; cf. Haarer (2006), ch. 2, and Meier (2009), 63–75, for more detailed discussions of Anastasius's elevation.

4. Brooks (1893) remains a terrific introduction to Isaurian involvement in Constantinopolitan politics; with Heather (1991), pt. 3, on the Thracian Goths.

5. There is no modern large-scale treatment of Zeno's reign, but *PLRE* 2, 1200–2 collects the evidence.

6. More detailed accounts: Haarer (2006), 21–8; Meier (2009), 75–84.

7. Haarer (2006), ch. 6; Meier (2009), 118–37.

8. On the careers of the nephews: *PLRE* 2, 577–81 (Hypatius); 898–9 (Pompeius); 912–13 (Probus). See Greatrex (1996) for a valuable discussion of their prospects; cf. Potter (2015), 68ff.

9. Lazica: Priscus fr. 31. 1–2; cf. Braund (1994), 271–2. On the overall pattern of cooperation, see e.g. Rubin (1986); Greatrex and Lieu (2002), chs. 3–4.

10. Sources and comment: Greatrex and Lieu (2002), chs. 1–2.

11. Huns: Heather (2009), chs. 4–5; Hephthalites: e.g. Greatrex and Lieu (2002), 58–61, for the sources; more detailed commentary in Christensen (1944), 293ff.; Kim (2013), 35–9, 183–8.

12. Key sources and commentary: Greatrex and Lieu (2002), 62–3. More detailed accounts: Haarer (2006), 47–53; Meier (2009), 174–94.

13. Sources and commentary: Greatrex and Lieu (2002), 63–77; more detailed treatments in Haarer (2006), 53–93; Meier (2009), 194–221.

14. An excellent introduction to the backdrop is Gray (2005), 215–21.

15. Acts of Chalcedon are now available in the translation of Price and Gaddis (2005). On the aftermath, see Frend (2008); Gray (1979), (2005).

16. For more detail, see Gray (2005); Haarer (2006), ch. 5; Meier (2009), 84–92 and ch. 7; Potter (2015), 62–8.

17. Best account: Meier (2008).

18. We know an enormous amount about the revolt of Vitalian thanks to John of Antioch fr. 214e 1–15; cf. *PLRE* 2, 1171–6. Anastasius and Hormisdas: Haarer (2006), 128–35, 180–2; Meier (2009), 289–319.

19. Ammianus 15. 8. 17.

20. Malalas 410–11 is the main source; *PLRE* 2, 650, lists the others.

21. *PLRE* 2, 648–51, for a full account.

22. It is also an old maxim of British political commentary that the original favourite never wins leadership elections.

23. *PLRE* 2, 650, for a guide to the available sources. Patricius: *de Cer.* 1. 93 cf. *PLRE* 2, 840–2, for his career in full. I follow here the general vision; cf. Croke (2007); also cf. Potter (2015), 70–2.

24. Amantius and Andreas: *PLRE* 2, 67. Celer: *PLRE* 2, 275–7. Marinus: *PLRE* 2, 727 (the bath story: Zachariah of Mitylene *HE* 8. 1). Hypatius: *PLRE* 2, 579–80.

25. For more detailed accounts with full references, see Moorhead (1992a), 194–200; cf. Noble (1993); Sotinel (2005).

26. For all the sources reflecting Vitalian's moment in the limelight: *PLRE* 2, 1175–6. Assassination: Zachariah of Mitylene *HE* 8. 2 (main account: the others are listed at *PLRE* 2, 1176). Procopius blames Justinian for the death (*Anekdota* 6. 27–8, also implicating him in the fall of Amantius: n. 24), but this is to underestimate Justin's influence: Croke (2007); Potter (2015), 83–4.

27. Hypatius was back in office by 7 August: *PLRE* 2, 580.

28. Justinian as *MVM Praesentalis: PLRE* 2, 646–7.

29. *CJ* 5. 4. 23, with the legal analysis of Daube (1966–67); cf. on the politics: Croke (2007); Potter (2015), 91–3.

30. For fuller discussion, see Potter (2015), 96–7. Just possibly, this gives us some insight into the methods of political violence by which Justinian was currently inserting himself into the political life of the capital; cf. Croke (2007).

31. Greatrex and Lieu (2002), 79–80 (source listing and commentary); Braund (1994), 275–8.

32. On the deeper background, see Dodgeon and Lieu (1991); Heather (2005), chs. 1 and 3; Dignas and Winter (2007), 9–32.

33. Procopius *Wars* 1. 11. 17–18. Of secondary commentators, only Jones (1964), 269, smells a rat, although he doesn't pursue his suspicions further.

34. *Wars* 1. 11. 23–30.

35. Alternative discussions taking the story much more at face value but with further commentary and more detailed discussion of the backdrop in, e.g. Greatrex (1998), ch. 7; Greatrex and Lieu (2002), 79ff.; Dignas and Winter (2007), 34–44; Leppin (2011), 87–8.

36. For sources and commentary, Greatrex and Lieu (2002), 82. Analysis: Braund (1994), 281–3.

37. Procopius *Wars* 1. 11. 31, 38–9, for the accusation. My reading of this is similar to Potter (2015), 106–7.

38. *Wars* 1. 9. 5. My overall understanding is strongly influenced by Croke (2007); cf. Leppin (2011), 43–91.

4. THE LAST DESPERATE GAMBLE

1. For more detailed accounts, see Gray (2005); Frend (2008).

2. Meier (2003), 215–23, with most recently Potter (2015), 89–90; Potter (2015), 78–82, also explores the origins of Theodora's ties to anti-Chalcedonian circles; see also 93–5, 97ff., for their possible early exploitation.

3. Persecutions: *CJ* 1. 5. 12; cf. Meier (2003), 198–209; Leppin (2011), 92–105; Potter (2015), 129–30, with full references. See pp. 118–9 on the first formal discussions of a possible compromise in 532.

4. *Deo Auctore* 1.

5. An excellent overview of the Justinianic Code project is Honore (1978), esp. ch. 7. On the earlier codes of Hermogenianus and Gregorianus, see Honore (1994). Matthews (2000) and Sirks (2007) provide modern and in some ways contradictory accounts of the Theodosian project, but the disagreements focus on the reasons for slow progress, not the fact that it was so slow compared to its Justinianic successor, nor do they differ much on the editing practices involved.

6. *Deo Auctore* 4–5.

7. Honore (1978), ch. 5. The Theodosian predecessor project was announced in 429 (*CTh* 1. 1. 5) but never actually undertaken.

8. Overview: Howard Johnston (1995). An excellent introduction to the northern front is Braund (1994), chs. 2 and 8. On the Arab world, see Sartre (1982).

9. New command: *CJ* 1. 29. 5, with Greatrex and Lieu (2002), 83–6, on the early exchanges.

10. *PLRE* 3, 181–224, provides an excellent, in-depth guide to Belisarius's career. On *bucellarii* and the training of officers, see p. 54.

11. Procopius *Wars* 1. 13–14; the quotation is from 1. 14. 54.

12. *Wars* 1. 15.

13. *Wars* 1. 16–17 on the run-up to the actual battle, with Greatrex and Lieu (2002), 92–3, for the other sources and commentary.

14. Procopius *Wars* 1. 18, with alternative account in Malalas 18. 60, which mentions suspicions about Arab loyalties but does not put the blame for the defeat so clearly on Harith, who continues fighting in Malalas after some other Arab auxiliaries and Roman regulars had fled.

15. For the full range of sources and commentary, see Greatrex and Lieu (2002), 93–6.

16. For more detail on the Fifty Decisions, see Honore (1978), 142–6.

17. *Wars* 1. 24. 37.

18. Alan Cameron (1973), (1976), provides the best modern introduction to the circus factions. Our main sources for Nika are Procopius *Wars* 1. 24 and the *Chronicon Paschale*, trans. Whitby and Whitby (1989), 115ff. For more detailed commentary, see e.g. Alan Cameron (1976); Greatrex (1997); Meier (2004), ch. 5; Leppin (2011), 142–8; Sarris (2011), 148–53.

19. As identified by Evans (1984). For Kaldellis (2004), 24ff., this is an excellent example of the extremely clever, extremely subversive Procopius at work.

20. But they may have been in the vicinity of the capital for quite other reasons, since Justinian may already have been contemplating a possible Vandal expedition; p. 118.

21. *Wars* 1. 24. 57–8.

22. John the Cappadocian was not brought back into office until October 532 (*PLRE* 3, 627–35, for his full career); Tribonian had to wait until November 533 (*PLRE* 3, 1335–9).

23. The quotations are from Justinian *Nov.* 30. 11. 2 (AD 536) and *CJ* 1. 27. 1. 1–2 (AD 534), respectively. Variations of the traditional vision of Justinian can be found in more academic commentators such as Jones (1964), 269ff.; Browning (1987), 55–7; Honore (1978), 18–19; and more popular studies: Norwich (1988), ch. 10. The one exception is Brown (1971).

24. Sceptical: Evans (2001), xxv; non-existent: Moorhead (1994), 63ff.; Meier (2004), 62ff.; Leppin 149–58.

25. Browning (1987), 57–60, is a typical exposition of the idea that affairs in the East had to be settled first, which is why it is so important to see that Justin and Justinian were actually engaged in an aggressive policy towards Persia.

26. For fuller discussion, see pp. 133–4.

27. On the role of religious persecution in the Vandal kingdom, see p. 134. On Hilderic and the Carthage spring, see e.g. Courtois (1955), 304–9; Steinacher (2016), 286–92.

28. On the rise of the Moors, see pp. 241–4. Gelimer's coup: Courtois (1955), 269ff; Merrills and Miles (2010), 74ff.; Steinacher (2016), 292–8.

29. Procopius *Wars* 1. 22–3. For other sources and commentary, Greatrex and Lieu (2002), 96–7.

30. See further pp. 4–5. Its defeat also marked the end of Eastern efforts to keep the Western Empire afloat: Heather (2005), 407–30.

31. The key anti-Chalcedonian Syriac source for the 'conversations' of 532 is translated in Brock (1981). It emphasizes that Justinian was desperate for a quick agreement. See Gray (2005) and Frend (2008), 260–71, for the broader context.

32. Procopius *Wars* 3. 10–11.

33. Procopius *Wars* 3. 11. 31–14. 13 recounts the voyage; cf. *Wars* 3. 14. 1–5 for Procopius's scouting mission.

34. Belisarius's authority: *Wars* 3. 11. 20–21; cf. *Wars* 3. 14. 14–17 for the moment of decision.

35. *Wars* 3. 16. 12–15; cf. Meier (2004), 62ff.; Leppin (2011), 149–52.

5. FIVE THOUSAND HORSE

1. Procopius hides this fascinating insight in his account of the African expedition's time in Sicily at *Wars* 3. 14; it is mentioned in the course of later negotiations between Justinian and the Ostrogothic court: *Wars* 5. 3. 33.

2. *Wars* 3. 11. 1–19 for its catalogue of Procopius's army.

3. Procopius *Wars* 4. 6. 6–9.

4. Highly accessible introductions to Roman North Africa are Raven (1993) and Manton (1988). Ennabli (1992) provides an introduction to the findings of the UNESCO excavations at Carthage, and Mattingly and Hitchner (1995) to the rural survey evidence.

5. Dracontius's poetry has been edited with French translations in Moussey and Camus (1985–8), Bouquet and Wolff (1995–6), and Moussey (1988). Relevant material in the Latin Anthology is translated partly into English in Kay (2006) and Rosenblum (1961). For more detailed discussion, see e.g. Merrills and Miles (2010), 97–108 and ch. 8; Conant (2012), ch. 3; Steinacher (2016), ch. 5

6. Merrills and Miles (2010), ch. 2, understand the Rhine crossers as a series of warbands. For some introduction to the issue of 'barbarian' identity, see Gillett (2002); Heather (2008).

7. Goths of 376: Heather (1991), ch. 4. Radagaisus: Zosimus 5. 26. 4 and Olympiodorus fr. 9, with fuller discussion in Heather (2009), 174–6.

8. I have argued the case for the views on motivation and scale laid out here more fully in Heather (2009), 173–88; cf. Steinacher (2016), ch. 2. Goffart (2006), ch. 5, and Halsall (2007), 195–212, have similar views on scale but dispute the role of the Huns.

9. Hydatius *Chron.* 59 [67]; cf. Goffart (2006), ch. 5; Steinacher (2016), 71–4; Merrills and Miles (2010), 41–7.

10. Hydatius *Chron.* 69 [77]; cf. Merrills and Miles (2010), 44–7 (I simply don't believe, as they do, that most of Castinus's defeated army attached itself to the Hasding dynasty at this point); Steinacher (2016), 74–83.

11. For more detailed accounts, see Matthews (1975), ch. 15; Heather (2005), 251–62.

12. Recent, more detailed accounts are Merrills and Miles (2010), 50–55; Steinacher (2016), 92–102. Courtois (1955), 155–84, remains invaluable.

13. Augustine's rallying call: *Ep.* 228. 11; cf. Victor of Vita 1. 10 on the torturing of bishops. The quotations from the *Vita* are (in order) from 28. 4, 30. 1, 28. 5–6.

14. Theophanes *AM* 5942. Merrills and Miles (2010), 112, dismisses the reported ship numbers, but Belisarius's fleet numbered nearly six hundred ships, and the expedition of the early 440s was a joint East-West enterprise, so I don't find them at all implausible.

15. For more on the strategic context and the details of the agreement, see Heather (2005), ch. 6; Merrills and Miles (2010), 111–16; Steinacher (2016), 120–46.

16. The discussion of Moderan (2002) is much more convincing than Schwarcz (2004); cf. the very full discussion of Steinacher (2016), 151–66 (which, correctly in my view, starts to think about Vandal-Alan social structure and how this would have affected land distributions, although there is little specific evidence), or Merrills and Miles (2010), 66–70.

17. Victor of Vita 1. 2; fuller discussion and references. Heather (2009), 174–7.

18. A few contingents of a few thousand men each are in line with such figures, such as the 2,000 men led by Gibimund p. 137) or the 7,000 by Tatzon p. 140. After the war was completed, ca. 2,500–3,000 surviving Vandals were turned into East Roman auxiliary troops on the Persian front p. 143). I am firmly in agreement here with Steinacher (2016), 164–6, on the fact that military service remained the privilege of a specifically endowed landowning elite in the Vandal kingdom.

19. Victor of Vita I–II for the key measures; with fuller discussion in Heather (2007a).

20. Good narratives of the development of the kingdom between Geiseric and the landing of Belisarius can be found in Courtois (1955), 215–71; Merrills and Miles (2010), ch. 3; Steinacher (2016), ch. 5.

21. On these previous attacks, see further Heather (2005), 385–407. Signalling arrangements: *Wars* 3. 13. 1–11. Fresh water: *Wars* 3. 13. 23–4.

22. Council of War: *Wars* 3. 15.

23. *Wars* 3. 16. 13–15.

24. *Wars* 3. 17. 1–5.

25. *Wars* 3. 18. 1 for Gelimer's plan.

26. *Wars* 3. 18. 5–11.

27. *Wars* 3. 18. 12–19.

28. *Wars* 3. 19.

29. *Wars* 3. 20–21.

30. *Wars* 3. 24–25.

31. *Wars* 3. 24. 7–18.

32. *Wars* 3. 23. 1–4 (headhunting); *Wars* 4. 1 (cutting of aqueduct and impaling).

33. *Wars* 4. 2–3.

34. *Wars* 4. 4. 9–41 (pursuit of Gelimer); 6. 6. 14–7.17 (the king's surrender).

35. Procopius *Wars* 4. 4–9; cf. *PLRE* 3, 192–3, for the many other sources which record the triumph and consulship celebrations. Beard (2007) is a good introduction to the Republican Roman ceremony, which was less rigidly choreographed than is often imagined; cf. Meier (2003), 150–65, on the Vandal triumph in particular.

36. Auxiliaries: *Wars* 4. 14. 16–19; Vandals after 534, see ch. 9.

37. *Wars* 4. 7. 20.

38. *Wars* 4. 2. 8–32.

6. ROME AND RAVENNA

1. *Wars* 1. 24. 57–8.

2. *Cod. Just.* 1. 27. 1. 1–2 (AD 534): quoted in ch. 4 p. 115).

3. Among recent commentators, Moorhead (1994), 63–4; Meier (2004), 65ff.; and Leppin (2011), 161–5, likewise see the astonishing ease of victory over the Vandals as the final piece of the mental jigsaw which led Justinian's regime to place so much emphasis upon western expansion.

4. Natural waterways of the Mediterranean: Braudel (1973), 103–37; Horden and Purcell (2000), ch. 5.

5. Theodahad: references as *PLRE* 2, 1067–8; Tuluin: *PLRE* 2, 1131–3. More detailed discussion: Heather (1995).

6. Procopius *Wars* 5. 2 (with 5. 4. 1–3 on the public shaming of Theodahad). But see Heather (1993) on the education of Theoderic's children and his overall attitude to classical education. Tuluin held large estates in Gothic Provence (which would count as a provincial command; Cassiodorus *Variae* 8. 9–10). One of the others might be Osuine, who at about the right time was appointed to an important and equally provincial command in Dalmatia; *Variae* 9. 8–9. Both then disappear without trace See further Wolfram (1988), pt. 5, ch. 9.

7. *Wars* 5. 3. 10–29.

8. The sources for Peter the Patrician are collected and discussed at *PLRE* 3, 994–8. Good news: *Wars* 5. 3. 30. Bad news: *SH* 24. 22–3.

9. *Wars* 5. 4. 4–16; cf. *Anekdota* 16. 4 for the assassination orders.

10. *Wars* 5. 4. 17–31.

11. *Wars* 5. 5 (both expeditions); cf. 5. 6 (Peter's exploitation thereof).

12. *Wars* 5. 7.

13. Cassiodorus *Variae* 1.1

14. On the overriding importance of claiming divine support, see p. 23.

15. For a fuller examination of the context of *Variae* 1. 1 and Theoderic's gains from the crisis of 507, see Heather (2013), 68–79, with *ILS* 827 for the inscription.

16. Fuller account: Heather (2013), 79–87.

17. See in more detail Heather (2013), 88–97.

18. Hilderic: references as *PLRE* 2, 564. Tuluin's punitive campaign (taking advantage of a Frankish intervention): Cassiodorus *Variae* 8. 10, 8; cf. *PLRE* 2, 1009 (on the Burgundian king Sigismund).

19. For a more detailed discussion, see Heather (1991), pt. 3, esp. 248–9, 253–4, on Malchus frr. 2, 18. 4, and 20, which provide the key numbers.

20. The argument of Amory (1997), which has been influential. Certainly, in principle it is possible to imagine Theoderic in the Balkans in 470s and 480s benefiting from the same kind of recruiting of disaffected Roman units as would help bolster the insurgency of Totila in Italy in the 540s (see ch. 9), although Amory does not exploit this potential analogue. But such a process is not at all what detailed contemporary sources for the 470s and 480s describe (Heather 1991, pt. 3), and it is also worth noting that most of the disaffected Roman units then redefected to Narses (pp. 265–7).

21. Amory simply asserted that 'only' Procopius mentions women and children and has been believed. But see Heather (2007b) for a full refutation. I would also underline that the Thracian Goths

are referred to as *foederatii* before joining Theoderic (Malchus fr. 2), like Heruli, well evidenced in Justinian's army, not Roman regulars, who always served under their own leaders and had a propensity to reassert independence accordingly (see pp. 51–2 and 292).

22. The clustered geographical distribution of Theoderic's followers emerges from the Gothic war narrative: in more detail Heather (1995); cf. the attempt of Bierbrauer (1975) to link this historical evidence to archaeological materials.

23. Procopius claims that Wittigis advanced on Rome an army of 150,000 men (*Wars* 5. 16. 11), but his own more detailed evidence suggests an overall Gothic field army of more like 25,000–30,000; Hannestad (1960).

24. Two warrior grades: Heather (forthcoming). Cassiodorus *Variae* 8. 26 gives one example of the appointment of a local-level leader at Rieti.

25. *Wars* 5. 1. 34–9 (Symmachus and the fish). Momigliano (1955) remains highly influential, the basic argument recently echoed in Bjornlie (2013).

26. General evolution of senatorial elite: Barnish (1988); cf. Heather (2016), extending its implications to the careers of Symmachus and Boethius. Theodahad and Boethius: Barnish (1990).

27. Deliyannis (2010), ch. 4, on the palaces; cf. ch. 5 on Ostrogothic church construction and mosaic decoration.

28. Good archaeological introductions to this key artery are Agostini et al. (1989) and Messineo et al. (1993).

29. Procopius *Wars* 5. 8–10.

30. Procopius *Wars* 5. 11. 1–9 (overthrow of Theodahad). Wittigis's initial moves: *Wars* 5. 11. 10–29; 13. 14–29.

31. *Wars* 5. 14. 16.

32. *Wars* 5. 14. 12–16. 4 (the surrender of Pitzas and his followers is recorded at *Wars* 5. 15. 1–2).

33. *Wars* 5. 17–18.

34. *Wars* 5. 21–3 (5. 23. 26 for the 30,000 dead, but see n. 22).

35. *Wars* 5. 24. 1–21 (the initial reinforcements); 5. 25–6 (settling into siege warfare). Mule sausages: 6. 3. 11.

36. First sortie: *Wars* 5. 27. 1–23 (recording a few more skirmishes from the initial period; cf. 5, 27. 24–9, on differences in equipment).

37. *Wars* 5. 28–9.

38. *Wars* 6. 4–5.

39. *Wars* 6. 6–7 with 6. 22. 22–5; 29. 1–2 for the specific terms of Wittigis under discussion.

40. *Wars* 6. 9 is a little incoherent, since Procopius does not exactly accuse Wittigis of negotiating in bad faith despite launching his final attacks on the city ostensibly in the middle of the truce, I am not quite sure what to make of the account.

41. *Wars* 6. 10. 1–8 (John's attacks); 9–20 (break-up of the siege of Rome).

42. *Wars* 6. 11. 1–3.

43. Ildiger, Martinus, and Rimini: *Wars* 6. 11. 4–9; Genoa: *Wars* 6. 12. 26–41.

44. *Wars* 6. 11. 10–13. 15 (cf. 6. 11. 22 for John's unwillingness to follow Belisarius's orders).

45. *Wars* 6. 13. 16–18; 6. 16; 6. 17. 12–24.

46. *Wars* 6. 18 (disputed command); 6. 21 (disaster in Milan).

47. The story of the Gothic embassy is told at *Wars* 2. 2; Justinian's worries about Persia: *Wars* 6. 22. 22–5.

48. Belisarius's strategy: *Wars* 6. 22. 1–8; 6. 23. Frankish intervention: *Wars* 6. 25.

49. Fiesole: *Wars* 6. 24. 18 and 6. 27. 25–7. Ossimo: *Wars* 6. 24. 1–17; 6. 26 (Burcentius); 6. 27. 1–24 (water battles).

50. *Wars* 6. 27. 28–34.

51. *Wars* 6. 28.

52. *Wars* 5. 1. 16–17.

53. *Wars* 6. 29. 1–31.

7. THE CULTURE OF VICTORY

1. *Buildings* 1. 2. 9–12. A drawing of the statue was made in the 1430s for Cyriacus of Ancona, and Pierre Gilles saw fragments of the leg and nose in the 1540s. Meier (2003), 599–608, is an excellent discussion of the apotropaic character of the statue.

2. *Buildings* 1. 10. 11–20.

3. Alchermes (2005) is an excellent introduction to the building projects with Meier (2003), 101–82, on the unashamed triumphalism of the regime between 533 and 540.

4. *Const Tanta* preface; cf. Honoré (1978), 170ff. for a projected reconstruction of Tribonian's working timetable.

5. The Theodosian predecessor project was announced in 429 (*CTh* 1. 1. 5) but never actually undertaken. Matthews (2000) and Sirks (2007) offer differing views of the evolution of the Theodosian project, but there is no doubt that the second, greater task was never begun.

6. The law of citations can be found at *CTh* 1. 4. 3; trans. Pharr (1952). This was originally meant to be applied to one particularly intractable case: Matthews (2000), 221. On the messy legal background which this reform needed to address, see Jones (1964) ch. 14 (arguably a little pessimistic); Harries (1999), ch. 1; Humfress (2007), pt. 1. Honoré (1982) is an excellent introduction to the work of the jurisconsult Ulpian and the whole jurisconsult 'system' in general.

7. Suppression: *Const. Omnem* 7; cf. Honoré (1978), 147–8, 163–70, which discusses the commission working with Tribonian, which included two representatives each from the schools of Constantinople and Beirut.

8. *Deo Auctore* 5; cf. Honoré (1978), ch. 150–64.

9. *Const Tanta* 13; 15.

10. Quoted in Humfress (2005), 175.

11. A good introduction to the medieval commentary-by-gloss tradition of Bologna which eventually made good on Justinian's claims is Stein (1999), 43–8.

12. Justinian's Institutes can be read in the translation of Birks and MacLeod (1987); cf. Honoré (1978), ch. 6, on the revised curriculum.

13. Only England and the Nordic countries stood apart.

14. Necessity and fortification work in the East and Balkans: pp. 224 and 282.

15. General introduction: Alchermes (2005); Leppin (2011), 191–202.

16. See, amongst many possibilities, Krautheimer (1986).

17. The sources for Anicia Juliana are assembled and discussed at *PLRE* 2, 635–6. *Anth. Graec.* 1. 10 records the inscription on her great church. Harrison (1989) discusses its physical remains.

18. *Buildings* 1. 1. 30–54 (excerpts). The same point was made in more elaborate language by Paul the Silentiary when the church was rededicated over the Christmas period in 562/3; Bell (2009), 195ff.

19. Alchermes (2005), 361–6. Justinian's supposed reaction is reported in *Narratio de Aedificatione Templi S. Sophiae* 27 (= Preger 1901, 105).

20. Procopius *Buildings* 1. 1. 54–65.

21. Procopius *Buildings* 1. 1. 61; cf. Demus (1976) on the developing schemes of mosaic decoration and Mathew (1963) on importance of light and colour.

22. Quoted by Krueger (2005), 298.

23. *Buildings* 1. 6. 5–8.

24. Meier (2003), esp. 489–528, and Croke (2005) discuss Justinian's use of Constantinople; cf. MacCormack (1981) on the broader tradition of Roman processional ceremonial.

25. Literature and the fourth century: e.g. Wilson (1975) on Saint Basil, but Augustine, of course, confronted the same issues—Brown (1967)—as did, from the opposite point of view, the Emperor Julian; Athanassiadi Fowden (1992). Science: Sorabji (1988), (2006). Classical philosophy: Wildberg (2005); cf. Watts (2006) on the contrasting fates and traditions of the Athenian and Alexandrian schools.

26. Croke (2005).

27. Background of dispute: pp. 78–9. Ending of Acacian schism and approach to pope: p. 87.

28. See p. 119.

29. Good introductions (among many possibilities) to the progress and eventual resolutions of the Arian and Donatist disputes are, respectively, Hanson (1988)—cf. Berndt and Steinacher (2014)—and very recently Miles (2016).

30. Gray (2005), 232–3, and Van Rompay (2005), 246, who bring out the further adjustments that Justinian continued to make after the Conversations of 532. Good further discussions of Justinian's evolving religious policies can be found in Meier (2004), 10; and Leppin (2011), 181–90, 293–307.

31. Meier (2003), 273–91; Van Rompay (2005), 246–7.

32. *CJ* 1. 1. 6–8 with commentary, in Gray (2005), 232–3.

33. Translation of the Latin summary (with related texts): Price (2009). On Vigilius's manoeuvres, see pp. 277–8.

34. Van Rompay (2005); Frend (2008), 283–95.

35. Fourth-century Antioch: e.g. Sandwell (2007), with e.g. Trombley (2014) on subsequent processes of conversion. On the development of more intense forms of piety: Krueger (2005).

36. John of Ephesus cannot hide the fact, although he desperately tries to excuse himself, that he took communion with the patriarch of Constantinople in the time of Justin II.

37. E.g. Gray (2005); Van Rompay (2005).

38. Van Esbroeck (1997) explores what Justinian may have had in mind.

39. Cf. the much fuller discussion of Meier (2003), chs. 4–5, who rightly emphasizes the significance of ill-omened natural phenomena like earthquakes.

8. 'OUR BROTHER IN GOD'

1. The quotation is from the preface to *On Virtues and Vices*; for an introduction to Constantine's project, see Lemerle (1971), 280–8.

2. *De Cer* I 89–90; trans. Greatrex and Lieu (2002), 124–8.

3. See ch. 4

4. Share of African wealth: *Wars* 1. 26. 1–4. *Limitanei: Anekdota* 24. 12–14; with *Wars* 1. 26. 5–12 (Dara) and 2. 7. 19–37 (unpaid deserters at Beroea). See p. 224 on the defensive improvements of the 540s.

5. *Wars* 2. 1.

6. Introduction to the physical remains of the city: Downey (1961). Role in the later empire: Liebeschuetz (1972). Religious communities: Sandwell (2007).

7. *Wars* 2. 5.

8. Diplomacy: *Wars* 2. 6. 17–25; 7. 14–18. Siege and fall of Hierapolis: *Wars* 2. 6. 1–8; 7. 1–13, 19–37.

9. *Wars* 2. 8–11. 13; with the earlier identification of the crucial weak point at *Wars* 2. 6. 9–16.

10. Wars 2. 12–14.7 with Tabari I. 898/157–8; trans. Greatrex and Lieu (2002), 107–8. There is no archaeological evidence for Chosroes's New Antioch.

11. *Wars* 7. 1. 2–3 (Procopius does not make this link).

12. *Wars* 2. 14. 8–13; 18–19. 46. *Anekdota* 2. 18–22. The other fragmentary sources for this campaign are translated by Greatrex and Lieu (2002), 108–9.

13. *Wars* 2. 20–21. 29.

14. On the plague, see ch. 11. Conclusion of 542 campaign: *Wars* 2. 21. 30–4.

15. *Wars* 2. 26–7 with Segal (1970) on the general wealth and significance of the 'Blessed City'.

16. Procopius has much to say about the refortification of the eastern front in *Buildings* book 2 (Mesopotamian frontier) and book 3 (Armenian sector). After Croke and Crow (1983) it used to be argued that much of this was fantasy, but Whitby (1986b) conclusively showed that what Procopius has to say about Dara could be believed, and Whitby (1985), (1986a), (1986b), (1987) convincingly extended the argument to the broader refortification programme. There is not much archaeological evidence for Antioch, but what there is again supports Procopius's account of the rebuilding: *Buildings* 2. 10. 2–25; cf. Foss (2000). And Antioch was certainly a major settlement centre again by the late sixth century.

17. Truce in Mesopotamia and aftermath: *Wars* 2. 28. 1–11 with Greatrex and Lieu (2002), 113–14, and ch. 9.

18. An excellent introduction to the tradition and its development is Jouanno (2002).

19. Braund (1994), 269–75, with Greatrex and Lieu (2002), chs. 4–5.

20. 387 partition: Greatrex and Lieu (2002), ch. 2. On Khavad's demands of Anastasius and the defections to Rome of the 520s, see pp. 76–7 and 91.

21. Braund (1994), ch. 2, esp. 41–4.

22. Gubazes's diplomacy and the backstory: *Wars* 2. 15; Petra: *Wars* 2. 17; Roman counter-thrust: *Wars* 2. 24–5.

23. Wars 2. 28. 15–30. Braund (1994), 276–87, is excellent on the general approach of the Lazi to life between two empires.

24. *Wars* 2. 29. 1–9.

25. *Wars* 2. 29. 10–30.

26. *Wars* 8. 8 for the 549 campaign; cf. *Wars* 8. 12. 21–7 for the triple water course which the Romans discovered only after storming the city in 551.

27. *Wars* 8. 9 with the helpful commentary of Braund (1994), 300–2.

28. Full career: *PLRE* 2, 226–9; Criticism of his Roman command: pp. 259–60. Falling over: *Wars* 8. 11. 11–62.

29. *Wars* 8. 11–12.

30. *Wars* 8. 16; Menander fr. 6. 1; Agathias 2. 19–22, 3. 2–4; 8–15 with Braund (1994), 308–9.

31. Agathias 3. 15–28 (Persian attack); 4. 13–23 (Roman counterstrike).

32. Protests in Constantinople and terms: *Wars* 8. 15. 13–18 with Greatrex and Lieu (2002), ch. 9.

33. Menander fr. 6.1: the full amount was thirty thousand solidi p.a., and there were seventy-two solidi to the pound.

9. INSURGENTS

1. *Wars* 3. 15. 2–17 with *PLRE* 2, 133–4 for his full career. He acted as Praetorian Prefect in Africa after the conquest until Justinian sent out a new appointment.

2. *CJ* 1. 27. Guntharis later offered the Berber chief Antalas command of 1,500 Roman *limitanei* in Byzacena, which may serve as a guide to the notional strength of each of these provincial forces.

3. Boniface and Laurus: ch. 5. *Wars* 4. 1. 7–8 refers to other Vandal-supporting landowners, and some peasants were willing to disrupt foraging expeditions: p. 140. Opponents of the Three Chapters also identify the now-Roman functionary Mocianus as a former Arian and therefore quite possibly a Roman ex-functionary of Vandal kings; see pp. 277–8.

4. * The kind of Roman landowners who appear in the *Tablettes Albertini* were edited by Courtois et al. (1952); cf. further recent discussion in Merrills and Miles (2010), 159–62.

5. *Nov.* 37 with Merrills and Miles (2010), 249–51.

6. *Wars* 4. 14. 11–15.

7. Wars 4. 14. 8–10.

8. 17 chieftains: Corippus *Joh.* 8. 627–36 (all killed; Jordanes *Romana* 385). General background: Courtois (1955), pt. 3, ch. 2, is the classic account brought up to date by Moderan (2003) and Shaw (1995). Rushworth (2004) and Merrills and Miles (2010), esp. 124–9, provide useful supplements.

9. Moderan (2003), 396–415, for the reading; with Merrills and Miles (2010), 124–9, for a useful English introduction.

10. I am confident that this kind of model plays a major role in processes of state formation in less developed societies on the fringes of larger polities in the first millennium; see further Heather (2009).

11. *Wars* 4. 10. 1–12.

12. *Wars* 4. 11–12.

13. *Wars* 4. 13. 1–38.

14. *Wars* 4. 14. 20–15. The sources for Stotzas are collected and discussed at *PLRE* 3, 1199–1200; cf. Merrills and Miles (2010), 248ff.

15. *Wars* 4. 16–17.

16. *Wars* 4. 19–20. For more discussion of Solomon's fortification programme, see ch. 10.

17. *Wars* 4. 21–28. 34.

18. Apart from Procopius, our main source is the *Iohannis* of the Latin poet Corippus, which can be read in the English translation of Shea (1998). Averil Cameron (2000) provides good secondary commentary. For Troglita's career in full, see *PLRE* 3, 644–9.

19. Corippus *Ioh.* 6. 478–81, 496–505; cf. p. 107 on Callinicum.

20. Corippus *Ioh.* 7 provides the information. Procopius *Wars* 4. 28. 48–50 has remarkably little to say about the victory, presumably reflecting the broader judgment he had by now come to about the effects of Justinian's wars in Africa and elsewhere; see further pp. 270–1.

21. *Wars* 6. 29. 33.

22. We do not know what happened to Pitzas and the Goths of Samnium. In 538/9 the garrisons of Petra, Clusium, and Tudra were transported away from the war zone to Naples and Sicily (*Wars* 6. 11. 19ff; 13. 2ff.; 27. 31ff.). Some at least ended up in the east fighting Persia in the 540s.

23. *Wars* 6. 29.

24. *Wars* 7. 1. 34–6.

25. See further p. 50.

26. *Wars* 7. 1. 24–33; cf. *PLRE* 3, 43–4, for his career and full references.

27. Urais and Ildebadus: *Wars* 6. 28. 35; 29. 39–41; Eraric: *Wars* 7.1. 25–2. 13.

28. *Wars* 8. 32. 20; with *PLRE* 2, 1112–13, on the career of Theudis.

29. The quotation can be found at *Wars* 7. 4. 32; the conclusion to a sequence of events recounted at *Wars* 7. 3–4.

30. *Wars* 7. 5; with *Wars* 7. 5. 18 for the Roman loss of mobility in fixed strongpoints. The point is repeated at *Wars* 7. 9. 1–6.

31. Cf. *Wars* 7. 9. 1–6.

32. Heather (1996), 327–8, provides a listing of the elements of the Roman army that Totila recruited at different moments. The majority joined on a contingent basis, usually because they had not been paid (like the mutineers in North Africa), and returned to an imperial allegiance once they had; pp. 246–7. *Wars* 7. 5. 19 records the transfer of allegiance on the part of (unspecified numbers of) Totila's initial Roman prisoners.

33. *Wars* 7. 6–7.

34. *Wars* 7. 10–11 with 7. 15. 1–8 for the attempt to get more troops inside Rome.

35. *Wars* 7. 10. 19–23 (Tibur captured); 12. 11–20 (Assisi and Spoleto); 15. 9ff. (capture of grain fleet).

36. *Wars* 7. 17.

37. *Wars* 7. 19.

38. *Wars* 7. 20.

39. *Wars* 7. 21. 18–25 (ambassadors to Constantinople); 7. 22 (Rome's defences); 7. 33. 7 (Franks and the Venetias).

40. *Wars* 7. 24; cf. 7. 37. 1–2 on the failed Frankish marriage alliance.

41. Reinforcements and their fate: *Wars* 7. 27–9. Antonina: 7. 30. 3. Rusciane: 7. 30. 9–14. Belisarius's return east: 7. 30. 25; cf. *Anekdota* 5. 16–17 and *Wars* 7. 35. 2 (fall of Perugia).

42. *Wars* 7. 35. 23–39. 5.

43. *Wars* 7. 37. 6–7; cf. 8. 24. 4.

44. *Wars* 7. 39. 6–24.

45. *Wars* 7. 40. 9 (death of Germanus); 8. 21 and 26 (Narses's appointment and build-up); 8. 22–3 (Totila's fleet).

46. *Wars* 8. 26. 17–25 (Salona to Ravenna); 28. 1–12 (Ravenna to Rimini).

47. *Wars* 8. 29–32 (the variant versions of Totila's death can be found at 8. 32. 29–36).

48. *Wars* 8. 33–5.

10. THE WESTERN EMPIRE OF JUSTINIAN

1. Corippus *Just.* 3. 1–84 describes Justinian's funeral. Theophilus *AM* 6057 records the death of Belisarius, and *PLRE* 3. 997f. discusses the evidence for Peter the Patrician.

2. Among earlier commentators, Stein (1950), 756–6, 1 and Jones (1964), 298–302, have a go at drawing up such a balance sheet, but both were writing before much of the latest archaeological evidence for the overall economic state of the empire became available.

3. Africa: *Wars* 4. 28. 52; cf. his broader diatribe at *SH* 18. 3ff.

4. Corippus *Joh.* 3. 443–50, tr. Shea; cf. Procopius's and Corrippus's reports of thousands of Berbers dying in battles with the armies of Solomon and John Troglita; pp. 245, 250–1.

5. Malalas 495; cf. *PLRE* 3, 366–8.

6. Exploration of Roman methods in detail: Heather (2001), with Heather (2009), esp. ch. 2, for further thoughts on longer-term consequences.

7. The inscriptions: *PLRE* 3, 1167–77; cf. Pringle (1981), 84–120 and ch. 4, which collects the more general evidence for fortification. Merrills and Miles (2010), ch. 9, is also helpful. An excellent introduction to the general evolution of North African public townscapes away from old rhythms and buildings of the classical city is Leone (2007), chs. 3–4.

8. On urban production in particular, see generally Leone (2007), 217–36, with Mattingly (1992), (2001), (2011) on Leptiminus. Wickham (2005), 637–44 and 720–8, discusses the evidence for continued urban prosperity and economic complexity in post-conquest North Africa.

9. Leone (2007), 208–13; cf. Merrills and Miles (2010), 241ff., on religious reconstruction.

10. Markus and Sotinel (2007), with Sotinel (2007), on Vigilius, and Moderan (2007) on the North African protests.

11. Moderan (2007).

12. Merrills and Miles (2010), ch. 9, surveys the evidence with full references; cf. p. 197 on the new processional liturgies and buildings of the sixth-century East.

13. The quotation is from *SH* 18. 20–1. Mundus: p. 152. 538/9: *Wars* 6. 11 and 13. Mid-540s: *Wars* 7. 6, 10, 30. Germanus and Narses: pp. 264–5, 279.

14. Cutrigur raids: Procopius *Wars* 2. 4; Agathias *Histories* 5. 11ff. Slav raids: *Buildings* 4. 7. 13 and 17f; *Wars* 7. 39–40. Ammianus on the Lentienses.

15. Raids of 548–50: *Wars* 7. 29, 38–40; cf. Curta (2001), chs. 5–6, for secondary commentary.

16. On the evolution of this situation from the chaotic collapse of Attila's empire, see in more detail Heather (2009), 238–56, 371–7, 392–406.

17. *Buildings* book 4, esp. 4. 2 (Thermopylae); 4. 9 (Long Walls of Constantinople); 4. 10 (Chersonesus). The lists can be found at *Buildings* 4. 4, 11. Good secondary commentary is now available in Curta (2001), ch. 4, with full references (mustering archaeological reinforcements), who convincingly argues against the previous tendency to dismiss the reality of Procopius's evidence for major Justinianic investment in the defences of the Balkans. Agathias *Histories* 5. 11–12, 19–20, 23. 5–9, describe the Avar raid of 559, 5. 16–20, which was held up by the new fortifications at both Thermopylae and the Chersonesus. Agathias 5. 16–20 is devoted to Belisarius's heroic defence of Constantinople.

18. Compare the lists at *Buildings* 4. 4 (Illyricum, north and south) and 4. 11 (the eastern Balkans).

19. Menander fr. 5. 1, trans. Blockley (1985), 49. Good introductions to Avar history are provided by Whitby (1988); Pohl (1988), (2003). For an introduction to Avar archaeology in English, see Daim (2003). Uldin: Sozomen *H.E.* 9. 5. 1–5.

20. Menander fr. 5. 1–2, trans. Blockley (1985), 50–1.

21. Agathias *Histories* 5. 24–5.

22. Justin's declaration: John of Ephesus, *H.E.* 6. 24, trans. Smith (1860), 429; cf. Menander fr. 8: trans. Blockley (1985), 97.

23. For a more detailed discussion of identity and political structuring within nomad empires, see Heather (2009), ch. 5.

24. Sirmium: Menander fr. 12. 5, trans. Blockley (1985), 135ff. Siege of Constantinople: *Chronicon Paschale*, trans. Whitby and Whitby (1989), 178ff. For a fuller discussion of the Hunnic parallels, see Heather (2005), ch. 8; (2009), ch. 5.

25. Menander fr. 11, trans. Blockley (1985), 429.

26. The price of the alliance is recorded at Menander frr. 24–5; cf. full references collected at *PLRE* 3, 38–40.

27. The Pragmatic Sanction is preserved as Appendix 7 to the *Novels* (new laws) of Justinian. *P. Ital.* 49 (cf. Amory 1997, App. I) records part of one of the consequent law suits.

28. Agathias *Histories* 1.6–2.4.

29. Agathias *Histories* 2. 4–9. Agathias does not date Casilinum, although it was certainly after the end of June, and it is just about possible that the Pragmatic Sanction was issued on news of the victory reaching Constantinople, although the timing is very tight and you might expect a more explicit reference to the victory.

30. Agathias *Histories* 2. 2–3; cf. 11. 1.

31. Belisarius: pp. 252–3. Narses: Agathias *Histories* 1. 1. 1 correcting Procopius's very odd remark that, after Mons Lactarius, the Gothic survivors agreed to leave Italy altogether; *Wars* 8. 35. 33–36.

32. Aligern: Agathias *Histories* 1. 8–9; Indulf: Procopius *Wars* 8. 35. 37; Ragnaris: Agathias *Histories* 2. 13–14. Ragnaris is described by Agathias as a Bittigur Hun in origin. This group figures in the narratives of the collapse of Attila's empire in the 450s and 460s, so his ancestors may have attached themselves to the Pannonian Goths (p. 158) at this point, or he may have been a much later renegade from Roman service. He is first explicitly named in connection with events of 552; Procopius *Wars* 8. 26. 4.

33. Agathias *Histories* 1. 20. 2.

34. Agathias *Histories* 2. 13–14; the 7,000 were presumably—after all the fighting, casualties, and recruiting—a ramshackle group of the former followers of Totila and Teias.

35. Widin: Paul the Deacon, *History of the Lombards* 2.2, with commentary at *PLRE* 3, 924.

36. Sindual: *PLRE* 3, 1155.

37. For an introduction to Constantinople's Italian holdings and the effects of Lombard invasion, see, e.g. Wickham (1981), 28ff.; La Rocca et al. (2002), 21–7 and ch. 3.

38. The story of Narses's invitation is told by Paul the Deacon, *History of the Lombards* 2. 5. For further discussion of the circumstances of the Lombards' move into Italy, see e.g. Jarnut (1982), ch. 1; Christie (1995), ch. 2. For earlier Hunnic-era analogy, see Heather (2009), ch. 4.

39. It was of course Justinian's own decision not to respond positively when Totila later put the same deal back on the table (Ch. 6). By then, however, imperial prestige was already decisively committed, following Belisarius's coup de théâtre in 540, to a complete conquest of the Italian peninsula, and it would have taken a great deal to accept the loss of prestige (and potential knock-on political consequences) inherent in even a partial defeat.

40. Brown (1984) for the evolving army of Italy; cf. Noble (1984) on the political functioning of militarized elites within the Roman ducate.

41. Sotinel (2007); cf. Straw (2007) on the arguments of Gregory I.

42. Wickham (2005), 728–39; cf. Wickham (2009), 140–7; Christie (2006), esp. ch. 5, for the evidence in more detail. Wickham's overall model in these works—see e.g. (2005), 708–17—is that the economic complexity of the late Roman period was built around the structures and operations of the late Roman state. If so, then the disappearance of that state was bound to generate substantial simplification, even if the Gothic war hurried matters along. A less state-centred view is Ward Perkins (2005), who explains the complexity more in terms of the general conditions generated by the empire than the workings of its own political economy. In this model, the violence associated with the end of the empire and its aftermath has a more important causative effect. My own view would be a combination of the models, which I do not find remotely contradictory.

43. The meagre sources for the expedition are discussed at *PLRE* 3, 140; cf. Thompson (1969), 320ff., for an English-language introduction to the broader history and eventual Visigothic reconquest of the annexed cities.

44. Jones (1964), 299–300, comes to the opposite conclusion, but he did not have the newer archaeological evidence for North African and southern Italian relative prosperity available when he wrote, and he limited the time frame of his discussion really only to the reign of Justinian itself, which to my mind is far too short. Stein (1959), 377, takes a suitably longer view of the significance of East Roman holdings in the Italian peninsula. The guesswork quoted by O'Donnell (2009), 289, suggests that Justinian inherited a reserve of 28 million solidi, that the conquests cost about thirty-six million, and that Italy and North Africa annually brought in maybe half a million each; no figure is given for Sicily. Even using these figures, which take no account of the looted royal treasuries, one still has to reckon that the conquests did indeed pay for themselves in the medium to longer term.

45. See pp. 288–9.

46. Effects of second-wave Arab expansion in Italy: Noble (1984), ch.2; cf. La Rocca et al. (2002), chs. 2–3, on the Lombard conquest of Ravenna. On the desperate Constantinopolitan struggle for survival in the early eighth century, see Mango (1977).

47. Whitby (1988), 156ff., explores the effective East Roman counterattack of the 590s. For a more detailed account of the slavicization of the Balkans, see Heather (2009), ch. 8, esp. 399–406.

11. THE FALL OF THE EASTERN EMPIRE

1. Quotation: *SH* 18. 23. Overall judgment: *SH* 18. 4.

2. See pp. 215–20. Jones (1964), 299, seems to me surprisingly dismissive of these losses.

3. Cf. chapters 6 and 9.

4. Pay arrears: pp. 246–7. Narses expedition: p. 265. The diversion of funds to North Africa with Germanus in 537 may also explain why it took so long for Belisarius's initial Italian expeditionary force to be reinforced.

5. Aside from general comments—e.g. *Anekdota* 8. 31–33—the text also names six specific aristocrats that Justinian and Theodora ruined: *Anekdota* 12. 1–11. The first four seem to have been based in Constantinople, but the other two were Dionysius of Lebanon and John of Edessa, emphasizing that richer provincial aristocrats (like the Apions: p. 66) needed to remain in good odour at court. We have no real way of testing whether six aristocratic bankruptcies is far worse than par for the course for a forty-year reign like Justinian's, although Procopius would obviously have us believe so.

6. A good recent account of Justinian's tax reforms is Sarris (2011), 151–3; cf. *SH* 12 for some examples of great men's fortunes being destroyed.

7. Much of the peasantry of early fourteenth-century England just before the Black Death e.g. seems to have been in such a position; Postan (1993).

8. Justinian *Nov.* 148, discussed by Sarris (2011), 227–8.

9. There is an excellent recent literature in English on every aspect of the plague: Horden (2005); Stathakopoulos (2000); Sarris (2002). McCormick (2015) is particularly good on the accounts of Procopius and John of Ephesus and for thinking in broad terms about what the archaeology of plague might look like. I generally follow Horden's guidance in matters of detail, but see also Meier (2003), 359–87. On the continued prosperity of the eastern Mediterranean post 550, see Ward Perkins (2000); Holum (2005); Wickham (2005), 443ff. (on rural production) and 626ff. (on the cities), with 548–9 for his particular analysis of the effects of the plague as 'marginal'. The footnotes to these studies give full references to the more detailed surveys and excavation reports on which this overview is based and which, to my mind, undercut earlier arguments that the Islamic takeover of the seventh century was a consequence of substantial sixth-century social and economic decline in the East Roman world; e.g. Kennedy (1985a), (1985b). On the specific rebuilding of Antioch, see Lassus (1972); cf. Foss (2000). There are two possible reasons why the economic effects were apparently limited. Half of everybody in the ancient world died by age fifteen, many from the effects of chronic low-level malnutrition. So population numbers could rebound quickly from major bouts of mortality as the resulting availability of food led, if briefly, to higher survival rates. Alternatively, perhaps, the Justinianic plague did not kill in the countryside on the scale of the fourteenth-century Black Death.

10. The overall picture from the first set of excavations was famously pulled together by Foss (1977); cf. Foss (1996) for greater detail. For a recent summary of subsequent material, see Wickham (2005), 626ff. Ward Perkins (2000) and Wickham (2005), 609ff., both emphasize the contrast

provided by the continued prosperity of old Roman cities in Egypt and the Fertile Crescent that fell under Islamic Umayyad rule.

11. Hickey (2012), 1–2, in particular, but cf. the remainder of this fascinating work on the estate's history and operations across the bulk of the sixth century. The point is unaffected by whatever stance one chooses in the broader argument between Hickey (2012) and Sarris (2006) on how to conceptualize the estate's economic operations.

12. Ottoman documents: Hendy (1985), 613–69; cf. more generally Haldon (1997) on the dramatic administrative, military, and political adjustments required.

13. Haldon (1997), esp. chs. 5 (tax) and 6 (military organization).

14. Haldon (1997), esp. chs. 8–9.

15. For a good in introduction to the end of Macedonian prosperity, see Angold (1997). Second phase of East Roman losses generated by Umayyad expansion: p. 301.

16. For an introduction to the source problems, see esp. Crone and Cook (1972); Crone (1987).

17. The point emerges very clearly from Sartre (1982); cf. more generally on Arabia in late antiquity e.g. Donner (2005); Dignas and Winter (2007), ch. 5. For parallels with the Germanic world, see Heather (2009), esp. chs. 2 and 11.

18. An excellent recent account in English (among many) is Kennedy (2007), esp. ch. 1 on the Ridda wars.

19. On the pre-Hunnic transformation of Rome, by the fourth century, into the 'inside-out' empire, see Heather (2005), chs. 1 and 3, with full references. Heather (2009) develops an overview of the economic, demographic, and political shifts of the first millennium which led to the rise of the north.

20. Syria, Palestine, and Egypt are the only areas of the former Roman world which seem to have maintained the same degree of prosperity in the post-Roman period as they enjoyed under imperial rule: for references, see n. 9. An excellent introduction to the political (not, of course, religious) eclipse of Arabia under the Umayyad and Abbasid caliphates is Kennedy (1986), chs. 3–4.

21. Some of the diplomacy with the western Turks is covered in extraordinary detail in the surviving fragments of Menander Protector, esp. frr. 10 and 13. For more detail and alternative views, particularly of Turkish motivation, see Dignas and Winter (2007), esp. 109–15; Sarris (2011), 226ff.

22. The best account of Maurice's campaigns is Whitby (1988), chs. 9–11. See also Sarris (2011), 232ff., for the 'Versailles moment'.

23. For more detailed narrative treatments, see e.g. Whitby (1988), ch. 6; Sarris (2011), 236–42.

24. The *Chronicon Paschale*'s account of the siege of Constantinople can be read in the English translation of Whitby and Whitby (1989), 168ff. The sources for the Persian wars of Phocas and Heraclius are brilliantly examined in Howard Johnston (2010). For more detailed narrative reconstruction, see e.g. Dignas and Winter (2007), 44ff., 115ff., and 148ff.; Sarris (2011), 242–57.

25. On the third-century crisis and Roman recovery, see e.g. Dodgeon and Lieu (1991), pt. 1; Potter (2004), chs. 6–7; Heather (2005), chs. 2–3.

26. In the tenth century, likewise, it was a Slavic dynasty established in Poland, further away from immediate Ottonian counteraction than its counterparts in Bohemia, which was able to build the larger, more independent power base: Heather (2009), ch. 10.

27. For more detail on Justinian's Arab policy, and Maurice's reversal, see the works cited in n. 17. The ambiguous evidence for the precise date of Arethas's promotion is collected and discussed at *PLRE* 3, 111–12, but the reactive, causal connection is clear.

28. Luttwak (1975) began it; Isaac (1992) is a sustained reply, concentrating on the early imperial period. Heather (2000) continues the discussion into the late Roman period.

29. Balkans: pp. 279–83. Lazica: pp. 228–30. Balancing Italy and the East: pp. 258–65.

30. Ch. 4.

31. Opening of the Italian war: pp. 148–53. Events of 539/40: pp. 178–9.

32. Conversations and Africa: pp. 118–9. Conquest of Carthage and the *Digest*: pp. 182–4.

33. *SH* 1. 1–3; cf. pp. 31–6.

34. Kaldellis (2004); cf. Bjornlie (2013) for what is in the end an unpersuasive argument that Cassiodorus's *Variae* were aimed at the same politically key Constantinopolitan audience.

35. An excellent introduction to the bureaucratic world of John Lydus is Kelly (2004). That such men had serious political opinions is clear; Bell (2009). But there is simply no evidence for them functioning as an effective power bloc. Justinian's overall initiative in church matters: pp. 203–9 and 277–8.

36. Hypatius: pp. 92–4. Anicius Olybrius: pp. 192–3.

37. See pp. 142 and 178–9.

38. Procopius *Wars* 7. 32; although implicated, Artabanes escaped capital punishment, it seems, only by a whisker.

39. The main source is Malalas 494/fr. 49; cf. *PLRE* 3, 219, for full references.

40. Corippus *Iust*. 1. goes to huge lengths to present the nephew Justin as Justinian's chosen heir and establish the new emperor's legitimacy by stressing that the transfer of power was smooth and absolutely inevitable and that just before his death, Justinian's final words had mentioned the nephew's name (*Iust*. 4. 357–63). But the supposed final words were heard by only one palace functionary, the eunuch Callinicus, and less partial sources fill in the full backstory of the two Justins and the eventual isolation and physical elimination of the son of Germanus: Evagrius *EH* 5. 1–3; cf. *PLRE* 3, 750–4 (the son of Germanus), and 754–6 (Emperor Justin II).

41. Corippus *Iust*. 3. 151–401; cf. pp. 269–70.

PRIMARY SOURCES

As per normal conventions, editions of standard classical works are not cited in the bibliography; most are translated in either or both of the Loeb and Penguin Classics series. All Christian authors are available, if sometimes in outdated form, in *Patrologia Latina* or *Patrologia Graeca* editions. More recent (sometimes competing) editions of most of the texts cited in the Introduction and notes can be found in *GCS* (*Die Griechischen Christlichen Schriftsteller der ersten Jahrhunderte*), *CSEL* (*Corpus Scriptorum Ecclesiasticorum Latinorum*), *CC* (*Corpus Christianorum*), and *SC* (*Sources Chrétiennes*). Many are translated in the Nicene and Post-Nicene Fathers and the Library of the Fathers collections. Otherwise, the following editions and translations of late Roman sources have been used.

Agathias, *History*: ed. Keydell (1967); trans. Frendo (1975).
Ammianus Marcellinus: ed. and trans. Rolfe (1935–9).
Anthologia Graeca (*The Greek Anthology*): trans. Paton (1916–18).
Bavarian Code: trans. Rivers (1977).
Cassiodorus, *Variae*: ed. Mommsen (1894a); trans. Hodgkin (1896); Barnish (1992).
Chronicon Paschale: ed. Dindorf (1832); trans. Whitby and Whitby (1989).
Claudian, *Works*: ed. and trans. Platnauer (1922).
Codex Theodosianus: ed. Mommson and Meyer (1905); trans. Pharr (1952).
Constantine VII Porphyrogenitus, De Ceremoniis: ed. Reiske (1829).
Corippus, *In Praise of Justin II*: ed. and fr. trans. Antès (1981).

Corippus, *Iohannes*: ed. Teurfs et al. (2007); trans. Shea (1998).
Evagrius Scholasticus, trans. Whitby (2000).
Hydatius, *Chronicle*: ed. Mommsen (1894b); trans. Burgess (1993).
John of Antioch: ed. Müller (1851–70); trans. Gordon (1966).
John of Ephesus: part 2, ed. and trans. Harrak (1999); part 3, ed. and trans. Brooks (1952).
Jordanes, *Getica*: ed. Mommsen (1882); trans. Mierow (1915).
Justinian, *Corpus Iuris Civilis*:
Institutiones, Digesta: ed. Krüger and Mommsen (1928).
Codex Iustinianus: ed. Krüger (1929).
Novellae: ed. Schöll and Kroll (1928).
Lactantius, *On the deaths of the Persecutors*: ed. and trans. Creed (1984).
Life of Daniel the Stylite: trans. Dawes and Baynes (1948).
Malalas: ed. Dindorf (1831); trans. Jeffreys et al. (1986).
Malchus: ed. and trans. Blockley (1982).
Menander rhetor: trans. Russell and Wilson (1981).
Olympiodorus of Thebes: ed. and trans. Blockley (1982).
Orosius, *History against the Pagans*: trans. Fear (2010).
Paul the Deacon, *History of the Lombards*: ed. Bethmann and Waitz (1878).
P. Ital.: ed. Tjäder (1955).
Priscus: ed. and trans. Blockley (1982).
Procopius, *Works*: ed. and trans. Dewing (1914–40).
Symmachus, *Works*: ed. Seeck (1883); *Relationes*: trans. Barrow (1973).
Synesius of Cyrene: ed. Garzya (1989).
Theophanes, *Chronographia*: ed. Niebuhr (1839–41); trans. Mango and Scott (1997).
Victor of Vita, *History of the Persecution in Africa*: ed. Kalm (1879); trans.: Moorhead (1992b).
Zachariah of Mitylene, trans. Hamilton and Brooks (1893).
Zosimus, *History*: ed. Paschoud (1971–89); trans. Ridley (1982).

BIBLIOGRAPHY

Agostini, C., et al. (1989). *La strada Flaminia Militare: Testimonianze archeologiche sulla dorsale sinistra del Savena tra Bologna e il Passo della Futa alla ricerca della strada del 187 a.C.* (Bologna).

Alchermes, J. D. (2005). 'Art and Architecture in the Age of Justinian', in Maas, 343–74 (Cambridge).

Amory, P. (1997). *People and Identity in Ostrogothic Italy, 489–554* (Cambridge).

Angold, M. (1997). *The Byzantine Empire, 1025–1204: A Political History*, 2nd ed. (New York).

Antès, S. (1981). *Corippe: Éloge de l'empereur Justin II* (Paris).

Athanassiadi Fowden, P. (1992). *Julian: An Intellectual Biography* (London).

Barnes, T. D. (1981). *Constantine and Eusebius* (Cambridge, MA).

Barnes, T. D. (1993). *Athanasius and Constantius: Theology and Politics in the Constantinian Empire* (Cambridge, MA).

Barnish, S. J. B. (1988). 'Transformation and Survival in the Western Senatorial Aristocracy, c. A.D. 400–700', *Papers of the British School at Rome* 56: 120–55.

Barnish, S. J. B. (1990). 'Cassiodorus, Boethius, Theodahad: Literature, Philosophy and Politics in Ostrogothic Italy', *Nottingham Medieval Studies* 34: 16–32.

Barnish, S. J. B. (1992). *The Variae of Magnus Aurelius Cassiodorus Senator* (Liverpool).

Barrow, R. H. (1973). *Prefect and Emperor: The Relationes of Symmachus, A.D. 384* (Oxford).

Bavant, B. (2007). 'Caricin Grad and the Changes in the Nature of Urbanism in the Central Balkans in the Sixth Century', in *The Transition to Late Antiquity on the Danube and Beyond*, ed. A. G. Poulter, 337–74 (Oxford).

Beard, M. (2007). *The Roman Triumph* (Cambridge, MA).

Bell, P. (2009). *Three Political Voices from the Age of Justinian: Agapetus, 'Advice to the Emperor'; 'Dialogue on Political Science'; Paul the Silentiary, 'Description of Hagia Sophia'* (Liverpool).

Berndt, G. M., and Steinacher, R., eds. (2014). *Arianism: Roman Heresy and Barbarian Creed* (Farnham).

Bethmann, L., and Waitz, G., eds. (1878). *Pauli Historia Langobardorum*, Monumenta Germaniae Historica: Scriptores rerum Germanicarum (Hanover).

Bierbrauer, V. (1975). *Die ostgotischen Grab- und Schatzfunde in Italien* (Spoleto).

Birks, P., and McLeod, G. (1987). *Justinian's Institutes* (London).

Bjornlie, S. (2013). *Politics and Tradition between Rome, Ravenna and Constantinople: A Study of Cassiodorus and the Variae 527–554* (Cambridge).

Blockley, R. C. (1981). *The Fragmentary Classicising Historians of the Later Roman Empire: Eunapius, Olympiodorus, Priscus and Malchus*, vol. 1 (Liverpool).

Blockley, R. C. (1983). *The Fragmentary Classicising Historians of the Later Roman Empire: Eunapius, Olympiodorus, Priscus and Malchus*, vol. 2 (Liverpool).

Blockley, R. C. (1985). *The History of Menander the Guardsman* (Liverpool).

Bouquet, J., and Wolff, E. (1995–6). *Dracontius: Romulea* (Paris).

Bowman, A. K., et al., eds. (2005). *The Crisis of Empire A.D. 193–337*, Cambridge Ancient History, 2nd ed., vol. 12 (Cambridge).

Braudel, F. (1973). *The Mediterranean and the Mediterranean World in the Age of Philip II* (London).

Braund, D. C. (1994). *Georgia in Antiquity: A History of Colchis and Transcaucasian Iberia 550 BC—AD 562* (Oxford).

Bregman, J. (1982). *Synesius of Cyrene, Philosopher-Bishop* (Berkeley, CA).

Brock, S. (1981). 'The Conversations with the Syrian Orthodox under Justinian (532)', *Orientalia Christiana Periodica* 47: 87–121.

Brooks, E. R. (1893). 'The Emperor Zenon and the Isaurians', *English Historical Review* 8: 209–38.

Brooks, E. W. (1952). *John of Ephesus: Ecclesiastical History*, vol. 3 (Louvain).

Brown, P. R. L. (1967). *Augustine of Hippo: A Biography* (London).

Brown, P. R. L. (1971). *The World of Late Antiquity: From Marcus Aurelius to Muhammad* (London).

Brown, P. R. L. (2013). *The Rise of Western Christendom: Triumph and Diversity, AD 200–1000* (Oxford).

Brown, T. S. (1984). *Gentlemen and Officers: Imperial Administration and Aristocratic Power in Byzantine Italy, A.D. 554–800* (London).

Browning, R. (1987). *Justinian and Theodora* (London).

Burgess, R. (1993). *The Chronicle of Hydatius and the Consularia Constantinopolitana* (Oxford).

Bury, J. B. (1889). *History of the Later Roman Empire (395 AD to 800)*, 2 vols (London).

Bury, J. B. (1923). *History of the Later Roman Empire from the Death of Theodosius to the Death of Justinian*, 2 vols (London).

Calo Levi, A. (1952). *Barbarians on Roman Imperial Coinage and Sculpture*, Numismatic Notes and Monographs 123 (New York).

Cameron, A. D. E. [Alan] (1970). *Claudian: Poetry and Propaganda at the Court of Honorius* (Oxford).

Cameron, A. D. E. [Alan] (1973). *Porphyrius the Charioteer* (Oxford).

Cameron, A. D. E. [Alan] (1976). *Circus Factions: Blues and Greens at Rome and Byzantium* (Oxford).

Cameron, A. M. [Averil] (1970). *Agathias* (Oxford).

Cameron, A. M. [Averil] (1985). *Procopius and the Sixth Century* (London).

Cameron, A. M. [Averil], et al., eds. (2000). *The Cambridge Ancient History*, 2nd ed., vol. 14 (Cambridge).

Campbell, B. (1984). *The Emperor and the Roman Army, 31 BC–AD 235* (Oxford).

Campbell, B. (2005). 'The Army', in Bowman et al., 110–30 (Cambridge).

Carrié, J.-M. (2005). 'Developments in Provincial and Local Administration', in Bowman et al., 269–312 (Cambridge).

Chazelle, C., and Cubitt, C., eds. (2007). *The Crisis of the Oikoumene: The Three Chapters and the Failed Quest for Unity in the Sixth-Century Mediterranean* (Turnhout).

Christiansen, A. (1944). *L'Iran sous les Sassanides*, 2nd ed. (Copenhagen).

Christie, N. (1995). *The Lombards* (Oxford).

Christie, N. (2006). *From Constantine to Charlemagne: An Archaeology of Italy AD 300–800* (Aldershot).

Conant, J. (2012). *Staying Roman: Conquest and Identity in Africa and the Mediterranean, 439–700* (Cambridge).

Cook, S. A., et al., eds. (1939). *The Cambridge Ancient History*, 1st ed., vol. XII (Cambridge).

Corbier, M. (2005a). 'Coinage and Taxation: The State's Point of View, A.D. 193–337', in Bowman et al., 327–92 (Cambridge).

Corbier, M. (2005b). 'Coinage, Society and Economy', in Bowman et al., 393–439 (Cambridge).

Courtois, C. (1955). *Les Vandales et l'Afrique* (Paris).

Courtois, C., and Albertini, E., eds. (1952). *Tablettes Albertini: Actes privés de l'époque vandale, fin du V. siècle* (Paris).

Creed, J. L. (1984). *Lactantius: De mortibus persecutorum* (Oxford).

Croke, B. (2005). 'Justinian's Constantinople', in Maas, 60–86 (Cambridge).

Croke, B. (2007). 'Justinian under Justin: Reconfiguring a Reign', *Byzantinische Zeitschrift* 100: 13–55.

Croke, B., and Crow, J. (1983). 'Procopius and Dara', *Journal of Roman Studies* 73: 143–59.

Crone, P. (1987). *Meccan Trade and the Rise of Islam* (Oxford).

Crone, P., and Cook, M. (1977). *Hagarism: The Making of the Islamic World* (Cambridge).

Curta, F. (2001). *The Making of the Slavs: History and Archaeology of the Lower Danube Region, c. 500–700* (Cambridge).

Dagron, G. (2011). *L'hippodrome de Constantinople: Jeux, people et politique* (Paris).

Daim, F. (2003). 'Avars and Avar Archaeology: An Introduction', in Goetz et al., 463–570 (Leiden).

Daube, D. (1966–7). 'The Marriage of Justinian and Theodora. Legal and Theological Reflections', *Catholic University Law Review* 360: 380–99.

Dauge, Y. A. (1981). *Le Barbare: Recherches sur la conception romaine de la barbare et de la civilisation*, Coll. Latomus 176 (Brussels).

Dawes, E. A. S., and Baynes, N. H. (1948). *Three Byzantine Saints* (Oxford).

Deliyannis, D. (2010). *Ravenna in Late Antiquity* (Cambridge).

Delmaire, R. (1989), *Largesses sacrees et res privata: L'aerarium imperial et son administation du Ive au VIe siecle* (Rome).

Delmaire, R. (1995). *Les institutions du Bas-Empire romain de Constantin a Justinien*, vol. 1: *Les institutions civiles palatines* (Paris).

Demus, O. (1976). *Byzantine Mosaic Decoration: Aspects of Monumental Art in Byzantium* (London).

Dewing, H. B. (1914–40). *The Works of Procopius* (London).

Dignas, B., and Winter, E. (2007). *Rome and Persia in Late Antiquity: Neighbours and Rivals* (Cambridge).

Dindorf, L. (1831). *Malalas Chronographia* (Bonn).

Dindorf, L. (1832). *Chronicon Paschale* (Bonn).

Dodgeon, M. H., and Lieu, S. N. C. (1991). *The Roman Eastern Frontier and the Persian Wars (AD 226–363): A Documentary History* (London).

Donner, F. M. (2005). 'The Background to Islam', in Maas, 510–34 (Cambridge).

Downey, G. (1961). *A History of Antioch in Syria from Seleucus to the Arab Conquest* (Princeton, NJ).

Drinkwater, J. F. (2007). *The Alamanni and Rome 213–496* (Oxford).

Dvornik, F. (1966). *Early Christian and Byzantine Political Philosophy: Origins and Background*, Dumbarton Oaks Center for Byzantine Studies (Washington, DC).

Elton, H. (1996). *Warfare in Roman Europe, AD 350–425* (Oxford).

Ennabli, E. A. (1992). *Pour sauver Carthage: Exploration et conservation de la cité punique, romaine et Byzantine* (Tunis).

Ennsslin, W. (1939a). 'The End of the Principate', in Cook et al., 353–82 (Cambridge).

Ennsslin, W. (1939b). 'The Reforms of Diocletian', in Cook et al., 383–407 (Cambridge).

Evans, J. A. S. (1984). 'The "Nika" Rebellion and the Empress Theodora', *Byzantion* 54: 380–2.

Evans, J. A. S. (2001). *The Age of Justinian* (London).

Fear, A. G. (2010). *Orosius, History against the Pagans* (Liverpool).

Foss, C. (1977). 'Archaeology and the Twenty Cities of Byzantine Asia', *American Journal of Archaeology* 81: 469–86.

Foss, C. (1996). *Cities, Fortresses and Villages of Byzantine Asia Minor* (Aldershot).

Foss, C. (2000). 'Late Antique Antioch', in *Antioch: The Lost City*, by C. Kondoleon, 23–7 (Princeton, NJ).

Frend, W. H. C. (2008). *The Rise of the Monophysite Movement: Chapters in the History of the Church in the Fifth and Sixth Centuries*, 2nd rev. ed. (Cambridge).

Frendo, J. D. (1975). *Agathias History* (Berlin).

Garzya, A. (1989). *Opere di Sinesio di Cirene: Epistole, operette, inni* (Turin).

Gascou, J. (1972). 'Les grands domains, la cité et l'État en Égypte byzantine: Recherches d'histoire agraire, fiscale et administrative', *Travaux et Mémoires* 9: 1–90.

Gillet A., ed. (2002). *On Barbarian Identity: Critical Approaches to Ethnicity in the Early Middle Ages* (Turnhout).

Goetz, H.-W., et al., eds. (2003). *Regna and Gentes: The Relationship between Late Antique and Early Medieval Peoples and Kingdoms in the Transformation of the Roman World* (Leiden).

Goffart, W. (1980). *Barbarians and Romans* AD *418–584: The Techniques of Accommodation* (Princeton, NJ).

Goffart, W. (1981). 'Rome, Constantinople, and the Barbarians in Late Antiquity', *American Historical Review* 76: 275–306.

Goffart. W. (2006). *Barbarian Tides: The Migration Age and the Later Roman Empire* (Philadelphia).

Goldberg, E. J. (2006). *Struggle for Empire: Kingship and Conflict under Louis the German 817–876* (Ithaca, NY).

Gonzalez, J. (1986). 'The *Lex Irnitana*: A New Copy of the Flavian Municipal Law', *Journal of Roman Studies* 76: 147–243.

Gordon, D. C. (1966). *The Age of Attila* (Ann Arbor, MI).

Gray, P. (1979). *The Defence of Chalcedon in the East* (Leiden).

Gray, P. (2005). 'The Legacy of Chalcedon: Christological Problems and Their Significance', in Maas, 215–38 (Cambridge).

Greatrex, G. (1994). 'The Dates of Procopius' Works', *Byzantine and Modern Greek Studies* 18: 101–14.

Greatrex, G. (1997). 'The Nika Riot: A Reappraisal', *Journal of Hellenic Studies* 117: 60–86.

Greatrex, G. (1998). *Rome and Persia at War, 502–532* (Leeds).

Greatrex, G., and Lieu, S. (2002). *The Roman Eastern Frontier and the Persian Wars: A Narrative Sourcebook* (London).

Gwatkin, H. M., and Whitney, J. P., eds. (1911). *The Cambridge Medieval History*, 1st ed., vol. 1 (Cambridge).

Haarer, F. K. (2006). *Anastasius I: Politics and Empire in the Late Roman World* (Cambridge).

Haldon, J. F. (1997). *Byzantium in the Seventh Century: The Transformation of a Culture* 2nd rev. ed. (Cambridge).

Halsall, G. (2007). *Barbarian Migrations and the Roman West 376–568* (Cambridge).

Hamilton, F. J., and Brooks, E. W. (1899). *The Syriac Chronicle Known as That of Zachariah of Mitylene* (London).

Hannestad, K. (1960). 'Les forces militaires d'après la guerre gothique de Procope', *Classica et Mediaevalia* 21: 136–83.

Hanson, R. P. C. (1988). *The Search for the Christian Doctrine of God* (Edinburgh).

Harrak, A. (1999). *John of Ephesus: Ecclesiastical History*, vol. 2 (Toronto).

Harries, J. (1999). *Law and Empire in Late Antiquity* (Cambridge).

Harrison, R. M. (1989). *A Temple for Byzantium: The Discovery of Anicia Julian's Palace-Church in Istanbul* (Austin).

Heather, P. J. (1991). *Goths and Romans 332–489* (Oxford).

Heather, P. J. (1993). 'The Historical Culture of Ostrogothic Italy', in *Teoderico il grande e i Goti d'Italia*, Atti del XIII Congresso internazionale di studi sull'Alto Medioevo, 317–53 (Spoleto).

Heather, P. J. (1994a). 'Literacy and Power in the Migration Period', in *Literacy and Power in the Ancient World*, ed. A. Bowman and G. Woolf, 177–97 (Cambridge).

Heather, P. J. (1994b). 'New Men for New Constantines? Creating an Imperial Elite in the Eastern Mediterranean', in *New Constantines: The Rhythm of Imperial Renewal in Byzantium, 4th–13th Centuries*, ed. P. Magdalino, 11–33 (London).

Heather, P. J. (1995). 'Theodoric King of the Goths', *Early Medieval Europe* 4, no. 2: 145–73.

Heather, P. J. (1996). *The Goths* (Oxford).

Heather, P. J. (2001). 'The Late Roman Art of Client Management and the Grand Strategy Debate', in *The Transformation of Frontiers from Late Antiquity to the Carolingians*, ed. W. Pohl and I. N. Wood, 15–68; Proceedings of the Second Plenary Conference, European Science Foundation Transformation of the Roman World Project (Brill).

Heather, P. (2005). *The Fall of Rome: A New History* (London).

Heather P. (2007a). 'Christianity and the Vandals in the Reign of Geiseric', in *Wolf Liebeschuetz Reflected*, ed. J. Drinkwater and B. Salway (London), 137–146.

Heather, P. (2007b). 'Merely an Ideology? Identity in Ostrogothic Italy', in *The Ostrogoths: From the Migration Period to the Sixth Century; An Ethnographic Perspective*, ed. S. J. Barnish and F. Marazzi (Woodbridge), 87–111.

Heather, P. (2008). 'Ethnicity, Group Identity, and Social Status in the Migration Period', in *Franks, Northmen, and Slavs: Identities and State Formation in Early Medieval Europe*, ed. I. Garipzanov et al., 17–50 (Turnhout).

Heather, P. (2009). *Empires and Barbarians: Migration, Development, and the Birth of Europe* (London).

Heather, P. (2012). 'Conclusions: The Politics of Accommodation', in Porena et al., 295–319 (Rome).

Heather, P. (2013). *The Restoration of Rome: Barbarian Popes and Imperial Pretenders* (London).

Heather, P. (2015). 'East and West in the Fifth Century', in Roberto and Mecella, 189–211 (Rome).

Heather, P. (2016). 'A Tale of Two Cities: Rome and Ravenna under Gothic rule,' in *Ravenna: Its Role in Earlier Medieval and Exchange*, ed. J. Herrin and J. Nelson, 15–38 (London).

Heather, P. (forthcoming). 'Freedmen: Forgotten Warriors of the Early Middle Ages', in *Common Men and Women at War*, ed. Leif Inge Petersen, Conference proceedings (Trondheim).

Heather, P. J., and Matthews, J. F. (1991). *The Goths in the Fourth Century*, Translated Texts for Historians (Liverpool).

Heather, P. J., and Moncur, D. (2001). *Politics, Philosophy, and Empire in the Fourth Century: Select Orations of Themistius*, Translated Texts for Historians (Liverpool).

Hendy, M. F. (1985). *Studies in the Byzantine Monetary Economy, c. 300–1450* (Cambridge).

Herrin, J. (1987). *The Formation of Christendom* (Oxford).

Hickey, T. (2012). *Wine, Wealth and the State in Late Antique Egypt* (Ann Arbor, MI).

Hodgkin, T. (1886). *The Letters of Cassiodorus. A Condensed Translation* (Oxford).

Hoffmann, D. (1969). *Das spätromische Bewegungsheer und die Notitia Dignitatum* (Düsseldorf).

Holum, K. (2005). 'The Classical City in the Sixth Century: Survival and Transformation', in Maas, 87–112 (Cambridge).

Honoré, A. M., (1978). *Tribonian* (London).

Honoré, A. M. (1982). *Ulpian* (Oxford).

Honoré, A. M. (1994). *Emperors and Lawyers*, 2nd rev. ed. (Oxford).
Honoré, A. M. (1998). *Law in the Crisis of Empire 379–455* AD: *The Theodosian Dynasty and Its Quaestors, with a Palingenesia of Laws of the Dynasty* (Oxford).
Horden, P. (2005). 'Mediterranean Plague in the Age of Justinian', in Maas, 134–60 (Cambridge).
Horden, P., and Purcell, N. (2000). *The Corrupting Sea: A Study of Mediterranean History* (Oxford).
Howard Johnson, J. D. (1995). 'The Two Great Powers of Late Antiquity: A Comparison', in *The Byzantine and Early Islamic Near East 3: States, Resources and Armies*, ed. Averil Cameron, 123–78 (Princeton, NJ).
Howard Johnston, J. D. (2010). *Witnesses to a World Crisis: Historians and Histories of the Middle East in the Seventh Century* (Oxford).
Humfress, C. (2005). 'Law and Legal Practice in the Age of Justinian', in Maas, 161–84 (Cambridge).
Humfress, C. (2007). *Orthodoxy and the Courts in Late Antiquity* (Oxford).
Isaac, B. (1992). *The Limits of Empire: The Roman Army in the East* (Oxford).
Janniard, S. (2015). 'Les adaptations de l'armée romaine aux modes de combat des peuples des steppes (fin IVe–début VIe siècle apr. J.-C.)', in Roberto and Mecella, 231–69 (Rome).
Jarnut, J. (1982). *Geschichte der Langobarden* (Stuttgart).
Jeffreys, E., et. al. (1986). *The Chronicle of John Malalas* (Melbourne).
Jones, A. H. M. (1964). *The Later Roman Empire: A Social Economic and Administrative Survey*, 3 vols (Oxford).
Jouanno, C. (2002). *Naissance et métamorphoses du roman d'Alexandre: Domaine grec* (Paris).
Kaldellis, A. (2004). *Procopius of Caesarea: Tyranny, History, and Philosophy at the End of Antiquity* (Philadelphia).
Kaster, R. A. (1988). *Guardians of Language: The Grammarian and Society in Late Antiquity* (Berkeley).
Kay, N. M. (2006). *Epigrams of the Anthologia Latina. Text, Translation and Commentary* (London).
Kelly, C. (2004). *Ruling the Later Roman Empire* (Cambridge, MA).
Kennedy, H. (1985a). 'From Polis to Madina: Urban Change in Late Antique and Early Islamic Syria', *Past and Present* 106: 3–27.
Kennedy, H. (1985b). 'The Last Century of Byzantine Syria: A Reinterpretation', *Byzantinische Forschungen* 10: 141–83.
Kennedy, H. (1986). *The Prophet and the Age of the Caliphates* (London).
Kennedy, H. (2007). *The Great Arab Conquests: How the Spread of Islam Changed the World We Live In* (London).
Keydell, R., ed. (1967). *Agathias Historiae*, Corpus Fontium Historiae Byzantinae (Berlin).
Kim, H. J. (2013). *The Huns, Rome and the Birth of Europe* (Cambridge).
Krautheimer R. (1986). *Early Christian and Byzantine Architecture* (New Haven, CT).
Krueger, D. (2005). 'Christian Piety and Practice in the Sixth Century', in Maas, 291–315 (Cambridge).
Krüger, P. (1929). *Codex Iustinianus* (Berlin).
Krüger, P., and Mommsen, T. (1928). *Iustinianus: Institutiones, Digesta* (Berlin).
La Rocca, C., et al. (2002). *Italy in the Early Middle Ages: 476–1000* (Oxford).
Lassus, J. (1972). *Antioch-on-the-Orontes* (Princeton, NJ).
Lee, A. D. (2007). *War in Late Antiquity: A Social History* (Oxford).
Lemerle, P. (1971). *Le premier humanisme Byzantine* (Paris).
Lenski, N. (2002). *Failure of Empire: Valens and the Roman State in the Fourth Century* AD (Berkeley).
Leone, A. (2007). *Changing Townscapes in North Africa from Late Antiquity to the Arab Conquest* (Bari).
Leppin, H. (2011). *Justinian. Das Christliche Experiment* (Stuttgart).
Lewitt, T. (1991). *Agricultural Production in the Roman Economy* A.D. *200–400* (Oxford).

Liebeschuetz, J. H. W. G. (1972). *Antioch: City and Imperial Administration in the Later Roman Empire* (Oxford).
Liebeschuetz, J. H. W. G. (2001). *The Decline and Fall of the Roman City* (Oxford).
Luttwak, E. N. (1975). *The Grand Strategy of the Roman Empire from the First Century A.D. to the Third* (Baltimore).
MacCormack, S. A. (1981). *Art and Ceremony in Late Antiquity* (Los Angeles).
Maas, M. (2005). *The Cambridge Companion to the Age of Justinian* (Cambridge).
MacMullen, R. (1988). *Corruption and the Decline of Rome* (New Haven, CT).
Maenchen-Helfen, O. J. (1973). *The World of the Huns* (Berkeley).
Mango, C. (1977). 'Historical Introduction', in *Iconoclasm*, ed. A. Bryer and J. Herrin, 1–6 (Birmingham).
Mango, C., and Scott, R., trans. (1997). *Chronographia, The Chronicle of Theophanes Confessor* (Oxford).
Manton, E. L. (1988). *Roman North Africa* (London).
Markus, R. A., and Sotinel, C. (2007). 'Introduction', in Chazelle and Cubitt, 1–14 (Turnhout).
Mathew, G. (1963). *Byzantine Aesthetics* (London).
Matthews, J. F. (1974). 'The Letters of Symmachus', in *Latin Literature of the Fourth Century*, ed. J. W. Binns, 58–99 (London).
Matthews, J. F. (1975). *Western Aristocracies and Imperial Court A.D. 364–425* (Oxford).
Matthews, J. F. (1986). 'Some Enemies of Symmachus', in *Colloque genevois sur Symmaque: À l'occasion du mille six centième anniversaire du conflit de l'autel de la Victoire*, ed. F. Paschoud et al. (Paris).
Matthews, J. F. (1989). *The Roman Empire of Ammianus* (London).
Matthews, J. F. (2000). *Laying Down the Law: A Study of the Theodosian Code* (New Haven, CT).
Mattingly, D. J. (2011). *Leptiminus (Lamta): The Field Survey. Report no. 3* (Portsmouth, RI).
Mattingly, D. J., et al. (1992). *Leptiminus (Lamta): A Roman Port City in Tunisia. Report no. 1* (Ann Arbor, MI).
Mattingly, D. J., et al. (2001). *Leptiminus (Lamta): The East Baths, Cemeteries, Kilns, Venus Mosaic, Site Museum and Other Studies. Report no. 2* (Portsmouth, RI).
Mattingly, D. J., and Hitchner, R. B. (1995). 'Roman Africa: An Archaeological Review', *Journal of Roman Studies* 85: 165–213.
McCormick, M. (1986). *Eternal Victory: Triumphal Rulership in Late Antiquity, Byzantium and the Early Medieval West* (Cambridge).
McCormick, M. (2015). 'Tracking Mass Death during Rome's Fall, Part 1', *Journal of Roman Archaeology* 28: 325–57.
McLynn, N. (2004). 'The Transformation of Imperial Churchgoing in the Fourth Century', in *Approaching Late Antiquity: The Transformation from Early to Late Empire*, ed. S. Swain, 96–112 (Oxford).
Meier, M. (2003). *Das andere Zeitalter Justinians: Kontingenzerfahrung und kintingenzbewältung im 6. Jahrhundert n. Chr. Hypomnemata* 147 (Göttingen).
Meier, M. (2004). 'Zur Funktion der Theodora-Rede im Geschichtswerk Prokops (BP 1, 24, 33–37)', *RhM* 147: 88–104.
Meier, M. (2008). 'Der Aufstand gegen Anastasios im Jahr 512,' *Millennium* 4: 157–238.
Meier, M. (2009). *Anastasios I. Die Entstehung des Byzantinischen Reiches* (Stuttgart).
Merrills, A., and Miles, D. (2010). *The Vandals* (Oxford).
Messineo, G., and Carbonara, A. (1993). *Via Flaminia* (Rome).
Mierow, C. C. (1915). *Jordanes Getica* (New York).
Miles, R., ed. (2016). *The Donatist Schism: Controversy and Contexts* (Liverpool).
Moderan, Y. (2002). 'L'établissement des Vandals en Afrique', *Antiquité Tardif* 10: 87–122.
Moderan, Y. (2003). 'Une guerre de religion: Les deux églises d'Afrique à l'époque vandale', *Antiquité Tardif* 11: 21–44.

Moderan, Y. (2007). 'L'Afrique reconquise et les Trois Chapitres', in Chazelle and Cubitt, 39–83 (Turnhout).

Moderan, Y. (2012). 'Confiscations, expropriations et redistributions foncières dans l'Afrique vandale', in Porena et al., 157–224 (Rome).

Momigliano, A. (1955). 'Cassiodorus and the Italian Culture of His Time', *Proceedings of the British Academy* 41: 215–48.

Mommsen, T., ed. (1882). *Jordanes Romana et Getica*, Monumenta Germaniae Historica, Auctores Antiquissimi 5. 1 (Berlin).

Mommsen, T., ed. (1894a). *Cassiodori Senatoris Variae*, Monumenta Germaniae Historica, Auctores Antiquissimi 12 (Berlin).

Mommsen, T., ed. (1894b). *Chronica Minora* 2, Monumenta Germaniae Historica, Auctores Antiquissimi 11 (Berlin).

Mommsen, T., and Krüger, P., eds. (1905). *Codex Theodosianus* (Berlin).

Moorhead, J. (1992a). *Theoderic in Italy* (Oxford).

Moorhead, J. (1992b). *Victor of Vita: History of the Persecution in Africa* (Liverpool).

Moorhead, J. (1994). *Justinian* (London).

Moussy, C. (1988). *Dracontius Oeuvres II* (Paris).

Moussy, C., and Camus, C. (1985). *Dracontius: De Laudibus Dei* (Paris)

Müller, K., ed. (1851–70). *Fragmenta Historicorum Graecorum*, vols. 4–5 (Paris).

Niebuhr, B. G., ed. (1839–41). *Theophanes Chronographia* (Bonn).

Nixon, C. E. V., and Rogers, B. S. (1994). *In Praise of Later Roman Emperors: The Panegyrici Latini* (Berkeley).

Noble, T. F. X. (1984). *The Republic of St. Peter: The Birth of the Papal State, 680–825* (Philadelphia).

Noble, T. F. X. (1993). 'Theoderic and the Papacy', *Teoderico il grande e i Goti d'Italia*, Atti del XIII Congresso internazionale di studi sull'Alto Medioevo, 395–423 (Spoleto).

Noble, T. F. X. (1995). 'The Papacy in the Eighth and Ninth Centuries', in *The New Cambridge Medieval History*, vol. 2, c.700–c.900, ed. R. McKitterick, 563–86 (Cambridge).

Norwich, J. J. (1988). *Byzantium: The Early Centuries* (London).

O'Donnell, J. J. (2009). *The Ruin of the Roman Empire* (London).

Oertel, F. (1939), 'The Economic Life of the Empire', in Cook et al., 232–81 (Cambridge).

Paschoud, F. (1971–81). *Zosimus Historia Nova* (Paris).

Paton, W. (1916–18). *The Greek Anthology*, 5 vols (London).

Pazdernik, C. (2005). 'Justinianic Ideology and the Power of the Past', in Maas, 185–213 (Cambridge).

Pharr, C. (1952). *The Theodosian Code and Novels, and the Sirmondian Constitutions* (New York).

Platnauer, M. (1922). *The Works of Claudian* (London).

PLRE = *The Prosopography of the Later Roman Empire.* (1971–1992). A. H. M. Jones et al., eds., 3 vols (Cambridge).

Pohl, W. (1988). *Die Awaren: Ein Steppenvolk im Mitteleuropa, 567–822 n. Chr.* (Munich).

Pohl, W. (2003). 'A Non-Roman Empire in Central Europe: The Avars', in Goetz et al., 571–95 (Leiden).

Porena, P., et al., eds. (2012). *Expropriations et confiscations dans les royaumes barbares: Une approche régionale* (Rome).

Postan, M. M. (1993). *The Medieval Economy and Society* (Harmondsworth).

Potter, D. (2004). *The Roman Empire at Bay: A.D. 180–395* (London).

Potter, D. (2015). *Theodora: Actress, Empress, Saint* (Oxford).

Preger, T., ed. (1901). *Scriptores originum Constantinopolitanarum* (Leipzig).

Price, R. (2009). *The Acts of the Council of Constantinople of 553: With Related Texts on the Three Chapters Controversy* (Liverpool).

Price, R., and Gaddis, M. (2005). *The Acts of the Council of Chalcedon* (Liverpool).

Pringle, D. (1981). *The Defence of Byzantine Africa from Justinian to the Arab Conquest* (Oxford).

Raven, S. (1993) *Rome in Africa*, 3rd ed. (London).

Reid, J. S. (1911). 'The Reorganisation of the Empire', in Gwatkin and Whitney, 24–54 (Cambridge).

Reiske, J. J., ed. (1829). *Constantine VII Porphyrogenitus, De Ceremoniis aulae Byzantinae* (Bonn).

Ridley, R. T. (1982). *Zosimus New History* (Canberra).

Rivers, T. J. (1977). *Laws of the Alamans and Bavarians* (Philadelphia).

Roberto, U., and Mecella, L., eds. (2015). *Governare e riformare l'impero al momento della sua divisione: Oriente, Occidente, Illirico* (Rome).

Rolfe, J. C., ed. (1935–9). *Ammianus Marcellinus*, Loeb Library (London).

Rosenblum, M. (1961). *Luxorius: A Latin Poet among the Vandals* (New York).

Rostovtzeff, M. (1926). *The Social and Economic History of the Roman Empire*, 1st ed. (Oxford).

Rubin, Z. (1986). 'The Mediterranean and the Dilemma of the Roman Empire in Late Antiquity', *Mediterranean Historical Review* 1: 13–62.

Rushworth, A. (2004). "From Arzuges to Rustamids. State Formation and Regional Identity in the Pre-Saharan Zone', in *Vandals, Romans, and Berbers: New Perspectives on Late Antique North Africa*, ed. A. H. Merrills, 77–98 (Aldershot).

Russell, D. A., and Wilson, N. G. (1981). *Menander Rhetor* (Oxford).

Sandwell, I. (2007). *Religious Identity in Late Antiquity: Greeks, Jews, and Christians in Antioch* (Cambridge).

Sarris, P. (2002). 'The Justinianic Plague: Origins and Effects', *Continuity and Change* 17: 169–82.

Sarris, P. (2006). *Economy and Society in the Age of Justinian* (Cambridge).

Sarris, P. (2011). *Empires of Faith: The Fall of Rome to the Rise of Islam, 500–700* (Oxford).

Sartre, M. (1982). 'Trois études sur l'Arabie romaine et byzantine', in *Revue d'études latines* (Brussels).

Schöll, R., and Kroll, G. (1928). *Iustinianus: Novellae* (Berlin).

Schwarcz, A. (2004). 'The Settlement of the Vandals in North Africa', in *Vandals, Romans, and Berbers: New Perspectives on Late Antique North Africa*, ed. A. H. Merrills, 49–58 (Aldershot).

Scott, R. (2012). *Byzantine Chronicles and the Sixth Century* (Farnham).

Seeck, O. (1883). *Symmachus quae supersunt* (Berlin).

Segal, J. B. (1970). *Edessa: 'The Blessed City'* (Oxford).

Shaw, B. (1995). *Rulers, Nomads and Christians in North Africa* (Aldershot).

Shea, G. W. (1998). *The Iohannis or De bellis libycis of Flavius Cresconius Corippus* (Lewiston, ME).

Sirks, A. J. B. (2007). *The Theodosian Code: A Study* (Friedrichsdorf).

Smith, R. P. (1860). *The third part of the ecclesiastical history of John, Bishop of Ephesus* (Oxford).

Sorabji, R. (1983). *Time, Creation and the Continuum: Theories in Antiquity and the Early Middle Ages* (London).

Sorabji, R. (1988). *Matter, Space and Motion: Theories in Antiquity and Their Sequel* (London).

Sotinel, C. (2005). 'Emperors and Popes in the Sixth Century: The Western View', in Maas, 267–90 (Cambridge).

Sotinel, C. (2007). 'The Three Chapters and the Transformations of Italy', in Chazelle and Cubitt, 85–119 (Turnhout).

Stathakopoulos, D. (2000). 'The Justinianic Plague Revisited', *Byzantine and Modern Greek Studies* 24: 256–76.

Stein, E. (1950). *Histoire du Bas-Empire*, vol. 2 (Paris).

Stein, P. (1999). *Roman Law in European History* (Cambridge).

Steinacher, R. (2016). *Die Vandalen: Aufstieg und Fall eines Barbarenreichs* (Stuttgart).

Straw, C. (2007). 'Much Ado about Nothing: Gregory the Great's Apology to the Istrians', in Chazelle and Cubitt, 12–59 (Turnhout).

Swain, S. (2013). *Themistius, Julian and Greek Political Theory under Rome: Texts, Translations and Studies of Four Key Works* (Cambridge).

Teitler, H. C. (1985). *Notarii and Exceptores* (Amsterdam).

Teurfs, C., et al. (2007). *Corippe: La Johannide; ou, Sur les guerres de Libye* (Paris).

Thompson, E. A. (1946). 'The Isaurians under Theodosius II', *Hermathena*, 18–31.

Thompson, E. A. (1969). *The Goths in Spain* (Oxford).

Tjader, J.-O. (1955). *Die nichtliterarischen lateinischen Papyri Italiens aus der Zeit 445–700* (Lund).

Trombley, F. (2014). *Hellenic Religion and Christianization c. 370–529* (Leiden).

Van Esbroeck, M. (1997). 'The Aphthartodocetic Edict of Justinian and Its Armenian Background', *Studia Patristica* 33: 578–85.

Van Rompay, L. (2005). 'Society and Community in the Christian East', in Maas, 239–65 (Cambridge).

Vinogradoff, P. (1911). 'Social and Economic Conditions of the Roman Empire in the Fourth Century', in Gwatkin and Whitney (1911), 542–67 (Cambridge).

Vogler, C. (1979). *Constance II et l'administration imperiale* (Strasbourg).

Ward Perkins, B. (2000a). 'Land, Labour and Settlement', in Cameron et al., 315–45 (Cambridge).

Ward Perkins, B. (2000b). 'Specialised Production and Exchange', in Cameron et al., 346–91 (Cambridge).

Ward Perkins, B. (2005). *The Fall of Rome and the End of Civilization* (Oxford).

Watts, E. J. (2006). *City and School in Late Antique Athens and Alexandria* (Berkeley).

Whitby, L. M. (1985). 'Justinian's Bridge over the Sangarius and the Date of Procopius' *De adeficiis*', *Journal of Hellenic Studies* 105: 129–48.

Whitby, L. M. (1986a). 'Procopius and the Development of Roman Defences in Upper Mesopotamia', in *The Defence of the Roman and Byzantine Near East*, ed. H. Kennedy and P. Freeman, 717–35 (Oxford).

Whitby, L. M. (1986b). 'Procopius' Description of Dara', in *The Defence of the Roman and Byzantine Near East*, ed. H. Kennedy and P. Freeman, 332–57 (Oxford).

Whitby L. M. (1987). 'Notes on Some Justinianic Constructions', *Byzantinisch-Neugreichischen Jahrbücher* 23: 89–112.

Whitby, L. M. (1988). *The Emperor Maurice and His Historian: Theophylact Simocatta on Persian and Balkan Warfare* (Oxford).

Whitby, L. M. (2000). *The Ecclesiastical History of Evagrius Scholasticus* (Liverpool).

Whitby, L. M. (2002). *Rome at War AD 229–696* (Oxford).

Whitby, L. M., and Whitby, J. M. (1989). *The Chronicon Paschale* (Liverpool).

Whittaker, C. R. (1976). '*Agri Deserti*', in *Studies in Roman Property*, ed. M. I. Finley, 137–65, 193–200 (Cambridge).

Wickham, C. (1981). *Early Medieval Italy: Central Power and Local Society, 400–1000* (London).

Wickham, C. J. (2005). *Framing the Early Middle Ages: Europe and the Mediterranean 400–800* (Oxford).

Wickham, C. J. (2009). *The Inheritance of Rome: A History of Europe from 400 to 1000* (London).

Wilcken, U. (1912). *Chrestomathie* (Berlin).

Wildberg, C. (2005). 'Philosophy in the Age of Justinian', in Maas, 316–41 (Cambridge).

Wilson, N. G. (1975). *St. Basil on the Value of Greek Literature* (London).

Wolfram, H. (1988). *History of the Goths*, trans. T. J. Dunlap (Berkeley).

Woolf, G. (1998). *Becoming Roman: The Origins of Provincial Civilization in Gaul* (Cambridge).

INDEX

www.ingramcontent.com/pod-product-compliance
Lightning Source LLC
Chambersburg PA
CBHW020642280125
20908CB00002B/8
* 9 7 8 0 1 9 7 5 0 0 5 3 8 *